This is dedicated to
The creator and nurturer of us
The Mother Earth.

AND

To the memories of my mother
Geetabai Kisan Wani

Watch the rising Earth from the Moon!!!

- As we see the sunrise and moonrise from the Earth, watch the rising Earth from the Moon.
- The sky is seen blue from the Earth. The same is seen black from the Moon.
- Such small seems to be the size of Earth from the distance of 384600 KM! If this is the Earth's standing, the human must think about his own transitory standing on the Earth.
- Now search on this tiny visible round of Earth if you can find your bungalow, car, wealth and your existence? These are the facts human must contemplate about!

The Sun rise in the country of first sunrise in the world!!!

Watch the Sun rise in the country of early sunrise, which is New Zealand!!!

Each and every country in the world witnesses the sunrise daily. But the speciality of the above photograph is that it captures the sunrise of the New Zealand where the Sun rises first in the world. The speciality of the sunrise of this city is that compared to other cities or countries in the world the rays of rising Sun first touch this city. This is the place of first sunrise in the world. We are taught in the school about Japan being the 'country of sunrise'. But that is not true. The first sunrise happens here in New Zealand. It is because the date is changed here first. Here after 12 O'clock the date of 7th is changed to 8th first; while in the rest of the places of the world the date still remains 7th. So it dawns here first on the Earth and later at all places the date is changed from 7th to 8th after twelve o'clock in phases. When New Zealand gets sunrise of the date 8th, the Sun is setting in London city of the date 7th.

The Sunset in the nation where Sun sets first in the world!!!

Watch the fascinating scenery of sunset in the Dunedin city of New Zealand where the Sun rises and sets first in the world!!!

Though the scenery of sunset is similar everywhere; this is the sunset of the Dunedin city of the country New Zealand where the Sun sets first in the world. As the Sun rises the earliest in the New Zealand it also sets the earliest in the world. After the sunset in this country, the Sun starts setting in the other places of Earth gradually. When the Sun is setting on the 8th date of any month in New Zealand, the Sun of 8th date is rising in London.

REAL LIVE GOD & HUMAN DELUSION

(With doctrine)

Eknath Kisan Wani

PARTRIDGE

* Translator *
Tripti Awade

* Cover, Photo setting & Typeset by*
Sunanda B. Agashe

ISBN:	Hardcover	978-1-4828-6879-1
	Softcover	978-1-4828-6878-4
	eBook	978-1-4828-6877-7

Print information available on the last page.

To order additional copies of this book, contact
Partridge India
000 800 10062 62
orders.india@partridgepublishing.com

www.partridgepublishing.com/india

Words of The Translator.......

Dear Ones,

Namaste!

This ancient Sanskrit word of Indian greeting literally means - I bow to the Divinity within you. This originates from the ancient spiritual scriptures of Indian philosophy that everything is God or Divine that is all pervading and yet more.

I am thankful to the author for the opportunity given and the patience shown. Translation of this book had been a different experience. The main motif was to keep the language simple & appealing and hence despite strong urges there is less use of official words or decorative literary language in this book. Being voracious reader and translator of articles from books like 'Only Love Is Real', 'The Tao of Physics', and 'The Seat of the Soul'; you may find the influence of their language in this book. But I have tried to keep as close as possible to the original Marathi book except few changes with the permission of author which brings the content of the book out of the framework of a particular country. I hope you will enjoy reading the book.

The concepts and content of the book solely belong to the author. As the author has correctly stated with the pride that this book is not written by him after reading or studying other books; it is solely based on his own thoughts and experiences. I have delivered the work just as a translator and do not necessarily identify with the thoughts or philosophy within the book.

Happy reading!
Love

Tripti Awade
10, Sheelaban Society,
Paud Road, Pune 38.
Phone 9422519814

I hereby permit the Author Mr. Eknath Kisan Wani to publish the above said article in his book 'Real Live God & Human Delusion' through Partridge Publishing India (A Penguin Random House Company).

With Regards,

02/12/15

(Tripti Awade)

The Intention

So far, means almost during past 25 years, I traversed all the six continents of the Earth. So I got the view of the entire Earth planet. I observed her in various forms during these journeys. I kept collecting information and knowing various things about the Earth incidental to these journeys. Along with it, I studied about the Sun and the Moon. I realized the roles of the Sun and the Moon along with the Earth in creation of the life on the Earth. After traveling in the six continents and studying the Sun and Moon out of curiosity; I published my first book of 680 pages in Marathi 'Me, Earth and the Travel' on February 2010 due to the insistence of my friend Dr. Purohit. I received the positive feedbacks from all the readers. During past 2 years the first edition of 1100 prints was sold like a hot cake and same is happening with the second edition of 1100 prints. The important thing is that without any publicity and distributor just the mouth publicity has helped the sale of two thousand copies of this book. Owing to the demand of the youth I plan to publish the third edition of this book in English.

Though I had included the three chapters on geographical & astronomical Earth and the life on Earth and today's human; I realized that due to the brief information many readers didn't understand the subject. In reality these three chapters include the secrets of human birth, life and death from the scientific viewpoint. Due to my minute observation and study during my Earth's travel so far, I got introduced to my real self and received the knowledge. With a thought of making our lives happy, joyous and prosperous by sharing the knowledge I received and helping you get your real identity; this second book 'Real Live God & Human Delusion' is born. This is written in an easily understandable language. Also, this book is not the thirteenth book written after reading some previous ten-twelve books; but all the doctrines and examples presented here are my own means suggested by the

Mother Earth. All statistics is discovered by me. So no reference of other book is possible. This book is written with the research based on the knowledge I received.

Unknown people question me, "In which college did you teach? Have you got the doctorate in this subject?" I reply them, "Please read my first book 'Me, The Earth and the Travel' which will inform about me." I am neither a teacher, nor a thinker, professor nor even a graduate from any university. Then how I handled such a big topic? This will be the obvious question from the readers. But there have been so many renowned scientists, who weren't much educated or graduated. The answer to your question is the sentence of the Albert Einstein, "Imagination is more important than knowledge." So with the strength of my imagination (thought) power I searched the answers to the questions I had. That's it! So I discovered that the Sun & Moon in the space never get eclipsed and the forms of the Sun & Moon that you see aren't the real Sun and Moon.

Discovery of the real and live God!!!

In this book I have proved the real God which no one has shown or proven so far. There is no other God on this Earth. Real God doesn't die. But when the Earth will be destroyed, the God proven by me too shall die. No animate being including human shall be alive that time to claim any God! You shall view and identify the real God in this book. I have discovered the real God and presented in front of you. Whether the manmade God is alive or not; it doesn't affect the humankind. But the destruction of any part of the God that I have discovered or any increase decrease in it; shall destroy the entire life on the Earth including human. This is the importance of the real God. This means the twelve vital factors which I have discovered! Since they belong to and exist on the Mother Earth let us call Mother Earth the God.

To get the real identity of self, the human needs to first identify his/her root, that is the Mother Earth. When and how was the Earth born? What was her original form at the time of birth? Knowing about this is necessary. The fundamental nature of the Earth is the huge ball of dust. The Earth was born out of this dust-ball. There wasn't any creation of life at that time. The continuous processing since her birth created the water. You will get to read the history next to this till the creation of the human in this book.

We humankind have been reciting the legends and religious stories so far. We have been trying to identify ourselves and discover the God from them. All the saints and preachers have been requesting the salvation to the Lord. Means they have been asking the freedom from the cycle of birth & death – be it of any other animate being or the human. It means no birth, so no question of death. But since we are born, living this life is inevitable. There is no escape from it. Then to make the life smooth till the death shouldn't one understand the life to know oneself? No, rather one needs to understand ones' own true self to make the life smooth. At least the human has got the eligibility to know the self, no other animate being has received it and they don't need it. Only the human needs to realize himself/herself. Just because only the human have been fighting against the rules of the creation structure. So if you need the birth-death like other animate beings; first the ignorance needs to be destroyed. It means the realization that there is no difference between the human being and the other animate beings. For example, there is no difference between the insects like ant, snake and animals or trees and the human. Understanding this is like warding off the big ignorance. How? I have given it in this book. All life is created due to Earth and her related 12 factors. No animate being is an exception to this. Knowing this is like knowing self to a good extent. Any manmade thing is for the human. That too for handful of human beings or a group of humans! The entire humankind has nothing to do with what the handful of humans have made. For example, the law in a particular religion; it applies only to the people of that particular religion. It doesn't apply to the people of other faiths or religions. The law of polygamy is for the Hindu religion. Other people in Muslim religion have nothing to do with it. This is about the group of human. But the adjectives created by the entire human race like rich, poor, wise, stupid are just limited to the humankind. Other animate beings have nothing to do with these adjectives. This means, other animate beings have nothing to do with the manmade laws or adjectives. But the rules of the creation are application to the entire living beings including humans.

The same twelve factors which are needed for the creation of other animates are needed for the creation of human too. So any law, adjective created by human is false from the point of view of other animates. For example the human attributes importance to the gold-silver, diamonds-gemstones. But these things hold no value to the other animates on the Earth. Suppose if you keep 50 KG of gold in front of some cow and tell her "Now this gold is yours, so please give me 2 Litre of more milk daily!" Do you think she will give more milk? Never! Whatever gold you offer her, it is in vain for her. Then why should the human, made up of the same 12 factors, value gold so much? It neither feeds the hunger nor quenches the thirst. Had it been the case, other animates too would have started running after and collecting gold. They too would have created some God and daily worshiped it. God is not the privilege of the human alone. Other animate beings too would have needed it. So hey human living the momentary life! Understand this! And with this knowledge walk through the life till death. Then your life too will be happy and not just the death, you will not be afraid of anything.

No doctrine, no example cited in this book of mine is imaginary. You experience at each breath each thing mentioned in this. So each thing in this book exists in reality. There is no scope for the imagination. Any increase or decrease in any of the twelve factors which are needed for the creation of the animate beings on this Earth; will create difficulties for the formation of this creation-structure. No animate being can challenge this statement of mine. So I will also be sending one copy of this book to the famous astronomical institute NASA. I assure you that after studying and understanding Earth and her twelve factors mentioned in this book your view towards your mundane life will certainly change.

Just as one gets fresh after the bath, you will be fresh to live this human life after studying, contemplating and reflecting upon this book. Just like the snake sheds the old skin; you too shall get fresh by shedding the old, meaningless thoughts to live the rest of life. Study this book from the start to the end of the last page and you will not need to study the scriptures, legends, sermons. It is because no point within this book is explained by spicing it up and is based on the reality. You are experiencing it with each breath.

Each person lives underneath the covering of an illusion. He takes this cover as real. He believes it to be the universe. He is never ready to come out of this cover. So he keeps sinking in the life and takes leave of the Mother Earth one day. Just like the frog in a well thinks of the well as the universe and doesn't know what is beyond it; human has the same attitude. He doesn't see anything beyond the illusionary materialistic casing. Thinking of this casing as the universe he makes a mess of everything. What is the root of the human? It is just the invisible sperm. What this sperm is made up of? From where did it come? After understanding this you shall come out of the illusionary cover. You will start new life shedding the skin like a snake. This is the characteristic of this book.

The human hasn't yet found the way out of this illusionary cover to live completely clean life. I have brought this way, this path in front of human through this book. What is the secret of your birth-life and death? This will be revealed after reading this book and your life will be worthy. Ending many of the trials, troubles, needs, demands, misunderstandings and wrong thinking in the life you shall be free to live happy life. So this book should go to each human on the Earth.

After studying the human creation in this book you will be convinced that the creation-structure doesn't approve of the cast, race, religion, God etc. manmade things. Excluding human no other animate being has such manmade concepts. So have you ever heard the wars between the other animals? Since billions of years the aquatic animals are dwelling in the water. Have you ever heard of the war where millions of aquatic animals died? But due to the creation of manmade concepts like religion, race, God etc. the human has been killing the human so far. Till today billions of humans are killed in the war, are being killed and will be killed. Such unfortunate things are happening only within the human race. Will humankind ever think that their own insane ideas are responsible for this? You will be convinced after reading this book about how the human has been holding to the insane concepts and harming himself enormously.

Have you ever tried to know about why the creation-structure has given you the birth? There is a big selfishness of the creation-structure behind birthing each of the animate. You aren't given the birth to merely enjoy the food or be a rich-poor person or a great leader or a scholar, a philosopher, the prime minister or president. Actually this rich or poor are your own concepts. These concepts are not agreeable to the creation structure. If it was acceptable, then there would have been the marked difference between all animate beings on Earth. You will know the purpose of creation-structure in birthing you after reading the book. Then once you understand your role here; the things like troubles, trials, worries, fear and greed get vanished from your life totally. Besides, after knowing the secret of your birth-life and death that is revealed in this book, your life gets full of joy.

This book is not like belles-letters or a romantic novel. So the philosophy in this book is not for common readers but the need of this knowledge is for anyone irrespective of the status and the titles like simple social worker to president, prime minister, big industrialist or a famous preacher. In short this book is very useful for entire humankind. Today the train of human life seems to have slid off the track. The knowledge and philosophy in this book shall be useful to bring it back on the track to offer happy and joyous life again. For the young generation this book may prove to be the rare opportunity. The door to the knowledge that was unknown so far is opened through this book. So the youth should necessarily study this book and demand the government and the society to include this book in the academic curriculum.

After reading this book the youth will realize the extent to which the false ideas, thoughts and things the older generation have inflicted on them. This shall immediately open their eyes wide and clean. For example, Japan is not the country of the rising Sun today, the mountain taller than the Mountain Everest exists but …, in reality the real Sun and Moon never get eclipsed. Such many things are kept in front of the youth which will make their life easier. Second thing is that many things out of these facts are not brought forward by the scientists or some studious person. These are brought forth by me, Ekanath Wani. Had they been already brought forth by someone, the prevalent wrong understandings would have been destroyed long before and the pomp of eclipse wouldn't have ever existed. I want the entire humankind to benefit from this book and hence have decided to publish this book in English.

Earth too is an animate being like human. She too has the body just as we do have. Just like the creation of your body needs the body of the parents; the creation of each animate being needs the body of the Earth. You should know the geological Earth to understand how our bodies and the existence are dependent on her body. Along with the surface of the Earth, her inner core, outer layers, distance from the Sun; you should also know about the real nature of Sun & Moon which are responsible for the creation and existence of the life on this Earth, about what makes the Earth and the planetary system float in the space, about what speed the Sun is revolving around himself, about what is the speed of revolution and rotation of Moon? Why do we always see only one side of the Moon? Also if owing to the rule of universe of 'creation is the root cause of the destruction' the Sun too has its death like any other animate; how his entire planetary family too is going to die along with our Earth? You will certainly enjoy reading such interesting information given in this book which is also related to your life.

We learnt in our school book of geography that the measure of counting the distance between celestial bodies is called 'light year'. But do you know that the distance of entire planetary system is nothing in front of just one light year? It is because the last planet within our solar system is almost 4500 million KM from the Sun; whereas one light year means the distance of almost 10 thousand billion KM! You will realize how negligible is the human being having the momentary existence in the universe that is spread out trillions of light years; after reading the elaborate information about light year in this book!

The commoners in India always have the fear about planets Mars and Saturn. But knowing the reality of these planets would change the outlook towards these planets. The one who studies astronomy or one who has understood the astronomy will not have the place for the superstitions in the life. S/he will spend the life happily without fears.

Out of all the planets in the solar system, only our Earth looks beautiful like a blue sapphire. The reason behind these beautiful looks is that out of her 510 million sq. km. area almost 360 million sq. km. (3/4th of the area) is occupied by five huge oceans and the bottomless water of 113 seas. Balance 150 million KM tract of land is covered by tall and long spread range of mountains, deserts, long range of great valleys, islands and wide spread dense forests. No other planet in our solar system has the life creation like it is on the Earth. Since there are no factors available on other planets like Earth which are favourable for the creation, these planets are dry and barren. Our Earth holds many geographical surprises like the valley and mountains of eight thousand KM, the lands never drenched with rainwater for century and at the same time huge snowy regions, ever green forests, mountains popped up through ever erupting volcanoes and the tract of land flowing the perpetual fountains of sulphur. You will get to read these surprises in this book.

Also the clock that we use to know the time is nothing else but the 'miniature Earth' itself. The self-revolution of the Earth means the clock! You will get to read the information about this in the book.

Our breathing, the perpetual cycle of birth-death of the entire life has its reason lying in the twelve factors which I have described in this book. I have concluded this through the ever dwelling thoughts in my mind and my observation during the Earth-journey. I have introduced each of these twelve factors independently which is your own identity. Increase or decrease in any single factor out of these shall destroy entire creation-structure. So if you wish to reveal the secret of your birth-death you need to read this book from the start to finish and contemplate and meditate upon it.

The scientists have discovered the DNA and RNA but the Earth herself is a big science. It is through the Earth science other manmade sciences are created. Understanding this Earth science will make human life fulfilled and worthy. After studying and knowing the truth about the twelve factors which I discovered, you will be convinced about the falsehood of the man made things like soul, super soul, God, future telling, architectural science called vastu shastra, astrological planet periods and miracles and how they don't relate to the human life. For example, what will be the effect, if one of these twelve factors - which is 'Earths' revolution' - stops? Or what will happen if the combustion of the hydrogen gas on the Sun stops? No soul, super soul or manmade God will come forward at such time to continue this cycle of creation on Earth. Means these twelve factors cut across the stupid human ideas. You will not get to read elsewhere about these twelve factors which I have described in this book. I have discovered them through my minute observation and study. You will know the Mother Earth in true sense after reading these twelve factors. Your own identification actually means the mixture of these twelve factors. Then you will understand that if YOU don't belong to yourself then to no one does the wife, children, husband, relatives, lands and property or fame actually belongs to! Understanding this true identification about yourself will create the happiness in your life, such is an importance of these twelve factors. Understanding this structure will lead to automatic elimination of the ignorance the human beings hold that is -of not seeing the similarity between themselves and other animate beings. Just because, be it insect like ant or shrubs, trees, plants, insects or human beings, none can be created without these twelve factors. All animate beings are the same to the creation-structure. Creation-structure isn't concerned about the manmade things. The human must understand that creation structure's work doesn't depend upon the manmade things. Human race is the most cruel and unhappy amongst all animate beings due to the misuse of their gifts of intelligence, thought and imagination powers. There are creation laid rules for the happy and joyous life; but due to violation of these rules the humankind suffers.

When you shall study the creation structure and Earth; you will find that the birth and life that any animate being lives is merely an illusion. It is a part of the creations' rule. But the humankind invites all troubles and trials by living in the illusion and assuming the illusion to be the truth. All phases from life to death are illusionary. Only death is the highest truth. Your origin is the droplet of semen, actually the micro form of it. Later embryonic stage, infant state, youth, adulthood, old age and the flat dead body! Who are you in all these stages? From birth to death all is illusion. All world around you too is an illusion. Understanding this by human is opening the door to live the life free from troubles, greed, animosity, worry and fear. Other rule of the creation is 'there is no valuable thing or relation than the happy and healthy life of the self'. Another rule of the creation is 'hunger means all living and non-living creation'. Even if you consider 'hunger' a trivial thing, it has a great importance. In the absence of the hunger this entire creation shall perish! What all things it doesn't make humans perform! There are various types of hungers. Some forms of hunger are necessary for the creation & existence of the living & non-living beings. But some types of hungers leave adverse effect on the social life of the humans.

To live happy and joyous life there are some laws which are –

1. Ill-gotten seldom prospers. 2. The creation-structure doesn't accept the manmade concept of God. 3. Possessing anything in excess is not a gift but the curse of the creation-structure. 4. Not having wealth of thoughts makes both the rich and poor the beggars. 5. Wealth of thought is the highest and most valuable asset of all the wealth. 6. Contentment contains all riches, discontented person is real beggar. 7. Creation-structure doesn't approve of the manmade things like soul, super soul, future or miracles. 8. No animate being has the reincarnation. Re-creation is creating similar multiples from

the single animate which is the plan of creation structure. So, creation-structure is not the factory of producing souls. 9. Kindliness is the needed trait for living the happy and successful life. You will find wide discussions on such various rules of the creation-structure in this book. Also the definition of the human mind is given. Mind is not the part of the body. If you understand the above rules of the creation and follow them; your life will be definitely successful.

As the birth is caused by the twelve factors, the absence of any single factor causes death. What is death? What is next to death? If you know this you will never fear death. Once you get introduced to your Mother Earth you shall know the secret of your birth death. It is because for all life on Earth including human beings, only Earth is everything. You will be convinced after reading this book that everything that you see around is the part of the Mother Earth. Everything is created from her and dissolves in her.

To live happy and content life one must have sufficient money to meet the needs. Proper financial planning is necessary for the same. Based on my own experience I have guided about how the poor and middle class person should plan financially. In short, the key word for ending the poverty and living tension free life is given.

After traveling worldwide, one thing conspicuously caught my attention that is huge population growth of the India. Government machinery and society too should put the efforts to control the population. The population of 300 million before independence has now reached to almost 1300 million. Is this the gift received by the India from independence? The body that observes the above rules of the creation should also end happily. For the benefit of the society, each one should get the right for the painless, joyous euthanasia. It is the need of the time today. Of course, those who wish to wait and accept the painful and troublesome life till death will not be forced into euthanasia. But today there are people in the society who are suffering from the incurable diseases and living a painful life, eagerly waiting for the rescue through death; they need euthanasia. The need of euthanasia is asserted. Readers should give it a serious thought and demand the same to the government.

After observing and studying the creation-structure and the Earth I realized that things like God, fate, vastushatra, future, miracles and ghosts etc. which have birthed from the human imagination do not actually exist. You too would agree with my opinion after reading this book by heart from start to end. Even then I do not force the readers to agree with my opinion. Or I am not interested in harming anyone's emotions. And I apologize if anyone's emotions are getting hurt. But whosoever will understand the Earth and her twelve factors and complete creation structure and observe the laws of creation after studying them will get free from the mundane thoughts and enjoy the life fully in true sense and happily take leave from the Earth. This is my own experience. Actually the information in this book needs to go beyond the boundaries of Maharashtra or India. It needs to reach to each person on earth; because so far there are lot of misunderstandings prevalent regarding eclipses, God, fate and miracles and I have narrated in the simple, understandable language about how these are false and what is the reality that I have discovered. No one has put the doctrine so far that the twelve factors mean Earth. I wish that it should reach to all and the life of entire humankind should be happy and prosperous. For this purpose I want this book to reach each country in the world. The book is intended and structured to be of use for the entire humankind in all ways.

It's a truth that in this endless universe, the life exists only on the Earth. This book finds the answer for 'Why life dwells only on Earth?' and reveals the secret behind birth and death of all living beings including humankind. Forget about reaching the other solar systems like ours, which are trillions of light-years away from us; humankind cannot even reach the planets within its own solar system. Despite having brains, the human being lives in ignorance from birth to death. They waste their life within the limited confines of the mundane & materialistic world that is visible to his/ her eyes, thinking that is the final truth. I have stated with doctrines the meaning of creation-state-destruction; i.e. the power behind birth-life-death of the human being about which the average human doesn't have knowledge in the real sense. Though I have tried to put it in a simple language in front of readers, due to lack of study they might not understand the importance and need of this book mere by reading it. For example, the things described in this book like - the Earth revolves around the Sun with the speed of 107000 KM per hour, or there is always a bright light or full moon like situation on the Moon, or the Sun of the size that is visible to our eyes doesn't practically exist in the space; these may not be understood mere by reading the book. You need to analyze, memorize and study each sentence of this book by heart. Unless you become one with this book you won't understand creation-structure or human life and your ignorance shall prevail.

Those having their bread-butter and fame dependent upon the illusionary things might find this book an obstacle. But what is the benefit of hiding the truth from the humanity by considering the livelihood and fame of these people? At least, henceforth the young generation shall not fall prey to such illusionary ideas and understandings. So this book is the gift for the young generation.

If the entire society and the government wishes to eliminate the harmful things like fate, God, soul superstitions, quackery, miracles from the humanity; then it is necessary to know the reality about the creation structure and accept the truth. For this purpose if the reality from this book is taught in the schools-colleges at least the coming generations shall have the conditioning about the truthful things and the superstitions, God, magic as discussed above shall be banished from the roots of the society. There will be no need of making laws or social movements to destroy the wrong modes and methods. But for this purpose the intense will of all social reformers and national leaders is necessary.

This book is not written by me on my own but since I became one with, blended with the Mother Earth, she has got this written through me. The entire animation structure is created by the Mother Earth and I am a negligible iota dwelling upon Her! Likewise the existence of each animate being is negligible too. This book mentions about the president, prime minister, philosophers, saints and intelligent & brilliant people and leaders from time to time. These are all the animate beings created by Mother Earth and everyone is the same for her whether it is an ant or a huge elephant, or tall tree or a human being. Everyone is same for her. She doesn't discriminate. So these people are not mentioned by me, Eknath Wani, but the Mother of all i.e. Mother Earth. One might think that the author is using the insolent language! But it doesn't belong to me but wishes of the Mother Earth.

The figures given in this book may not be the exact values. These are the approximate figures used to give an idea to the readers. So the author is not legally responsible for any shortfalls in the accuracy of the figures.

Eknath Kisan Wani

Note of Thanks

One shouldn't boast about 'I worked, due to me the work got completed' while delivering the work. In reality no one can work alone. So despite being author of this book, without the valuable co-operation of others I wouldn't have been able to complete the difficult task. So it is my duty to thank the ones by mentioning their names who helped me in the process. My first sincere thanks go to my colleague Sunanda Agashe, without her this book wouldn't have been possible. From writing to desktop publishing step; everything is done by her and this book is in front of the readers. She is assisting my work since past 30-32 years. My previous book, 'Me, Earth and the Travel' was brought in front of readers due to her. So if I must, I will give the credit to my assistant; Sunanda Agashe.

The dummy of the book in Marathi language was ready almost since a year. But I wasn't getting anyone to translate it in simple and neat English as I wanted. But one day I got introduced to Advocate Sunil Naik. During talks when I expressed my agony that my work is bogged down due to unavailability of a right translator, he removed the hurdle in a flash. He himself introduced me to the correct translator for this book, Ms. Tripti Awade. So I am very thankful to him.

The most important thanks I wish to express for the translator Ms. Tripti Awade who translated my book into English. She translated the book in the very simple, lucid English language, which is in front of you today. I am very much thankful to her.

Whosoever I gave the prepublication dummy for reading, those people from different walks of life and society gave the feedback about the book being amazing and admired. I am thankful to those who gave me their feedback after reading the prepublication dummy.

Almost 20 photographs which adorn this book were available to me from the public domain which I have used in this book. I am also thankful to the institutions like 'NASA' and personalities from whom I could get these photographs. I sincerely thank them all very much.

I also lovingly thank Rtd. officer Mr. Jayajirao Jadhav and my granddaughter Ms. Pallavi Wani for the English proof reading of the translated writing and co-operating despite her important and busy 12th standard schedule. Also, I am thankful to my second granddaughter Juhi Wani for contributing to this book.

Also I am very much thankful to our family doctor, Dr. V. N. Annachhatre and an inventor and mechanical engineer Mr. Yogesh Barbhai for allowing me to publish their feedbacks in this book.

I have an intense desire that this book should be read and contemplated in every household of the world and to complete this task, I cannot at present mention the name of the agency who would take this important responsibility; but I thank them in advance.

Besides this; whosoever institutes and personalities directly or indirectly may have co-operated and assisted me from the inception to the actual publication of this book, I sincerely thank them all!

Eknath Wani

The pre-publication dummy of the book was given for reading to the selected personalities from the different areas of the society to get the feedback. Out of them, the feedbacks of two persons - one doctor who is masters in medicine and a mechanical engineer who is an inventor of an invention centre; are given here.

Feedbacks

Dr.V.N.ANNACHHATRE M.D.

*Consulting Physician *Cardiologist *Diabetic Centre *Intensive Care Unit

*CONSULTING ROOM *POOJA NURSING HOME

80, Surekha, Tulshibagwale Colony, Pune 411 009 M.S. INDIA. Contact:

Respected Mr. Eknath Wani Sir, I have read your both books – 'Me, The Earth and the Travel' and 'Real Live God & Human Delusion'. First book is now my reference book. As I too am an avid traveller, I first get the information reading your book, which benefits me a lot. There are very few places which aren't mentioned in your book. The short information about Earth, Sun and solar system is in your first book too but you have taken a detailed review of the same in your second book 'Real Live God & Human Delusion'.

Indeed, the Earth herself is responsible for birth, good life and real joy of life, protection and ending of the humankind. Earth is the only Mother, father, mentor, friend and God – everything for the human. She gives the human a quality life, but by avoiding the natural laws the human has started the self-destruction.

In the childhood we could read some chapters about Astronomy; but that information used to be very short and abrupt and non-convincing. But reading your book has expanded all four directions of the intellect. Due to this book I got the basic information of some topics and also became aware of the misunderstandings about some facts. I also got to know some new things. Mr. Wani has boldly and earnestly written by giving examples and canons; about the falsehood of certain things taught to us or read by us so far.

The author has wonderfully discussed the astronomical Earth, geographical Earth, creation of Earth and vastness of the solar system. The doctrine of 'twelve factors' was new to me. But the author has systematically convinced their importance in our creation and life. Our creation and life seems impossible without each of these factors. So I found the structure of the book very neat. Mr.Wani has put forth many doctrines and convinced upon them from the base. He has tried from his heart to make the common man understand many of those doctrines.

One realizes that the human is very negligible compared to this creation and the solar systems; and after studying the expanse of the universe we, feel the human to be the frog in a well! After reading the book we do feel how hollow are money, power, pride and revengeful mind! The author has put up his straight thoughts along with the doctrines about the beliefs of birth-death, sin-virtue, ghosts and rebirth prevalent in the society and has tried to convince about the falsehood of present heritage, traditions, customs and conventions. He has convinced that compassion, tension free and fearless life is the only key to the joyous and prosperous life.

The only real live (not dead) God is Earth and her related twelve factors and it should be experienced by the human. God is not in any statue of human or a charlatan. God doesn't have form, but we can experience her with each breath. The author has reprimanded the things like sin-virtue, fortune, miracle, fate, soul & super soul and rebirth. Also he has countered the illusionary ideas about eclipse, Moon, Sun, Saturn, and Mars and has put forth the real doctrines convincible to the conscience, which can be noted by the scientists of the world.

Since this book is written by an author in simple words fearlessly and earnestly; the government and the society should take a note of this book in time and include it in the academic curriculums of the school-colleges to spread this knowledge worldwide. Understanding the reality since the childhood will help create a healthy, good natured and fearless society. The peace and prosperity shall dwell in the entire world. The differences of small-big, rich-poor will not be created. The author has tried to deliver the sight of real live God to the entire humankind and remove the darkness of the ignorance present so far in humankind. Actually if the so called monks and saints try to remove **the ignorance** of the humankind by keeping the reality in this book in front of their devotees the charlatans, and hypocrite preachers will not get the footing in the society. Not just this, but this book is a knowledge bank. The author has discovered and put forth to today's human, the knowledge and the real God unknown to the humankind so far. So that keeping away the wrong understandings, ideas, customs and superstitions the human shall live a clean, spotless, and fearless and tension free life, which will be the success of this book. This knowledge is given by an apparently common man and I am proud that he is a Maharashtrian (resident of a Maharashtra state in India) and an Indian. I truly wish that this book be translated in as many languages as possible. This philosophy has to be reached to the citizens of all countries then only it shall be true fruition of Mr. Wani's efforts.

Dr. V. N. Annachhatre (M.D.)

EDISON
Invention Centre
Calibration Laboratory

1 A, Trio Chambers, 1414, Sadashiv Peth, Near Renuka Swaroop Girls High School, Pune - 411030. Maharashtra (India) Telephone: + 91 - 20 - 24481822 Telefax: + 91 - 20 - 24471238 Email: chaitrayogesh@yahoo.co.in

---

To,

Respected Mr. Eknath Wani Sir,

Warm Greetings,

First of all I congratulate and thank you that you are bringing such book with revolutionary thoughts and doctrines in front of the world. The revolutionary thoughts put forth in the book are proven by giving examples and doctrines, leaving no room for the doubts.

You have done the big task of blowing the thoughts, bearing and the concepts of God/religion on the basis of doctrines adhering to rationalism and science through book writing.

I am sure that whichever reader will study this without prejudice with full rational; will certainly get answers to the questions like how to live the joyful life? Why have we come here? What responsibility has been given to us by the creation structure? What is our birth? When should we leave this world? So it will bring the awareness of up to what level one should keep the desire of living.

There is no comparison to the rules of creation-structure that you have put forth after your continuous Earth travel and bizarre observation power. The reader who will observe these rules accurately will certainly find his life prospering. Not just once but twice I have studied and contemplated this book and it has changed my life thoroughly.

What is the definition of the universe? What makes all the eight planets float in the space along with the Earth? What is the gravitation power of each planet? What is the distance between each of these planets? What is their size and mass? What is inside the core of the Earth? All this enigmatic information expands the periphery of knowledge.

The information about the planet Earth you have given is surprising. Perhaps the more surprising thing is your invaluable discovery that 'to create any animate being in this universe the twelve factors are necessary'; which you have elaborated in the book. You have given the entire humankind an invaluable gift.

The entire humankind must study this discovery so that human can be free from the present unwanted customs, traditions, ideas, cast and religion systems and would be able to live the life more joyously and abundantly. Also the proper contemplation of this discovery will create the harmony, love and peace between people.

So this book will be the rare opportunity for old-young alike and specially youngsters. Everyone should take the full benefit of this knowledge as I have already taken.

Your discovery about the twelve factors necessary for the creation would compel the world famous American institute NASA scientists to study because the said institution is searching the life on other planets since many years.

You can get riches by sincere and good methods, but how? You have stated the financial calculations about this in a simple language. It shall certainly guide the readers and the generation today which runs behind money.

Also you have whipped the greedy Indian politicians and handful businessmen who try to make more money using money, which is a wonderful work and you have the right to whip them because you have closed your multi-million making business overnight by keeping money just necessary for your living.

I am short of words to write about this book; such a wealth of knowledge is comprised in this book. So I express good wishes that this book reaches on the Earth wherever the human habitat is found. My good wishes that let the reader definitely be benefited.

Yogesh Barbhai

Contents

Watch the most beautiful of all solar planets, our Earth!!

Watch our real Mother....Everything is Earth!!!

Our real God is the Earth. Only the Mother Earth has given us the birth. Only she nurtures us. We too are nothing else but the fraction of Mother Earth. Without Earth we are nothing. If you wish to know yourself, you must know and understand the Mother Earth which is your and everyone's Mother. This will make your life tension free, joyous, fearless and greedless and you will happily say final goodbye to her when time comes. Knowing the Earth is the highest knowledge of all.

1

The open secret about our life and death…

The Mother Earth

The greatest ignorance above all is taking birth on this Mother Earth and not knowing about her! Means your life is just a waste!!!

Friends, do you really wish to know yourself? Do you also wish to reveal the enigma of life, birth, death, incarnation, god, soul, supreme power etc.? Then you must read this book wholeheartedly- from this first chapter 'Mother Earth' till the last page. Everything-- your breath, your food, air, water, wealth and all that is visible to your eyes-- is Mother Earth! Nothing else but Mother Earth, Mother Earth and just Mother Earth!! Yes my friends and this fact will be revealed to you through this book.

Do you really wish to be fearless, live peaceful and happy life? Yes? Then please throw the laziness and read! Only then would you be able to reveal the enigma of your birth & death. It will wipe off your ignorance and make your life easy and really meaningful.

YOU REALLY DON'T KNOW YOUR TRUE IDENTITY!!!

What are you? Who are you? My friends, the titles like prime minister, minister, president, MLA, lord, super star, rock star, royal, prince, duke, head, leader, master, philosopher, rich, poor, industrialist, wise, mad, special, blind, disable are not REAL YOU.

These are just the labels you have attached to yourself! The real YOU actually are just the Mother Earth and Her twelve factors!! This is it; anything else is a false identity!!! To understand this canon you must read & inculcate this chapter 'Mother Earth'. And once you read & understand the next chapters, just know you are transformed! You are free in the life!! You shall get rid of the entire material burden that you have been carrying on your head and start living like a human in the true sense. Such is an importance of knowing your real identity. So, let's know what this Mother Earth really is.

For this, first we must know the birth enigma of our creator Earth. Because no element of, whatever that is visible on the Earth, can be separated from Earth. Just as our birth and death, our creator Earth too has her death. So we shall first try and know when and how the Earth was born. This will help you understand and ensure the truth about birth and death. Henceforth I am going to reveal all secrets Pandora's Box one by one. You will know how you have been in the illusion so far and had wrapped up your life in attachments, illusion, anger, selfishness, jealousy and ego.

BIRTH OF MOTHER EARTH! INCLUDING HUMAN BEINGS, ALL LIVING BEINGS ARE THE CHILDREN OF EARTH!!!...

All the animated life that we see on Earth is the creation of Earth my friends!. There is not any power on Earth that will create something without the Mother Earth. The age of our Mother Earth is approximately 4600 million years. Considering this very large figure, the human is a very recently created; existed lately

WATER WAS THE FIRST CREATION ON EARTH!!!...

The original nature of Earth is the collection of bundle of dust, a hot ball. Upon the cooling of its surface a thin crust was formed. Later with the shocks & strokes of other planets the craters or cavities were formed. The layer of clouds was formed by the growing amount of steam that was thrown out along with other gases through the lava bursting out of Earth. As the temperature of sun decreased gradually, the rains started. It simply was a natural phenomenon of the cooling of the steam that was thrown out. The accumulation of rain water in the craters eventually created seas and oceans on the Earth.

FIRST LIFE WAS CREATED IN THE WATER! VEGETATION AND OTHER LIFE CAME INTO EXISTENCE LATER!!!...

As the temperature on Earth decreased, the water on Earth was cooled. It gave birth to the first animated being approximately

3500 million years back. Later till approximately 450 million years before from today, other than fishes no other living being or vegetation was created. Approximately 350 million years before vegetation was formed and 300 million years before reptiles of 7 to 8 feet long, crawling animals as well as grasshopper type flying insects with wings came into existence.

First dinosaur which could turn on its two feet was born approximately 230 million years before from today! It was non vegetarian. Later, approximately 140 million years before from today, the next generation dinosaurs were created. They were around 20 meter long with long neck and as long tail and pointed teeth. Due to their long neck they could eat the leaves and branches high up on the trees. Later approximately 35 million years before from now the mammals like monkeys etc. were created.

When our ancestors, humanlike animals were created?...

During next 4600 million years after the birth, Earth had undergone many transformations that kept changing her environment. There was a huge period gap before the existence of human. Just 4 million years before from now a humanlike animal was born on Earth. Later approximately 2.5 million years before, monkey like man with hands was born first in the continent of Africa. He was advanced enough to create stone weapons to hunt and feed self. He started living in a group and eat cooked meat approximately 0.5 million years before. He could protect himself from other wild animals. He used to live naked those days.

Start of farming...

Approximately 30000 years back from now, he faced difficulty getting prey. So 12000 years back he discovered & started farming. This gives an idea of how recent the human is when compared to earth! Later he started settling near water i.e. river banks, ponds. If you think of it, on the Earth aged 4600 million years, the human being came into existence just 12000 years before now! Just the existence of Earth has caused the rest of the creation of living and non-living.

Earth is the Mother of all living beings!!!...

In our solar system there are seven other planets like Earth. But as of now there is no creation of life yet on any of them! Then the question is why this creation is only on our Earth itself? There is a good reason for this. The things necessary to create all living nature, including human being are available only on our Earth.

This means, whatever we see in the nature on this Earth is nothing else but the fraction or part of Mother Earth itself!

Only Mother Earth has the power to create!!!...

However progressed the human may be, whatever he may have invented, he won't get power like Earth. There is no other power on this Earth equal to the power of Earth itself, friends. So the human must realize its limit. He should happily celebrate the life given by Mother Earth and surrender it happily to the Mother Earth itself!

Now in this universe is there another planet like Earth that has living nature? Discovering this is beyond the capability of a man. Even if there is such a planet, the man cannot reach there. Man must know this limit. I am giving further the reasons of why life exists only on this Earth. In this expanse of living nature the man takes birth in ignorance and perishes in ignorance. Thus, till death he does not realize his true identity. My intention is to give him back this identity.

Except the thin outer crust the Earth is still a hot lump!!!...

In this universe, there are millions of planets like Earth. But we cannot give a guarantee of a life similar to that on Earth on these other planets and reaching there is just impossible. Basically Earth itself is a 4600 million year old hot lump of our solar system. Even today, we just believe whatever we see, but even today Earth is a hot globe. Inner Earth is still 5500 degree Celsius hot. Just like a fruit has an outer layer and inside pulp, just the same way Earth has an outer thin shell of cool crust and inside super-hot kernel.

Earth's surface is just like a football!!!...

Friends, the amazing fact is that Earths is actually a huge hot lump of minerals like iron and the cool outer crust is just 35 to 70 KM thin. This crust is not even or uniform but is made up of 15-20 patches, just like a football is made up of different colour patches. Now we may guess how thin is this outer layer? Friends, if we talk about an apple, the thickness of a peel of an apple is nothing compared to the large pulp inside it! The Earth's crust is so much thinner compared to the ratio of an Apples inner pulp and its peel!!

Just like we see the leaves of water lily floating in the pond, the thin patches of Earth's crust are gently floating on the lava of inner hot lump of earth. The thickness of the same crust of an earth at the base of oceans and seas is just 5 to 10 KM! Hence the earthquakes or volcanoes erupt much more inside the seas or oceans than on land of Earth.

What does these 15-20 patches of crust hold?...

It is amazing that this thin surface, the crust of Earth made up of 15-20 patches holds five oceans, 113 seas, huge mountains like Andes, approximately 9 million sq. kilometres of deserts like Sahara, 14 million sq. kilometres of ice covered Antarctica, millions of sq. kilometres forests and rest of the land covered by life of humans and other animals!!

What is the main reason behind the creation of animates?...

As the environment on the Earth underwent the gradual transformation, the creation of animates or living beings began. Even today life is created and perished. The environment is the main reason behind this. Favourable environment creates many living beings and the change in environment destroys them.

For example, there are seasonal plants, fruits. During rainy season we suddenly see much vegetation, plants sprung which are unseen otherwise throughout the year. We see specific insects for the temporary periods and later see them dead. Means these plants or insects or any other animals are created when they get favourable environment for their creation. They die when the environment changes and becomes unfavourable. We see the growth of fungus when food is kept in humid environment for a long time. We watch pest formed on farm crops due to change in environment. The environment favours the creation of this pest.

This during Earth's life of approximately 4600 million years, as the environment changed, the life was created and it also got destroyed with the unfavourable change in the environment, as in case of dinosaur.

During my journey of Europe i.e. northern hemisphere of Earth, I did not see any tree of Mango or Coconut which is very common in India. The trees that grow in the tropical countries do not grow in the countries having cold environment as in Europe. Likewise, the trees growing in the cold environment of European countries do not grow in tropical countries like India. For example, I was amazed to see the splash of apples on the roads of Moscow, the fruit that is so expensive in our India and not seen in so many other countries. Even within India, I saw the splash of a fruit called 'Pear' in northern India which I have never seen in my own state of western India. Within India, the environment changes around coastal area, northern region, southern region and different fruits are available in abundance at different area. Environment is the reason for this creation of fruits in abundance. This is an effect of environment and nothing else.

Similar to other planets, the Earth too has a place which is without environment and life!!!...

Our Earth has a place that has no environment! So the place has no vegetation, animals, humans or insects! It is even devoid of aquatics!!

This is what we may call the bottom of Earth, the region of Antarctica. It covers the area of 14 million sq. Kilometres on Earth crust. Birds like penguins exist just at the banks of South Ocean and Antarctica. But inside the Antarctica where the temperature is minus 57 degree Celsius we do not find a single bird! This is the result and effect of environment!!

So much is the importance of environment for the creation that while travelling through the northern region of Earth I found very less vegetation and animal or any other life in Norway, Sweden,

Finland and Siberia of Russia. Human inhabitation is very less and scanty. The environment kills the desire of sex. Due to slow reproduction rate within such cold regions, the governments of some of these countries honor the couple producing the child with prize and helps in the upbringing of the child. In tropical countries the scene is very opposite! The Indian government encourages family planning program and offer facilities to the families limiting the birth of children to maximum two!! This is the situation of the Earth that has the environment, leave aside the planets that has got no environment!!!

There is no sign of life on the Antarctica which has a temperature of minus 57 degrees. Similarly, if the temperature of the Earth rises to 70 degrees, there will be no relating existence of life on this Earth.

How and why was the first man, our ancestor on Earth was born?...

Many people ask me how and when the first man came into existence on this Earth. It took 4597.5 million years for the creation of environment favorable for creation of human. The humanlike animal with hands was created that time. Earth's age is 4600 million years. So scratch the head, how and when did man come into existence on the Earth? You shall get the answer here.

Each animate beings form is originally in its micro appearance. 3500 million years before from now 1st life was created in water. What does this mean? It is not as though the fish was formed and started swimming in the water. But it means the first life was created in the form of an egg. Even today each life starts in its micro appearance. For example, large banyan tree, what is its original form? A miniature seedling! From that micro form is created next leaves, branches, large trunk…the large form of the tree. But basic creation is in a micro appearance. Likewise the man does not come suddenly with his grown up form, but the fraction of recreation of the man is the microscopic sperm and egg in human body. This is its first micro appearance! This encompasses all, the hands, legs, heart, brain, eyes and ears. This microscopic appearance gets the form of an animate with the 12 factors of an Earth, and this work is done only by Mother Earth.

This can be elaborated by an example. Take a groundnut and check the small budlike prick that it has at the front. This tiny fraction has hidden everything that is flowers, leaves, stem and many groundnuts. We nip off this bud and there is no chance of recreation.

Means no body of an animate has reincarnation, but the fraction of recreation within the body of an animate has an incarnation. Each life has this life cycle. A sterilized man cannot reproduce. Understand this arrangement of the mysterious nature system!

But without understanding this knowledge, man has created out of his own ignorance the things like soul, super soul, god, miracles!

This in short is the relationship between environment and creation. Next I am going to explain how the suitable environment was formed on the Earth. I am going to analyse each of the 12 factors which are associated with Earth, which will give you the identity that you never realized so far!

Example of how without the environment some life gets dead!!!...

There was news on the TV news channels and newspapers in March 2012. In India, within a city of Nagpur a full 9 month pregnant woman was admitted in a hospital. But she died during the treatment. So what about the fetus in her womb? Doctors advocated the kin to get the child out of womb within half an hour, else it shall die too. The reason for giving this example is as long as mother was alive; the fetus was getting the nourishment like food and air of Earth through the placenta connected to mother. But with mothers death this supply of nourishment was broken endangering the life of fetus. So the decision was made to take the fetus out of womb immediately. Means the connection to the Earth through physical mother was severed and a direct connection with Earth was established for the survival of the fetus and it remained alive like other new born babies.

Where is Soul- Super Soul?...

In religious literature statements are made like 'Soul is immortal' 'God is the only savior'. In above example where is soul and where is god? If the connection of placenta to mother was not severed in time and Earth connection not established, would the baby have survived? What is meant by his soul? If baby wouldn't have been taken out, where would have been that soul and god? Would it have remained in the baby? Here the baby survived because of the direct connection established with the 12 factors with Earth and not due to soul. If the Earth's 12 factors were not connected to the baby, it wouldn't have been survived and hence there is no such thing as soul!

Friends, we have seen the history of creation structure on the Earth. Now tell me where did you find creation of the God & Soul? That is why I have proved Real Live God by researching 12 factors, which you will see ahead.

****

Watch the galaxy that is made up of billions of solar systems!!!

The Galaxy

Despite the existence, the human on Earth is nothing. So negligible is his nature. The Earth on which he is born, she herself is nothing in this gigantic Universe. Our solar system has eight planets and these planets have many Moons. Our Sun is the controller of all them. Such billions of huge Suns like this and their solar systems together form the galaxy, which is again just a small part of the gigantic Universe. The Universe is made up of such billions of galaxies!! Just think about it! Where we stand in all this? The picture above shows a minute part of this Universe means our galaxy – Milky Way. Mere 60-70 rotations of earth around the Sun mean our life. Means our existence in the gigantic Universe is simply zero!!

Watch our solar system!...

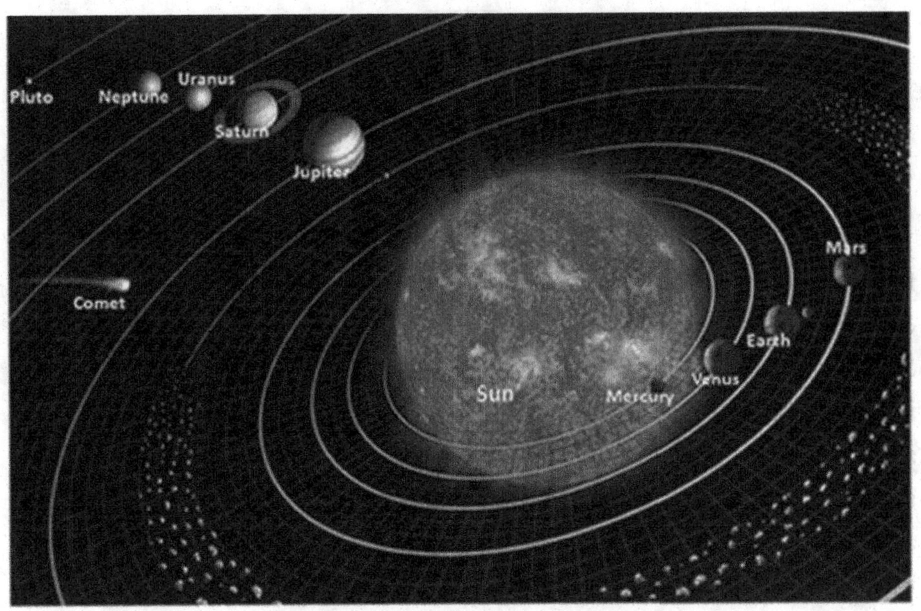

Sun and his family members!!...

All the eight planets of the solar system are rotating around the Sun within their specific orbit. The star that manages and controls them all is the Sun. Only the Sun's gravitational force is the reason for them to float in the space and rotate around Sun. End of the Sun's gravitational pull may make them all wander and perhaps collide with the planets in other solar systems. Each planet of the solar system is revolving around self and also rotating around Sun in a specific orbit at the same time due to Sun. Sun is the bearer of all these planets. The description of Sun and the other planets is given in the chapter 'Astronomical Earth'.

2

The Introduction of Astronomical Earth

The root of all knowledge and sciences is Mother Earth!!

Friends, the most necessary for the life on Earth and what we experience with each breath is Earth, Sun and Moon. The life on Earth is deeply related to these three. If a human being desires, rather he should desire peace, happiness, joy and freedom from stress then he must have information about these three in order to know the nature's design.

Even the top ranked person doesn't understand the natures' design!!!...

After travelling throughout the Earth I realized that whatever is taught in schools and college curriculum about Earth is so sparse! Hence even the top ranked person doesn't understand the natures' design! The man takes birth in the ignorance and dies ignorant. Then even if he may be a great person from world's point of view like prime minister, president, industrialist or master, If he does not understand about the Earth, his life is in vain!

We can site an example of one kind of con man in India. All who's who like prime minister, ministers, cricketers all rich & famous folks protest themselves before him to experience his alchemy, without using their mind or understanding the facts. If they had some knowledge of what we discussed before, these folks wouldn't have even looked at him. Instead, they would have prohibited such fraud people by law. No living being on this Earth has the power to create even a simple dried grass stem. At the most, con man can use sleight of hand to change the place of things by taking advantage of people's ignorance. It is surprising to see the big wigs and knowledgeable people being victims of such con men showing so called miracles of changing places of golden rings, lockets, etc. using the sleight of hand!

No living being on Earth can create even a simple grass flake! Whatever you see just has Earth at its root...

For this reason I am going to describe in this book about what it takes to create a simple dry grass stem. The ignorance of geological Earth keeps man in illusion about this. Do you want to know more about the importance of Earth? Whichever sciences exist on Earth; have Earth at their root. No Earth, no science! The root of gold, food, water and everything is Earth. Whatever you see, whatever you experience here has just the Earth at its base. Not just that, due to our Earth, for us we have this expanse of universe. No Earth for us, no expanse of universe for us. How is this? You will get to read about this more in this book. We discussed about how this geological Earth came into existence, now we shall see the place of our Earth in this universe.

What is Universe?...

Friends, what we call universe is simply beyond our scope! Ours is a small solar system. Such billions of solar systems and their planetary systems create one galaxy. This space has such billions of galaxies. The globular group of such galaxies is known as universe!! Phew! Does this give you some an idea of the expanse of the universe? Not only this universe, but there are innumerable universes!! Considering all this, in such a span where is our Earth? It is negligible! From the Sun of our own solar system, it looks like a sago size! Nothing in its existence!!

Our solar family and its member Earth! The importance of 150 million KM distance!!!...

There are 9 main planets like Earth in our solar system. Right now, the Pluto is removed from this planetary system, so just 8 remain.

Brief about the planets in the solar system...

Mercury: the nearest planet of the Sun.

Diameter of Mercury: 4880 KM

Approx. solar distance: 58 million KM

Single day of Mercury: Equals to 58.6 Earth days

Mercury's one year: Equals to 88 days on Earth

Temperature on Mercury: Minus 180° to max. 430° Celsius

Venus: The second planet in the solar system after Mercury.

Diameter of Venus: 12105 KM

Approx. solar distance: 108 million KM

Single day of Venus: Equals to 243 Earth days

An year of Venus: Equals to 225 days on Earth

Temperature on Venus: 490° Celsius

Earth: The third planet in the solar system after Venus.

Diameter of Earth: 12756 KM

Approx. solar distance: 149.7 million KM

Single day of Earth: 23 hours 56 minutes

An year of Earth: 365.26 days

Temperature on Earth: Minus 70° to max. 55° Celsius

Earth has one moon too.

Mars: The fourth planet in the solar system after Earth.

Diameter of Mars: 6797 KM

Approx. Solar distance: 228 million KM

Single day of Mars: Equals to 24.6 Earth hours

An year of Mars: Equals to 687 days on Earth

Temperature on Mars: Minus 87° to minus 5° Celsius

Mars has two moons.

Jupiter: The fifth planet in the solar system after Mars. (12 times larger than Earth!)

Diameter of Jupiter: 143884 KM

Approx. solar distance: 778 million KM

Single day of Jupiter: Equals to 9.8 Earth hours

An year of Jupiter: Equals to 11.8 years on Earth

Temperature on Jupiter: Minus 150° Celsius

Jupiter has sixteen moons!

Saturn: The sixth planet in the solar system after Jupiter.

Diameter of Saturn: 120514 KM

Approx. solar distance: 1427 million KM

Single day of Saturn: Equals to 10.2 Earth hours

An year of Saturn: Equals to 29.5 years on Earth

Temperature on Saturn: Minus 180° Celsius

Saturn has sixty two moons according to new research of NASA!!

Uranus: Seventh planet in the solar system after Saturn.

Diameter of Uranus: 51118 KM

Approx. solar distance: 2869 million KM

Single day of Uranus: Equals to 17.2 Earth hours

An year of Uranus: Equals to 84 years on Earth

Temperature on Uranus: Minus 210° Celsius

Uranus has eighteen moons.

Neptune: the eighth planet in the solar system after Uranus

Diameter of Neptune: 49557 KM

Approx. solar distance: 4496 million KM

Single day of Neptune: Equals to 16.1 Earth days

An year of Neptune: Equals to 164.8 years on Earth

Temperature on Neptune: Minus 220° Celsius

Neptune has eight moons.

Pluto: the ninth planet in the solar system after Neptune

Now this planet has been removed from our solar system.

Diameter of Pluto: 2300 KM

Approx. solar distance: 5914 million KM

Single day of Pluto: Equals to 6.4 Earth days

An year of Pluto: Equals to 248 years on Earth

Temperature on Pluto: Minus 220° Celsius

Pluto has one moon.

The head of all these planets in our solar system is Sun. Earth is the third planet from Sun in the solar system. Its distance from the sun is approximately 150 million KM. This distance is of prime importance from the point of view of life on Earth. A permanent difference of few million kilometres in this distance will destroy the life on our Earth. When the distance between Sun and Earth reduces to a small extent than 150 million KM, the temperature on some parts of Earth hits to more than 50 degree Celsius and is unbearable to the life on the Earth. It causes death of much life including human beings during that particular year. And when this distance increases to a small extent than 150 million KM, we experience hailstorms in some parts of Earth. It causes such a drastic reduction in the temperature that it gets unbearable to the life on Earth and we hear about the deaths due to freezing. Isn't this distance important?

THIS INFORMATION IS IMPORTANT TO KNOW THE SECRET OF YOUR PRESENT BIRTH AND DEATH!!!...

The Earth is rotating lifelong around herself from west to east. Besides rotating round her, she is also rotating around the Sun. Friends, isn't reading this information boring? But to know the self-identity and drive away the ignorance it is important to read on and UNDERSTAND this. Because your each breath is dependent on this, these things are connected to our breath!

CLOCK IS A MINI EARTH!!!...

It takes 24 hours for Earth to rotate around itself and 365 days 6 hours to complete the rotation around Sun, which we call as year. These two velocities of Earth create the time calculations of seconds, minutes, hours, days, months and year. Other than Earth, nowhere in the space time calculation takes place!

****

See what is hidden inside the Earth's belly?

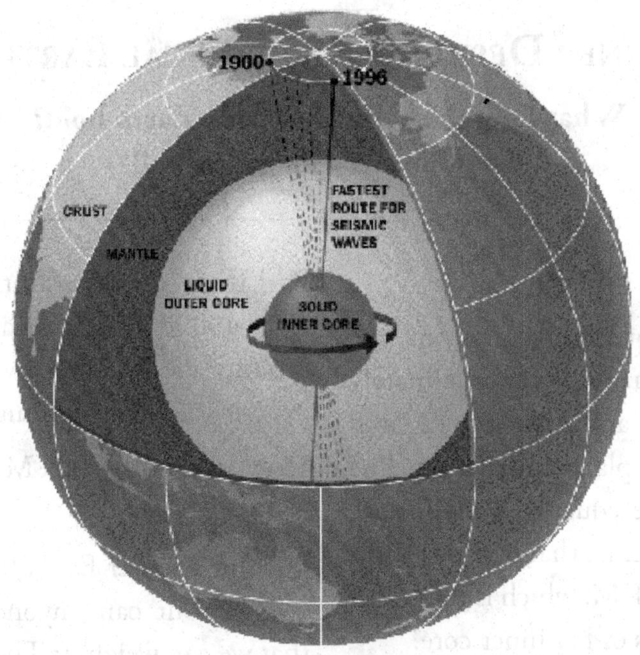

Earth's inner structure...

Everyone is curious about what is hidden inside the Earth's belly? The inner structure of the Earth is seen in the above picture. Earth has a diameter of 12756 KM and the radius of 6378 KM. The thickness of the tract out of the visible surface of Earth is just 35 to 70 KM whereas at the bottoms of seas and oceans it is mere 5 to 10 KM. Our Earth's surface is made up from almost 20 to 25 pieces combined together. These pieces are floating on the lava flow layer of approximately 600 KM thickness flowing underneath. Below this is the layer of flexible rocks of 2300 KM thickness. Then there is a 2200 KM layer of nickel mixed iron. There is a revolving solid iron ball of an approximate radius of 1250 KM in this layer. It has bestowed the nature of magnetic ball to the Earth. It has caused the creation of animates on this Earth. You will get to read the detailed description about this in the chapter 'Inner Design of Geological Earth'.

2.1

Inner Design of Geological Earth

What does the belly of Mother Earth hold? Earth means a magnetic ball

---

The size of Earth...

The equatorial girth of the Mother Earth is approximately 40075 KM and diameter 12756.8 KM. If we plan to put a pipeline through the equator, we will have to put a pipeline that has the length of 12756.8 KM, which is the width or thickness of her inner core.

What is the girth of Earth on equator?

I was lucky enough to get the chance of being at equatorial line during my visit to Kenya. This line that connects the southern and northern hemispheres passes through approximately 100 KM distance from Nairobi, the capital city of the country Kenya. The complete length of this circular line that is total length of equator is 40075 KM. Due to this, the Earth makes a round of approximately 20000 KM from sunrise to sunset and again of approximately 20000 KM from sunset to sunrise, that is total 40000 KM within 24 hours around itself. This gives us the experience of day and night.

How much does our Mother Earth weigh?

Our Mother Earth has its own weight. But can anyone imagine that we can weigh it? The scientists have done this miracle. The great scientist Isaac Newton discovered the weight of the Earth and scientist Henry Cavendish endorsed it further with his research.

5974 trillion metric ton is the weight of our Mother Earth!!!...

Friends, so far we have seen that our Earth is 4600 million years old. I described briefly the transformations she underwent since her birth. I have been telling that these descriptions and the upcoming descriptions are related to the human birth and death, every breath of ours; it is not my opinion or some imagination or thought but is a mere reality! But humanity must attempt to understand it.

See what Mother Earth holds in her belly!!!...

We have seen the size, diameter, girth of the Earth. We saw how and when the man was created first on the Earth and also how the clock was created due to Earth's rotation around herself. Now let's know what she holds in her belly and what it means or how it affects us, her children. What is beneath the rivers, mountains, seas and oceans, deserts, forests, farms and all that we see on the surface on Earth? I am coming to it and revealing this secret!

As the outer case or the crust of the earth looks solid and hard, we imagine the same about her inner core. But reality is different. The cities, buildings and all infrastructures we see on Earth are resting on such a thin peel that we just cannot imagine. Imagine the ratio of apples' inner pulp and outer thin peel. Earth's crust is thinner than this ratio of apples' outer peel to its inner pulp. It is just like a thin film or a thin flake compared to its inner core. And it is amazing that on this thin film the entire life dwells!!

If we imagine Earth as a round ball, its radius shall be approximately 6600 KM. If we make an opening or a hole of this length, we shall find it changed much. As we go deeper, we shall find it getting hotter. Approximately after every 100 meter, means 325 ft we shall see the temperature rising by 3 degree Celsius. As we go further the temperature will rise so much that we shall see the molten rocks!

Earth is divided into four layers...

Earth's first layer is called the 'crust' which is a hard outer case, the land that we see.

Second layer is called the 'mantle' that acts like a covering.

Third layer is called 'outer core' which is the outer case to inner core

Fourth layer is called the 'inner core' which is the inner core or pulp, the Kernel.

Now let's know more about each layer friends, as this relates to our life.

1. CRUST: THE OUTERMOST HARD CASING OF EARTH...

Friends, we feel that the outermost hard casing, the land, of earth is even and consistent, isn't it? But that's not the reality! The casing of our Earth is like a football, made up of many different patches those are connected together. How many are these patches? There are main 7-8 patches besides 12 -15 small patches. These patches are called 'tectonic plates'.

Our existence is dependent on these patches. These patches do the task of creating life and handling, nourishing it. This is not seen on any other planet.

Tectonic plates are plots or lands or continents. There is a difference of opinions amongst the geologists about the numbers of continents or lands. However, roughly following continents or lands are agreed by majority.

1. African 2. Antarctic 3. Australian 4. Eurasian 5. Indian 6. North American 7. South American 8. Pacific 9. Arabian 10. Caribbean 11. Cocoas 12. Juan de Fuca 13. Nazca 14. Scotia 15. Philippine Sea

THE CRUST OF EARTH IS NOT CONTINUOUS AND IS MADE UP OF THE THIN PATCHES FLOATING ON LAVA!!!...

As mentioned earlier, the crust of an Earth is much thinner compared to the ratio of the peel of an apple to the pulp of an apple. And on this thin film we have large and tall buildings, seas, oceans, huge dams, heighted mountains, mega cities, huge rivers etc. Now friends, it will surprise you to know that the patch on which your home is situated has a thickness of mere 35 to 70 KM! And at the base of seas and oceans it is just 5 to 10 KM!

'Yellow stone national park' in the United States has the thinnest layer or land patch on Earth. It always experiences the outbursts of volcano and fountains of sulphur. The islands of Hawaii too are formed due to such volcanoes. You cannot imagine the temperature beneath these patches. It is as high as 1500 degree Celsius! And these patches are just floating on the lava that is in the layers below! The places where the edges of these patches or plates climb upon each other or get scratched to each other experience the volcano or earthquakes.

Why does city of Tokyo in Japan frequently experience earthquakes and tsunamis?...

The city of Tokyo in Japan frequently experiences earthquakes and tsunamis. The reason behind this is that three plates have come together at this place on Earth! So their activities cause earthquakes, tsunami, and volcanoes. Usually the base of seas or oceans experience earthquakes or volcanoes because of the thinness of the layer of Earth's crust.

On such main 7 to 8 plates and small 12 to 15 plates of Earth crust our life dwells.

On a thin patch floating on Lava is our abode!!!...

Friends, do you know this fact? that our abode is on just one of these thin patches floating on hot lava! Our existence depends on this patch. If the patch moves, oops! Experience the earthquake or volcano depending on the extent of its motion!! Increased motion makes doom inevitable!

We and all life breaths due to these patches!!!...

These cooled patches of Earth crust have a deep connection with us. We owe our existence to these patches! You breathe due to these patches. You are getting your food grains, fruits water, vitamins, and minerals due to these patches! These patches help you farm and produce the crops you need. No other planets on our solar system has such patches, hence friends make a good use of whatever existence you have received! Live in a good manner and let others live in a good way too!!

These patches belong to all living beings, then why some people starve?...

The food, shelter and clothing created by these patches do not belong to you alone. It is not an exclusive property of someone but is available for all living beings on the Earth. So have you ever thought that you snatch the food, shelter and clothing of others for your selfish reasons and leave these patches one day? None have been given the exclusive rights to collect this for just oneself, but it is for all! It should be distributed to all. Remember this! The man indulges in unethical practices under the name of industrialization, business and politics to snatch the wealth given, things created by these patches. Does he think that time why 800 million people are starving in India? Or why worldwide there are small children dying in countries like Africa due to malnutrition?

For the tiny belly of self, keeping the wealth of others worth million dollars only for self, be in the form of food, gold or money, would this clan ever think about the starvation they are causing? Would this clan ever know their true identity?

I too belong to a human clan of animates. But I too had faced moments of suicide due to lack of food, just due to these selfish hoarders! Would such people read this book, have the knowledge and realize their true identity?

2. Mantle - covering of core means the second layer below the Earth crust...

We now know much about the thinnest layer of Earth that is the crust of Earth. Means what we see and imagine about the Earth contradicts with the real interior nature of Earth. Such a huge Earth and its land, but including the humanity situated on its surface, all the life dwells on such a thin layer floating on hot flow of lava!

What is your standing? Who are you compared to this Earth?...

After knowing the facts above we realize the grave illusion the humanity lives in! They talk like "some educationist has 200 acre of land! Some XYZ owns so many sq meters of land! Some industrialist owns 50 factories in the world!" Some politician says he has a backing of 200 MLAs! Wow! What an illusion of ego! Grandeur in the air!

I would like to ask them, have they ever studied the Earth? Do they know on what ground are they dancing? On the wafer thin crust patch of Earth that may move anytime! They are dancing on a huge mass of fire that may burst anytime!

Do they know whose wealth are they claiming as their own? It is Mother Earth's wealth given for all beings dwelling on her! I urge the government authorities and social reformers to include this information about Earth as the compulsory curriculum of schools and also colleges. So trust me all would know the reality and would change their thinking. All my efforts are to show the difference between the reality of Earths true nature and the ignorant buccaneer are dwelling on her!

The second layer in Earth's belly is hot lava with temperature of 2000 degree Celsius! The thin patches floating on it has our abode!!!...

The first layer described is the Earth's round crust. The layer below this is also circular which is called 'Mantle'. Its thickness is approximately 2900 KM and it is divided in 2 sub layers. The outer 600 KM thick layer out of this thickness of 2900 KM is lava which is called 'magma'.

The 35 to 70 KM thick surface of Earth that we live on has rivers besides mountains, hills, tall buildings, green forests, deserts, farms full of crops. We are enjoying all these things living on Earth. But we cannot imagine that below the layer that we live on flows lava juice with temperature of 2000 degree Celsius! And our existence is on the crust of such hot lava. Considering this our ego drops! Think, who are you?!

How earthquake takes place and volcano erupts?...

Due to the pressure below the lava erupts breaking the crust at the place that has thinner crust on Earth. We call it volcano. So fragile is our existence as all life dwells on thin crust of lava! This existence can end anytime. We have already watched on television how it caused earthquake and tsunami in Japan that destroyed houses, cars and entire city.

As is described earlier about the surface of Earth, the 5 to 6 large and 12 to 15 small patches are floating on the flowing lava. So while floating, when the joints of these patches brush up each other or climb on each other then at the city or town of that place the earthquake is experienced. This is the alchemy of the 600 KM thick lava layer under the Earth crust!

The elastic layer of moving plastic like rocks of 2300 KM thickness!!!...

Below this lava there is 2300 KM thick elastic like soft molten plastic and slow moving layer of rocks.

Thus we are getting into the Mother Earth's belly. We have come up to 2 layers deep. This would have helped you understand the grandeur of Mother Earth. Now let's get to the third layer in her belly.

The root of existence of all animates and human breath in Mother Earth's belly!!!...

The third layer in the mother Earth's belly is so important that all other things necessary to form life like land, water, air and light etc. are dependent on this and fourth layer. Your birth too is dependent on this layer.

So involved is human being in the daily chores of earning bread and butter, fame, name and wealth that he spends whole life just for it. But he never gets queries like who am I? What am I made up of? Who made me? What is the reason of my being? Do I really own myself? And up to what period this body is formed? He never thinks about it. The root of all these things is the third and fourth inner layers of the Mother Earth. Whatever wealth or fame one may have accumulated, however rich and smart industrialist one may be or however public might have adored him, if that person does not know about this basic knowledge then he has taken birth in ignorance and will die ignorant. So I as I have been writing that the root of each animate in inside the Earths belly, that I am going to describe elaborately in twelve factors. Now we shall turn towards third and fourth layer.

3. The third inner layer 'outer core' of Earths belly...

After the layer of lava and solid yet elastic cover the inside of Earth suddenly changes. As in case of any animates body design, this too is the part of Earths body design. The description that I am going to make will surprise you! You may not have imagined that Earths' belly holds something that has given us the birth! You will be amazed to know that this layer causes the birth of all animates.

So far we have read the descriptions about the rocks, stones, dust, hard rock and molten rock. But now this layer means the start of molten metals! How thick is this? You will be amazed to know that it is approximately 2200 KM thick circular and is made up of the fluid mixture of the iron and nickel!! This mixture of both metals is fluid and flowing like water! They are rotating within the Earth's belly! The Earth is rotating around Sun with the approximate speed of 107000 KM per hour and also around itself with an approximate speed of 1610 KM. This speed of her dual rotation gives tremendous flow to this 2200 KM thick molten iron and nickel layer.

The ocean of molten iron and nickel and the formation of Earth's magnetic power!!!...

Friends, the third layer means 3000 degree Celsius boiling ocean of 2200 KM thick molten and free flowing iron and nickel! Can you imagine the temperature at this layer? 3000 degree Celsius! An ocean with such a huge temperature, many times greater than any ocean on Earth's surface, is inside the belly of an Earth! The largest ocean on Earth's surface is Pacific Ocean and what is its thickness? At the most 11 KM! And what is the thickness of this ocean of molten iron and nickel in the Earth's belly? it is approximately 2200 KM!! And that too free flowing like water! Isn't this a big surprise in the belly of Mother Earth?

Now, the motion of Mother Earth gives motion to this huge ocean of metals inside her belly and the waves of this ocean create a magnetic field on Mother Earth and give her the gravitational force! That's what; Earth is the big magnetic ball with a gravitational force within our solar system. She draws all things to herself! Jupiter and Neptune have more gravitational force than that of Earth. But neither of them has the situations or elements favorable for creation of life and has no life.

What helps you give food, drink water, AND BREATH air? Just check!!!...

Such is the third 'outer core' means an ocean of flowing iron and nickel having temperature of an approximately 3000 degree Celsius. This has created the gravitational force on Earth which has created the life including you and me. How? I would explain further about it.

Of course, the fourth layer in Earth's belly too is responsible for creating this magnetic field means gravitation force. Some may find this description boring and lengthy. But one must know this, because our breathe depends on this third and fourth layer within the Mother Earth. All living beings need oxygen for living and the existence of this oxygen is caused by this third and fourth layer. If the gravitational force is not created by third and fourth layer, then the life on Earth shall perish and she will be barren as Moon. Means we must know that our existence depends on these layers.

4. Inner core: internal kernel means solid iron ball...

Now let's know about the fourth layer inside the Earth's belly. This is the last organ in the body of Earth. Creation means getting birth. After birth each life starts its needs. Each needs air, food, light and water. It gives growth to each living being. We have bread, vegetables, milk and so many other things in our meals. The root of all these things is the fourth layer within the Earth's belly.

Earth's fourth layer is smaller than Moon in size...

Third and fourth layer causes the magnetic power due to which we can enjoy the things on Earth. Then what is this fourth very important layer? The man accustomed to routine life will get very amazed. Because inside the belly of Earth that has the ocean of liquid iron and nickel at the temperature of 3000 degree Celsius, is floating a solid iron ball of approximately 1250 KM radius, means having approximately of 7857 KM circumference. This is the fourth innermost layer i.e. inner core of the Mother Earth!

The size of this ball is just a quarter smaller than the size of a Moon. This layer has the intense temperature that we cannot imagine, i.e. approximately 5500 degrees Celsius! Thus the Earth has the temperature that may be found on the surface of the Sun. This huge iron ball is rotating in the ocean of iron and nickel in liquid form which causes the magnetic waves, giving huge gravitational force to the Earth.

THE MAGNETIC POWER CAUSED BY THIRD AND FOURTH LAYER HELPS YOU SEE THE MOON!!!...

The Moon that you see in the sky is at a distance of approximately 384600 KM from the Earth and yet floating and rotating in the space due to the magnetic power of this Earth and the same magnetic power causes the Earth to rotate around the Sun at a huge speed of 107000 KM along with this Moon!! Can anyone copy this miracle?

Not just this, the influence of this magnetic power is spread to the heights of hundreds of kilometres from Earth. That is why the faulty airplane falls down on Earth from such a height. Even more we must know is what we call environment is nothing but the layers of different gases and Mother Earth hold them near itself due to her gravitational pull. Earth pulls to herself anything that comes within her orbit.

Now you all may be wondering, if this fourth part has a temperature as high as it is on Sun's surface, then how this iron ball is formed and remained a solid ball? The reason behind this is that this part has a pressure million times more than that of Earth's surface. So here all molecules of iron come together to form a ball holding each other tightly that makes this ball of approximately 7857 KM circumference.

You may say who has gone and seen what is hidden inside Earths belly? No one has gone so far and no one can go ever, this is a reality. But these discoveries are the alchemy of our great scientists. They have studied the waves of earthquakes happening on Earth and the meteoroids fallen on Earth from time to time to discover the inner facts of Earth. These are the things beyond ordinary man's reach but knowing the reality is important. Humans have drilled at the most 15 KM deep inside the Earth's belly.

Owing to this inner structure of the Mother Earth we exist and can consume, enjoy the beauty of everything created on Earth. Whatever we see here, we see because of this, else we wouldn't have been able to see Moon in the sky too! Neither would we get created to see it nor would anything worth seeing be created! Did you ever read about this reality that I am keeping forth now? You won't read about these facts in any religious scripts.

What is the secret of your birth? What is your real identity and what is the cost of your existence?...

My sole aim to put forth all this information is to let you know your real identity. Till today who is responsible for your, mine and entire life's creation and existence? Moreover, the 'I', the one you think of yourself, who is this 'I'? From what did this 'I' is made up of? What is the meaning of being born? What is your life? What is the value of your existence? Who is mother who is father? Your relatives? If you don't belong to yourself, then who are these people and where from they came? Then what about fame, name, assets & property created by man? To remove these delusions and illusions, to know your true identity each page of this book is important.

If you really wish to enjoy the life, live the life in true sense, know the causes of sadness and happiness then know about the Earth's structure, her creation and creation upon her. This book is dedicated to it. If you study this book you will get the answers hidden in this book.

The gravitational force of each planet in our solar system...

The following chart denotes the gravitational force of each planet in our solar system, compared to our Earth. If anything weighs on Earth as 100 KG, we can derive the weight of the same thing on other planet in comparison to this weight on Earth knowing how many times the gravitation force is more or lesser than that of Earth.

The Planet	Approx weight (KG)	Gravitational force compared to Earth
Sun	2822	28.22 times more
Mercury	38	2.63 times lesser
Venus	91	1.09 times lesser
Earth	100	Same
Moon	16	6.00 times lesser
Mars	38	2.63 times lesser
Jupiter	214	2.14 times more
Saturn	74	1.35 times lesser
Uranus	86	1.16 times lesser
Neptune	110	1.10 times more
Pluto	8	12.50 times lesser

When and how was the human created on Earth?...

While studying the inner structure of the Earth I realized that 4600 million years ago the Earth was created. The man was not created even after so many million years means approximately 4597.5 million years were passed. Before 2.5 million years the man with hands was created on this Earth. And as recent as just 12000 years before he got developed and turned to farming. He started protecting himself from heat, rains using leather, mulch to make hut. He started using leather as clothes. The time before Christ passed in this state. Until 16th century after Christ, means approximately 400 years before from now the humanity was unaware of gravity, magnetic power etc.

Just 400 years from now the scientific knowledge dawned upon humanity...

Isaac Newton discovered gravity during 17th century. Until then neither any saint was aware nor was it ever mentioned in the manmade religious scriptures that Earth has a gravitational force and is the major cause for life's existence. We can just imagine the ignorance of the mankind. But humanity is so much stuck to the old religious, superstitious methods even today that it is still ignorant despite various discoveries made by scientists in 21st century. We see examples of so called famous, intelligent people prostrating themselves before clever god men!

The real saints interested in the wellbeing on humanity are scientists! They discovered new things which have made our life easier and we are enjoying the fruits of the gifts they have given. Thus humanity is ignorant even in this 21st century. Not much difference has taken place since long time! How much percentage of Earth's population knows the facts elaborated above? How unfortunate it is for humanity to not know the facts related to the life's breath! So I wish whatever is described here, should be incorporated and taught in the compulsory study curriculums from school levels to college levels. I sincerely feel this will ward off ignorance of humanity and challenges thrown by fanatic religious leaders, selfish politicians and likes can be eradicated at the root.

****

Many pieces combined together make the Earth's surface!!!

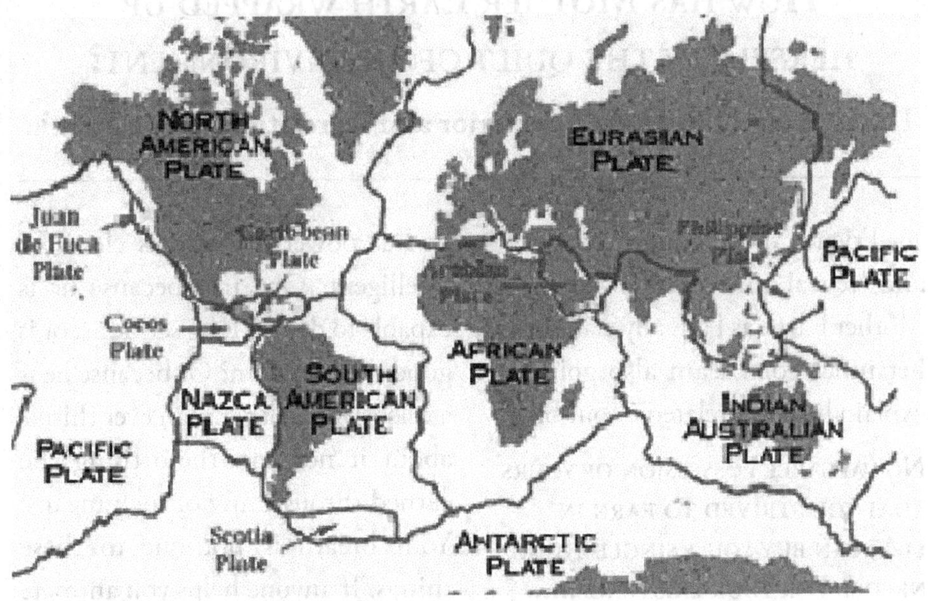

Main tectonic plates...

The above picture is not the map of the countries on Earth; but you can see how the surface of the Earth is connected by different pieces combined together. We take the Earth's surface to be monolithic; but in reality it is made up of many patches combined together just like a football. Out of the 20-25 tectonic plates that it is made up from; you can see some major continents in the above picture. The thickness of these pieces or plots or continents at the place of tract is approximately 35 to 70 KM; whereas the thickness at the bottoms of seas and oceans is only about 5 to 10 KM. All these tracts are floating on the 600 KM thick flowing lava in the Earth's belly. There is always a slow movement between these tracts. But when these tracts rub or climb on each other the earthquakes and volcanoes are experienced on the Earth at those places. The human and other animal life dwelling on these tracts is affected resulting in the economic and life disaster. You will get to read the complete description of the Earth's inner core in the chapter 'Inner Design of Geological Earth'.

2.2

How has Mother Earth wrapped up herself in the quilt of an environment?

The breadth of the Earth's exterior and its relation to our breath.

Friends, I am going to describe and reveal the exterior part of Mother Earth as I already elaborated her inner core. I am also going to explain how it is related to our birth.

No valuable possession of yours that you strived to earn in life, can buy you a single thing needed for your existence!!!...

As described in earlier chapters, the Earth has inner parts and they are deeply related to the life on Earth. Likewise, Earth has its external parts and that too is related to the life on Earth equally. The breath of animates including human beings is due to this external coat on Earth. Think about it, whatever life we are living, the breath on which our existence depends, our life and death depends; does the man earn the things necessary for this breathing through hard work or earns them because he has lot of money, gold, precious stones? Or earns because he has powerful body, is clever or intelligent? Or earns because he is capable to deliver long sermons, or is good as a con man? Or because he is a celebrity? Neither man ever thinks about it nor can these things be earned through any of such means! Your breath is not due to these things. If anyone helps you animate your life, helps you breathe, it is just Mother Earth, Mother Earth and only Mother Earth!

Now let's know the environment from Earth's surface to what we call sky, how it is and how many layers it has.

Mother Earth rotates in space along with her quilt!!!...

Friends what we call sky is comprised of different layers of gases which are spread many kilometres wide. The color of these layers is bluish due to which we see blue sky. But the real sky if we wish to see, it can be seen beyond these layers spread over many kilometres, it is totally black!

We term these layers widespread over many kilometres from Earth's surface as environment. Within such thick environment that spans over many kilometres from her surface, our Earth is clad, as if clad in a quilt! Only she has the quilt! In the entire solar system, no other planet has this environmental quilt! The main reason for this valuable possession of hers is the inner structure in her belly. Owing to it Earth has become a huge ball with a gravitation force. Due to this gravitational force she has pulled towards herself these layers of gases spanning through kilometres over kilometres from her surface. She has pulled and held them circularly due to her gravitational pull and rotates along with this quilt around the Sun with the speed of 107000 KM! Due to this environmental quilt that surrounds her, the life dwells happily on her surface!

Which all gases this environment is made up of? How many layers it has?...

This environment has many gases and it consists mainly of nitrogen gas which is 78%, oxygen 20.95%, 0.93% argon and 0.035% carbon dioxide. Besides this it has some amount of ozone and water steam approximately 1%. We call this mixture 'air'. What Earth would be without this layer of air? You would say it would be devoid of life. But just that is not the enough fact. Besides life, this Earth would be devoid of any water drop. There would be no rivers, seas, oceans but just a barren land as is Moon. Have they, running behind money and fame ever thought about this? You have now cleared enough idea about what has given you the life and breath! No precise explanation is required.

The approximate quantity of gases in the environment is as given below.

Gas in the environment	Approximate quantity in percentage
Nitrogen N2	78
Oxygen O2	20.95
Argon Ar	00.93
Carbon Dioxide Co2	00.035
Neon Ne	00.0018
Helium He	0.00052
Methane CH4	0.00014
Krypton Kr	0.00018

Nitrous Oxide N2O	0.0000325
Nitrogen Dioxide NO2	0.000002
Hydrogen H2	0.00005
Xenon Xe	0.000009
Ozone O2	0.000007

The environment that we are talking about is divided into four main parts.

1. Troposphere 2. Stratosphere
3. Mesosphere 4. Thermosphere

WHAT WE OWE OUR EATING OF FOOD, DRINKING OF WATER TO?...

The very important task these four layers perform from the point of view of life on Earth is absorption of the ultraviolet rays emitted from Sun. This reduces the intensity of the sunlight and heat that is coming on Earth. Thus sunlight and heat is made bearable and most importantly, nourishing for the life on Earth. Due to this humanity is alive, nature gift trees are standing, varieties of plants, flowers, leaves, and fruits are visible. Due to this we are eating our food, drinking the water!

Let's see the nature and width of these helpful layers of the environment.

1. TROPOSPHERE - THE FIRST LAYER OF ENVIRONMENT...

The temperature in the air is affected by the density and sparseness of this layer of the environment. Earth has two poles i.e. north pole and south pole. Viewing the Earth, environment spans up to a height of 7 KM from these poles as a thick layer. On equator, it has a width up to 17 KM height from the Earth's surface. The airplanes fly approximately 11 KM from this layer.

Troposphere is the nearest layer to Earth's surface. Of the total air, this layer comprise a very small i.e. 1/70 part and rest 4/5 part is divided amongst other environmental layers. The height of 16 to 17 KM which is beyond this layer has a temperature as cold as minus 55 degree Celsius. Such a layer called Troposphere. You would hear about this temperature when the airhostess usually announces to remove your seatbelts after crossing this layer in an airplane.

2. STRATOSPHERE - THE SECOND LAYER IN THE ENVIRONMENT...

Importance of Ozone gas!!!

From 7 to 17 KM up to 50 KM wide, this second layer mainly consists of Ozone gas which protects the life on Mother Earth from the dangerous ultraviolet rays of Sun. Because these rays absorbed by the ozone gas present in this layer.

3. Mesosphere - the third layer in the environment...

This is spread from 50 KM to 80 KM wide in the environment. The meteors entering into Earth's environment get burnt and destroyed in this layer. Here the temperature lessens with the increase in height.

4. Thermosphere - the fourth layer in the environment...

From 80 to 85 KM up to more than 640 KM wide is this layer. In this layer the temperature increases with the increase in the height. The usual temperature here is approximately more than 1400 degree Celsius! The environment is very sparse in this layer. After this, approximately 700 to 800 KM onwards starts exosphere. Space shuttles travel from this height means outside the environmental orbit. From 700 to 800 KM onwards space starts.

The orbit of Earth's environment...

There is no specific orbit between Earth's environment and space. This is because the environmental layers get sparse and fade away with the increasing height from Earth's surface. But in the field of aeronautics usually 100 KM from the Earth's surface i.e. 328000 ft height is considered as environmental boundary or orbit.

'Carman line' means the orbit of Earth's environment...

The Hungarian - American engineer Theodore Van Carman, working in the field of aeronautics and material sciences first researched that after the height of 100 KM the environment gets sparse and is sufficient for the aeronautical use. According to him outside this orbit the space shuttle can take on maintaining enough speed for itself and can travel faster than it can with the speed within the orbit. This orbit of Earth's environment is named after the scientist Carman, called 'Carman line'.

The travellers travelling above 80 KM height from the Earth's surface are termed as 'astronaut' in the United States.

Clouds -The clouds that we see in the sky are nothing else than the miniature particles of ice or millions of micro drops of water held together. Or the mixture of these two. Being micro particles they have negligible weight and float in the air. Clouds are formed at different heights from the Earth's surface. They get different forms. These can be formed near Earth's surface too.

Rains and snowfall is caused by such clouds in the air...

The clouds of the type 'stratus' cover the sky fully while the type Nimbo stratus usually are responsible for rain and snowfall. The clouds of type Cumulo Nimbus appear to be on the heights more than 500 meters. The grayish or black light group of clouds with white silver lining denote electricity and storm.

Earth's age is 4600 million years. During this period the life started forming as the environment started forming. This environment favorable to creation of human life was formed much later means just 2.5 million years ago. Then first human was created. Much of life was already created by then. First animate was born millions of years after the birth of Earth. Since the effect of Suns heat was lesser in the water than on the Earth's surface, first animate was born in the water. Favorable environment was the reason for its creation! Even today the environment is one of the main factors out of 12 factors that cause the birth of an animate!

Environment means our birth and death! How?...

An environment is of a grand importance. Even today you will not see any life taking birth if the Earth gets the temperature of 70 degree Celsius! The existing life will perish. Earth will be a barren land. If the temperature gets to minus 50 degree Celsius, then too no life will take birth. Earth has a place where temperature is minus 57 degree Celsius. It is Antarctica. Due to unfavorable environment at this place, neither in water nor on Earth's surface life is created. Forget the human; this place doesn't even produce ants, insects, and plants!!

The root cause of birth of the animate is environment! One part of your identity!!

After studying all this, I found that just environment or atmosphere is the root cause of the creation of animated life. 'I' am not created by any manmade god but the environment is the main cause of 'my' creation. And hence you won't find the animate on any other planet or even if you keep any animate on the other planet it will not survive there. Not just that, the oxygen gets sparse on the height of 20 to 25 thousand ft from the Earth's surface! No life is created at that height. You won't find any plant, vegetation or animate on Mount Everest! Many visitors to Kailas Mansarovar have died due to insufficient oxygen. Due to prolonged cold climate for the majority of year, the northern pole of Earth has a very slow reproduction rate. So the population of the countries there counts just in single million or lesser.

You must read this if you wish to spend your life in happiness and joy!!!...

My parents are just the cause for my birth. But the 12 factors needed to create the body of each animate are only on this Mother Earth! So the Earth creates you, she feeds you and only she causes the reproduction from you! Once you know this identity of yours, your pseudo 'I' will drop and you will get the identity of real 'I'! Once you identify your real self, you get the keys to which things are to be given importance and spend the time between your birth and death happily. I ensure you, if you know about 'who am I, from where I came, what after me and what is my highest good' then in real sense there will be no sorrow in your life, no dangers in your life. Greed, selfishness, jealousy would vanish from your life. The human on this Earth will be able to eat enough, no one will starve. No one will accumulate wealth more than necessary.

This is the reality unfolded!!...

This is not because I am mentioning, but this is the reality unfolded. Each child must learn in school and college this complete identity of Mother Earth. If these things are taught in childhood from schools, told in stories then it certainly will naturally shape a better human. Imbibing the stories in old legends will never solve problems. Since thousands of years saints and elderly have been telling the stories of manmade god, has that brought any improvisation in human? But what I have understood and revealing here is quiet different! If you know and understand the things that you experience at each breath, the life will so much smoother!

See this importance of environment. Except Earth no other planet in our solar system has the life. No divine power, no god, no almighty can create any life on these other planets. Because the twelve factors necessary to create the life are unavailable on any other planet except Mother Earth! This is not enough, it is just impossible for a human being to go to any other solar system! It is not the cup of tea of the man having a limited life span of just 60 to 70 Earth's rotation to Sun! Whatever NASA says or any other space system concludes, reaching there is just impossible for man! Hence Earth means environment, environment means the life on Earth and you and me existing here are the negligible fractions of Mother Earth! This is our identity. Letting you know this real identity is the purpose of this book!!

Any manmade adjectives of religion, race, and sect are not approved by Earth!!!...

In the process of description that I have about creation on Earth, where does religion play role? Where is race? What sorrow and what happiness through these? Are these things created by Earth? No. The natural design doesn't approve of this! These have sprung from the thought power, mind and imagination that man received and man has created the trouble for himself! I am going to share such more realistic actions of Earth further. It will make you understand who are you? Where you came from? Where are you going? What is your life and death?

What is so called sorrow and happiness that you experience? For your creation so much process has to undertake so many things go in it and they are available only on Mother Earth. Once you leave the Earth, no soul no divine soul! You are nothing but a negligible particle of Mother Earth with a momentary existence! Means your creator your savior everything is Mother Earth, Mother Earth and end product is Mother Earth!

STUDY MOTHER EARTH AND HER LIFE OVER RELIGIOUS SCRIPTURES! EVERYTHING IS HER!!!...

You are now convinced that you owe your existence to Earth's inner structure, cooled patches of crust and the environment! Otherwise who are you? To know yourself, understand pulse of Earth and her life design is sufficient than reading religious scriptures. It will help you dissolve your ego. And hence be insistent for inclusion of this knowledge of Mother Earth in study curriculum which will add to the true knowledge of entire humanity. Friends, I am not describing anything imaginary or hearsay but the truth, only the truth! No one can prove this wrong! This is not connected to any manmade god. No manmade god can interfere the earthquakes, tsunami, and life design. So if god must be imagined, it is Mother Earth, Mother Earth and just Mother Earth!

****

2.3

One Part Related to The Astronomical Earth

Light Year

A Unit to measure the distances between Celestial Bodies of the universe

The difficulty of expressing the huge distances between planets, stars, galaxies in figures led the scientists to discover the unit of measure based on light that has the greatest speed of all.

Friends, you may have heard the word 'light years' while learning geography in primary school. Usually the deeper knowledge is never given about this word either in school or college. How the term light year was created? In this universe of ours there are millions of planets like Earth and millions of stars like Sun. The distances between them are so huge that it is difficult to express them in usual mathematical figures. Just as we tell the distance in figures; say between India to United States is roughly 13576 KM, or from Boston in US to Shanghai in China is roughly 11725 KM, we cannot express the distance between planets and stars in such figures. So the scientists discovered the unit **'light year'** to express the distance between two planets or stars. This unit is used to count and express the distance between stars, planets or any celestial body.

Do you know what would a light year be when counted in usual figures? Some of you still may like to know it. So, just one light year expressed in our usual figures is approximately 10 trillion kilometres! Anyone interested in counting zeros? No? So light year (symbol is 'ly') solves the issue of expression, it is easy to express.

The fastest speed in this universe is that of the light speedily travelling from any star. We may know the speed of light. But while explaining light year we must mention this speed. The time taken for a Sun's light to reach any planet is the speed of light. Let us take an example of our Mother Earth. The light emitted from Sun is travelling to Earth at a speed of 300000 KM per second. So how much is the speed per minute? It shall be 18 million KM. Thus per hour this speed would be 1080 million KM. Hence for a day i.e. for 24 hours it will be 1080 x 24 = 25920 million KM. Now, the earth takes 365 days 6 hours to rotate around the Sun. We call it an year. If speed for a day is 25920 million KM, then **for a year it would take approximately 10 trillion KM, means one light year.**

Henceforth wherever you read the distance between two planets or stars is some xyz figure, then multiply that figure with 10 trillion KM and it will give you the distance. For example, the distance of our Earth from the Sun is 150 million KM. There are so many Suns in our universe that we have no reason to consider them. But their distances would be measured in light years.

The second nearest Sun to Earth is Proxima Centaury at a distance of 42 trillion Kilometres!!!...

Besides the present Sun that we know, there is another Sun nearest to the Earth. His distance is 4.2 light years. Sounds a small figure right? But in real it is at a distance of 4.2 light years x 10 trillion KM = 42 trillion KM. This is the second nearest Sun to Earth from our Sun in our galaxy. His name is Proxima Centaury.

The expanse of the universe is approximately 13 billion light years!!!...

It is said that this universe is spread approximately 13 billion light years from our Earth! Keep counting figures! Thus, in this huge expanse of universe; Earths' position is nothing! And the human and politicians living on Earth keep jumping about their own positions! What they think of themselves? Ignoring the duty of serving people, without sharing with other humans they just hoard money and wealth that is so momentary!

If so negligible is the position of Earth in the expanse of universe, what position the humankind hold? Would these human beings ever think about the negligibility of their prospect of life? Those who never aware about this must read this book, this is for them!!

If you don't have the knowledge of your own creator, rest of your knowledge is a waste!!!...

After I comprehended these facts, I came to a conclusion that the top positioned politicians within humanity, the philosophers having deep knowledge on any subject, brave ones, the richest people on Earth, people skilled of making lot of money, the clever con men, religious leaders willing to control humanity and all such so called experts; if have not understood the Earth and her life design, then they have poor and incomplete knowledge! Because the root of all philosophies, sciences, principles and even the root of people who preach & teach these philosophies, sciences and principles is just the Mother Earth! Only the people who know thoroughly whatever I am describing about the Earth and her life design; have the complete & full knowledge. Whatever I am describing is the root of all and if root is not known; all other knowledge is incomplete! They haven't understood themselves. I am going to explain this further. Person talks about mundane or material knowledge. But what about it's root? He never talks about that! Life is created due to Mother Earth. Due to her the human is created. But the one who doesn't know this, his or her knowledge is a waste! Without the existence of Mother Earth who is the human? What is life? Who are the leader and what stand priest has?

****

See the Moon shining in the pitch darkness of the space!!!

Moon is the life of people on the Earth!!!

See how the Moon looks in the photograph above. Are you even aware that our existence depends upon the existence of the Moon? She rotates around the Earth with the speed of 3689 KM per hour from the distance of approximately 384600 KM. Due to her this rotation the 20-25 pieces or tectonic plates of the Earths' surface are stable. With the end of Moon's existence these pieces of tracts on Earth would get unstable and entire animate creation will end. Are you aware that a day of the Moon is 656 hours? It means continuous sunshine of 328 hours and the night of 328 hours. The detailed description about the Moon is available in the chapter 'Astronomical Earth- Actual Moon'.

The human to set the first foot on the Moon!!!

The flag of USA and the first footstep of human on the Moon...

The photograph above is about the human's first footprint set on the Moon. The flag of USA and the footprints of the men alighted on the Moon are seen in the dust of the Moon's surface. There will be no change in these footprints and the flag hoisted there even after the millions of years get passed, they shall remain the same. The main reason for this is that there is no environment on the Moon. Due to this nothing on the Moon ever moves.

2.4

One Part Related to Astronomical Earth

Actual Moon

The Existence and breath of each animate including human is Moon!

The moon too rotates around Sun at the speed of 107000 KM per hour along with the Earth. As the day on Earth is made up of 24 hours, that of is Moon is of 656 hours. The maximum temperature on Moon is 105 degree Celsius and minimum temperature is minus 85 degree Celsius. Without one moon, no life would have been created on Earth! Such surprising facts will be revealed in this chapter about Moon.

We saw the information about Mother Earth and the life on Mother Earth. One more such important factor related to Earth is Moon. Let's see the history of Moon's birth.

How and when was the Moon born? Moon means the life on Earth!!!...

Before 4400 million years there was no environment on Earth and her surface was not cooled. So the other planets used to hit the Earth often. In such one instance, one planet hit the Earth harder and caused a small piece or a chip of Earth's surface to escape away from Earth and get steady in the space. This separated chip of Earth is what we call Moon. Since the chip was a fraction of primitive Earth, it doesn't have the minerals and metals that the inner core of Earth has. So the Moon doesn't have the gravitational force equal to Earth's. Many of us count the Moon as a planet. But in reality it is neither the planet nor the star in our solar system. It is just a ball of rocks rotating around Earth that we call a satellite of Earth. The light that is emitted on Earth from the Moon is not Moon's own light but it is Sun's hot light. The Sun's hot light is reflected from Moon to Earth, so it feels cool.

Moon too has a major share of causing animated life on Earth. It causes the high tide and flow in the seas and oceans of our Mother Earth. The cool light from Moon helps the creation of animated life on Earth. Now let us clear our misunderstandings about this Moon.

What is the Moons' distance from Earth?...

You may ask, 'how far is the Moon from the Earth?' Its approximate distance from Earth is 384600 KM. The reason of the Moon's steadiness at this distance is Earth's gravity. Due to the gravitational force of Earth, the Moon is rotating around Earth. Moon's size is four times smaller than the Earth's size. So the diameter of Moon is 3476 KM and its circumference is 10900 KM. The surface of this Moon is dry and barren. When I read in the newspaper or hear on TV that 'Humans will settle on Moon! The sale of plots on Moon will begin!' I take it like a joke! Because the temperature on one side of Moon is 105 degrees Celsius while on the other side it is minus 85 degree Celsius! These humans could not make any proper habitat on Antarctica of their own Earth so far; and they are talking about settling on extremely cold and hot Moon! And plot sale!! Isn't it a amusing humour? I get entertained with such news!

The Moon is barren and dry, without atmosphere!!!...

The twelve factors which are responsible for the creation of life on Earth are totally absent on Moon. So she has no life of any type, no creation. Insects, animals, vegetation or birds nothing is there. And yes! It never rains on the Moon! You will never see any clouds in the sky of the Moon. She doesn't have the gravitational force of Earth. Her gravitational force is 6 times lesser than that of Earth. So any stuff weighed as 100 kilograms will weigh mere 16 kilograms on the Moon!

The environment described on the Earth is just non-existent on Moon, she has no atmosphere. There are no layers of gases from the surface of Moon as they are in case of Earth. So there is no question of ozone gas, which protects the life. This causes the ultraviolet rays from Sun to directly hit the Moon's surface! This is the reason it has such a high temperature i.e. 105 degree Celsius! As there is no environment around, the sky appears pitch black from the Moon. Oh yes! Our Mother Earth looks like a decorated beautiful blue sapphire from the Moon!

Sitting in the arms of Mother Earth, Moon too rotates around the Sun!!!...

Earth rotates around the Sun at the speed of 107000 KM per hour; but her this rotation is caused just by the gravitational force of Sun. But the Moon's rotation around the Sun is not at all dependent on Sun's gravitational force. As each thing on Earth and; even though, atmosphere and aeroplane in the sky too rotates around the Sun due to her own gravitational force, Moon too is affected by her gravitational force and rotates along with Mother Earth as if a child sitting on Mother's lap or in her arms! As mother moves, the child sitting in her arms or lap too moves with the same speed. Likewise as Moon too is sitting in the Mother Earth's arms she too is rotating around the Sun along with Mother Earth.

The doctrine of the Moon's rotation speed around the Earth!!!...

As Earth rotates around the Sun, the Moon too rotates around the Earth in an oval orbit! Her speed is usually not mentioned anywhere. Due to my curiosity, I studied and discovered the canon of Moon's rotation speed around the Earth. It is as given below.

We can assume the distance of Moon from Earth as the approximate radius of Moon's rotation around Earth. It is 384600 KM; with rounding off it is 385000 KM. Now let us calculate how much the Moon has to rotate. For this we can use the formula 'radius x 44/7 = circumference' from geometry.

385000 x 44/7 = 2420000 KM, means Moon has to rotate a distance of 2420000 KM around the Earth.

It takes 27 days 8 hours, means 656 hours for the Moon to cover this distance. So 2420000 divided by 656 hours gives us the figure of 3689 KM. This is an hourly speed of Moon's rotation around Earth. Thus with study I discovered the Moon's rotation speed around the Earth.

What about the Moon's own rotation speed around self?...

First, we will derive the circumference of the Moon to know the speed of her own rotation around self. We will have to use the formula 'diameter x 22/7'. So, 3476 KM x 22/7 = 10900KM approximately. So to rotate around self, the Moon has to travel the distance of 10900 KM. She takes the same time to rotate around self as she takes to rotate around the Earth. Her speed of rotation around self is unimaginably slow! We shall divide her circumference with the time it takes to complete the rotation around self. It shall give us the speed of her self-rotation. Thus, we arrive at the figure of 10900KM / 656 hours = 16.61 KM.

With such slow speed she rotates around self. We don't get such information elsewhere. But we must know this because Moon is the part & parcel of Mother Earth as we are!! We along with the Earth's life share a deep relationship with Moon just like a one related by birth!

If you properly read the Moon's speed of rotation around self and around Earth, we will notice that the time she takes to rotates around self-i.e. 656 hours is also the time she takes to rotate around Earth. We shall see the effect of these similar periods of Moon's rotation.

Why do we see only one side of the Moon from Earth?...

We are so engrossed in the mundane life that we cherish the cool light of Moon but we never try to know more about her! Moon is an inseparable part of our life. In fact while the Moon is rotating around Earth while rotating around self; the human has been able to see just one side of the Moon! The other side is never visible. Why? There is a reason which lies in a magical number that I have discovered. That number is 222 times! Now I shall describe how I arrived at this number and its canon.

How magical number of 222 is the reason for single side visibility of Moon?...

Now check that Moon has her rotational orbit approximately of 10900 KM. Similarly, her rotational orbit around Earth is 2420000 KM. This is 222 times higher than her rotational orbit around self! How? As 2420000 KM / 10900 KM = 222 times. Means her rotational orbit around Earth is 222 times higher than her own rotational orbit around self. Similarly we shall consider her hourly speed of rotation around Earth and also around self.

We have seen earlier that Moon rotates around Earth with the speed of 3689 KM per hour and around self only with the speed of 16.61 per hour. As we derived the measurement of the rotational orbits, we shall derive the same for the speed. Means rotation speed around Earth divided by rotation speed around self.

Hence, 3689 KM / 16.61 KM = 222 times

1. The rotational orbit of Moon around Earth and around self
2. The hourly speed of Moon for rotating around Earth and around self

The similarity in the measurement denotes that as Moon takes 656 hours to rotate around herself, she also takes same, means 656 hours to rotate around Earth. This similarity gives permanent visibility of only one side to the human on Earth!

Deep knowledge of Moon is as necessary as food!!!...

Engrossed in the mundane life, human is just concerned about daily bread and butter. But this reality is as connected to our life as daily bread and butter is. How?

Suppose, if Earth had two moons as in case of Mars and their gravity would have been more or lesser compared to Earth's. Or second Moon would have been closer than the first Moon and her gravitation force would have been more; then it would have affected almost ¾ of Earth's water. It would have caused high and low tides in the seas and oceans in enormous way, causing water to spread everywhere. It would have caused chaos because the life on

Earth is situated just on 20 patches and they are floating on lava. The gravitational force of second Moon would have caused the movement in tectonic plates or patches. It would have resulted in big earthquakes and volcanoes! It would have endangered the animated life on Earth. So, for the existence of life on Earth it is important to have ONLY one Moon and her being at such distance. Did we ever think about this? We just weren't aware of it!

The surface of the Moon...

Moon's surface is not similar to Earth's surface which has football like 20 patches. It is continuous. It is uninterrupted like a hard covering of a wood apple and is thicker than Earth's surface.

Are there earthquakes, volcanoes on Moon?...

Moon's surface is like a barren land. But it has large craters. As the surface of Moon is continuous and thick, there are no earthquakes or volcanoes. Have you ever heard on TV or read in any newspaper that Moon had earthquakes or volcanoes? But similar to Earth, Moon too has many high mountains. The tallest of them is called Mons Huygens. It has a height of approximately 5500 meters. The spots appearing on the Moon may be these heighted mountains.

There is an elongated plateau on the Moon and it has no stones. It has the crater of a diameter of approximately 2100 KM with the depth of 12 KM, which is the largest one in our solar system. United States of America had sent two astronauts on Moon. Their footprints and the flag they hoisted would remain as they are for trillions of years. Because there is no atmosphere to cause any change in them, there is no air to wipe off the footprints! Just because of Earth Moon is floating in the space and rotating around herself and Earth.

The tide and ebbs at the oceans of Earth...

The five oceans and 113 seas on the Earth get affected by the gravitational pull of the Moon that causes tide and ebb. With the proximity of Moon during full moon day, we observe huge waves i.e. tidal waves in the seas. When the Moon goes away from the Earth, i.e. during no Moon day, we can observe ebb or low tide. So the Earth needs only one Moon which would never interfere the life on her. The important fact is, even a slight permanent difference in the present distance of 385000 KM of Moon from Earth will endanger the life on Earth! There is a deep relationship of the life on Earth and Moon, but man will never be able to create a life on Moon.

WHERE IS GOD, HEAVEN AND HELL?...

Human being has created the ideas of god, heaven, soul and hell from his imagination. If we send 5 to 10 different pairs of male and female on Moon, not only would they die soon but also would not be able to reproduce. Then where is god? And other imaginations like soul, heaven? So whoever will study and understand the Mother Earth and the creation of life on her, will never believe in these things. They will know the reality.

THE ILLUSION OF EYE SHOWS THE SAME SIZE OF SUN & MOON FROM EARTH!...

We see the Sun & Moon daily. Actually Moon is the satellite of Earth and four times smaller than the Earth. Its circumference is about 11000 KM. While Sun is 100 times larger than Earth and 400 times larger than Moon. But upon gazing at sky we see the Sun and the Moon of the same size, isn't it? Why is it so? The vague explanation given by the scientists is that there is a difference of 400 times between the sizes as well as the distances of the Sun and Moon. The similarity of difference in the distance and size is the reason scientists give for our visual illusion. But I didn't understand one thing that was, the difference of 400 times between the sizes was understood, but difference of distance was vague. After deep thinking for many days I got the answer. We are looking at Moon & Sun from Earth. The distance between Moon and Earth is approximately 385000 KM; and 400 times of this distance is the distance between Moon and Sun! The Moon is 400 times far away from Sun, but from which reference distance? It is from the reference distance of her distance of 385000 KM from Earth! Thus due to the similarity of differences between the distance and size, Sun and Moon appear to be of the same size to us from Earth.

NOW LET US SEE THE SIZE OF BOTH...

Moons diameter is approximately 3476 KM and circumference is 11000 KM. Sun's diameter is approximately 1.4 million KM and circumference is approximately 4.4 million KM. Considering these figures the size of the Sun is 400 times larger than the size of the Moon.

Similarly, the distance between the Earth and the Sun is 150 million KM. For the person viewing from the Earth, the distance between Sun and Moon is 400 times more than the distance of 385000 KM between Moon and Earth. So to his/her eyes the huge Sun looks similar to the size of Moon! So the fun is, it seems like the Sun having total solar eclipse, but it is just an illusion. How? I am going to explain this further.

THE SIZES OF SUN AND MOON AS VIEWED FROM THE EARTH ARE COMPLETELY FALSE AND ARE AN ILLUSION!!!...

Yes! How the sizes of the Sun and Moon as appearing from Earth are an illusion? This is just the alchemy of the distance between the Earth and the Moon! I will elaborate this again. Suppose we travel 100000 KM towards Moon from our Earth, the Moon will appear to be much larger than the Sun. Because you are going nearer to the Moon and at the same time Sun will appear smaller comparatively, right? This example will clear that the Sun & Moon's appearance of similar size is just an illusion of a viewer from the Earth! So I will also explain how the eclipses too are false!! If you properly study this book, you will know that the human from Earth 'feels' that there is total solar eclipse due to Moon, but the reality is different. The main reason for this is the 'illusion of appearance' of Sun & Moon; they appear to be of same sizes from the Earth! Once you know this, you will realize how eclipse too is an illusion!

THE DAY AND NIGHT OF MOON!!!...

You may not have read the information I am going to reveal here about the day and night of the Moon. It is very surprising. The diameter of Moon on an average is 3476 KM and the circumference is 10900 KM. The Moon rotates around herself as she rotates around the Earth. Earth rotates around herself at an average speed of 1610 KM per hour and hence takes 24 hours to complete her circumference of 40000 KM. So her one part is facing the Sun for 12 hours, that is the day, and the other part that is not facing the Sun for 12 hours means the night. Thus total 24 hours are needed for a full day (day and night). How many hours form the full day of Moon? You will be surprised!

The Moon rotates around earth with an hourly speed of 3689 KM. But she rotates around herself with an hourly speed of just 16.61 KM. So to complete the round around her own circumference of 10900 KM, she needs 656 hours. The Earth has a full day of 24 hours, but the full day of Moon takes 656 hours! Out of them, for 328 hours her one side is in front of the Sun and the other side that is not facing the Sun, which is the night of Moon is of 328 hours too! Though this is the reality, from our Earth we assume the night and day on Moon to be similar to the Earth's i.e. of 12 hours each! Have you read this? One must study astronomy to know such fun and reveal the mysteries! It increases the depth of knowledge. Moon takes 656 hours to complete the rotation around Earth. So the viewer from the Earth sees Moon's Sun facing side growing each day till full moon day. When Moon is viewed as a complete circle, we call it a full moon day. Likewise, further from this full moon day it appears to be reducing phase by phase each day till no or new moon day. When it goes behind the Earth we don't see it in the sky, we call it no moon day.

Why Moon changes its shape each day?...

For the human being watching the Sun & Moon in the sky daily from Earth, some facts about them are hard to accept. But the truth is not the mere appearance, the reality could be different. For example as I explained earlier, viewed from Earth the Sun and the Moon appear to be of the same size. But are they really of the same size? The sky appears to be blue when viewed from Earth, is it in reality blue? The light emitted from the Moon on Earth appears to be cool, but is it really cool? Friends, so many such things that 'feel' or 'appear' to our eyes could be deception or illusion of eyes. The reality may differ.

So now, when viewed from the Earth, the Moon appears to change its shape each day. This is another 'feeling' or 'appearance' or say deception to our eyes and in reality the Moon never changes its shape! It is an illusion of the viewer from the Earth. What could be the reason behind this illusion? Take a note that while rotating around self; Moon is also rotating around Earth in an 'oval' shaped orbit. So the viewer from the Earth can see only the illuminated, Sun facing part of the Moon.

Illusion about the Moon's phases!!!...

As the Moon keeps coming in front of the Earth from no moon day to full moon day, she appears to be increasing her size daily. When the she is completely freed from the Earth and is fully Sun facing, she is fully illuminated. We call it the 'full moon day'. From this day till no moon day as she keeps on hiding behind the Earth, her Sun facing illuminated part keeps reducing. We say Moon is reducing. When she completely hides behind the Earth, she disappears to the viewer from the Earth. Thus this is just the illusion of appearance of the viewer from the Earth.

The cool full moon night is the hottest Moon!!!...

We enjoy and find the cool moon light on full moon day to be very pleasant. But do you know the irony about it? Do you know that when we are feeling pleasant under the moonlight, the Moon has such a blazing sunlight on her that the temperature on her is whooping 105 degree Celsius!! Would anyone survive at such temperature?

The human on Earth enjoys the coolness of the moonlight because the actual blazing sunlight on Moon is reflected on Earth. What causes this magic? This magic is caused by the distance of almost 384600 KM between the Earth and the Moon!

What we see is not the real Moon!...

Now what is this? The lunar disc that we see is an illusion! It is not the real Moon. Simply because there is no such lunar shape in existence! But there is just one Moon, and then what do we see? Again this is the viewer's illusion. If you march towards the Moon, it will appear to be bigger, but that too an illusionary Moon. But if you go to 384600 KM from Earth, you will see the real Moon. That is her real existence. But if the same Moon is seen from the planet Mars, it wont even be visible. Or will appear as a tiny dot. Means it is not the real Moon. Such Moon does not exist. It is your illusion.

THE BIG ILLUSION OF HUMAN! THERE IS NO LUNAR ECLIPSE!!!...

As I said, every scene as it appears may not be real and may be an illusion. Same way eclipse is a deceptive vision. The lunar disc that you see in sky, is it the real Moon? As we have seen earlier, we know the description of the real Moon. She has dry, barren surface, she has huge craters, high mountains, and her circumference is almost 10900 KM and diameter 3476 KM. Have you seen such Moon in the sky? Your answer certainly will be 'no'! Such huge Moon appears to be just of 15 cm diameter to us from Earth. Then is the Moon of 10900 KM circumferences true or the Moon of 15 cm diameter as it appears to us is true? The answer would be 'the real Moon is the true Moon'. We see her from the distance of 384600 KM. So instead of real Moon we see the small delusionary Moon of 15 cm diameter. Then does the real Moon ever get an eclipse? Never! The deceptive image of Moon appears to be eclipsed! So the lunar eclipse that you see is a false concept!

Now you would know that there is no effect of an eclipse to the real Moon. Because if you see Earth from the Moon, it will appear to be just of 2 ft diameter or less! Then, will the Moon of almost 10900 KM circumference and 3476 KM diameter be covered by this apparent Earth disc of 2 ft or lesser diameter? It is impossible! Means the real Moon is never affected. Then what about the eclipse that we see in the sky? The Earth rotates around the Sun and Moon rotates around the Earth. When Sun, Earth and Moon come in a straight line; the viewer of the Earth feels as if the image of Moon is covered due to the image of Earth. I say image, because the real Earth, the real Moon and the real Sun are much different than the sizes they appear to be of in the sky! So the human on Earth 'feels' the deception of the lunar eclipse, but in reality there is no effect on the real Moon. And such eclipse is not visible to all from Earth. But it appears from the specific locations on Earth. So eclipse is an Illusion.

The sizes of the Moon and Sun as they appear in the sky are illusionary! Their actual sizes are different!!!...

The shapes that we see of Sun and Moon in the sky have no existence in reality. There is no Sun or no Moon of such shape. So the eclipse that you see is of non-existent Sun and Moon. Means there is no real phenomenon called eclipse based on any real objects. The real Moon and Sun never get eclipsed. The Moon is 400 times smaller than Moon. If viewed from the Sun, the Moon just won't be visible! Then would she ever cause total solar eclipse? The scientists should bring this reality to common public. Why not institutes like NASA bring these facts to notice of people openly? With my explanation above, you must be convinced by now about the truth of the Sun & Moon. That which is not a reality but your eyes see is an illusion. Illusion is falsehood. So the Sun and Moon that you see, both are illusionary.

What an ignorance of humanity!!!...

Due to the ignorance of humanity, the eclipse gets related to the religious rituals. Some people, without giving the true information play with human emotions and exploit the innocent and ignorant humans. The real Moon has nothing to do with the eclipse. Only the humanity of Earth has this illusion. I hope, after knowing the reality your misunderstanding about eclipses is cleared.

What you see is not necessarily what it is in real!!!...

The things are not the same as the man's eyes see. You must note this and must understand this. Because 'change is the rule of nature.' 'Change at every moment' is the law of nature. Nothing is permanent, nothing is eternal. If this is understood, you would realize that the ideas of happiness and sorrow, fear or joy are nothing but your imaginations that you are stuck up with. For example, the fragrance, cleanliness are desirable and pleasing to the human being but the same are undesirable to the pigs, flies, mosquitoes and such other living beings. Pig likes dustbins; human has disgust for it! For pig it may be a heaven; for humans it is the hell!! Actually, there are living beings in multiples of humans. They are created by our Mother Earth herself. But human race lives in its own illusions and ignorance. Man thinks of himself as something different. So the vices not attached to any other living beings like sorrow, greed, manipulations, urge to lie are stuck only to him! He does not obey the laws of nature but believes in illusions. This has resulted in increasingly hard and unhappy life for him!

See, how Moon is weighed!!!...

You may wonder about how like any other object; the Moon's weight can be decided? But the scientists have attempted this. Scientists have derived the weight of Earth too. It is 5974 trillion metric ton! We have already discussed and know about the size of Moon and the size of Earth. Earth is four times more in size than the size of Moon. So you may think that Moon's size may be four times lesser or just a quarter of the Earth's size, isn't it? But to the contrary it is not that simple!

Even though the Moon is just four times smaller than the size of Earth, she weighs whooping 80 times lesser than the Earth!! Isn't it funny! But how is it? Do you remember the birth of Moon that we described earlier? Moon is but a chip separated from the surface of Mother Earth and does not have the properties of the inner structure of Mother Earth. Oh yes! Further, Earth was later cooled and has undergone many changes with respect to her inner and outer structure. So owing to the hard rocks on her and the huge iron ball in her belly; Earth weighs 80 times more than the Moon! Well, sometimes simple human assumptions go totally wrong!

Earth's weight / 80 = Moon's weight. That's why 5974 trillion metric ton / 80 = 74.675 trillion metric ton; this is the weight of the Moon that we see.

Would humanity take a note of this reality and responsible politicians show their generosity?...

Would this reality be included in the school and college curriculums? Would the politicians and responsible socialites show this generosity keeping away their own illusionary image?

While giving the most possible information, I have tried to remove the misunderstandings regarding eclipse, phases about the Moon that is so deeply connected with our life. And I have also thrown the light upon the falsehood of prevailing misconceptions. My request to humanity is to not to connect illusionary things like eclipse with the religion and add to the ignorance of people. The truth must be described and elaborated to all instead of keeping public in ignorance. Especially the Asian continent should get rid of ignorance about eclipse. It is necessary to give the information about the truth behind eclipse to children through school syllabus. Knowing the truth described in this book will be useful to make the life of the human easy, peaceful and satisfied on Earth. Whatever is taught today about the eclipse in schools and colleges is misleading. The reality about eclipse must be taught in all schools on Earth. I have put up my efforts. Whether to know the reality about this is the question of the human race.

This was just dispelling the misconception about Moon. Just read to remove the other misconceptions that you may have!

****

See the closer view of the Moon!!!

Moon's surface...

You can see that the surface of the Moon is covered by the craters. Do you have an idea that the maximum temperature on the Moon is 105 degree Celsius? But the same light on the Moon feels so cool to us. So how is it possible to make an abode and stay on the Moon? At this place there is no air, water, sound or sky, except sunshine as we have on Earth.

This is our Sun!!
The ball of hydrogen gas!!!

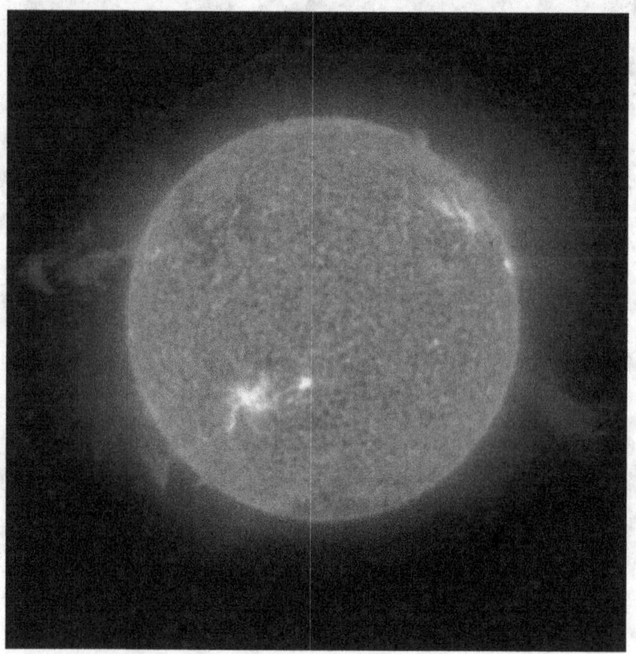

Sun means the mundane human life and existence of life on Earth!!!

The real nature of the Sun that is at a distance of 150 million kilometer from the Earth is huge. What is visible to us is just the hot ball of mere 15 cm diameter. But the real Sun has a diameter of whooping 1400000 kilometers and the circumference of 4400000 kilometers. Almost 0.4 million ton hydrogen gas is combusted per second on the Sun due to which we breathe, the animate beings are created and exist. Due to the gravitational power of the Sun the huge ball of Earth is floating in the space. Due to that the creation of animates is dwelling on the Earth. You can read the complete information about the Sun in the chapter of 'Astronomical Earth- The Real Sun' of this book.

2.5

The Real Sun

The size of the Sun that you see is not the real size of the Sun!

Deceptive Appearance of Sun's Size Leads to the Falseness of Total Solar Eclipse!

The entire life's existence on this Earth and the reason of our every breath is just the Sun!!!...

Sun plays a major role in every living beings existence and creation on Earth including human. Forget about you and me and the entire living nature, but even our creator, our beloved Mother Earth too depends on Sun for her existence! But without understanding this truth, the entire humanity spends all her energy and time on earning more and more possessions of gold, money, vanity and fame. Also she is so much absorbed in consuming the man-made, artificial things! She is lost in imaginary stories. Some priests, god men & swamis are making millions of dollars by narrating imaginary stories and adding to the public ignorance. They build big ashrams, tombs, religious centres. These people are responsible for creating the gap between rich and poor by getting the investment of million dollars for the religious places. On the one hand poor people are searching for the food, shelter, education & health care. And on the other side the rich people are snatching these basic rights of these poor people. And without spending a single penny on these needy people, they spend millions on the man-made god! Where do they have time to know about why they breathe?

The living beings on the Earth are of two types! How and which types are they?...

You take food & water daily, enjoy the married life and reproduce. You breathe continuously till death. Each living being is enjoying its life. What is living being? You should know the definition of 'living being'. The whole humanity on Earth, animals like elephants, horses, snakes, ants, water dwellers like fishes, food, all plants form the gamut of 'living beings'! It is the definition of 'living being' that has a very wide scope. I have divided them further in two types; mobile beings and fixed or immobile beings! Mobile beings are the ones who can move around. Immobile or fixed beings are the animates who cannot move around without the help of others, like plants. On these fixed elements depends the rearing of all life. Without the consumption of these fixed beings the mobile animates cannot exist. On these fixed living beings depends the creation, nurturance and existence of mobile beings. Some mobile beings are meat eaters and some are plant eaters like cow, goat, and deer, buffalo who cannot exist without eating grass, fodders and plants. They are also called 'herbivorous' or grass eaters. The omnivorous animals' existence depends on these herbivores. Like lion, tiger have to depend upon these herbivores to survive. This is a food chain, which exists only on Earth. The reason to describe all this is to emphasize that to create these beings, the Sun is majorly responsible.

The Man-Made Legends and Concrete Reality!!!...

Owing to the energy of the Sun; the living and non-living nature dwells on the Earth. In truth, the man-made scriptures, legends and stories should ward off the ignorance of humans by telling reality than narrating imaginary stories. Because of whom this animate and inanimate nature exists, who is responsible for the creation of this nature? This humanity never tries to know. The Human race turns the back at what they experience at each breath, at that which is always visible to their eyes; and believes the legends, stories and the imaginary things mentioned in them that they have never seen, that which is absolutely unrelated to their existence. Assuming such imaginary things and imaginary god as real, the human race spends literally million and billions of dollars on them; and thus wasting the invaluable time of their lifetime one day departs from this world in the ignorance! What an ignorant humanity! The humankind has neither improved in the past nor will ever improve in the future due to such legends!

Scientists, the real dutiful children of Mother Earth and obligators to human race!!!...

If anyone has obligated the human race, they are the scientists! Does anyone keeps the photographs of those scientists at home who have made the life of humanity easier, happier and of those who have completely changed the life of human race in this twenty first century? Does any one of you remember them while using the facilities and modern technology enabled easy life that they have gifted us? No! No one remembers Thomas Alva Edison while lighting the bulb light at home or office; or no one remembers Alexander Graham Bell while using the telephone! But singing the praise to the imaginary god, performing out dated meaningless rituals, spending lifetime on it and fostering the charlatanry or quackery is what humanity still doing! It dances for the gods it has never seen and for those who have absolutely no connections to human life and existence! Isn't it regrettable?

For whom is the creation of imaginary god? For the fearful and selfish children of Mother Earth!!!

To tell you the truth, the imaginary god came into existence due to the fear and selfishness in humanity! The fear does not touch to those who are dwelling in harmony with the nature and her laws without any misdeeds. So he does not need god. Also the ones who earn enough for their own necessity with their own clean efforts and carry selfless love for all in their hearts do not need the god.

Suppose the kids of two acquaintances are appearing for exams. One puts clear sincere efforts, while other goes to the religious place and prays "let me pass with good marks without much efforts". What do you think? The selfishness coming out of laziness creates god! If their god is real, and just the prayers come true, why one needs to put efforts and study?

Which is actual god? Is it only humanity's god?...

Originally the concept of god is not natural. Is god only the monopoly or privilege of humanity?

What about the other living beings? Is god not for them? Is he limited just for Humanity? The animal kingdom does not worship any god or recite the religious scripts. Where is the god when daily thousands of goats, hens get slaughtered? The mockery is that this slaughter happens in the name of this human created god! So my request to humankind is, if they want to honor someone as god then why not they honor the Sun, Moon and Earth who are responsible for their every breath, their whole existence, their creation?

To disobey the nature human needs god, other beings obeys the nature and depart without sorrow!!!...

You may wonder 'what is the relation of above description to the Sun?' But you forget the Earth and the Sun who have created you. You do not wish to obey their unwritten laws. You constantly break the unwritten laws of nature and so you need god! Other beings take birth and dwell happily complying with the unwritten law and depart happily without needing the god! Have you seen any animal sitting sad or sorrowful expecting something from some imaginary deity? They are so much in the presence of 'now', one with the nature, always responsive to your love.

Your each breath is related to the Sun and the Earth, not just that, but your life & death, your existence depends upon them. Not only human but the entire living and non-living nature is dependent on the Sun. It means all your activities like eating, walking, talking, sitting are dependent on the Sun. But we pay no attention and neglect it. This is what I try to relate with whatever I described earlier about the faddism of man-made god.

Now how this creator is Sun belongs to us? Let us see how he is responsible for our creation.

How is Sun? What is the size of Sun?...

In reality, what your eyes see is virtual, ostensible! But whatever is seen to eyes, we humans assumes it to be the truth. You may have noticed that the technology sellers have to specifically advertise that they are delivering 'WYSIWYG' means 'What You See Is What You Get'! It is because we have a saying 'things are not what you see!' Our Sun is no an exception to that!

As has been described earlier too, the Sun that we see in the sky appears to be the ball of just 15 CM diameter. But is it really so? Whatever you see is the 'virtual' Sun or 'illusionary' Sun. How big is the real Sun, if you haven't read anywhere, I am anyway going to explain.

The real Sun of our solar system!!!...

Our Sun is nothing else but a huge hot ball made up of 3/4th hydrogen and 1/4th helium gases. He has such a grand size that just the diameter of him is 1.4 million KM and the circumference of almost 4.4 million KM! It takes 25 days means 600 hours to complete the rotation around self. It also means that he rotates at the speed of almost 7333 KM around self. Such super-hot huge ball of hydrogen and helium we call the Sun. It will never be possible for us to go and see even some kilometres near to him!

Our existence would end if we try to go near him! The astronomical institutes of the repute like NASA has sent and will send the spaceships on other planets like Moon, Mars, Jupiter, Saturn; but have you ever heard of having sent something on Sun?

The family of Sun that too has the secrets of your birth & death!!!...

The huge planet from the human viewpoint, but with its negligible existence in the expanse of the universe, Sun maintains the family of 8 planets. We should know a bit about this family as our Mother Earth too is a part of it.

Mercury is at a distance of almost 58 million KM from the Sun, while Venus the next planet is at a distance of 108 million KM. Third planet is Earth, the place of our inhabitance. She is 149 million KM far away from the Sun. Fourth planet is Mars having the distance of 228 million KM and fifth planet Jupiter is a distance of 778 million KM. Sixth planet is Saturn which is almost 1.42 billion KM far away from Sun and seventh planet Uranus is 2.86 billion KM far away from Sun. Eighth planet Neptune is farthest planet of the solar system with its distance from the Sun being 4.49 billion KM. This is the wide scope of the Sun's family or our solar system!

How Sun upkeeps the members of his family?...

Though negligible in the expanse of the universe; the Sun upkeeps the family of 8 planets. Now what is meant by maintaining the family of planets? It means the gravitational force of the Sun is much larger than any of these 8 planets. We have seen the chart depicting this earlier. Due to the gravitational power of Sun, these planets are rotating around the Sun in the specific orbit of theirs. Our earlier chart depicts the time or earth years they need to complete the round around the Sun.

Without the huge gravitational power of Sun, all these planets may have hit each other and strayed away somewhere. But due to control of Sun, they don't leave their own orbit. The gravitational force and the control of solar system is one of the main twelve reasons for the creation of life on Earth including human. The Earth would not have existed without this gravitational force of the Sun and the life on Earth would never have been created. We shall know about this further.

Now you must have noted that the Sun is the 'guardian' or 'host' of these huge planets! And it is related to each of your breath and activity.

How we get energy on the Earth from the Sun?...

We have seen that Sun has huge store of hydrogen. This Sun has been maintaining the Earth since 4600 million years. What is meant by he maintains or upkeeps the Earth? Means the energy generated by combustion or burning of the hydrogen gas on the Sun comes to Earth. Due to this energy, the life on Earth is created and humanity is happily dwelling. Each life that is created on Earth needs energy. Life cannot be created without energy, and Sun gives that Energy.

Almost 4 million ton hydrogen burns per second from Sun surface to keep your breath going!!!...

What creates energy on Sun? You will not read this explanation in any religious scriptures! It may surprise you but the fact is that out of the huge storage of hydrogen on the Sun, almost 4 million ton hydrogen is combusting each second. Due to this continuous burning process, the rays of Sun reach the Earth. The life on Earth gets the sunshine. Each life gets energy. And this energy gives existence to each life. This has caused our births. Once the energy in body is over, it gets dead. So the reason behind all this is the burning of the hydrogen at the rate of 4 million ton per second on the Sun surface! Why is this energy useful only to the life on Earth? The reason behind this is the distance of 150 million KM between Sun and the Earth. Any change in it will make this energy from the Sun useless to the Earth! This energy is so blazing that if it had directly hit the Earth, we wouldn't have taken birth. We wouldn't have been able to give birth to anyone. For this, Earth has got the gift of environment. From the surface of the Earth far wide in the space there are so many layers of the gases. Out of them, due to the layer of ozone gas, the intensity of ultraviolet rays gets reduced and we get mild light rays on the Earth. It makes the sunshine of Earth bearable and keeps up the warmth. This warmth fosters the creation and existence of life. Moon does not have such atmosphere and the blazing ultraviolet rays of the Sun directly hit her surface making the temperature as high as 105 degrees Celsius. This temperature is not bearable for life and its creation.

So by now you must have noticed that amongst the reasons behind our birth and sustained existence, two main reasons are combustion of hydrogen gas on the Sun at the rate of almost four million ton per second and the huge gravitational force of the Sun.

THOUGH THIS IS NOT THE INTERESTING NOVEL, BUT IS A SORT OF KNOWLEDGE TREASURE; THE CONTINUOUS READING OF WHICH WILL WARD OFF YOUR IGNORANCE! THIS TRULY ANSWERS THE QUESTIONS OF YOUR AFFECTION & CLARIFIES YOUR IDENTITY!!!...

Friends, as food, water and air are important for our living, our true identity is as important for our living. The true answer of 'Who am I?' should be known to us. Not the imaginary answer! Why am I here? Who is responsible for my creation and existence? We shall get truthful sincere answers of all these questions in this book. This is not a romantic novel, not at all a novel, but is related to the information concerning your birth and death. So if this book is read and studied by each human being on the Earth in depth, I assure them the real knowledge of the root cause of their existence that will add true meaning to their life. This is NOT my personal opinion that I am writing! I am not writing for the fancy of my own. Each chapter in this book sticks to the sincere truth. There is no scope for imagination! It is because this writing is based on the doctrines and not opinions. The important part is that, the human is very much lost in the mundane life and would leave this world one day. But he never gets to know the reality or no one informs him. In the ignorance human is born and in the deeper ignorance s/he lives! Without knowing the information given in this book s/he wastes the life in unwanted things and one day leaves this precious life! So the unknown things are elaborated and described in this book to impart the knowledge, the true knowledge about the things. You must know that they are the truth and you are experiencing them at every moment.

This book may get boring because there is no scope for story or drama in this book. But just like you take bitter pills for the cure or follow a hard routine to build your body, reading and studying this book without laziness will cure your illusions, ward off your ignorance! Then your life will be free from stress and sorrows, it shall be happy. You shall live the life fully knowing the value of its existence and depart from this world. The life will come to fulfilment.

****

NO ONE MIGHT HAVE TOLD YOU OR YOU MIGHT NOT HAVE READ ABOUT THE TRUTH THAT THIS LIFE GIVING SUN TOO HAS ITS DEATH ONE DAY!

While studying this solar system and the nature of life, I realized the hidden truth behind the saying 'Creation is the root cause of destruction'.

IF YOU FULLY REALIZE THE ABOVE TRUTH, OUR LIFE SHALL BE FREE OF WORRY, FEAR, STRESS AND WE SHALL SURELY LIVE HAPPY, JOYOUS AND SATISFIED LIFE. IF EVERYTHING IS TO GET DESTROYED ONE DAY, WHY SHOULD THERE BE AN ATTACHMENT, GREED, WEALTH AND ANGER, SORROWS, UNHAPPINESS AND MISERY? EVERYTHING IS TO PERISH!! NO GOD, NO RELIGION WOULD SUSTAIN, BECAUSE THESE ARE MAN-MADE, THEY WILL DIE TOO...

Anything that gets created in this world gets perished. It carries the seeds of destruction with its creation. Every living being is born with its specific life span and an inevitable death. From the humankind's point of view, how much ever courageous the person may be, or whatever strength, intelligence, great philosophy and knowledge he may possess and whatever titles and simile people may confer to him; he has a death! That is something of the law of nature, life on Earth! Rest, all his possessions, simile and titles are man-made and nature has nothing to do with it!! Whosoever has taken the birth has the death! The humans may have created the great wonders like Tajmahal, but it will decay in the process of time. The human's life will be much easier if he keeps this fact in the mind that you are to perish one day; then why to gather the wealth and possessions in excess? And, more important is why to waste this gift received of a precious lifetime in longing for each thing, every possession? The intention of this book is to make you aware of the reality, give you your identity so you can think of better ways of spending the lifetime happily. Each line written in this book relates to your life's reality. But whether to understand the reality or not is your choice! If you understand, it will bring about 100%

changes in your behaviour from the root! This is because you have been leading the illusionary life due to lack of your true identity.

SUN TOO HAS ITS DEATH ONE DAY!!! HERE IS THE EXPLANATION...

Now back to our main point of this chapter. Every creation has a seed of its destruction. With this law our life giving Sun too is going to die one day. What it means? The storage of hydrogen gas on the Sun is burning only with the speed of almost 4 million ton per second at present. Just like we get tsunami in our oceans and with huge waves everything around gets flooded with the water, there will be tsunami on the Sun too at the storage of hydrogen.

As a result, the hydrogen gas will spread out and its combustion too will speed up. As the hydrogen gas will be burnt in more and more quantities, the size of present Sun too will get larger and larger. He will be glowing much more than what he seems to be at present. He will become a huge star. The scientists have termed such Sun 'The Red Monster'.

Due to the growing piles of burning hydrogen, huge energy will be created. Such blazing energy will be intolerable to the life on the Mother Earth and it will start getting destroyed! The water storage on the Earth in the forms of ponds, rivers, seas and oceans will vaporize and disappear in the space. The excess heat will prevent the cloud formation and rains. All seas and oceans will get dried. At this time the temperature on Earth will be very high i.e. almost 1500 degree Celsius. This would start melting of the rocks and the quilt of environment on Mother Earth will get destroyed and so will be life on her! Along with the human the man-made gods' existence too will end!!

More and more fuel will come out and burn on Sun. His size will keep growing till finally the outer mass means the crust of the Sun falls down. The storage of hydrogen too would have exhausted by then. So the Sun's size will be drastically reduced to a white dwarf ball. Later his glow will disappear and he shall be a cool, wasteful black dot. His gravitational force too would end by then and so will his

relation and control with other planets in his family. As a result, these planets may get strayed away somewhere and may hit the planets on the other solar systems. Suppose the Earth hits something or halts at something, her both types of rotation will halt. Environment and life too would have already ended due to heat. The twelve factors responsible for the creation of life on the Mother Earth will get destroyed and the natures' life cycle will completely come to a halt. Thus the death of Sun will be the death of the Mother Earth too!!

With the end of the head of family in our solar system, all the eight planets dependent on him will end too along with their corresponding Moons. Creation has the seeds of its destruction. Sun too is not an exception for this!

NOW THINK HARD! THINK ABOUT YOUR VALUABLE LIFE AND THE LIFE GIVERS AND THINK ABOUT YOUR OWN BEHAVIOUR ON THIS EARTH, YOUR DEEDS IN THIS LIFE! PEOPLE MUST THINK AND IMPROVE THEIR LIFE!!!...

The greedy people, the selfish wealth collectors, corrupt leaders, black market mafias, capitalists thriving on the blood of common people-will this completely ignorant lot of people ever think that if the great Sun is not an exception to natures law, aren't their own activities have the seeds of their own destruction? Would they ever think that if the huge Sun has the death, they too have the death?

IF THIS IS THE LIMITATION OF EXISTENCE OF SUN, WHO ARE YOU? WHAT ABOUT YOUR MOMENTARY EXISTENCE? IDENTIFY YOURSELF!...

In the expanse of this huge universe, our Sun is the smallest Sun of the million's of galaxies. Compared to other Suns he is so negligible! This is his position. Then should not the human think about this? Our human race exists due to this Sun! This is a momentary life! Yet the man wants to embrace entire universe in his arms, but it doesn't happen and within a moment the man leaves this world with one way ticket!!

****

2.6

The part of an Astronomical Earth is eclipse...

SOLAR AND LUNAR ECLIPSES ARE NOTHING BUT THE HUMANKIND'S VISUAL ILLUSIONS!

If the visible Sun & Moon are not real then what do you see? You see a visual illusion!!

The Sun that you see in the sky is not the real Sun. To tell you this, I am no scientist, not intelligent think tank; neither a researcher of religious scripts, maker of ephemeris nor even a graduate of any faculty. I am the commonest of common man! So when I talk like this, some people warn me that other people will not trust. They will declare you lunatic and insane. Actually there is nothing wrong with these people! The truth bringer, fact revealer has been a lunatic for the society and the humankind! The great scientist like Galileo Galilee was tortured and killed by the elites of humankind, where do I stand? I am just a simple commoner! No wonder people may call me eccentric! To anyone whom I told, "the Sun that you see is not the real Sun", they questioned back, "If it is not the real Sun, then what about that everyone sees in the sky?" Being an observer and having some study of Earth, Sun and the Moon, I knew at heart that the Sun as seen in the sky is not the real Sun; but didn't know how to convince people about what I knew. But later, I discovered a doctrine that not only would convince the people but also the scientists.

THE SUN AND MOON AS SEEN IN THE SKY ARE NOT THE REAL! HERE IS THE DOCTRINE!!!...

The Sun that is visible to our eyes is just of a 15 cm diameter. But there is no Sun that has this size. Means what is visible is actually non-existent. Then what is that your eyes see? The answer to that is your illusion! Because our solar system has only one Sun, and it is so huge that his diameter is of 1.4

million KM and circumference is of 4.4 million KM. The hot ball of this huge size is the only Sun in our solar system and the real Sun for humankind of Earth. Any Sun visible other than this is the illusion! I say 'any other Sun visible' because, rather than from the distance of 150 million KM that Earth has to Sun, if you go to the Venus that is at a distance of just 108 million KM from Sun to see the Sun, the visible Sun will be even larger to your eyes than it is from Earth having a distance of 150 million KM from Sun. It will be very large if seen from Mercury due to the proximity of Mercury to Sun. Of course, it is impossible to go so near to the Sun. I just explained effect of going near to Sun. Now we shall see the effect of going away from Sun.

If we decided to watch the Sun from the planet Jupiter that is at the distance of 778 million KM, then he will appear to be five times smaller than what he appears from our Earth! The distance between Saturn and Sun is 1427.7 million KM. Means from the Saturn, the Sun would appear to be a small dot! Means other than the real Sun, all these Suns of the sizes they appear of are illusions, isn't it?

Now we shall check the actual sizes of the Sun and the Moon. The Moon, the satellite of our Earth has a diameter of 3476 KM and circumference is 10900 KM. But to the eyes of the person on Earth it appears only of a 15 cm diameter. The reason behind this is the person on Earth is seeing the Moon from a distance of almost 384600 KM. So it appears to be of a 15 cm diameter.

If we assume what we see is the real Moon, then the life that we see on Earth today, and the waves in the ocean caused by the gravitational force of Moon and the other benefits to the life on Earth caused by Moon (we shall see them next); would they be available due to your imagery Moon of a 15 cm diameter?

Would Earth bathe in the moonlight of just a 15 cm Moon? So the Moon as she appears in the sky is not the real, it is just the illusion to the eyes. What is visible is not the real.

Now we shall see the size of Sun. We have seen the huge size of Sun in the earlier chapters, haven't we? With a diameter of almost 1.4 million KM and the circumference of 4.4 million KM, Sun is a huge fireball and yet appears to be of a just 15 cm diameter!! The reason is the distance of Sun from the Earth i.e. 150 million KM! Means we see the Sun from 150 million KM distance and it appears to us only of a 15 cm diameter!

From the above description, one thing must have been clear to you is that neither the Sun that is visible in the sky is the true Sun, nor the Moon that you see in the sky is the true Moon. Had they really been of the sizes of what they appear to be in the sky, then this Earth wouldn't have been existing, forget about the life on Earth!

No one has revealed this to the humankind. My curiosity led me to the study and I was convinced that the Sun and Moon as visible in the sky are not the real Sun and Moon.

THE REAL SUN AND MOON NEVER GET ECLIPSED! IT IS MY OWN DOCTRINE, HOWEVER I CAN SCIENTIFICALLY PROVE THIS FUNDAMENTAL EQUATIONS!!!...

As I had mentioned earlier, most of the things that we see are deceptive or illusions. The solar eclipse too is not an exception to this. What your eyes see is actually the deception of eye! The influences of old doctrines imbibed on our minds are so strong that any one telling 'solar eclipse means an illusion to eye'; like me will be recognized as a lunatic. You may even think why to read the book of this impulsive man? But wait! Just read on! After reading the analysis that I have made for above statements you may decide whether you wish to continue the reading or else!

We shall first find out the root cause of the illusion of eclipse. We all human beings dwell on the surface of the Earth and assume the things as appear from there to be true. We shall take a peek at the process happening in the space at the time the Sun is said to experience the total solar eclipse, means on the no moon day.

Around the real Earth the real Moon rotates, and the Earth rotates around the Sun. This is a lifetime cycle. So one day comes when the Sun Moon-Earth come in one straight line. This illusion happens only to the people viewing from Earth. Thus, only the people in some part of the Earth get the illusion of solar disc being completely covered. We call it the total solar eclipse. But if you go out of the Earth's orbit, you will not get this illusion.

Now why the complete Sun appears to be covered? The root cause is that, Sun and Moon appear to be of the same size to the eyes of a viewer on the Earth. From Earth the Moon appears to be of the size of almost 15 cm diameter and the Sun too appears to be of the 15 cm diameter. This appearance itself is the illusion to the human eyes. If you go near the Moon and see, will it appear to be of a 15 cm diameter? Is really the Sun and Moon are of the sizes of 15 cm diameter each? The answer will be no. Their actual sizes are very big. Then isn't their appearance of the same size to your eyes an illusion?

THE SUN AND MOON DO NOT GET ECLIPSED. ECLIPSE IS DECEPTIVE AND IS YOUR ILLUSION. JUST KNOW, HOW?...

Doctrine 1:

The Sun and Moon as we see in the sky are not the same in reality. They are not the real Sun and Moon. You will be convinced of this, only when you will know the actual sizes of real Moon and real Sun!

The circumference of real Moon is almost 10900 KM and that of real Sun is almost 4.4 million KM. These are not the imaginary figures. These are actual figures. If we divide the size of Sun by the size of Moon, we shall find the size of Sun 400 times bigger than the size of Moon. The reason to describe this in so much detail is that even with such a huge difference in their sizes, Sun & Moon appear to be of the same size when viewed from the Earth. But in reality their sizes are not the same. Means this 'appearance of same size' is the illusion to your eyes. It is because we see them from a far distance. So what we see happening on the day of eclipse too is an illusion. Because the solar and lunar discs as you see on that day are not the real Sun and Moon. But if we assume the Sun and Moon as we see to be true, then since the actual Moon is 400 times smaller than the Sun the Sun should appear larger than the Moon. But it doesn't appear that way.

Now realizing the facts above, answer me the question. Will the Sun ever get completely covered by the Moon which is 400 times smaller than him?

The viewer from the Earth sees the Sun to be of just of a 15 cm diameter though he is 100 times larger than Earth! Is it the real Sun? Same way, if we decide to view the Earth from the Sun, means from 150 million KM distance then being 100 times smaller than the Sun, the Earth shall appear to be 100th part of this 15 cm diameter Sun, means as small as a sago! Will the Sun ever get covered by this sago sized Earth? And will you call that sago size Earth as the real Earth?

Same way, if we plan to view Moon from the Sun, she won't even be visible! Such invisible is the position of Moon from the Sun! Then how the Sun will ever get covered by such Moon?

Doctrine 2:

We have only one Sun in our solar system. With this, from each planet of our solar system the Sun will appear to be of different size. So are there 8 Suns in our solar system? As explained earlier, the Sun as we see from Earth will look so much bigger if seen him from Mercury. And the same shall look like a white dot if seen from Saturn! Then which is the real Sun? Means every Sun that you see is the illusion. So the Sun you see in the sky is illusion too and not real Sun. It is the same with the Moon. So the eclipse of the Sun or Moon as it appears is a mere illusion of our eyes.

Doctrine 3:

The Sun and the Moon of a 15 cm diameter that you see in the space are not existent. If you decide to go on the Sun or Moon of the 15 cm diameter size that you see from the Earth, you will not get them anywhere in the space! Because the Sun and Moon of the size visible to your eyes are just not available in this space! So their eclipses too do not exist. The eclipse that you see is your illusion. In the space no actual event of eclipsing of Sun or Moon ever happens! I can justify and prove. Eclipse is just the illusion of the human living on Earth.

Actual 'seeing' and 'being' are two contradictory things. Seeing the Sun of a 15 cm diameter is your illusion. This is your visual fantasy. The actual Sun of having 1.4 million km. diameter is visible as just of a 15 cm diameter. Does this mean the real Sun is just of a 15 cm diameter? This all analysis proves that the illusion of eclipse that the humans get from the Earth happens to these illusionary discs of Sun and Moon. The actual Sun or the Moon never gets eclipsed!

What we see as the Sun & the Moon are the illusionary figures. These illusionary figures are not in existence therefore, human on Earth is ignorant and believes in concepts such as eclipse and phases of moon. Such concepts do not affect or make any difference to the real existent Sun & the Moon. The illusionary figures which we see are nothing but non-existent figures of moon and sun. Then how can the eclipse and phases of moon occur to the non-existent Moon & Sun.

To explain you more, we shall consider the actual celestial bodies of Earth, Sun and Moon. Even though they come in the single straight line, they actually casting their shadows on each other is just impossible. It is because just the distance between Earth and Sun is more than 150 million KM. And the Moon is 400 times smaller than the Sun. Means the Moon won't be visible to our eyes if we try to see her from the Sun. Then how will the Moon that is invisible and 400 times smaller than the Sun will cover the self-shining Sun? So the eclipse is an illusion of the viewer.

Till today the human has been making a big mistake of assuming the visible Sun and Moon in the sky as the real Sun and Moon. So he gets the illusion of solar and lunar eclipse. But the actual Sun and Moon never get eclipsed.

One professor asked me that, "If the Sun & Moon as visible to our eyes do not exist, then how do we see the shadow from Earth at the time of eclipse?" Apparently his question will sound logical. But the reason behind the visible shadow is the distance of approximately 384600 KM distance between the

Earth and the Moon. But if the Moon has been at almost 6 million KM distance from the Earth; then it would have appeared as the small dot to the viewer on the Earth and there wouldn't have been the illusion of eclipse to him.

In the space the planets like Mercury and Venus can come in between the Earth and Sun but due to millions of KM distance between Earth and them their shadow never falls on the Earth. This doctrine of distance that I have stated here for shadowing is scientifically correct.

Now let us take an example of Eiffel Tower. This Eiffel tower is much taller than any human. Would this tower be covered by your finger while standing below this tower? The answer is obvious 'No'. But if you see this tower from the distance of 3 kilometres, then you can certainly cover the illusionary image that is visible to your eye by a single finger. But you cannot cover the real Eiffel Tower with one finger. The image captured by your eye from 3 kilometre is existence less or absent and illusionary. An illusion is created of covering this existenceless illusionary image by the finger. Does the small sized Eiffel Tower that you see from 3 kilometre distance, exist in reality? The image you covered by your finger is not Eiffel Tower in reality. The image that is seen or visible from a long distance is illusionary and existenceless. Similarly, the image of Sun and Moon that appears to be covered in the space is illusionary and existence less.

But the thing called eclipse is so much imbibed on the human mind that without using the brain; the human keeps more faith on the things imbibed. So the humankind is usually not ready to accept the truth. After such descriptive explanation the professor got convinced and satisfied on my speech.

Not just the eclipse, but everything in the space is the illusion for the viewer from Earth. For example the phases of the Moon that are viewed from the Earth. Due to this, the viewer from the Earth sees the full moon only once in a month! But in reality, there is no **phase** for the Moon; there is **always** full moon day on the Moon!!

Some people in the humankind impart undue importance to such illusions by relating them to religion and creating ignorance in the public. They exploit the people with this ignorance. Now tell me, why this truth not be there in the school curriculum? Why not any scientist brought these characteristics at the base of the humane race?

Are you now convinced that solar eclipse and lunar eclipse are the illusions or deceptions to the eye? Neither actual Sun nor the actual Moon, none of these celestial bodies gets eclipsed. This is my discovery against the assumptions of the human race. Not for fame or greatness, but to ward off the ignorance and superstitious rituals, I want these things to reach to the entire humankind through this book.

Is the light of Sun illusionary?...

As I said earlier, visible things are illusionary. Now check this. Out of the storage of the total hydrogen gas, almost 4 million ton per second is getting burnt. Due to this we are experiencing the light and sun shine on the Earth. We see the light on Earth usually whitish in color. But if we decompose this Sun light, we get 7 different colors. When there is sun shine on the Earth and it is raining, we see a beautiful rainbow in the sky, isn't it? Actually the Sun light gets decomposed due to the drop of water and we see the rainbow.

Similarly, the leaves of the plants appear pitch green to our eyes. In reality, these leaves absorb the other 6 colors except the green color. And this **non absorbed** green color is reflected to our eyes! So we feel the leaves to be green. If the green color too is absorbed, the leaves would appear white! This way, one must remember that this entire world is an illusion! Our life too is not an exception to this! Happiness, sorrow, joy, difficulties all these things are just illusions. The things that are not steady, not permanent are all an illusion. So considering this, live your mundane life.

****

2.7

Illusionary Are The Lunar Days Which are based On The Phases Of Moon!

All lunar days means full moon, no moon and other auspicious days as are observed in different continents are Based on the phases of the Moon. They are all imaginary. People believe in ephemeris, auspicious and inauspicious days and moments because they don't know the reality...

From the Earth only one side of the Moon is visible to us. The Moon gets bathed in Sun light every day. Means it is always a full moon day on Moon in actual. But as the Moon hides behind the Earth she appears to be getting lesser and lesser in the size to the viewer on the Earth, and when she gets free from the Earth, she appears to be getting fuller or increasing. So we humans have made up the lunar days. In reality there is no change in the Moon. Her one side that is visible to us is actually illuminated daily. As there is a day and night on this Earth, Moon too has day and night. As daily half the Earth is bathed in the Sun light, one side of Moon too gets bathed daily in the Sun light. On the contrary, the day of Moon is much bigger than the day of Earth. Day of Earth is of 24 hours. The day of Moon is 656 hours. As the Earth has 12 hours a day and 12 hours a night, the Moon too has 328 hours of day and 328 hours of night! So what is full moon and what is no moon or any such lunar days? What is auspicious moment? Each day is a good day! Has this cleared your misunderstanding? Actual auspicious moment means just now! But human being is engrossed in the ideas of auspicious day and moment, good day or bad day and wastes the time in checking ephemeris. In reality all these lunar day, auspicious, inauspicious, lucky & unlucky moment are unintelligent and imaginary! These are limited only to the human kind! Other animates have nothing to do with these! As the offspring is born in human race it is also born in the other animals. But they don't make birth charts, but human being is lost in imagination and abstract idea! He keeps making the birth horoscope of the new born and observing the rituals!

You must have understood from above that the lunar days are based on the phases of Moon which can only be seen from the Earth, but do not exist in the reality. As Earth is the planet, Moon too is a sub planet or satellite. Do we experience the phases of Earth like Moon? No, we do not experience. The half part that is illuminated on Earth is a day. The other half has the night. But as the Moon's speed of rotation is slow, there is a day of 328 hours and the night of 328 hours in a single day. Once you realize this, you will be sure that lunar day, lunar month, auspicious moment, lucky and unlucky days, eclipses are entirely man made. It has nothing to do with the reality.

See the illusion of a man! The day you call no moon day, is the day when Moon is actually blazing like a full moon day in the sky! The space doesn't have such no or new moon day! The viewer on the Earth cannot see the Moon as she is behind the Earth. You call it a no Moon day. But even though invisible, the Moon is blazing in the space with the Sun light. So many times on the no Moon day it appears as if there is total solar eclipse!

The scientists have not brought such true information freely in front of masses. It is brought to your kind notice by me.

****

2.8

The Part of Astronomical Earth

Planet Mars

Poor fellow! Does not trouble us at All!!

The Earth's nature system has arranged the 12 factors of creation for all! No scope for influence of other planets exclusively for a human being as in astrology!!!

Friends, we got introduced so far to the Earth, Moon and Sun of our solar family. They are closely related to our life. Now let us know others too. Our Earth's neighbor is the fourth planet in the solar system Mars. How is he? What is his daily routine and atmosphere? We shall explore this information.

In the astrology of Hindu religion Mars is an important planet. The Hindu human being's aspect to Mars is retrograde! Because in Hindu astrology, with the Mars in a particular position in the birth charts of bride or a groom, arranging the marriage becomes a herculean task! No groom accepts the bride who has her Mars in such position, and also no father of bride wants to marry his daughter to a boy who has the Mars in particular position in his birth chart. People have such a deep faith on the retrograde Mars of a birth chart! They think this Mars will bring troubles to the married life. Actually the poor Mars has nothing to do with anybody's marriage! In reality he is far away; almost 80 to 100 million KM from our Earth! From our huge Mother Earth he looks like a dot. He has nothing to do with your daughter's or son's marriage. But the human race! The most whimsical of all living beings on the Earth! Is Mars just for human race? Doesn't it affect the other living beings on the Earth other than humans? It is unpredictable how the human being will use his or her gift of thinking power! They are not ready to take the responsibility of their own misdeeds! Then they sometimes hold either Mars or Saturn responsible for all their problems. With such beliefs human being tries to derive some satisfaction, even if it is false!

Friends, we are digging the very root of humans and all living beings. We are studying the doctrines of how the humans, entire animate nature is formed. It has no relation to any man made god, astrological faiths of tyranny of planets like Saturn or Mars or alchemy of quackery! These things are not acceptable to the design of life on Earth. In her design, no other power than herself can be created or will ever be created on this Earth. So the human should not misuse the gift of imagination, thinking power and intelligence!

Poor Fellow Mars who never troubles you!...

The fourth planet in the solar system, the Mars is at a distance of almost 228 million KM from the Sun. There is no life on Mars as it is on the Earth. But it has four seasons similar to Earth's seasons. On the middle equator of the Mars sometimes in the summer; the temperature is minus 5 degree Celsius. But since this planet is far away from the Sun, the temperature goes down to minus 87 degree Celsius too! Just like Earth Mars too have high mountains, hills, valleys, deserts and dry rivers. According to scientists, Mars too has the ice on both of its hemispheres as it is on the Earth. Mars is the planet with a barren land. The color of the soil there is orange. Mars has very less gravitational power when compared to the Earth. Anything weighing 100 KGs will weigh just 38 KG on Mars. As it has just twice as much the gravitational force than the Moon, there is no environment on the Mars and no life existence or formation is possible. It will not be possible even in the future, whatever Researcher Bodies may claim!

The size of the Mars...

The Mars is almost half the size of the Earth. His diameter is 6797 KM and the circumference is approximately 21362 KM that is almost double of the Moon's circumference. To cover the distance of 21362 KM to rotate around self, the Mars needs 24.6 hours. Means as the Earth's day is of 24 hours that of Mars is of 24.6

hours. Means, he rotates around himself with an hourly speed of 868 KM. Earth revolves at a speed of 1610 KM around herself. As Earth needs to travel almost 940 million KM to rotate around Sun, the Mars needs to travel more means almost 1433.1 million KM to complete the rotation around the Sun. He takes 16488 hours to complete this rotation. Means the 687 days on Earth is an year of the Mars. Mars needs to rotate at the speed of 86917 KM per hour to complete the rotation around Sun. This is lesser than the speed of Earth. Earth revolves around Sun at the speed of almost 107000 KM per hour.

As Mars does not have any of the twelve factors necessary for the formation of the life on Earth, there is no life on the Mars. Besides, Earth has just one Moon. But Mars has 2 moons. The most heighted mountain on Earth is called **Mauna Kea** that has the height of almost 33000 ft. But the characteristic of the Mars is that it has more heighted i.e. 20 KM heighted mountain.

Such is the harmless fellow of our solar system Mars! But people consider him as an enemy! Now he too rotates around the Sun. There is a huge distance of so many million KM between Earth's and his position in the solar system. With this fact, how will it affect one of the miniature animates 'human' on the Earth? This must be considered and instead of thinking about him as an enemy he better be viewed as our neighbor.

If we decide to view the Earth from the Mars, she looks like big sago. Then who is the human living on this sago shaped Earth? What is his standing? This is the position of huge Mother Earth from Mars and then what is the existence of the human? From Mars he is non existent! What effect he will have of Mars? Please man, living in the 21st century, at least now would you leave your whimsical ideas?

If the Mars has a retrograde aspect on human, why should he choose just human out of millions of living beings on the Earth? These other beings don't get retrograde aspect of Mars? Have we heard that the tiger has a trouble of Mars or elephant suffers from the retrograde Mars? No one has any problem from Mars. But the notion of only few within

human race getting affected by Mars is a complete ignorance of the human race! Humankind is just selfish. They never think of other living beings. If selfishness is left, all living beings are the same.

Mars on the Earth, means the enemies of the Earth!...

In reality the fraud and corrupt people on this Earth, the hoarders of wealth, food and resources, trouble makers, terrorists and religious fanatics, makers of the weapons like atom bomb-these are the real enemies of Earth in the form of humans! With this fact, what right do humans have to call some planets as enemies?

****

2.9

The Part of Astronomical Earth

Planet Saturn

Harmless fellow! How can he trouble from the distance of 1300 million KM at All?

Some people exploit the public imposing the fear of seven and half year Saturn transit.

The astrologers have imposed so much fear of the Mars and Saturn on the masses that the people are ready to do any remedial rituals out of this fear! Then it may include offering expensive oil in the temple of Saturn or any such wasteful ritual, even youngsters take out their productive time to make a queue in the temple. I feel pity on them. This book will help eradicate the wasteful misunderstanding about these two planets, Mars & Saturn from its root. For this reason the information about them is elaborated here to depict their true nature.

Rituals, astrology, miracles are all man made things and ideas. They do not exist. They are not applicable to the other living beings on the Earth. Then how they have effect on handful people in human race? Probably after reading how far the Saturn is from the Earth and his true nature, your fear would vanish.

Just like Sun, Saturn too is a ball made up of hydrogen and helium gases. But he is not hot like Sun. On the contrary he has a very cold temperature! It is as cold as minus 180 degrees Celsius. The ice formation starts at zero degrees Celsius. But here temperature is so low. He is 1427 million KM far from Sun and almost 1300 million KM far from Earth. There is zero possibility of him troubling the humanity on Earth in any way from such a distance, isn't it? If you see the Earth from Saturn, it won't be even visible to the bare eye! He is unnecessarily defamed by humans on the Earth!

Saturn is almost 10 times larger than Earth and his diameter is almost 120514 KM and the circumference is around 378758 KM. His speed of self-revolution is 37133 KM per hour, hence his one day equals to 10.2 hours on Earth. His speed to rotate around Sun is 34710 KM per hour. So to complete one round around Sun he has to travel the distance of almost 8960 million KM. So one year of Saturn is equivalent to 29.5 years on Earth. According to the new discovery of NASA Saturn has 62 Moons. He rotates around Sun with all these 62 Moons.

With the deep study of Earth and solar system, you will realize that the planet from which our Earth is not even visible, the humanity on such non visible Earth is so existence less! And yet few from human clan claim to experience the 'anger' of such distant Saturn! Having any effect of such planet on your life is just impossible. The idea of some planet that is invisible to the bare human eye troubling few human beings on Earth leaving other beings is hilarious! Saturn, Mars or any other third planet is not troublesome to humans on Earth. There are so many millions of planets in the other solar systems; they too should cast their bad shadow on the humans on Earth, isn't it? The fact is if you are not selfish, greedy, hoarder no one can trouble you!

****

3

Geographical Earth

A part of Earth's body design!

Means the entire life on Mother Earth including Human!!

For a common man, however educated s/he may be, geography is the boring subject! This is like calling your parents, who gave you the birth, boring. Saying you don't have any interest in them! Or 'what and why we got to know about them? We are eating, drinking and living merrily; they have done the arrangement of home and all other things for us. When everything is just cool, what is the need of getting information about the parents? Are they such big figures that we should know about their biography? What is the need?' how would such exclamation of a mischievous child about his/her parents would sound to the ears of the listeners? Definitely unpleasant! As this is not appropriate, not knowing about the Mother Earth who has given you the birth, gave you the gifts of intellect, thinking power and imagination; Mother Earth who takes care and accepts you from birth to death and is providing you the vital things needed for your life is a sad thing. More than this, not knowing about such Mother Earth on whose existence your life existence depends is really sad. Leaving this Earth again resting back in her arms, without knowing her is such ungratefulness!!

Forget about the other animals, the humans having intellect to know and imagination and thought power has a duty to know this Mother of all. I insist because it is important to know self and know about our Mother Earth after taking birth on her laps! It is the success of your life. So without getting bored it is necessary to know our Mother Earth geographically to know ourselves too. Once you know yourself deeply, it will help you get stability, peace, satisfaction and joy in your life. If you wish to know your existence, you must know the wholesome information about the Mother Earth.

If you want to reveal the secret of your birth and death then you must know the Mother Earth!!!...

Till now we got the information about the astronomical Earth necessary for the creation of life including human being and also the factors arising from Sun and Moon and how they are necessary for the creation of entire life including ours. Now we shall know about the creator and the bearer of our life design, the true god visible to our eyes, the geographical Mother Earth!

I request the readers that if you bring the round of Earth from the market and compare the geographical description with this round, understanding her will be much easier. To tell you the truth, whatever old religious scripts you read to get the self-satisfaction, peace, happiness and joy; they are all imaginary. But here there is NO place for imagination. Whatever is the description, it is based on the reality and doctrines. To get your true identity, you need the knowledge of reality. If you want to get this knowledge, to get the secret of your birth and death, you cannot depend on the imaginary scriptures and legends. You will never get it from them. Study your creator, the Mother Earth, who provides you the nourishment, who sustains your existence. And then you will be hundred percent convinced that god is nothing else but our Mother Earth!

Now we shall know the description of Mother Earth's geographical nature, means what all she holds on her body, what she bears on her shoulders. And we shall also know how each aspect of hers is connected to our Birth, nurturance and breath.

The area of the Mother Earth...

Just like we calculate the area of any agricultural land or plot same way the scientists have discovered the area of this Earth floating in the space. Contrary to the commoner's wonder whether the area of the huge Earth really can be calculated, scientists have really done this alchemy. Well, won't stretch your curiosity. Including all the huge seas, oceans, mountains and valleys the total area of our Earth is almost 510 million 66 thousand square KM or 510066000 km^2.

Shouldn't we know how big is our Earth on which we dwell and due to which we have taken birth?

The area of the water on the Earth and its importance!!!...

Viewed from the space, Mother Earth looks very beautiful like a blue sapphire. No other planets look as beautiful as Earth looks! The real reason behind this beauty of Earth is the round of Earth is almost covered by the water. Some sad reader may think what we got to do with how much water or land the Mother Earth has got? But this human being does not know that his own birth, his existence, his food and his pumping heart all are related to this water on Earth. Not just that, but his own body is composed of much more water just like his Mother Earth! Our body has almost 70% of water! If this amount in the body reduces, we get dehydrated and in extreme case we succumb. Water on the Earth has a very high importance for the existence of our life. There is no living being on this Earth who is devoid of water and doesn't need water.

Out of the 12 factors that our and every living being's body is composed of is 'water'. We shall see the description of what creates the human body.

What are the factors responsible for the creation and existence of water on Mother Earth?...

The much more area of Earth is covered by the storage of water through ponds, rivers, dams, seas and oceans. Water is an important factor for the life to dwell on Earth. Actually we have learnt in the schools and colleges that the mixture of two molecules, one of Hydrogen and another molecule of oxygen is the water. But the water creation needs many more things than this. And they are available only on Mother Earth and hence only Mother Earth is found with the abundant storage of water. We don't find water on any other planet. As formation of the living beings body needs 12 different factors, likewise, just hydrogen and oxygen are not enough for the formation of water. It needs more things. So, even if you go on the Moon or Mars with hydrogen and oxygen, since other necessary factors are missing there, you won't be able to create the water by mixing these two gases. I would present this analysis next.

Thus, taking this storage of water along, the Earth rotates around the Sun at the speed of 107000 KM per hour and at the speed of 1610 KM per hour around herself. One 80 year old had questioned me about why water does not spill from Earth though she rotates with such a speed? We will get an answer for that.

MUCH LESS IS THE DRINKING OR FRESH WATER FOR THE LIFE ON THE TERRAIN!!...

The water existent on Earth has covered the area of almost 360 million km2 or 361637000 km2. This has given the existence to each living being on the Earth. But there is some twist in this reality! Though Earth has almost 3/4th of water, the life does not get created with this fathomless water!! Now what I am going to tell will surprise you. Even though Earth has huge water storage, 97.5% of this water is not useful for the life! It is because this water is so salty, saturated with minerals. This water is useless for existence and creation of life. Thus excluding this 97.5%, only 2.5% is useful for drinking or available as usable fresh water. The more fun is that this remaining 2.5% water too cannot be used completely! This 2.5% has almost 68% of it in the form of ice!!

So on this 32% water out of this 2.5% total useful water; dwells our living and non-living world! Only 750 millilitre fresh water is available out of total 100 litre salty water on the Earth and causes us to take the birth and exist! This is the reality, your real identity. No god! No reincarnation, super soul and soul!! So you must have realized the importance of water on this Earth. The animate needs water at each moment. Means if water is there, we are there, and this entire life is there. Now you may be clear about how much space the water occupies on the Earth.

The lady in Margaret Thatcher's cabinet was amazed to get the information about Fifth Ocean on Earth and requested me to send the book when ready!!!...

People know the oceans having huge storage of salty water, but most of them know only 4 oceans! Many do not understand the difference between ocean and sea. Earth has total 113 seas and five oceans. I realized that most of the people don't know this fifth ocean. Not just in India, but it seems people of many countries are unaware of this. I would narrate an incident depicting this.

In India once I was waiting for a train going to Kunnur on Ootacamund railway station. Just like me, some foreigners too were waiting on the station platform. Two-three foreign guests came and sat on the same bench that I was sitting on. Since I am a hard-core traveler, I started getting introduced and chatting. In the course of discussion I introduced myself and told that I have travelled the Earth and have realized many facts and so writing a book on it to share the knowledge with all. That time I was writing 'Me, Earth and the travel' which is published now. When I told them about the fifth ocean and asked them about it, they counter questioned me "we don't know, where that is?" Then I explained them "You must know the southern hemisphere of our Earth. At this hemisphere there are three capes. One is Cape Horn of Chile country, second is the Cape of Good Hope at South Africa and third one is the southeast Cape of New Zealand. After these three capes, whole water of our Mother Earth gets together and after 60 degree latitude the fifth Southern Ocean starts up to the boundary of Antarctica and that is called Southern Ocean."

They were very surprised. They introduced about themselves. The lady was working with the ministry of the Prime Minister of England of that time i.e. Margaret Thatcher. She told her husband to give her visiting card to me and told me to send the book when it gets ready. But that first book 'Me, Earth and Travel' It was in Marathi so I could not send. But will be sent when it gets translated in English. But this new book in English I will send, because I want to reveal to all the unknown information in it.

The 'Cape' of Southern hemisphere and what is 'Cape'?...

The 'Cape' that I mentioned above are the three points of land jutting out into the water of ocean or as a projecting point of land. These are called 'Capes'. I was delighted when out of these I visited the city of Cape Town in South Africa. It is because this city is situated on the last point of the African continent.

The definitions of Sea and Ocean!!...

Many of us don't know the definitions of Ocean. Out of the total area of our Earth, almost 3/4th is covered by the abysmal or fathomless salty water. Huge storage of salty water that is spread fathomless having area larger than the continent and forming the boundary of the continent is called an Ocean.

So, we can say from the definition that the oceans are adjacent to the 'continents' and seas are adjacent to the 'countries'.

The old school textbooks that we studied taught about four main Oceans of the Earth to the students. 1. Pacific Ocean 2. Atlantic Ocean 3. Arctic Ocean and 4. Indian Ocean

1. Huge Pacific Ocean covering the 1/3rd area of the Earth...

This is the largest compared to other oceans on the Earth. In Latin it is called 'Mare Pacificum'. Portuguese researcher Ferdinand Magellan gave the term 'pacific' to this ocean. The meaning of pacific is 'peaceful sea'. This ocean is spread over from Arctic of north to the Southern ocean in south and from America eastward to Asia and Australia westward. Her area is almost 155557000 km2. Almost 1/3rd part of the Mother Earth is covered by this ocean. This means almost half the area of 3/4th water body on Earth is covered by this huge ocean alone.

Even the most heighted top of Mount Everest would sink in the depths of Pacific Ocean!...

The Pacific Ocean is the deepest of all oceans. The average depth of Pacific Ocean is the 13215 ft. The deepest measure is 36198 ft means almost 11 KM. The peak of heighted Mount Everest too will sink in this ocean.

The size of Pacific Ocean...

Half of the circumference of Earths' equator is covered by Pacific Ocean alone! The maximum width of this ocean is almost 19800 KM, means almost five times of the Moon's diameter. But due to the movements of tectonic plates this ocean is getting contracted and Atlantic Ocean is increasing.

Ocean of 25000 islands...

Can you imagine how many islands are there on this ocean? There are around 25000 small and large islands on this Ocean which are more than the total number of islands on the other oceans!

2. Atlantic Ocean covering 1/5th of Earth's surface...

This is the second largest ocean on the Earth. This ocean is connected to the Arctic Ocean at the north and is mixed with Pacific Ocean on the south west and connected to Indian Ocean on the south east of Earth. The adjacent continents to this ocean are Eurasia and Africa on east side and North America, South America on the west side. Due to equator the northern part of this Ocean is known as Northern Atlantic and southern part is known as Southern Atlantic.

This ocean has covered almost 76762000 km2 area of the Mother Earth and has the average depth of almost 12880 ft. The maximum depth is almost 30246 ft near the Puerto Rico, which is one point of the famous 'Bermuda Triangle'. Almost 22% of the total Earth's surface area is covered by this ocean. Spread over forming the shape of English alphabet 'S', the width of this ocean is almost 2848 KM to 6400 KM.

3. Fontanel of the Earth is Arctic Ocean...

If we see the round of the Earth, the northern pole of the Earth means the rounded part of the Earth like fontanel is covered by the Arctic Ocean. This ocean has occupied the area of almost 14056000 km2 on the Earth's surface. The average depth is 3953 ft. while the maximum depth is 18456 ft. in the basin of Eurasia.

The maximum part of this ocean is surrounded by the tract of land. The length of the banks of this Ocean is almost 45390 KM. Adjacent continents are Eurasia,

Norn America and Greenland and many big, small islands. The Ocean is connected to Pacific Ocean through Bering strait and to Atlantic Ocean through Greenland Sea and Labrador Sea. The surface of this island is covered by the ice throughout the year. The floating research centres of Russia and United States are on this Ocean.

4. Indian Ocean starts from Indian Peninsula i.e. Kanyakumari...

The third largest Ocean of the Earth is Indian Ocean that covers 20% tract of the Earth's land and is named after the subcontinent India within Asian continent from where it starts. The water of this ocean is spread over the area of 68556000 km^2. The width of this ocean is approximately 200 KM to 1000 KM with an average depth of 13002 ft and maximum depth 24460 ft at the islands of Sunda and Java. Indian Ocean is mixed with the Atlantic Ocean near Cape Town southward and is connected to Pacific Ocean near Tasmania southward of Australia. Adjacent to westward of this Ocean is continent of Africa and on eastern side Indo China, Sundae Island as well as Indonesia and Australia. The Islands that are independent countries in this Ocean are Madagascar, Comoros, Seychelles, Maldives, Mauritius, Sri Lanka and Indonesia. The major path for oceanic communication between the continents of Africa and Asia is through Indian Ocean.

Many people don't know the fifth Ocean and its importance!!!...

When I talk with the people or discuss with friends about the Oceans, I find that many of them don't know the names of Oceans, and those who know only name four Oceans. But when I tell them about the fifth Ocean they get surprised. It is because only four Oceans were taught in the earlier school curriculum. So many students, teachers, parents don't know about the fifth Ocean. We shall see this information below.

Our Earth has the fifth Ocean too!...

If we bring the south hemisphere in front of our eyes we shall see three peaks or headlands jutting into the water of Ocean. There is no land next to them. These are called 'Cape' in English.

The first Cape of Southern Hemisphere...

I was thrilled with joy when I visited the city of Cape Town in South Africa. It is because that is based on one of the last southern peak of African continent. At this point Indian Ocean and Atlantic Ocean get mixed into each another. At this peak the tract of Earth's land of one continent gets over and the abysmal water of the Ocean starts and next to it starts the Antarctica continent. There is no land in between. I have a satisfaction of visiting the last point of African continent, touching my feet at 'Cape of Good Hope' near Cape Town city.

The second Cape of Southern Hemisphere...

Second peak of land is 'Cape Horn' of the country Chile in South America. Here the Atlantic and Pacific Oceans mix together. There is no land after this headland or Cape.

The third last Cape of Southern Hemisphere...

Third one is 'South East Cape' the last headland or peak of Tasmania Island in Australia. There is no land next to it. Here Pacific and Indian Oceans come together. Thus, the land of Earth's Southern Hemisphere ends; after which the water of all four Oceans come together. I am saying four Oceans because the Arctic Ocean at the top is already mixed with the Atlantic and Pacific Oceans at north.

From these 3 Capes of Southern Hemisphere means the Earth's 60 degree of latitude; the abysmal continuous water spread till Antarctica is counted as fifth Ocean by International Hydro graphic Organization since 2000 and the same is called as Southern Ocean or Antarctic Ocean.

5. The peculiar or strange fifth Ocean or the Southern Ocean...

The abysmal water spread continuously from the 60 degree latitude of Southern Hemisphere to Antarctica is called Southern Ocean. Thus, this Ocean is not endowed with the long northern bank or land boundaries that other Oceans enjoy; this is the peculiarity of this Ocean. As is mentioned above, the water of all four oceans have come together here.

The area of this Southern Ocean is approximately 20327000 km2 and average depth is 13100 ft to 16400 ft. The Maximum depth found is 23736 ft.

The peculiarity compared to other Oceans...

The peculiarity of this Ocean is that she has the inner currents of 21000 KM length are flowing eastward in circular motion around the Earth at the speed of 130 million meter 3 per second at the north of Antarctica. These are called the circumpolar currents of Southern Ocean and are the only continuous flow that surrounds the globe. This flow is 100 times larger than the flow of all rivers put together! Also the length of this flow is the longest of all the flows in the Oceans!!

Many people don't know the difference between a sea and the Ocean. Actually all these things are related to our existence. So the importance of this knowledge is equal to that of our daily meal. So some deplorable reader may find this all uninteresting. But this knowledge is necessary for life.

What is sea and how many seas are there?...

The large storage of the salty water which is connected to the Ocean is called sea. Or it also can be called as the part of Oceans' salty water barged into the tract of land. The banks of the Ocean are adjacent to the continent's tract of land; whereas the bank of sea is adjacent to the nation or a country of a continent. This is one of the main differences between the Ocean and the Sea.

Actually there are approximately 113 seas of salty water on our Earth. There is an exception to the definition given above and out of these 113 seas 1) Aral sea, 2) Caspian sea, 3) Dead sea, and 4) Salton sea are surrounded by land on all sides and though they are the storages of salty water they are counted into lakes.

Also the 'Sea of Galilee' near Israel is not actually a sea but is a lake of fresh water which is identified in Israel as 'Tiberias' or 'Kinneret' lake. But due to the term 'Sea of Galilee' it gets counted in the seas.

THE SEAS JOINING THE FIVE OCEANS OF THE EARTH...

Total 36 seas join in Atlantic Ocean, 32 seas in Pacific Ocean, 21 seas in Arctic Ocean, 10 seas in Indian Ocean and 10 seas in Southern Ocean. Four seas are surrounded by the land. Such there are 113 seas in total.

10 SEAS OF INDIAN OCEAN...

Arafura Sea	Gulf of Oman
Andaman Sea	Mozambique Channel
Arabian Sea	Persian Gulf
Bay of Bengal	Red Sea
Gulf of Eden	Timor Sea

THE 21 SEAS OF ARCTIC OCEAN...

Amundsen Gulf	Baffin Bay
Barents Sea	Beaufort Sea
Bering Sea	Cambridge Bay
Chukchi Sea	Cold Bay
Davis Strait	Denmark Strait
East Siberian Sea	Greenland Sea
Hudson Bay	James Bay
Kara Strait	Labrador Sea
Kara Sea	Laptev Sea
Lincoln Sea	Norwegian Sea
White Sea	

36 SEAS OF ATLANTIC OCEAN...

Adriatic Sea	Gulf of Mexico	Argentine Sea
Gulf of Sidra	Aegean Sea	Marmara Sea
Alboran Sea	Gulf of Venezuela	Bay of Bothnia
Ionian Sea	Ligurian Sea	Bay of Campeche
Bay of Fundy	Irish Sea	Baltic Sea

Gulf of Saint lawrence	Black Sea	Mediterranean Sea
Bothnian Sea	Mirtoon Sea	Caribbean Sea
North Sea	Celtic Sea	Chesapeake Sea
Sea of Crete	Central Baltic Sea	Sea of Azov
Sea of the Hebrides	Sargasso Sea	English Channel
Gulf of Bothnia	Tampa Bay	Gulf of Guinea
Thracian Sea	Gulf of Finland	Tyrrhenian Sea

10 SEAS OF SOUTHERN OCEAN...

Amundsen Sea	Bass Strait
Bellingshausen Sea	Davis Sea
Great Australian Bight	Ross Sea
Gulf of Vincent	Scotia Sea
Spencer Gulf	Weddell Sea

32 SEAS OF PACIFIC OCEAN...

Arafura Sea	Banda Sea	Bering Sea	Bismarck Sea
Bohai Sea	Bohol Sea	Camotes Sea	Ceram Sea
Chilean Sea	Celebes Sea	Coral Sea	Flores Sea
East China Sea	Gulf of Alaska	Halmahera Sea	Koro Sea
Gulf of California	Java Sea	Gulf of Carpentaria	Molucca Sea
Gulf of Thailand	Savu Sea	Philippine Sea	Seto Inland Sea
Sea of Japan	Solomon Sea	Sea of Okhotsk	Sulu Sea
South China Sea	Timor Sea	Tasman Sea	Yellow Sea

THE SEAS BOUND BY TRACT OF LAND I.E. LAKES...

Aral Sea	Caspian Sea
Dead Sea	Salton Sea

Such total 5 oceans and 113 seas are there on our Mother Earth.

Salty water seas but are called lakes...

Our Earth has Caspian Sea, Aral Sea, Dead Sea, Salton Sea of salty water and Galileo Sea of a fresh water. These 5 are seas but are called lakes because they are surrounded by land from all sides. So they are counted into lakes.

Rest other seas meet the Ocean and so they are not called lakes.

Why is the sea or oceanic water salty?...

When it started raining on Earth, the minerals on the tract of land flowed with the water and this water was accumulated in the craters. This salty water gets vaporized and we get fresh water. But the amount of fresh water is very less on Earth.

The deeper most part of Earth in the Ocean below sea level... Challenger deep (Mariana Trench)

For the commoners like us it is very difficult to get the idea of the depth of Oceanic water. But the Pacific Ocean is curiously deepest Ocean on Earth! How much could be the depth of this Ocean at Gaum Island near Mariana Island southwards to Japan? It is good enough to completely sink the 29000 ft. most heighted Mount Everest peak in Himalaya! The part of this depth is famous as Mariana Trench. Its depth is almost 11 KM means 35798 ft. or 10911 meter!

How the term 'Challenger Deep' given for this deepest place on the Earths' Ocean?...

Many scientists tried to find the depth of this place. In its first effort of year 1951, Royal Navy discovered the depth of this place as 10900 meter from the 'Challenger' ship with the help of speed of sound. This place was named after this ship 'Challenger' and was known as a Challenger Deep. Later in 1957, the Russian ship Vitiyaz noted the depth of approximately 11034 meters. In 1962, M V Spencer F Beard concluded of the depth being 10915 ft. Later Japan sent the special ship 'Tokyo' in 1984 which noted the maximum depth of 10924 meters with the help of 'narrow multi beam echo sounder'. Again on 24 March 1995 Japan observed with the help of 'Kyoko' ship and discovered the exact depth of 10911 meters which prevails as of now. (The speed of sound is approximately 1530 meters per second)

Second deepest place under the sea 'Tonga Trench'...

In this same Pacific Ocean, north-eastwards to Australia, the place having an approximate depth of 10822 metre is known as 'Tonga Trench'. This is the second deepest trench. Similarly, the trench of an approximate depth of 7460 ft. is in the same Pacific Ocean. There are such 8 trenches in this Ocean alone.

The lakes on Earth...

Most of the lakes of Earth are in the hilly areas. Of all total lakes almost 50% lakes are in Canada alone. There is common notion that lakes are storages of fresh water. But the amount of vaporization is more in the dry place which makes the water salty to some extent.

1. The largest lakes on Earth with Salty water...

They are Caspian Sea, Dead Sea, and Great Salt Lake.

2. The biggest group of fresh water lakes...

The Great Lakes on the border of United States and Canada

3. Most deep lake from sea level of very salty water i.e. Dead Lake...

Dead Sea is the lake approximately 400 meters deep from sea level the water of which is 10 times more salty than the sea.

4. The biggest lake at the place highest from the sea level...

Titicaca Lake is at approximately 12500 ft. height from sea level. It is situated at the border of North American continent's countries Peru and Bolivia in the rows of Andes mountains. The sea trade happens between these two countries through this lake, such big is this lake. Also there are small floating towns are situated on it! As if this is not enough, the farming too takes place on the surface on this lake!!

5. Lake having biggest storage and depth of fresh water!!!...

The Baikal Lake in Russia is not only the deepest i.e. having the depth of 5712 ft. lake on Earth but also the largest storage of fresh water. Almost 20% of Earth's fresh water is in this lake alone!

The dry most part on Earth without rains for hundreds of year!!!...

There is also a place on Earth where it doesn't rain for hundreds of years! This is desert of Atacama in the country Chile of South American continent. Also the place Arica here is so devoid of rains that filling of a single coffee cup will take hundreds of years!

The amazing bridge sinking in the water!!!...

In the Greece there is a bridge on Corinth canal, near Athens which completely immerses in the water when the ship is passing through and comes back to its position for the road transport after the ship is passed.

The rainiest place on Earth!!!...

As we have seen the dry place, there is an over pouring place too. For many years the 'Cherrapunji' in India was known as the rainiest place. But now it is 'Mawsynram' in Meghalaya State of India in Asian continent. Here it rains on an average 1143 cm.

The bridge covering five Islands in Japan!!!...

In Japan Shimotsui Seto is the bridge having the length of almost 13 KM and it covers 5 Islands. Rail and road, both types of transports take place over this bridge. This is the biggest bridge in Japan.

The area of Earth's terrine...

We are nothing else but the part of Mother Earth. No other god has given us the birth but all the life including the human being is borne by Mother Earth. So the human must know the land or the terrine of Earth. We have seen above that almost the 71% means 361637000 km^2 area of Earth is covered by water.

Then how much is the area of Earth's terrine? Including the deserts on Earth, hilly areas, snowy region of Tundra, large & small forests; all these in total make the area of approximately 148429000 km^2 means 29% of Earth's total area.

The human has divided Earth's terrine in 7 parts, which are called continents. According to area they are as follows. The largest continent amongst them is Asia and the smallest one is Australasia (Oceania).

Name of the Continent	**Area (km^2)**
Asia	4,42,50,000
Africa	3,02,64,000
North America	2,43,97,000
South America	1,77,93,000
Antarctica	1,40,00,000
Europe	1,04,53,000
Australasia	89,23,000

Out of seven continents above, Antarctica continent has no life. Rest six terrines have the population of approximately 7000 million according to the 2012 census. The highest population is in Asia.

THIS PLACE GETS SUNRISE ONLY ONCE IN A YEAR!...

There is a place on Earth where Sun shines only once in a year! It is Antarctica. Isn't it surprising?

THE LONGEST RIDGELINE ON EARTH...

There are many mountains on our Earth, amongst them Mount Andes of South America is spread over the longest length north–southwards. Its length is more than 8000 KM. The animals Lama and Alpaca which appear here are not found anywhere else on the Earth.

IT IS THE PEAK HIGHER THAN THE MOUNT EVEREST BUT...

Mount Everest is known as the highest peak but there is the taller mountain peak Mauna Kea which is approximately 33000 ft. in height in U.S on Hawai Islands, taller than the Mount Everest. Yet it is not acclaimed as the 'tallest peak of mountains'. It is mainly because more than half the part of this peak means approximately 19000 ft. is immersed in the water and rest 14000 ft. is above water. But since the Mount Everest is approximately

29000 ft. higher than the sea level, it is counted as the tallest Mountain peak in the world.

The ridges of most height...

There are three ridges of the tallest peak heights. Out of these, Himalaya alone has 45 tall mountain peaks and Andes alone have 49 tall mountain peaks. Karakoram Mountain has 10 tall peaks.

The length–width of the great Himalayas and the tallest peak in the world!!...

Having the most famous and tallest peak of Mount Everest and many most heighted peaks in the world, the great Mount of Himalaya has the length of approximately 2500 KM with a width of approximately 450 KM.

The second tallest peak on the Earth...

In the Karakoram ridge situated between China and Pakistan there is second tallest peak in the world called K–2 (Godwin Austin). It has a height of approximately 28250 ft.

The Mountains on Antarctica too!...

We imagine the flat icy surface in front of our eyes with the mention of Antarctica. But there are ridges on Antarctica too and the Vinson Massif is the tallest peak of them with an approximate height of 5140 meters.

The smallest country on the Earth!!...

We shall be surprised knowing the area of this smallest independent country on Earth! It is the abode of 'Pope John Paul' in the city of Rome in Italy of European Continent. It has got the status of an independent country. The country is 'Vatican City'. The area of this country is just 0.4 km^2.

The two largest countries on the Earth

1. The largest country on Earth is Russia. Though divided, its approximate area is whooping 17075400 km^2!

2. The second largest country is Canada with an approximate area of 9958319 km^2

The neighboring nations with longest distance between capital cities!...

The capital of Australia Canberra and capital of New Zealand Wellington, these two cities of the adjacent nations have the distance of approximately 2330 KM. There is no capital of any other nation in between. This is the longest distance between two capital cities of any adjacent nations.

The hottest part of Earth!...

The place called Daloll within Danakil Depression in Ethiopia of African Continent has an average temperature of 34.4 degree Celsius throughout the year.

The last city of Earth!...

Ushuaia in the country of Argentina in South American Continent is the last city on Earth.

The place of chilliest weather on Earth!...

As there is a hottest place on Earth, you can chill out at the chilliest place on Earth! It is Plato station of Antarctica. The average temperature here is minus 56.7 degree Celsius.

The Forestland of the Earth...

Approximately 9.4% area of the Earth's surface is occupied by forests. Some part is occupied by Taiga, some rainforest and some is flourished with tall dense trees.

Of the total forestland area, 16% part of United States and Canada, 21% part of previous Soviet Union, 20% of Africa and 24% of Latin America is occupied by the forests.

Forests of Taiga...

The largest part occupied by forests on Earth is circularly spread from Siberia to Canada (Sweden, Alaska and Canada). This is the belt of evergreen plants growing in cold weather, full of varied living creatures. **In Canada alone approximately 4.2 million km^2 area is occupied by forests.**

Rainforest...

There is abundant occurrence of rainforests near the equator. It is because; it rains throughout the year in this part of the Earth, besides the warm weather. With the abundance of these favorable things the forests are in large amount. Out of this the most of the rainforests occur at the middle part of Africa, South America, Southeast Asia and Madagascar Islands. Besides these there are some at the Australia, Central America.

Woodland...

On the Earth where there is intense summer and as equal cold, means in Western Europe and eastward part of United States and eastward Asia such type of forests are found in abundance.

How many types of plants Mother Earth has created?...

Do you know how many types of plants are on our Mother Earth? There are almost 20 million types of plants on our Earth. Out of these, 50000 types are edible as food. Yet we use just 200 types as food. Today almost 80% food supply of the world is derived by just 8 types of plants!

How many types of birds are on Earth?...

Our Earth has many type of birds with wings. We may not be able to imagine but there are almost 9000 types of birds dwelling on Earth!

The biggest flying bird on Earth!!...

In the Andes ridge of the Southern America occurs the bird 'Andes Condor' which is the biggest flying bird on Earth. The length of his wings is almost 9 to 10 ft! He weighs 15 kg. Once spread his wings, he can cover the distance of many kilometres without making the noise! Actually Ostrich is the biggest bird but it cannot fly!

Is West Indies one country?...

If you watch game of cricket, you must know West Indies! Normally all think of it as one country, right? But in reality it is the group of small Islands in the continent of North America. Some of these Islands have received the status of a country. This group of Islands is divided in three main parts.

1. **Bahamas**: This includes almost 3000 Islands!

2. **Greater Antilles**: This is comprised of Cuba, Jamaica, Haiti, Dominican Republic, and Puerto Rico which are considered as independent nations.

3. **Lesser Antilles**: This is comprised of many small, small Islands and is divided further into Leeward Island and Windward Island. Now this group of West Indies Islands is also known as 'Caribbean'

WHY THESE ALL ISLANDS ARE CALLED WEST INDIES?...

According to the historians, the great European sailor Christopher Columbus sailed in 1492 on his mission of searching the India, he first boarded on Bahamas. He thought he reached East Indies in east and in Asian Continent. In the joy he named this land 'Indies'. But later when he realized that he has landed westward Islands on Atlantic Ocean instead of India, he named these Islands as West Indies.

IF THERE ARE 'WEST' INDIES ISLANDS, AREN'T THERE 'EAST' INDIES ISLANDS?...

In those days, famous for the spices were the Islands of Java, Sumatra, Bali, Bornio which were known as East Indies Islands. Now they are known as 'Indonesia'.

THE BIGGEST WATERFALL THAN NIAGARA ON EARTH!!!...

This waterfall that I have seen is a group of almost 270 waterfalls at one place, having the width of approximately three km. This is 'Iguassu' or Iguazu waterfall on the Iguassu River on the borders of Brazil and Argentina. At some places the water falls down in three phases. It appears to be three waterfalls

THE MOST AMAZING WIDE RIVER ON EARTH!...

The widest river with the width of amazing 220 km is called Rio de Plata. It is situated near Buenos Aires in the country of Argentina in the continent of South America.

THE NON-VEGETARIAN PLANTS!!...

It is amazing that there are some plants which eat flies, crawlers and such other insects! They clench hard the flies, crawlers sitting on their leaves to crush them and absorb their bodies!! Here the jungle law of 'life is a food of life' applies!

The Desert on Earth...

Almost 1/8th area of the total Earth is occupied by deserts. Besides this, 140 million km2 area of Antarctica too is counted in desert. So this is counted as the largest desert on Earth. The second largest desert after this is Sahara desert of North Africa.

Desert Is Not Just Sandy!...

It is commonly thought especially in Asian continent that the desert is full of sand. But the word desert encompasses much wider meaning. Excluding Antarctica, only 20% area is sandy and rest of the area is a rocky desert.

Antarctica, a type of desert...

Antarctica is a snowy region and yet is counted in deserts. This place has no plants, vegetation of any kind, animal or human inhabitance. Just at the shores we can see scanty population of penguins, seal fishes. So this is a kind of 'deserted' area, isn't it? Hence this icy region is called a cold desert.

Continent without Desert!...

While the deserts are spread over a large area on our Earth, European continent is an exception to it. There is neither rocky nor sandy desert in this continent.

****

See the Creation-structure's wonder!!!

Have a look at this wonder of almighty nature!!!

Some species of plants are carnivorous. Let's see how. The above photograph is of the carnivorous plant, 'Venus Fly Trap'. This plant species dwells in the marshy coasts of the United States. The plant, as its name suggests traps & devours at flies, crawlers, and other such insects. On both the inner surfaces of the leaf-like structures, myriad thorny hair-like outgrowths are seen. These hair senses when they are suppressed by any prey and if suppression is sensed within 20 seconds of the first sensation, the open mouth of the leaves shuts, to feast at its prey. This merely implies that even the non-locomotive organisms on the earth-plants can also be; or rather are; carnivores. One organism preys on the other to ensure its survival. This is the true rule of nature.

Hence, the allegorical secret of this book is that humans should not interfere between the nature's ways of functioning. Mobs of men make attempts to make vegetarianism pervasive. If this futile urge is followed by the Venus Fly Trap, it has a futuristic doom. It should be considered by mankind that nature does not accept its demands and delusions.

3.1

How was the clock created?

Clock is nothing else but the 'Mini Earth'!!

The human on Earth uses the wrist watch or a wall clock. What is the time now? Friends, we always keep watching the time in the morning, afternoon, evening and night. Actually we keep watching how much the Earth has revolved around self! And we call this watching the time! Means the root of clock's creation is in the self-revolution of the Earth, isn't it? Friends, please read this without any excuse as we are going to reveal some interesting facts!

Actually the dial of the clock is divided into two segments. One is the day of 12 hours and the other is the night of 12 hours. On the equator, the circumference of the Earth is approximately 40000 KM (actually 38640 KM according to hourly speed). Earth takes 12 hours of a day and a 12 hours of the night to complete the self-revolution, means total 24 hours to complete the circle of 40000 KM. The same method is used in the clock. Clock has 3 types of 'hands'. One short hand that points to the hours, another longer hand points to the minutes and some have the third 'sweeping' hand for seconds. From the sunrise till the sunset_ that is suppose from morning six to evening six o'clock _ the Earth usually completes the self-revolution of around 20000 KM distance. Means the hour hand takes 12 hours to complete a dial, isn't it? And the minutes hand takes one hour to complete the dial which equals to the distance of 1610 KM that our Earth covers per hour. Our Earth's rotation speed is 1610 KM per hour. Same is the case with the third seconds' hand. When seconds' hand completes the dial, the Earth has revolved 27 KM around self! Phew! Means to complete the minute, the seconds hand has to revolve around 27 KM. Earth completes the rest 20000 KM revolution from evening six to morning six In the same way, in 12 hours. Thus to revolve 40000 KM to complete the rotation around self, the Earth takes 24 hours. So we count one day as 24 hours, isn't it? Our clock or watch is based on this count. But the common man is oblivious to this, aren't we? If we divide the time taken by the Earth to complete her self-revolution in equal parts, we call it an hour. An hour divided in equal parts is called minutes. And a minute divided in equal parts is called seconds. Actually the clock must be comprised of just 24 hours. But for our convenience, the clock is divided into 12 hours of night and 12 hours of a day. The clock made up to show full 24 hours would have become very large, isn't it? Yet in railways, airports etc. the clock displays 24 hours. When the flight time is shown as 23.15, we minus the 12 hours from that time and assume that the flight time is at night 11.15. Clock is divided into AM i.e. Ante Meridiem (Before Noon) and PM i.e. Post Meridiem (After Noon) to indicate the time. Thus to make the dial of clock smaller for the convenience, the clock of 24 hours is fitted into 12 hours division. Clock is nothing but the 'Mini Earth'. Phew!

WHERE IN THE GALAXY IS THE CONCEPT OF YEAR? ONLY ON THE PLANET EARTH AND JUST FOR THE HUMANKIND! HAVE YOUR PET EVER ASKED YOU THE TIME?...

The 24 hours of the Earth's revolution is the criterion of a day. But Earth revolves around the Sun from the distance of 150 million KM. This means to complete this rotation around Sun she has to travel approximately 940 million KM. The time taken for this travel we identify as a 'year'. Means this chronology or calculation of time is purely based on the 'Earth's self-rotation and rotation around the Sun.' Hence only on Earth this chronology is used. Knowing this one realizes how baseless the birth charts and birth dates are, aren't they? This subject is discussed ahead.

When needed, the chronology of the Earth is taken as a base for the calculations regarding other planets. For example, a day on Venus is 243 days on Earth. A year on Neptune is 164.8 years on Earth. The Moons' day has 656 hours of Earth, which is a satellite of our Earth.

All these things must be covered during the schooling days of the human life. I don't understand why students are kept in the dark about such important things!

The things appearing on the Earth are the illusions!! Real nature of them is different!!!...

Earth revolves around self from west to eastwards. It gives an illusion of the Sun appearing on east in the morning and moved to the west in the evening. Actually Sun does not budge an inch from his place at all! For the Earth, the Sun is stationary at one place. Due to the Earth's revolution around self, the day, night, noon, morning and evening is not experienced by all on the Earth at the same time. For example when we see the Sun rising in San Francisco of America, it is not necessarily seen rising in all other parts of the world. Now how is this Sunrise illusionary? For example, if we go to Mumbai city in India when the Sun is rising in San Francisco, we will see it setting in India! It would be sunset at Mumbai. Mumbai time will be found to be almost 12 hours ahead of the San Francisco time! The day would be starting at San Francisco, when it would be ending in Mumbai! San Francisco citizens may be experiencing wonderful sunshine and a hectic day ahead and people of Mumbai must be leaving their offices to go & reach home! At the same time, the city of London in European continent will be experiencing the noon!

When it is evening six o'clock in the city Mumbai or Pune of India, the time at Auckland in New Zealand would be one past thirty minutes of the night. While it is sunset at Mumbai city of India, the ten thousand KM away westwards on Atlantic Ocean time would be 12 noon. Owing to the Earth's self-revolution things appear in this fashion.

What exactly happens when we experience the day and night?...

While the Earth is self-revolving from west to eastwards, and also revolving around Sun during sunrise to sunset, Sun appears to be rising at morning in the Sun facing part of the Earth. And Sun appears to be setting at evening on the non-Sun facing, other part of the Earth.

When this non Sun facing part of the Earth comes in front of the Sun due to the 20000 KM peregrination of Earth, then Sun appears to be rising in that part. Means what was experienced as sunset in that part of Earth now appears to be sunrise due to Earth's revolution of 20000 KM! Sun is steady. But the Earth has self-revolved 20000 KM from sunrise to sunset and again 20000 KM from sunset to sunrise. Means she completed one round of 40000 KM around self. So we experience day and night. Whoa!

The reason to elaborate this so much is that everything of this is related to your breath. Your existence is dependent on your breath. If this does not happen, there will be no life existent on the Earth. And with it, even human existence will end. If you don't understand this, your condition will be like 'all his life, lived in a fool's paradise'.

Now you must have realized that due to Earth's self-revolution the clock is created. Thus, clock is just a small Earth. As the Earth revolves, the hands of clock too are revolving keeping up to her speed.

Everything here is just an illusion!!!...

Friends, as sunrise and sunset are the illusions; the sunshine that we see too is an illusion. Actually sunshine is a mixture of red, orange, yellow, green, blue, white and purple colors. But it is visible only as white color to us, isn't it? Also what are always visible to our eyes are the pitch green leaves of tree and the rich blue sky. But in reality the green color unabsorbed by the leaves is reflected to our eyes; and they are visible as green to us. Had the leaves absorbed the green color too, we would have seen the leaves too as white colored just like the sunshine! That is because the mixture of seven colors gives the appearance of white color.

Also, the sky that is visible to us is nothing else but the layers of gases pulled and held together by our Mother Earth. The unabsorbed blue color thrown out by these layers of gases after absorbing the other colors is what is visible to us spread all over in the sky. If we leave the Mother Earth's orbit, say after approximately 300 KM away from Earth, or also from the Moon; we will see the real sky or space which will be pitch black. It is the same thing with water. The fluid water that we see is actually the mixture of two gases. The banyan tree is huge; but has its root in the tiny size of poppy seeds! Means each visible thing is an illusion. The things appearing on the Earth has a very different looking root in reality!

Whatever our eyes see has its root in the Mother Earth! So everything is just Mother Earth, Mother Earth and Mother Earth! Here we just saw the relation between the self-revolution of the Earth and the clock. Now we shall see the Earth's revolution around Sun.

Can anyone believe this reality?...

Earth is actually revolving around the Sun at a whooping speed of 107000 KM! But she appears to be steady to our eyes, isn't it? Do you know one reality? Actually, we too are rotating with her around the Sun with the same speed!

Who says we are rotating 107000 KM per hour? Here is the doctrine!...

Friends, aren't you wondering as to from where this figure of 107000 KM has come from? I too was curious about this in the beginning! This question was lingering in my mind for 2 to 3 months. I am a commoner and not at all a big wig to be able to consult any scientist. I used to think for hours in the solitude about how speed could be so great and why don't we even feel it. And one day this riddle was revealed to me! Something that I had never read about, that knowledge was received through my thinking power. Earth revolves around the Sun in an oval shape which everyone knows as I too knew. But the riddle of speed was unresolved, which finally was revealed as below.

I knew that the Sun is 150 million Kilometres away from the Earth. The scientist who discovered it and was credited for it was Captain James Cook. In 1769 Captain Cook discovered the Earth's distance from the Sun. I was fortunate enough to visit twice and see the house of such a great person while in Melbourne. I was so overwhelmed that I observed the minute details including his bed, utensils, chair and table in the home!

Well, the reason I am telling you all this is, due to this distance I could find the answer to how the speed is hourly 107000 KM! While thinking one day I visualized the rotation of Earth around Sun. Then I recollected the compass using which we drew the circle during schooldays. With this recall I drew a circle on the paper. To derive the circumference of that circle I used the geometrical formula of 'radius x 44/7 = circumference'. This gave me 150 million x 44/7 = 942.8 million KM as circumference. This is the Earth's distance of revolution around the Sun. Means to complete the rotation around Sun our Earth has to rotate the distance of 942.8 million KM. How much time she needs to traverse this distance? It is 365 days and 6 hours. Means in 365 days and 6 hours the Earth revolves 942.8 million KM. From this amount it is realized that in a day Earth traverses the distance of approximately 2581245 KM. Then from this I got the answer that she traverses the distance of 107000 KM per hour which is her rotation speed per hour! I was thrilled with joy! It is because I had discovered the answer to 'how the speed of Earth's rotation is 107000 KM per hour'? Then of course I felt astonished!

Your life is 60 to 70 revolutions of the Earth! Means your birth to death!!!...

So many things we do since our birth to death; means from being a new born baby up to an old age! After coming out of our mother's womb we start crying; because we know our needs have started, we need clothes, we need milk, we need the warmth and affection -- though we may not understand anything we need the company of parents and others!

As we start growing we crawl, we sit in the arms of our parents, start babbling and in some days we start walking independently. These transformations keep happening. Then while crossing the phases during education -- preschool, pre-primary, primary, high school and in college we graduate and enter into the youth. After completion of education we get the job and then get married and have kids. Performing the responsibilities of their upbringing and nurturance we enter the old age and in the due course leave this world. This duration from birth to death is nothing else but the 60-70 revolutions of Earth around the Sun, which is a human's average life period. Now you may think, we know this about the life period, what different is the author telling? Everyone knows it! Though you know this life period, it will be hard for you believe what I am going to tell you! The reality is that I call this life time as the 60 to 70 revolutions of Earth around the Sun. We call it 60-70 years. If on an average the life is assumed to be of 60-70 years, during this time each human from his birth to death rotates 66000 million KM and traverses the life! After death this travel ends!!

YOU ARE IN THE SPACESHIP CALLED EARTH SINCE YOUR BIRTH; AND TILL YOUR DEATH YOU ARE REVOLVING AT THE SPEED OF 107000 KM PER HOUR!!!...

As you go from Pune to Delhi and after coming back to Delhi you say 'I travelled approximately 2000 KM'. In the same way, would you believe the figure of the distance you travel in the space during your life time? But this is the reality. All of us are sitting in the spaceship of Earth. All our eating, drinking and stay is in this spaceship of Earth. This ship is rotating in the space at the speed of 107000 KM per hour and within a year covers the distance of almost 940 million KM. If we calculate our average life span to be of 60 to 70 years, it becomes the distance of whooping 65800 million KM!! You can check the truth about this with any scientist. So many things are related to our life to which we are oblivious! Here, unless we revolve like this, we shall not be able to keep our breath going! So much our existence is related to this reality! Without this travel the entire life on Earth shall end. But engrossed in our mundane life we never think or even know about this reality. That is why I am putting much ado of making you realize all this! Each person at least should know what helps him or her breath and who s/he is!

This is one of the reasons on which your breath is dependent. Just think if the Earth stops travelling with this speed, what will happen? The cycle of seasons that we experience is due to this continuous revolution of the Earth. Season's cycle is summer & winter and rainy seasons in various parts of the globe. During summer the clouds are formed due to excessive heat vaporizing the water. In rainy season these clouds drop water on Earth making her green. Crops get ripe which is our food and our life depends upon it. Winter fosters many plantations, fruits, food grains by giving the much needed weather to them. This cycle of seasons is perpetually on and so all life is safe and secure.

Just due to revolution of Earth the cycle of seasons exists which fosters the life by feeding it and watering it. The Earth's revolution benefits you in many such ways and you must have realized its importance. You also must have realized that there is no intervention or contribution of any imaginary man made third power like God. Everything is just Mother Earth, Mother Earth and just Mother Earth! What does this mean? This only means that you, me and all the life we see on Earth is nothing else but the part of Mother Earth!

Why don't we feel the huge speed of the Earth's rotation?...

Many people asked me, our Earth rotates with such a great speed then why don't we feel it? The simple explanation of the canon here is that when two things are travelling parallel at one direction at the same speed, they appear to be steady to each other. While travelling by the bus, plane or train the vehicle is running at a speed of at least 60 KM per hour, train is travelling by the speed of at least 80 KM per hour and plane is the fastest. But while sitting in any of it, we are travelling at the speed of whatever vehicle we have taken along and your co passengers too. The co passengers sitting in the vehicle appear to be steady to each other isn't it? Only if you peep out of the window of a bus or a train you will find trees, mountains and things on the road to be running, isn't it? In the plane that travels the fastest; everything appears to be steady isn't it? Barring take on, take offs and the times of air pockets; nothing inside the plane even moves, no shaking, no jolts. It feels super steady inside though it is travelling at the fastest speed. It is because of the same speed with which everything is travelling. The air hostess is travelling too; other passengers are travelling too with the same speed and so they appear to be steady. But you peep out of the window of a bus or a train and as other things on the road are stationary and you are travelling at a speed, so they appear to be running in the opposite direction! But your co passengers travelling with you at the same speed appear to be steady. Had the things on roads like tree, mountains, outside people been travelling with you at the same speed, they too will appear to be steady. This analysis explains that since we too are travelling with the Earth at the same speed and our entire life around too is travelling at the speed, i.e. at the speed of 107000 KM per hour, we don't feel the speed.

THE SKY AND THE PLANE IN THE SKY TOO ARE TRAVELLING WITH THE EARTH AT THE SAME SPEED!...

The fun is that the Mother Earth is also taking the sky that we see along with her and the sky too is revolving with her at the same speed! The sky that we see is not the real sky and is an illusion, I will explain this later.

Friends, when you travel in plane at least from that height too do you see the Earth revolving? Do you feel her speed? No! The reason for this is that the sky and also the plane that you are travelling in are revolving at the same speed along with the Earth! Just like even if the passengers in your plane are moving around within the plane but appear to be steady to you because they too are travelling with you in plane at the same speed; similarly, the plane is sitting in the spaceship of Earth and travelling with the Earth! So there is no question of the speed of the plane itself. So even from the plane the Earth doesn't seem to be revolving and appears to be steady. All the things which are within the orbit of Earth's gravitational force are revolving around the Sun with the same speed and hence 'Earth' doesn't appear to revolve from their point of view.

You must have experienced that if two vehicles are travelling parallel in the same direction at the same speed, they appear to be steady to each other. This happens more in train travel. When at station junctions the other train is moving too along with your train in parallel speed, you would find it to be steady along with the passengers in that train. I have experienced this many times.

Now you must be clear about why Earth's speed is not felt by us though she is travelling at the speed of whooping 107000 KM per hour! **THE REVOLUTION OF EARTH IS THE LIFE OF EVERYONE AND EVERYTHING ON EARTH! HALTING OF HER REVOLUTION IS DEATH OF EVERY LIFE AND EVERYTHING ON THE EARTH!!...**

Remember, you are revolving with the Earth at the same speed as hers and so you exist. The day your revolution along with the Earth stops, that is your death! Also since the time you are born you are revolving with the Earth and so you are existent. Now tell me which fanatic religious head and which God contributes this? Everything is Mother Earth and nothing else! She conducts her duty of just giving, without expecting back anything in return! So she is the Goddess, she is the Almighty! She doesn't need flowers, essences, garlands! So now you decide which is a real God, real super power! Water is Mother Earth! Food is Mother Earth and your soul too is Mother Earth! Everything is just Mother Earth. You will know yourself in truth and you will get your true identity if you understand this and your life will be joyous and tension free! You will experience who really you are. Actually you are experiencing this at each breath but are so unaware about Mother Earth!

So far we have seen two speeds of Earth, one of self-rotation and other of revolution around the Sun. There is one more, the third speed of the Earth. It is that this solar system of ours including its planets rotates around the galaxy. Why is it not felt? Because our solar system is rotating with the same speed at which the Sun is rotating around the galaxy!

****

Watch how the clock ticks according to Earth's rotation!!!

Clock is 'Mini Earth'!

The clock visible in the above picture that we tie on our wrist or fix on the wall is nothing else but the 'Mini Earth' itself. The total circumference of the Earth is approximately 38640 KM. In her self-revolution from west to eastwards the Earth takes 24 hours to complete this circumference. It means by revolving at 1610 KM per hour she completes half round in 12 hours, which we term a day; and the remaining round she completes in next 12 hours which we call night. The concept of clock is based on this and it is easier for us to calculate the time. The circumference of the clock seen in the above picture is approximately 20000 KM. To complete the same, means one complete circle; the hours hand takes 12 hours. Means the hours hand has to traverse 1610 KM to complete one unit. Whereas, the minutes hand needs to travel 1610 KM to complete one dial and the seconds hand has to travel 27 KM to complete one dial. Means the hands of the clock travel based on the speed of Earth's own revolution. Such is the structure of the clock. Please read the complete information in the chapter 'How the clock was created?'

3.2

JAPAN IS NOT THE COUNTRY OF THE RISING SUN!

Which are the real counties of rising Sun and why?

You may not get to read this anywhere. Owing to the self rotation of the Earth I am going to disprove the prevalent concept of Japan being the country of the rising Sun.

To understand this you should know about the zero longitude means the Greenwich Time and the International Date Line at 180 degree longitude. For those who don't know, our Earth is divided by lines imagined at a specific distance which are called meridians or longitudes and latitudes.

The distance between the two longitudes of the Earth that is divided conceptually among 360 meridians is usually four minutes. The median of these 360 meridians means zero longitude, which is known as Greenwich Line and passes through the city of London. Total 360 meridians are divided into 180 longitudes or meridians eastward and westward each to this line. This line of 180 longitudes is assumed to be the International Date Line. The time of the countries westward to zero degree i.e. the Greenwich Line lags behind 12 hours and the time of the countries eastward to Greenwich Line is ahead by 12 hours. Suppose if the time at London is 6 PM in the evening, the time at the eastward countries on 180 longitudes at the same time would be morning 6 AM. As the eastward countries are 12 hours ahead regarding time, the countries on International Date Line i.e. Kiribati, Nauru, Marshal and New Zealand change the date first on the Earth after night 12 o'clock. For example, in New Zealand at night 12 o'clock the date of 9th August changes to the date of 10th August first; while at all other countries on the Earth it still would be 9th August. Even the Alaska which is westward to the London too changes the date from

8th to 9th; though Alaska is very near to the meridian of 180 degree.

Now when in New Zealand the date changes from 9th August to 10th August at midnight, that time in Japan the time is yet around 8.30 PM at night of the date 9th August. As Earth keeps traversing from Japan to New Zealand; in Australia the date changes from 9th August to 10th August after New Zealand. After New Zealand almost 3.30 hours later the date in Japan changes from 9 th August to 10th August When there is a sunrise in the New Zealand at 6 AM of 10th August; in Japan it is still 2 to 3 PM at night of 9th August!

If this is the case, isn't where the date changes first on the Earth is the country of rising Sun in the real sense than the country having the previous date? Since the first date change and accordingly the first sunrise happen at New Zealand even before Japan, the countries of rising Sun in real sense are New Zealand, Kiribati, Marshall and Nauru. Japan cannot be the country of rising Sun because it is on the 140 degrees longitude. This factual information must be included in the school curriculum.

In Japanese language the earlier names of Japan were 'Nippon' and 'Nihon'. They mean 'rising Sun'. So based on this Japan may have been called as a country of 'rising Sun' in the old days. It is no where mentioned properly about why otherwise Japan is called the country of the 'rising Sun'. One explanation is that when the western countries weren't discovered, the Japan was at far eastward for the eastern world and so they called it the country of sunrise. Later with the discoveries as the larger world was identified all definitions have changed.

****

3.3

Earth's Rotation Around Her Axis Created the Directions

The illusion of directions!!!...

Directions were created for the convenience of the humankind. Otherwise if you go to the space there are no directions. But some greedy people on Earth try to take disadvantage of the mass ignorance about this. They divide the directions into the auspicious or inauspicious, connect them to religion and coating it with the nice name of 'architectural science' ask the ignorant people to break their existing houses, structures and mint money. Actually all this is bogus! The origin of directions is Earth's rotation and it has nothing to do with all this. This is all the imagination of those who are intolerant of life's challenges and have money more than necessary to spend on such corrections!

I am staying in city of Pune in India. I am born in a very poor family of a small village. After coming to Pune, I have spent almost 20 years of my life on footpath, below the bench of a private mess, later in a small hut and after spending the some life in a small room, I built my own home in Pune. The kitchen platform of this home is in south direction, one of the doors too open in the south direction. I have taken the tube well wherever the water was found, without any consideration of a direction. It has abundant water. In such house I am living happily since past 30 years. I have travelled all over the world myself and along with the family too, while living in this house. I have arranged this house according to my convenience and not at all according to the convenience or guidance of the architectural consultants i.e. vastu shastra!

Each place at the same time is at the East and West! At the same time North and South too. Then which is the real direction out of this? Directions have no real existence. They are not fixed, but are imaginary. Check this. The east that you see in the morning becomes west in the evening because the Earth rotates, Sun is steady! For example, London is in the west to India, North to Argentina, East to Canada and it is in the south of the Greenland! Which direction out of these is auspicious? It is in the all four directions at the same time to some country or the other, isn't it? One city but can be viewed in all directions. So these directions actually are illusionary. It is actually a non-existent but just a man-made imaginary thing.

Each animate on the Earth including insects are alive because we are rotating along with the Earth at the speed of 1610 KM. The day you will not rotate with her, you would have died! Our each breath, our very existence is dependent on Earth's rotation on her own axis. So if you need to imagine God, it is only Mother Earth, Mother Earth and Mother Earth! It is because she is rotating for a life time, without any rest so that the life on her including you and me happily dwell!

This is one true identity of yours, due to the rotation of the Earth. You are alive due to Earth's rotation. Now we shall see what happens due to her revolution around Sun, next!!

****

4

The Twelve Factors Responsible for the Creation and Existence of the Life on Earth

YOU AND I AND THE LIFE ON EARTH ARE NOTHING ELSE BUT THE 12 FACTORS OF EARTH! HOWEVER GREAT YOU MAY THINK OF YOURSELF THAT ARE THESE 12 FACTORS. IT IS YOUR TRUE IDENTITY WHICH I ENDEAVOUR TO YOU...

Till now I shared with you how the Mother Earth, the creator of you, me and all life; was created and when she was created. I shared what is the contribution of the Sun and Moon along with the Mother Earth in the creation and existence of all life including you and me. In short I informed you about the astronomical and geographical Earth. That informed you about when the animate was first created on Earth? When and how was the human created? How many factors were first created by Earth to create a human on the Earth? What is the relation between the Moon and the Earth? What is the Moon's relation with the animates on the Earth? Which factors were created through it? All these questions were answered through this information.

Later I informed you about the Sun. Which and how many factors responsible for the human creation and existence were created from the Sun? And discussed about how he is responsible for the creation of the life on Earth. Then described about how many factors of the environment been useful to the life, how the distances between the Earth and the Sun, Moon have been useful to the creation of life on Earth and how is the geography of our Earth.

THESE ARE THE SAME 12 FACTORS WHICH EMBED THE SECRET OF YOUR LIFE AND DEATH. ONCE YOU UNDERSTAND THESE, YOU HAVE GOT, YOU HAVE REALIZED YOUR TRUE IDENTITY. DUE TO THIS CONSIDERED VIEW YOU WILL BE FREE FROM ALL THE HAZARDS IN THE LIFE!!!...

Following 12 factors are responsible for the creation and existence of the life on the Earth, or the creation structure on the Earth including human.

1. Rotation of Earth
2. Earth's revolution around Sun
3. Earth's gravitational force
4. The Moon's particular distance from the Earth and her desired gravitational force.
5. The availability of the oxygen on the Earth.
6. The ice on the south and north pole of the Earth
7. The ¾ water on the Earth.
8. The Ozone gas in the environment held by Earth.
9. The quilt of environment clad around Earth containing various gases
10. Earth's distance of 150 million KM from Sun.
11. The combustion of 4 million ton hydrogen per second on the Sun
12. The greater gravitational force of Sun than other planets.

Just due to these 12 factors you and I take birth! Not our parents but these 12 factors give us the birth! The omission of just one factor out of these 12 factors will cease the process of birth!!

KNOW THE SECRET, THE ENIGMA OF OUR BIRTH AND DEATH ALONG WITH ALL ANIMATES!!!...

Combination of all these 12 factors means the on-going breath of all animates including human and their existence!

Now I am going to explain in detail how the human and other animate were created due to these twelve factors, elaborating them one by one! This will help you realize your true identity. Each thing out of these explanations you experience at each breath. Due to these twelve factors you breathe and you exist. These are your true creators. Friends, have you heard about the four elements in Buddhism or five elements of Hinduism i.e. Air, Water, Fire, Earth and sky? Means only the visible was brought to the humankind. But to identify yourself or to know the secret of your creation, just these four or five elements are not enough. They do not reveal the meaning or the secret of creation. So to know this secret of the creation, one must know and understand these 12 factors along with the Earth. Though I am saying this is the truth, this is the truth, all these things are illusionary. I have given the description of this ahead.

Just identify! an invisible sperm till your death; which is real you? All is illusion!!!...

The physical size developed from a non-visible sperm! But so many transformations it undergoes! The fetus in the mother's womb, the new born just out of mother's womb, an infant, toddler and a child, then an adolescent turning into a young man, the father of the small children, old man with weaker eye sight and no teeth and reduced hearing power, tired body and then a non-existent animate! A single invisible sperm to the old man on death bed, who are the real you out of these? If we assume one out of these to be true, then who are the others? Illusions! Zero created out of zero is a zero. What should one think about such a life? This life is an illusion. But the person never thinks about this while living. Never tries to know him. Never identifies himself. From the childhood he is just taught 'me' 'mine'. But actually there is nothing that belongs to him! This is all illusion.

Root is the sperm!! The root belongs to the Mother Earth!!...

We say we are created from the sperm and egg. But where it belongs? Has the sperm or egg been really created by your parents on their own? Is it formed without the support of the Mother Earth? The real identity of the sperm is that the combinations of the twelve factors described above have formed the sperm. The one who call 'I' is nothing but the sperm that is formed together by these 12 factors. It is the form that this sperm has given to you. If there is one factor short out of these twelve, no sperm, no egg will be formed and you won't get your form too! This is human's true identity. Human race doesn't understand this till the end. Human just keeps taking false pride in 'I', 'Me' and 'Mine'!

'My 10 bungalows, my 50 factories, I am a billionaire, I am the leader, I am the prime minister, I am the president, I am the royal, I am the duke, I am this and that!' These manmade titles and adjectives are all illusionary. Nothing is the truth. The only identity you have is the invisible sperm made up of twelve factors. But the man's illusion doesn't end till death and one day his connection to the Earth breaks, he dies. Thus in the illusion he takes birth and in illusion he dies. No one has been an exception to this process so far.

We shall know more about each of these twelve factors responsible for the form that each animate on the Mother Earth has received.

****

4.1

The first factor of your creation, your first identity...

The continuous East to Westward Rotation of the Earth at the speed of 1610 KM Per Hour

Part of Real LIVE GOD & signs of life and secret of your birth and death are hidden here!

Till date no one made you realize your true identity. Here is your true identity!!...

Living our mundane life, we never try to know the importance of these factors related to our breath. One of the factors is the Mother Earth's rotation around her axis. If I tell that this has relation to your birth, you will say, "What absurd talk! What is the relation between Earth's rotation and our birth?" But human being is ignorant about this phenomenon. However intelligent he may be but just unaware. S/ he is not well aware of creator or nurturer Mother Earth! Here is how his birth, his each breath and his existence and the rotation of Earth are related.

Earth's rotation means your birth, your existence, your eating and drinking, breathing!!!...

You must have read the description of the Mother Earth. Her circumference at the equator is almost 40075 KM, and if you don't know this, how will you know that your existence, your birth is dependent on this factor? The Mother Earth having the area of 510066000 km2 that we dwell upon is floating in the space. Not just floating but is rotating around self continuously. And due to this rotation our trees bear fruits, the crops get ripe, the tall big trees and useful forests are standing. Due to this it rains, the birds sing, variety of animates like tiger, cow, bull, elephant, buffalo, goats including humans are taking birth and living their life. While living the life, supporting to this life, to rest and rejuvenate the tired bodies something called 'night' takes place on this Earth due to Earth's rotation.

There is a consciousness filled in all the life of Earth due to the energy received from Sun due to Earth's rotation. Due to her rotation the environment necessary for the life on her is created. You are enjoying the day and night due to her rotation and enjoying your life.

What if she doesn't rotate? Death to ALL!!!...

Now suppose the Earth stops this rotation; can you imagine what would happen? To tell you the truth, no life will exist on this Earth! The on-going cycle of birth and death shall stop. If Earth doesn't rotate around her axis, we won't experience the day, night, noon, evening. There will be sunshine just on one part of the Earth forever. So the temperature there will be too high. It becomes unbearable to us humans when on some parts of the Earth the temperature crosses 50 degree Celsius, isn't it? Then if the Earth doesn't rotate, in half the part the night won't be experienced at all. There will be a continuous day. And due to high temperature; including humans all the life will not sustain and life will come to an end. And the new life will not be born at such an adverse climate. Not just humans, even the insects won't be survived. Forget about the nature trees, even simple vegetation like algae will not be formed. Earth will be a dry barren desert. This will happen on half of the part that will be under the continuous sunshine. Opposite to this will happen on the rest half part of the Earth. It will have continuous night. Not only the new life will halt the formation due to lack of Sun's energy; but the present life's existence will be endangered. The seas and Oceans won't get vaporized due to the lack of sunshine and so clouds won't be formed. So there will be no rains, the cycle of nature will be disturbed. No animate will be created as there will be no water due to the lack of rains. The water is a necessity for each animate. Nothing will be formed, not even a small flake of grass, forget about the human! This is the effect of no rotation of Earth. This is the importance of her rotation around her axis. The religious preachers and philosophers give long lectures, but they may not know this fact. So they are just adding the spice to the religious legends and adding to the ignorance of the people, but cannot share such true facts. Now do you identify yourself?

The rotation of Earth is your birth, your eating and drinking, your breathing, your being alive. Out of the twelve factors that make your existence, one is rotation of the Earth. No rotation, no existence! This is your identity. No man made God interferes, no soul or super soul intervenes this!!

WHO STANDS PRIME MINISTER, PRESIDENTS, LEADERS, INDUSTRIALISTS AND PREACHER IN FRONT OF EARTH'S ROTATION? THEY ARE NON-EXISTENCE!!!...

Now I say, even if someone is prime minister, president or owner of the whole industry but do not have this knowledge then everything is in vain! Out of so many animates dwelling on the Earth, only human being has got the gift of intelligence. Using that one must know Mother Earth and know oneself. Else what is the use of this intelligence? But human does not wish to make the right use of the gifts received! When things are out of control, only concept s/he has to support is 'God' and that has fostered the selfish clan exploiting such dependent and ignorant people.

NOW WE SHALL SEE HOW THE DIRECTIONS WERE CREATED ON THE EARTH...

The Earth is perpetually rotating from west to eastward. If the circumference of Earth is assumed to be almost 40000 KM; she is traversing 20000 KM in the day time and rest 20000 KM at the night time. So the Sun appearing in the east at sunrise appears to be setting in the west at Sun set. But actually he is steady at one place. He does not set as it appears. But due to the Earth's rotation speed of 1610 KM; the Sun facing part in the morning is not facing the Sun in the evening. So the people experiencing the sun rise in the morning have the deception of sunset after 12 hours means after the Earth's rotation of 20000 KM. Actually the Sun is a shining star in the space. At the same time the non-Sun facing part gradually starts facing the Sun. So the people dwelling on this part have the deception of the Sun rise. Means due to Earth's rotation from west to east the illusion of sunrise in the east and sunset in the west is experienced. Night in the half part of Earth and day in the other half part, such cycle is perpetually on. For the own convenience the human uses the directions east, west, south and north. Actually this too is an illusion for human. Once you leave the Earth and go to the space, the connection to the Earth's rotation is severed and there is no east, west, south or north! Space is directionless!

What if Earth's rotation speed increases or decreases?...

The life on Earth is happily dwelling only due to her rotation speed. If her speed changes, it would affect the life on her. For example 24 hours is the Earth day, while 656 hours of Earth is the Moon day. The day of Venus comprises of 243 days on Earth. If such day would be there on Earth what would be the effect? Had the Earth's speed decrease to such an extent, the life wouldn't have sprung on her!

We have seen what would happen if the Earth revolves with a very slow speed. But if she rotates with the speed higher than the current speed of 1610 KM per hour then there won't be any trace of life on the Earth. Due to the hourly rotation speed of 1610 KM; the day and night of 12 hours each are favourable for the life on Earth. It causes the creation of the life including human beings and her existence remains. But check the results if she rotates more than this speed. Suppose if she rotated with an hourly speed of 5000 KM then she would just take 8 hours to complete a rotation of approx.40000 KM; means it would have caused a day and night of 4 hours each. This would have resulted in no creation of any animate being on this Earth. So now you would understand how important is the hourly rotation speed of 1610 KM for the creation of life and its existence on this Earth. So I say our breath, our eating drinking and your existence is the Mother Earth!

The illusion of sunrise, noon, evening and night!!!...

See how sunrise, sunset, noon, night all is illusionary. When sunrise is experienced at London, it is afternoon in many Asian countries like India, Sri Lanka or Pakistan. When it is night almost 9.30 PM at San Francisco in American continent, it is morning almost 8.30 in Moscow of Russia and the same time it is dawning around 6.00 at Algiers of North Africa. At the same time it is afternoon around 1.00 PM at Shanghai and Singapore! When it is night around 11.30 in the city of Edmonton of Canada in North American continent, it is next day morning around 10.30 in the city of Islamabad in the Asian Continent!

When in India of Asian Continent it is dawning at 6 AM, the Southern east side of this country, in Australia, New Zealand, it is afternoon. If we traverse the far off distances on the Earth at the same time, we shall find the time zones changing, the day, night, sunrise and sunset changing. This is all illusionary.

DIFFERENT TIMES CAUSED IN DIFFERENCE PLACES DUE TO ROTATION OF THE EARTH!...

According to longitudes, the countries eastward to any nation are ahead in the time of that nation. Similarly, the countries westward of that nation lag behind the time of that nation. For example if we take India, the eastward countries are Myanmar, Cambodia, Vietnam, Singapore, Thailand, Australia, New Zealand all have the time running ahead of India. When it is morning 11.10 at Mumbai of India, it is almost 3.45 after noon at Sydney of Australia. When it is 12 noon at Delhi of India, it is night 7.30 at the city of Auckland. Let us take the city of London that is westwards to India. So the time of this city is four and a half hours behind the time of India. When it is night 9 PM in India, London's time is 4.30 PM after noon. This is the miracle of Earth's rotation.

Friends, I would like to sight one more amazing example of Earth's rotation below. This is the amazing fact about the direction and time. I have brought this reality to your kind notice.

THERE IS A SUNRISE AT 180 LONGITUDE WESTWARDS OF LONDON CITY AND ALSO AT 180 DEGREE LONGITUDE EASTWARD BUT IN THE CITY OF LONDON THE TIME IS 6 AT EVENING!!!...

Our Earth is divided in the 360 longitudes. The Greenwich Line of zero degree longitude passes through the city of London. The Earth is divided into 360 degrees i.e.180 longitudes westward to London and 180 longitudes eastward to London. The eastward countries to London city are like Kiribati, Nauru, and Marshal, New Zealand. These are 12 hours ahead of the London city. Similarly, the westward countries like Alaska in USA are 12 hours behind the London city time. If you understand this, you will realize that when it is sunset at 6 PM in London city, the countries on 180 degree longitude eastward being 12 hours ahead would be having the next day sunrise at 6 AM. And at the same time i.e.at evening 6 in London the cities on 180 degree longitude westward to the London, as they are 12 hours behind, they too would have a time of a 6 AM at sunrise. Means it is sunset at London, but at the countries on 180 degree longitude eastward, there is a sunrise and also at the countries on 180 degree longitude westward, there is sun rise! Isn't it an astonishing fact?

****

See how the Earth rotates around Sun And how Moon rotates around Earth!!!

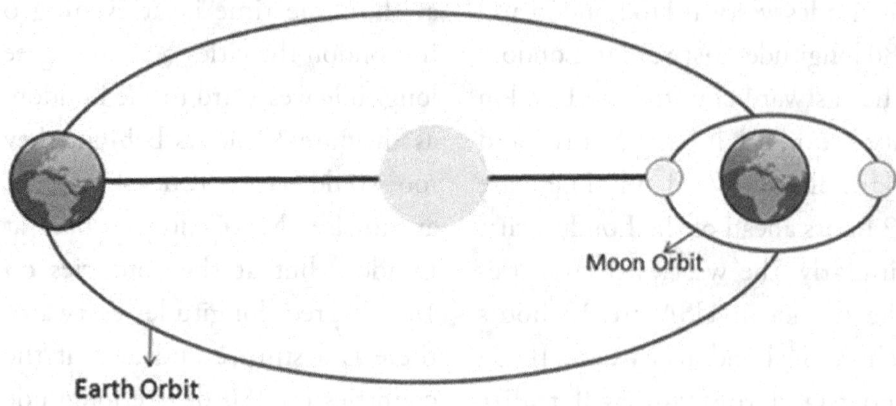

Visible in the above photograph is the Earth's rotation and her rotational orbit. The distance of Sun from the Earth is 150 million KM. So to complete one round around the Sun she has to traverse the approximate distance of 940 million KM. The oval shape circle seen in above picture around Sun has the length of 940 million KM. The time taken by Earth to complete this circle is termed as the year of 365 days. We can derive from this that the Earth rotates around Sun with the speed of 107000 KM per hour and we too rotate with the same speed till our death. Also the circle seen around the Earth is the Moon's rotation line around Earth. The circle seen in the picture has the actual length of 2420000 KM; it is the distance the Moon has to traverse to complete one rotation around Earth. It means the Moon rotates around Earth with the speed of 3689 KM per hour. You will get to read the detailed description about this in one of the factor out of 12 factors 'Revolution of Earth around Sun'.

4.2

The Second Factor of your Creation, Your Real Identity

THE REVOLUTION OF EARTH AROUND SUN AT THE SPEED OF 107000 KM PER HOUR...

Part of Real LIVE GOD & signs of life and secret of birth and death are hidden here!

EARTHS REVOLUTION AROUND SUN IS THE SECOND REASON FOR OUR BIRTHS AND ON-GOING BREATH!!!...

As rotation of the Earth is important for our ongoing breath and existence, it is also important that she revolves around the Sun. However, human busy with 'I', 'Me' and 'Mine' does not understand that just due to the perpetual revolution of Mother Earth around Sun since whooping 4600 million years has caused his birth. This continuous revolution of Mother Earth has caused the life to spring on her surface and even today the life is happily dwelling due to her revolution around Sun. **Your real identity is revolution of Earth around the Sun.**

HUMANKIND DOES NOT LIKE REALITY. TRUTH HAS ALWAYS BEEN DIFFICULT TO ACCEPT FOR THE HUMANKIND. SO THEY NEED CHARLATANS, INEXPERIENCED SCHOLARS, AND MISLEADING LEADERS! THE TRUTH TELLERS HAVE ALWAYS BEEN GIVEN A HARD LIFE!!!...

One doesn't get time to know ones' own real identity. So called scholars, religious heads, and leaders are still misguiding masses and are hiding truth. They only add to the ignorance of the people. Of course, since they too don't know themselves in this real manner, they just try to spice up the old legends & stories of Gods and narrate to public for their livelihood. They really earn good! But ask these masters at what speed does the Earth revolve? And what is the proof? Then you will know their knowledge! If they start telling such real knowledge to public then their own importance will end! And to tell you the truth, masses too desires such con men & misleaders! They believe in such phony scholars, masters. Masses too have an allergy to the truth! Masses and all elites fall for the charlatan's jugglery of manifesting golden locket, ring and wrist watches. Even prime ministers bow to such charlatan, forget about the commoners! I am just trying to give the real identity to what you are.

The description of the Earth's revolution to Earth and its effects on life that I am describing here is not written in any myth book, scriptures or no one has ever preached you. I am neither telling anything imaginary nor did I get an idea which I am just sharing. What I am narrating is experienced by you at each breath of yours. You are just ignorant of these realities!

You want to see the real God? Here it is!!!...

If you want to know and worship the real God, then know about the definition of the God. Study deep about the Earth and her 12 factors and you will know the real God. You will be convinced that the beats you are hearing in your heart are just because of the Mother Earth and her related twelve factors!

We shall know how the Earth's revolution around Sun keeps our breath going.

What makes your identity, your existence and breathing? Know it!!!...

It is hard to believe that the Earth is revolving around the Sun at such a huge speed. No commoner would believe because no preacher, no priest, no leader has told this before. No one is to blame. This huge ball of the Earth is revolving in the space without any fulcrum. Our Earth is revolving around the Sun with a huge speed of 107000 KM per hour against the speed of the hands of the clocks! Are you shocked? You may wonder from where this figure arrives. Aren't you in disbelief that Earth revolves around Sun at this speed? Even I was shocked earlier. But the scientists have discovered this speed. I am the commonest of common man. I used to wonder too about how the Earth's revolution with this speed is possible. Almost two months I was thinking on this fact. But finally this riddle was solved to me, how it was revealed that I have shared with you in the astronomical Earth chapter. Also I have explained with example about how this huge speed of Earth's revolution is not felt by us in the same chapter.

SEE HOW EARTH REVOLVES ROUND SUN AND WHAT IS THE EFFECT OF THIS ON HER?...

Earth's revolution around Sun is necessary for the creation of life on her including humankind. We all know that the distance of Sun from the Earth is 150 million KM. And at this distance the Earth is revolving around Sun in an oval shape. Due to this oval shape orbit of revolution of Earth, sometimes she goes near to the Sun more than usual and sometimes she goes away. When she goes away from the Sun, her distance from the Sun is 152099000 KM. At that time, the date on Earth is 21st June. It is the summer time in the North hemisphere and winter in South hemisphere. Similarly, when she comes near to Sun, her distance from the Sun is 147097000 KM and it is on the date of 22nd December. Means almost by the distance of 3 million KM than the usual orbit distance she goes nearer to the Sun. Even if she is nearer to the Sun, the North hemisphere experiences winter and South hemisphere experiences the summer.

The oval shaped orbit of revolution of Earth around the Sun causes the cycle of seasons. So the animate on the Earth experiences the seasons like summer, winter and rains. These seasons affect the life on Earth.

SEE HOW THE EARTH'S REVOLUTION AROUND SUN KEEPS OUR BREATHING AND HOW CREATION OF EACH ANIMATE!!!...

As the heat rises in summer; the salty water of Seas and Oceans get vaporized and get transformed into the clouds. After the summer it rains as fresh water in the rainy season, sufficient enough for all the animate throughout the year. The humankind cultivates different grains, fruits to satisfy their need of food for existence. Also the other animates other than human survive on the vegetation and plants that are sprung in the rainy season. Many new animals are born during this season. During the cold climate of winter coming after rainy season are fostered various plants and grains and fruits. This preserves the life on Earth.

So the reason behind your breathing, your existence is the Earth's revolution around Sun at the speed of 107000 km per hour which causes the cycle of seasons. The fresh water that you get to drink is due to this cycle of seasons caused by Earth's revolution around Sun! Some of the salty water out of the ¾ surface it has occupied on Earth gets converted into the fresh water in some quantity. It gives life to all on Earth. Also it helps preserve the 70% water in your body. The decrease in the amount of water from your body can lead to death!

Now are you convinced how our and all life's existence is dependent on the Earth's revolution around the Sun?

Had Earth not revolved around Sun or revolved with more speed or less speed, what would have been the effect?...

Now let's think contrary. If Earth doesn't travel in oval shape orbit around Sun at all, and then what would happen? If the Earth stays steady at one place, the cycle of the seasons that we experience i.e. the four months summer, four months winter and the rainy season; would stop! So only one season would have been experienced, if summer then only summer throughout the world, if winter then only cold winter throughout the world at all times. Have we thought what will have happen then? Then the life that is created and existing would end and the Earth would become either a very cold ball or a very hot barren desert. No life would be created on her. Then neither me to write this book, nor you to read this book would have got created and existed. Means to keep the cycle of this life on Earth, the necklace of each of the twelve related factors that I described earlier are necessary. If any bead drops out of this chain, the life on Earth will perish. I have just generally described to you about what would have happened if the Earth would not have revolved around Sun at the given speed. But actually the Earth exists because she revolves around Sun. She is revolving due to the gravitational force of the Sun. If it ends, the Earth just wouldn't exist to not revolve! Forget about yours and mine existence the Earth won't survive she will cease to live or exist! We shall read the information about this Sun's gravitational force ahead in these 12 factors. Also if there would be slight difference in the speed of revolution around Sun, which is 107000 KM per hours; means if it would be more or lesser; then too no one will survive on the Earth.

Earth has a year of 365 days. Means she takes 365 days to complete the rotation around Sun. Owing to her this specific speed the living and non-living nature dwells happily on her. Other planets, like Mars have 687 days a year and Jupiter has 11.8 Earth years as a year. Had Earth got such year, would she have had created life? **So, if you spend the life knowing the importance of our Mother Earth and her related 12 factors, the life would be successful.**

To know the identity of Mother Earth, identity of universe means to identify self, she has given the power of thinking and imagination only to the human being...

The human has got the intelligence to get the idea of and comprehend the Earth, the solar system, the galaxies comprising many solar systems and the universe made up of many such galaxies. This is a great gift conferred to human by Mother Earth! Excluding human being, no other animate has got such comprehending power.

Had Earth not revolved around Sun, forget you and I, even a flake of dried grass wouldn't have been created, survived on the Earth, then whose alchemy is this?...

Friends, after reading above information do you realize that if Earth wouldn't have revolved with such a huge speed around the Sun, forget about us, but even a flake of dried grass wouldn't have been created? If you realize this, the importance of people using the jugglery to take out golden chain, rings to impress public and the greedy religious heads raising their umpires exploiting the commoners by adding to the ignorance and the quacks whose bodies are nurtured by this Mother Earth and her 12 factors will reduce. They will be exposed.

Not just a dry flake of the grass but the creation of whole life on Earth plane and sustaining its existence is not dependent on just her revolution around Sun but on all such total twelve factors as they are. Without these related twelve factors, no life is born till now on this Earth and will never be born! Even a particle of dust cannot be created by anyone on Earth other than Earth! The creation is only the forte of Mother Earth! No ascetic, no godfather or any other animate can ever create anything on their own! The significance of life must be understood by each of us.

****

4.3

The Third Factor of Your True Identity

The Gravitational Force of Mother Earth

Very important factor for the creation of life
Part of Real LIVE GOD & signs of life and
secret of birth and death is hidden in this!

Friends, so far we have understand the necessity of two factors out of twelve factors required for our birth and the creation of life. The third very important factor out of these factors is the **gravitational force** of Mother Earth.

Our ancestors wrote the legends and religious scripts but there is no mention of the very necessary factors for the creation of life on Earth, if not all factors. If there was such mention, or if the script writers knew about it, we wouldn't have heard the names of scientists like Galileo or Newton. It means, the fact that the main reason for the life to happily dwell on our Earth is her gravitational force, was not known to humankind till the 17th century. Else the religion whose scripts contained this information would have shut the voice of Newton as they already knew it. The scientist Sir Isaac Newton was born in 1642; he first discovered the Earth's gravity.

How on Earth was the gravity discovered first?...

The scientist Newton was once sitting under the Apple tree when the ripe Apple fell down from the tree. He started thinking about the event. Why the Apple came down and why didn't it go up or stayed where it was? He discovered the answer to these questions. That time the humankind on Earth realized that the Earth has a gravitational force and due to this force the apple on the tree does not float or does not go up when separated from the tree. It falls down. It also means that if the humankind was ever benefitted for their human life by anyone, it was by these great scientists like

Newton, Galileo, Louise Pasture and Thomas Alva Edison; and not really by the makers of legends, big industrialists, famous and rich businessmen or philosophers!! Isn't it?

If you wish to worship, worship such great scientists!!!...

I believe that if someone should be worshiped with garlands, these great scientists should be worshiped, shouldn't they? Just think about it! Had these scientists not been born, had they not made such great discoveries, would the wild and uncivilised human have developed as s/he is today? Due to these scientists the world came closer. The facilities, the gadgets we are using now have scientists at their base. But as I have said earlier, the humankind is allergic to the truth! To call spade a spade is a crime today for the humankind! Also praising the worthy is a crime in some way! Those having the emotions cannot bear this. What humankind! I express so much gratitude to Newton and you will be convinced of his worthiness after reading the further information given here!

How is the water on the Earth steady despite her ultra-speedy revolution at 107000 KM per hour?...

This huge ball of Earth is floating in the space. While rotating on her axis she is also revolving around the Sun. Though this is the condition; the trees, rocks, mountains, big oceans and 113 seas on her crust and not even a drop of the water in these seas spill anywhere! This would have been a big riddle for the humankind and Newton has resolved this!

Once while chatting with my friends about the Earth, one old man of 80 years questioned me, "Mr. Wani, you claim that this Earth is revolving with speed of 107000 KM per hour. But she has so many oceans and so much of water; shouldn't it spread over on the Earth or spill over in the space?"

Then I answered that the Mother Earth pulls each thing towards herself, including mountains, trees, tall buildings, rivers, oceans and seas. Due to her gravity the vast water on her surface cannot cross its limit! Such many questions may come to our mind; the answer to them is 'gravitational power of Mother Earth!' So the humankind and everyone on Earth are very fortunate that they enjoy this gift and so they exist! So, I am going to explain and prove how this magnetic power of Earth is created. Then you will be convinced that the real Divine Power, the God is Mother Earth!

WHAT CREATES THE AIR, WATER AND FOOD ETCETERA THAT IS NEEDED BY ALL ANIMATES? JUST WATCH! ALL THE FOOD IN YOUR PLATE MEANS THE GRAVITATIONAL POWER OF THE EARTH!!!...

The existence of each animate is dependent on the gravitational power of the Earth! Human birth too depends upon the gravitational force. The gravitational power of the Earth is responsible for all the human actions like sitting, walking, jumping and standing! You travel to different places, different cities by trains or planes. On what basis does this train run or plane flies? The gravitational power of Earth! Mother Earth has held your train or your plane towards herself. So the train doesn't stray away from the rail lines and plane is not lost in the space!

Here is one more thing to convince you. The food in your plate that you eat nurtures you. How is it created? It is due to the gravitational force of Earth. The gravitational force of the Earth is at the base of the grains like oats, wheat and rice that you eat, the different fruits that you eat, the water and other beverages that you drink!

How do you get the rice? The seed of the rice that we sow in the crust of Earth is held steady by Earth's gravitational power! The rain fall that is needed for its germination and also happens due to the gravitational power of the Earth. Later the sapling too is held tight due to the gravitational power and also that helps its growth. The grains form in the cob due to gravitational power. The gravitational power is responsible for this entire process of the plants growth. The food, fruits that we get to eat, the water we get to drink is due to this gravitational power.

Now, have you ever thought about how this water is created? Mother Earth pulls towards herself the vast salty water; it gets evaporated due to Sun's heat. Means it transforms in the light gas and goes up in the sky to form clouds. At the height it gets cooled by cold air and the water molecules are formed. These molecules from such heavy clouds are pulled down by Earth due to her gravitational power, it means the rain falls. Thus, the salty water is transformed to fresh water which we can use. Means the gravitational power is necessary for the each thing that is created here.

You and I and every animate is breathing because of the gravitational power of the Earth. Do you know how the air that you inhale in and exhale out is made available on the Earth? The layers of gases are on some distance from the surface of the Earth; they contain 78% nitrogen, 20.90% oxygen, 0.93% argon, 0.38% carbon dioxide and 1% steam of water & ozone. We call this mixture an 'air'. The layers of such gases are spread wide many hundreds of kilometres from the surface of Earth to which we call environment. Cladding this aura of an environment around herself the Mother Earth is revolving around the Sun with the huge speed of 107000 KM per hour. Earth has held this aura of environment towards her due to the gravitational power. The air that this layer of environment has created and the existence that each animate has received due to this air are caused by the gravitational power of Mother Earth. Our heart beats due to this air in the environment. All plants, animals, aquatics are living the life due to the air pulled over by the Mother Earth using her gravitational power.

Severing the connection with the Earth's gravity means death!!!...

You are nothing else but a part of the Earth's gravitational power. Your body is full of the Earth's gravity. With each breath you are experiencing it. So I say that the mixture of these Earth related twelve factors are you and each living being on this Earth! The creation taking place from each part of reproduction is a part of Earth's gravity. The day you or any animate are born on Earth, including a small flake of the grass ends their connection with the Earth's gravity; they need to leave this Earth. Means die. I am explaining the 'death' so it will help to destroy your fear and misunderstanding about the death. When the connection with the Earth's gravity gets severed, any animal however large it is, any human however great s/he may be or any plant however tall it may be, lies flat on the Earth permanently means dies!

WHAT GIVES YOU THE ENERGY OF LIGHT FOR YOUR SURVIVAL?...

Light- Due to the ozone gas in the environment pulled by Earth towards herself, the blazing rays of Sun do not directly hit the Earth but loosen their intensity and come to the Earth as mild, bearable rays. As the intensity of the heat is lessened and it became bearable, these rays foster the growth and nurturance of the animates on the Earth. So each animate births the offspring and the cycle is continued for long or indefinite. Does human think of this? Due to the ozone gas pulled by the Earth which gives the favourable Sun light; the flowers bloom, fruits ripe, and the spirit of life is experienced in each animate. Every moment of each animates' life is related to the Mother Earth and her gravitational power! The animation of each life on Earth is due to the gravitational power of Earth! This description and the reality you will hardly get to read in any religious scripture.

We are so engrossed in our mundane lives that we don't have time to think about the consequences if Earth didn't have gravitational power!

Friends, if Earth's gravitational power would have been as less as other planets like Moon, Mars; what would have been the consequence?

THERE IS NO LIFE ON OTHER PLANETS AS THEY DON'T HAVE AS MUCH GRAVITATIONAL POWER AS EARTH!!!...

Out of the twelve factors needed for the creation of life one is the gravitational force. Moon doesn't have air, doesn't have water and also direct blazing Sun rays hit her surface. The man landed on Moon's surface using high technology but wasn't able to even stand properly! Planet Mars too has the same situation.

The gravitational power of Earth is responsible for the food that we get to eat today, the water that we get to drink, the huge tall trees, plants and crops are standing due to this power. But on Mars or Moon no plant can grow because it has less gravitational power. You cannot move around, sit, walk, build tall buildings, grow tall trees and ripen the crop on other planets as they have less gravitational power.

IF EARTH DIDN'T HAVE GRAVITATIONAL POWER, NO ANIMATE WOULD HAVE BEEN BORN INCLUDING YOU AND ME!!!...

The picture on the Earth, as it is today, would not have been visible had the Earth not got her gravitational power. We wouldn't have been born! No life would have been born. The sperm and egg is the root of the human reproduction and it is created with the help of Earth's gravitational force. The fetus lies steady in the womb of the mother due to gravitational force of the Mother Earth. Without the Earth's gravitational force even a flake of grass wouldn't be visible. The blue sapphire like beauty of Earth would look like dry and barren surface of Moon. Not a drop of water would have existed on the Earth. But large craters like Moon would have been visible on Earth. The temperature of Earth would have been intense as it is on Moon, Mercury and Venus. It is because the Sun rays would have directly hit the Earth's surface in the absence of environmental gases layer. The rock melting heat would have been produced on the Earth.

LOOK AT THE GREATNESS OF THE GRAVITATIONAL POWER!!!...

The greatness of the gravitational power is that the air and water that you need since your birth till death is available due to this power. In the absence of air and water no life will be formed, it hasn't been formed. The people who landed on the Moon carried along with them air and water so they could stay there for the short time. Friends, you know that this air is available because of the gravitational pull of Mother Earth that has held the environmental quilt close to her crust. In the absence of the gravitational power this environmental quilt - the layers of gases would have got diffused away in the space. Thus whatever is created on the Earth or is being created, gravitational power has an important stake in it.

Had humankind studied and understood these things earlier, the religious fanatics spreading unrest and quakes showing unnecessary miracles would not have been created on this Earth! Continents like Asia and Africa are invaded by such people and the whole world suffers from the religious fanatics. At least the next generation should know the importance of Earth and these Earth related factors through academic institutions to eradicate these unwanted evils on the Earth. Friends, shouldn't we thank Newton? All the description above gives an idea of the importance of the Earth's gravitational force. If these things are told in the discourses, won't it help ward off the ignorance of the people? We have been just hearing the word 'gravity' so far but did we ever understand the alchemy behind it?

Let's see on what the 'weight' is dependent on!!!...

Weight-density-form

In the daily life we talk about weight. Ten kilograms of rice, two kilogram Silver, half kilogram gold or one kilograms of potatoes. These measures we use in our mundane transactions. The primitive man didn't know of weight. The transactions in olden days were based on exchange of goods. But in the due course of time the measure of 'weight' came into an existence. Each animate on the Earth is fortunate. It is because the Earth has a more gravitational power than some other planet. So from all perspectives it is beneficial to the life on the Earth.

The weight is dependent on the size and the density of the object. Suppose we take the piece of an iron and a wood of the same size. Though the sizes of these two appear to be the same, there is a difference in the weight of them, because the weight depends on the density of the molecules of the object.

To bring the equality in the life and transactions of the humankind the measure of the 'weight' was created, which has gravitational power of the Earth as its base. Earth's gravitational force is 6 times more than the gravitational force of the Moon. So any object weighing 100 kilogram on the Earth shall weigh only 16 kilograms on the Moon! Different planets have different gravitational power. It is more in stars than in planets. So in our solar system, the Sun has the most gravitational power.

Due to the gravitational power of the Earth our bodies and the bodies of other life on Earth are created!!!...

As we go higher up, away from the gravity of the Earth, the influence of gravitational power of Earth decreases. So when any spaceship goes up in the space, the astronauts in the ship become weightless or light and float in the ship. Same is the case on other planets. So there is no sight of life on any other planets. Your bodies are created due to the Earth's gravitational power; this is your real identity.

How the gravitational power is created in the belly of Mother Earth? Here is a glance at it!!!...

In the chapter 'Mother Earth' I have analysed in detail about how the gravitational power is created in the belly of our Mother Earth. Yet, to narrate briefly; under the crust of 35-70 KM thickness lies the 600 KM of boiling lava in a circular form. Beneath that lies the flexible molten rocks of 2300 KM and further beneath to it is the ocean of the molten iron and some part of nickel. The depth of this ocean is almost 2200 KM and it encircles the solid rotating iron ball of the circumference of almost 8000 KM and 1250 KM radius.

This causes the electric currents resulting in a huge magnetic power which makes the Earth a huge magnetic ball. So she pulls everything towards her. The covering of atmosphere is no exception to this pull. This results in the perpetual cycle of life's creation-existence destruction of living and non-living beings. Since eons many people birthed here and died. It makes one consider about who are we? We are the mixture of the twelve related factors mentioned above! Once this is understood, the human will earn just enough for one's own existence and enjoy the life and let others reciprocate too.

This is the proof! The sound exists only on Earth!!...

Sound

Friends, you will not even imagine that the sound on Earth, whether it is of the conversation between two persons, cooing of the birds, beautiful sound from musical instruments like organ, guitar, sitar, piano, flute or the strokes on Drum, banjo, or vocal music or frightening noise of bomb blasts-- all these different sounds are heard only on the Mother Earth!!

On any other planets of the solar system, may it be Moon or Mars you will not hear anything even if you shout to each other! If you go there you won't be able to converse with each other using your mouth, because no sound waves are produced there. The medium that is needed to create the sound is air; it is present only on the Mother Earth!

'Sound' is the root cause for happy dwelling of the life on Earth!!!...

One of the root causes why the living and non-living nature is dwelling happily on Earth is 'sound'. Imagine how difficult our life will be if we do not hear any sound! We will not be able to express to each other through conversation, will not get delighted with the sweet songs of birds and will not get alerted about the upcoming rains with the thundering sounds or know the that the baby is hungry due to his/her cry. The life without the sound will have no meaning. Sound is such an important factor.

What is the relation between the 'sound' and the 'gravity'? There is no sound where the air of the Earth ends!...

Now you may wonder about what is the connection between gravity that we are talking about so far and the sound. Let us see how these two are connected. To create any sound, as low pitched as the rustle of the leaves on a tree or as high pitched as a bomb blast, needs air as a medium that carries it. Except Earth, no other planet has 'air'. The sound waves are carried through the air and we hear the sound. If there is no air, there will be no sound waves created and even if you have intact ears you won't hear any sound.

If you go far away from Earth in the airless space, you won't hear any sound. If you try to talk to each other, you would only see the mute lips moving, but there will be no sound created through them! Such is the relation of the air and sound. The environmental quilt that Mother Earth has clad herself in, she has pulled it towards her with her gravitational power. Had she left this quilt in the space, there wouldn't have been any air and also no sound would have been created on the Earth. Without sound there is no existence of the animate. Means due to gravity there is air, due to air there is existence of life on the Earth and due to this life there is sound. Such great is the importance of the gravity of the Earth. Due to the gravitational power of the Earth; the life is dwelling, animates are interacting.

Would the knowing of the fact that no preacher, or any other animate can create anything on the Earth without the Earth; ward off the ignorance of the humankind?...

After reading this description above you would have realized that even to create a small flake of a grass on the Earth, the gravitational power in the Earths belly is responsible. And we have seen what situation is needed to create that gravitational power. So I want to ask, how the quacks or so called religious preachers - who themselves are created due to Mother Earth's gravitational power- would be able to create the objects like golden chain, ashes and rings with their own miracle? No object on this Earth will be created by such miracles; it is only the sleight of the hand! After reading this book and knowing the realistic situation would people's ignorance go away? Would creation of such quacks stop? For that all this information must be included in the educational curriculum.

****

See how the Earth has woven the magnetic web around herself!!!

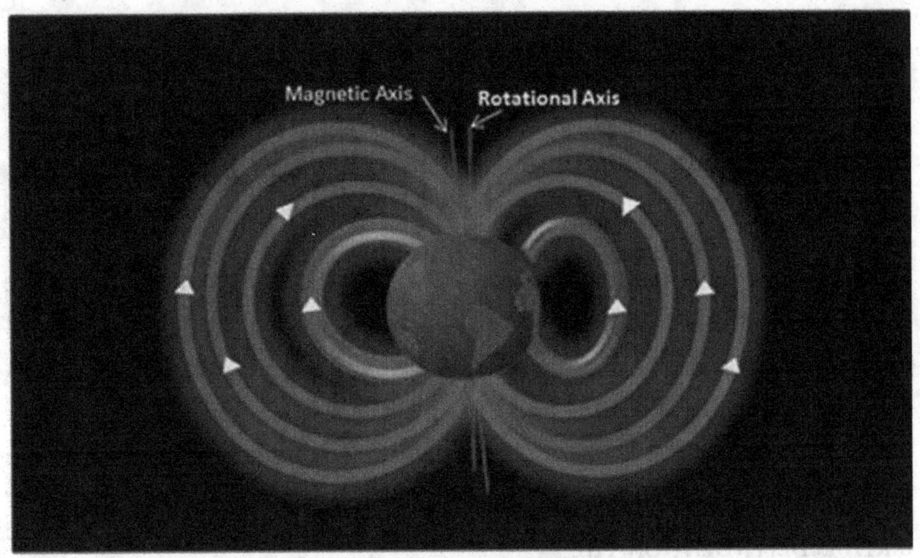

Check how Earth is a magnetic ball!!!...

We get to see from the above picture about how the magnetic web is spread around the Earth due to the magnetic power created in her belly. Earth essentially is a magnetic ball. Newton discovered the gravity only due to this magnetic web. Earth pulls anything towards herself; whether it is tree, water or a human being. Owing to this magnetic web the animate creation exists on this Earth. You will get to read the detailed description about this in the chapter twelve factors related to Mother Earth- 'Earth's gravitational power'.

4.4

The Fourth Factor of Your Creation means True Identity

The Mother Earth's Moon!

Part of Real LIVE GOD & signs of life and secret of birth and death is hidden in this!

So far we have seen the three factors responsible for the creation of life on the Earth. Now let us take the information about the fourth factor.

See how our and each animates birth is dependent on the Moon!!!...

We have seen the description of the Moon in previous chapters. Now we shall see how this Moon is closely related to the life of humans. So many people are born on this Earth and also died. But how many people have known what the Moon really is? Even today your each breath is dependent on the Moon; how many people know this? How many people know what has given each of the animate his/her body? Amongst the Earth's related twelve important factors available on Earth, the satellite Moon has a very important stake.

We see Moon daily from the Earth. So we don't understand her value. Of course, human undervalues anything close to him. Due to Moon the Earth has life dwelling on her. If Moon wasn't there, or if Moon disappears; what would happen? That is what I am going to explain to you.

When Earth gave birth to the Moon, Moon was looking much bigger due to her proximity to the Mother Earth!!!...

Almost 4400 million years back Mother Earth gave birth to the Moon. Almost after 200 million years after the Mother Earth's birth the Moon was born. There was no life on the Earth at that time. Today the Moon we see in the sky is almost 384600 KM away from the Earth. But she was just 20000 to 30000 KM away from the Earth when she was born. So in the sky she used to look much bigger than now. But to see such a big lunar disc, no animate was born on the Earth at that time. How big the visible lunar disc at that time would be? Almost 20 times larger than what she looks at present; means a ball of almost 15 ft. diameter must be visible.

If the distance of the Moon from the Earth increases or decreases, the entire life on Earth will perish!!!...

Due to Moon's proximity, means very less distance from the Earth; the effect of Moon's gravitational power on the lava below the Earth's crust was very high. Means she used to cause as huge waves in the lava in the Mother Earth's belly as she causes in the Oceans of the Earth today; the lava in the Earth's belly was surging and the temperature in the Mother's Earth's belly was very high.

Later as the distance between the Earth and the Moon increased, the effect of Moon's gravitational force on Earth decreased gradually; and also the activity and temperature in the Earth's belly decreased. Hence the crust of the Earth cooled gradually. Due to Moon the Earth's crust is in the patches, no other planet has such patches. Their crust is continuous and hence there are no volcanoes or earthquakes like Earth.

If the Moon comes nearer to Earth than her present distance, there will be huge activity on the Earth's patchy crust which will destroy all the life on the Earth. So when the Moon was nearer to the Earth, the life was not created on the Earth. Thus, for the creation of the life and its preservation on the Earth, the Moon just needs to be at the same distance that she is today. Due to Moon the life is stable on the Earth. In the absence of the Moon, the life will not be created due to the destruction of the environment of the Earth.

The human should have the deep knowledge of the Mother Earth, the creator of you and me and the entire life. Actually this information must be taught since the childhood so that human will not get engrossed in the imaginary false stories and legends.

See how the Moon affects the environment of the Earth!!!...

While rotating on the axis, our Earth is revolving around the Sun.

Also the peculiarity of our Earth is that she is tilted at the northern pole by an angle of 23.5 degree. It has affected the environment of the Southern and Northern Poles of the Earth. In some part of the Northern Pole and on Southern Pole too there is a night and day of 6 months each due to this tilted position. Rest of the part has a stable environment. I have told you before that the creation of life needs the 'favorable' environment.

We shall see the effect of Moon on the Earth's environment. Earth rotates on her axis but also the Moon is revolving around the Earth from her distance of 384600 KM. Due to Moons' gravitational force the Earth is tilted at the angle of 23.5 degree and is steady at that angle due to Moon. Think about it if there would have been no Moon at the distance of 384600 KM. And suppose if she would have been at a greater distance or at a lesser distance than she is at present to the Earth; do you know what would have been the effect? Have you thought about it? Perhaps you may have never thought about it. Had the Moon not been there, I wouldn't have been created to write this book or you wouldn't have been created to read this book!

What would have been the effect had the Moon that is with the Earth not been there? Read on!...

In the absence of the Moon, the largest planet of solar system Jupiter which is 12 times bigger than Earth and the and 100 times larger Sun would have influenced the Earth with their multi fold greater gravitational force and she would have tilted more than she is at present. Means she would have tilted almost at the angle of 90 degree and due to this plus in the absence of the Moon; one side of Earth would have always faced Sun and other side would have always been in the dark. In short, the absence of the Moon would have created hurdles in the creation of life on the Earth.

Other thing is, as an effect of the gravitational force of the Moon the 15-20 patches of the Earth's crust are steady. In the absence of the Moon there would have been constant huge commotions between them that would have erupted volcanoes continuously and caused earthquakes to destroy the life on Earth. Without Moon there would have been many ill effects on the Earth and no life on Earth including human would have left behind. Apart from this, due to the revolution of the Moon we see the phases of Moon, which are important for some animates on Earth as their life depends upon them.

Had Moon been at a distance far away than she presently is, or would have been smaller than now, there wouldn't have been the environment favorable to the creation of life on the Earth. I have said earlier, **atmosphere is the root cause of the creation.** This all means one thing; that is due to Moon we are breathing and we get food and water for existence. The main reason behind this is the Moon causes the favorable environment on the Earth.

Had Earth got more Moons at different distances...

Entire life on Earth including humankind is fortunate because Earth has got only one Moon. The planets of our solar system have got more than one Moon or many Moons. For example, Jupiter has got 16 Moons, Saturn has got 18 Moons. Had this been the position of Earth, the life wouldn't have been created on Earth. So having one Moon and its specific distance from the Earth is necessary from the Earth's point of view. Due to Earth's gravitational force the Moon is revolving from the distance of 384600 KM around Earth. Due to this and the Moon's gravitational force because of her slight proximity to the Earth on full moon day the Oceans and Seas of the Earth get high tide and when she goes away means on new or no moon day she causes the low tide to the Oceans and Seas. So just think, if we got one more Moon to Earth at a distance lesser than present Moon's distance what would have happened? The equilibrium of the water on Earth would have collapsed. Perhaps the Oceans and Sea water would have crossed the boundaries and flooded all over the Earth! More than that, if this second Moon had more gravitational force then it would have caused tremendous commotion in the tectonic plates and they would have climbed on each other causing calamities like earthquake, volcano severely harming the life on the Earth. So having just one Moon, at a proper distance that she is at is the fortune of Earth dwellers!

If in your mundane life you have any philosopher, intelligent person, capitalist or president or prime minister-would they ever think of these twelve factors? From their point of view, the presence or absence of the Moon doesn't make them any difference. But we have seen the chaos the absence of the Moon would cause on the Earth. But to understand this, studying the Earth and her natural system is necessary.

JUST BECAUSE THE REVOLUTION OF MOON AND EARTH TOGETHER THE HUMANKIND AND LIFE ON THE EARTH IS ALIVE!!!...

Gravitational powers of the Moon and the Earth affect each other. Their revolution orbits and revolution around Sun together doesn't change and so the Earth dwellers happily live their lives. But if the Moon leaves the Earth, Earth will leave her revolution orbit and will be pulled towards the Sun; enormously increasing the temperature on her and destroying the life on her. Of course, till the time Mother Earth has pulled the Moon towards her with her gravitational power, humankind need not bother about Moon's absence, isn't it?

I want to assert again. Your true identity is the twelve factors on the Earth. No soul, no man made God or reincarnation! Use wisely very short life you have received due to the twelve factors of Earth and one day happily leave this earth.

****

4.5

The Fifth Factor of Your Creation means True Identity

The Oxygen Necessary For The Earth Dwellers!

Part of Real LIVE GOD & signs of life and secret of birth and death is hidden in this!

Necessary for human's, your and mine and all animates' birth is Oxygen (air). These twelve factors are your birth, your breath and existence! The absence of these twelve factors is your death!!!...

Friends, out of twelve factors necessary for the birth and existence of the life on the Earth, we have described four factors till now. Fifth factor is the oxygen gas surrounding the Earth's surface. We shall see its importance.

Some institutions some time comes up with strange dilemma for the humankind!...

In this universe the planet having twelve factors necessary for life is the Earth. Till now the humankind has been boasting about finding the potential for life on some planet or the other. But are in vain!

Once USA had sent two astronauts on the Moon and they came back safely. Just this is the leap of the humankind so far! Some research institutions come up with new finding. Though this argument is rather ingenious there is actually no merit in it. They have found an Earth like planet. It has much water on it. So they also assumed the existence of life to be there. The people on Earth too admired. Wow! Another Earth like ours is found! All were happy. But I wasn't impressed at all. It is because the human exists on this Earth just from the birth to death! From this period, excluding childhood and old age years just 25 to 30 years are of consciously active existence.

Later death is inevitable. From such human, finding another planet and some human reaching there is not easy or convenient.

Some research institutions says they found other Earth 600 light years away from our Earth. Now, this won't be even properly understood by the people who don't know about light year, or whose knowledge about light year is nothing more than having heard this word in the schools geography book. I have shared the knowledge about the light year in the chapter 'Introduction of Astronomical Earth'. Light year is the unit of measure to calculate the distance between two celestial bodies like planets, stars in the space. It is because of the difficulty in expressing the huge distances in the normal figures they are expressed in terms of the speed of light travelling per second.

Here is the definition of one light year. The human cannot reach that other Earth like planet! Here is the proof!!!...

Now do you know how much distance is one light year? As I have already described in the chapter 'Introduction of Astronomical Earth' **one light year is whooping 10000 billion KM!** Try to write it down if you can! So the planet recently found is said to be 600 light years away from the Earth, isn't it? Means, if we calculate it i.e. 600 light years x 10000 billion KM =6000000 billion KM. Now considering the average active human life of 25 to 30 years, is it ever possible for any human to reach at such distance even if s/he spends their entire life? So, does it make any sense to talk about the impossible things? There is no speedy thing on this Earth other than light. So, even if you decide to travel by the speed of light, how many kilometres can you travel? Such many generations too will not reach to that other Earth like planet. For me such statements are ridiculous!

That all pervading power that you think exists and accept about, the God is just Mother Earth and Mother Earth!!!...

The reason I described all above is to bring the entire realistic situation that in this universe the human on Earth finding another Earth and reaching there is never possible. The twelve factors that I am describing in this book means your body, means the Earth. Such another Earth can never be found by the human of the Earth. So, that all pervading power that you think exists and accept about, the God that is just the Mother Earth and Mother Earth! The reason to convince you upon this is that the oxygen that exists on Earth is pulled and held by Mother Earth towards herself which has caused the birth of you and me and the entire life on the Earth. In India it is called 'Pranvayu' out of which 'Pran' literally means life. Thus the word literally means 'Life gases!

NOW LET US CHECK THE FACTOR 'OXYGEN'!!!...

As all animals need oxygen, the plants need carbon dioxide. Plants absorb carbon dioxide and release oxygen in the day while at the night they absorb oxygen and release carbon dioxide. Since the availability of all gases like carbon dioxide, oxygen and nitrogen is only on the Earth, the creation of living and non-living beings takes place just on Earth. Also the systematic mixture of the hydrogen and oxygen gas takes place just on Earth and hence the water much needed for the creation of animates is available only on the Earth. Occupying the huge area of almost 361 million KM on the Earth's surface is this mixture of hydrogen and oxygen.

OXYGEN, THE CREATOR TO ALL ANIMATES! LET US SEE HOW!...

Each being on the Earth needs oxygen. Without oxygen the part of reproduction will not be produced. The examples are the eggs or sperms of all animals including human. All animals lay eggs which is a seed for reproduction. From these seeds new breed of animate is formed. Due to this, the cycle of life continues on the Earth. It doesn't matter whether they are animals from deserts or in water or on the land or inside the land. The day the connection with the oxygen is severed for any animal, for him/her end is certain. Also, the day the connection with the oxygen is established, it is the birth for that animal. When this is the reality, the man-made religious books emphasis unnecessary imaginary things. As I said earlier, the human has an allergy to the truth and has been embracing falsehood. Actually the writer of these religious books is made up of these twelve factors.

But the unfortunate one could not identify the root of his being!

THE FOOD WE EAT, THE WATER WE DRINK IS DUE TO THIS OXYGEN!!!...

Friends, not just the breath of the human goes on due to oxygen, but the need of food is also completed by the oxygen. The fire needed to cook and prepare this food is ignited due to this oxygen. Do a small practical. Light a candle and completely cover it with a pot, you will see it extinguished due to lack of oxygen. Food, air and water are the necessary things for the existence of life and we get them due to oxygen. Due to oxygen the entire life births, such is the importance of this oxygen.

When USA had send two astronauts to Moon, they carried the cylinders of oxygen, and their landing and stay on Moon including the duration spent in space was timed according to the oxygen supply they had carried along with them. At almost 10000 ft height from the Earth's surface the oxygen gas starts diminishing. The human will not survive at further heights of 15000 to 20000 ft. We hear the mountaineer worldwide or the visitors at places of high altitudes like Kailas Man sarovar or Mount Everest dying due to lack of oxygen at the height.

MY TRIP TO SOUTH AMERICAN CONTINENT WAS TROUBLESOME JUST DUE TO THE LACK OF OXYGEN!!!...

I travelled in South American continent during which I had to stay almost 8 to 10 days at Cuzco, Puno, and Titicaca Lake in the country of Peru and the city of La Paz in Bolivia. I have a good memory of these 8 to 10 days. I had gone to enjoy the trip and see new places. But during those 10 days my health gave up badly. I was left in the lurch. Nausea, over sleepiness, fatigue, headache, anorexia and whirling were the symptoms experienced. These places are at almost 12000-14000 ft. height from the sea level and had scarce oxygen, which was the reason behind this trouble. I was more than eager to come down from this troublesome place! Not just this, I experienced such trouble at the place called Gangtok in India. At a height more than Gangtok means almost 15000 to 16000 feet height I visited one military camp and was surprised to notice that neither a flake of grass was seen grown nor any tree or insect was seen; no life other than the human beings! It was due to the lack of oxygen at that height, such is an importance of oxygen!

Far heighted distances from Earth's surface do not have oxygen and hence even too tall mountains lack the existence of life!!!...

Friends, till now I have enjoyed lot of air travel. International flights usually travel from a height of 45000 ft. height. So the oxygen supply is carried in the plane from the Earth itself before the flight. Otherwise getting the oxygen at such height is impossible. Mountaineers and Sea divers always carry the oxygen cylinders along with them. At almost 10000 ft. height, one doesn't feel the lack of oxygen much.

What is air? A definition of air...

A mixture of nitrogen, oxygen, carbon dioxide, argon, ozone and water vapors is the environment of the Earth. In this mixture, the amount of oxygen is almost 20.95%. It keeps the life on Earth active. As Earth has pulled together this covering of gases towards herself, the life cycle on Earth is permanently going on. Out of the twelve necessary factors to keep this cycle going oxygen is an important factor. Barring Earth you will not see any animate born or tree grown or any animal existent on other planets, because there is no environment. So other than Earth all other planets are barren. They are either too cold or too hot for the life to prosper. Of course, in truth it is difficult for the human to reach on them.

See your own identity! Who are you? Many countries on the Earth don't even know the name your country, so who are you?...

Though variety of life dwells on the Earth, the power of thinking and imagination is gifted only to the human being. Use it and calmly think, who are you on this Earth? Who is your creator? How long is your stay? Are the twelve factors which made your body are real or your imaginary concept of man-made God is real? Or the money, gold and wealth of any kind that you earned, the recognition that handful people have given you is real? Leaving handful people, no life being recognizes you, your value is zero for them, and no one knows you!

What is your real position? Friends, for this, I would like to share the experience. When I visited the country of Bolivia in South American continent, the locals there queried us "Who are you? From where did you come?" We told them that we are Indians and have come from the country India. They were surprised and asked us, "India? Where is this India? We never heard of this name?" If this is the position of a large country having area of 3287263 km^2, then who is the prime minister, president or leader or preacher of that country? The country is not recognized outside then who are these people? No one knows you outside! You may be from any country and think you are someone, belong to some republic, or belong to some kingdom, but if you are globetrotting don't get surprised that some other nationals don't even know the name of your country! Even you may not know where some country is; barring some famous 210 countries! So just think! What is your position in this vast universe? Your position is just like some tiny insect! A frog ramping in a small pond!!

Knowing our own identity is very important!!!...

That experience was like a rude awakening to me. It helped me think and discover my real identity. Each one should check and know ones' true identity and your ego will automatically drop. Also if you identify the twelve factors which created you, you automatically will get your self-identity! Then your greed will end. You will earn just sufficient enough for yourself and let others earn. Then no one will be hungry, no one will be homeless.

Knowing your real identity will make you free in the life. You will be fearless. So many benefits this self-identity will give you. I am experiencing them. I am no more afraid of the death and prepared to welcome it any moment!

****

4.6

The Sixth Factor of Your Creation means True Identity

The Temperature Controller of The Earth South and North Pole!

Part of Real LIVE GOD & signs of life and secret of birth and death is hidden in this!

We owe our existence to the icy southern and Northern poles; else all life will perish!! How?...

Friends, these two poles help preserve the life's existence on the Earth. Actually human of the Earth has no proper knowledge of the Earth. But while living the human life, it is necessary to know more about the Earth.

Each human on the Earth should know about Earth!!!...

I am an Indian resident. But whenever I travelled to the different parts of the Earth, I used to gather information about location of visit on the Earth's map, the geographies the plane would fly over, the geographical situations and life at that place. One enjoys the travel more if one knows the destination country's continent, geographical location. Even the learned people don't know the Earth and show their ignorance.

Many people are ignorant about the location and continent of the country Mauritius on our Earth. Once a known chartered accountant had informed me about this country's location being in Asian continent! Actually this country belongs to an African continent. I think the abundance of the Indian population in this country made him think about it being in Asia. Well this shows the ignorance about the Earth despite much educational qualification, isn't it?

Such is the Northern pole of our Mother Earth!!!...

The head of the Mother Earth is the Northern pole. It is completely covered by Arctic Ocean. The snowy tracts of land like Tundra are besides the Ocean. Thus this usually has a freezing cold temperature. Major part of the year there is a snowfall. Earth's area of 14056000 km^2 is occupied by the Arctic Ocean and the surface of this Ocean is covered with snow almost throughout the year.

My travel in Northern pole and my observations...

I traveled by train Oslo to Voss when I visited Northern pole. This journey felt unusual. Our train was passing through complete snow white land. The window view was scenic. The trees were hardly visible while this train was running by the sides of snowy mountains. But passing through snowy white tunnels in every 5 to 10 minutes was a fun. It was really admirable of this country to have laid down this rail road. There is a snow fall very often. The residents of Southern Asia do not experience snow fall. But it is very common for the people living here. You would be amazed to read that during the year of 1967, there was such a heavy snow fall on this rail line that a snowy layer as thick as almost 67 ft was formed! Such is the fun of the climate on Northern Pole.

The gift to the life on Earth is the snowy Northern part of the Earth!!!...

The reason to describe this as above is that compared to the middle part of the Earth, the topmost part, Northern pole is usually snowy. So the temperature is very low compared to the middle part. This is the gift to the life on Earth. The twelve necessary factors that I mentioned already include this part of Northern Pole. Though the reproduction process in this part is slow, these poles play the important role in lowering the intensity of temperature of the middle part of the Earth which is densely populated.

The bottom of the Earth means Southern Pole, Antarctica! The temperature here is minus 57 degree Celsius!!!...

The Southern Pole of the Earth is equally important as is the Northern Pole. As the head or fontanel of the Earth is the

Arctic Ocean of Northern Pole, the bottom or butt of the Earth is the Antarctic Continent of the Southern Pole. The complete area of 14 million km2 is covered with the snow. This continent is larger in size than the Continent of Europe comprising 52 countries and Australasia comprising 15 countries together! There is a vast globular spread of water from the latitude of 60 degrees on Earth to the latitude of 66.5 degrees; which is termed as Southern Ocean. Further stretch from 66.6 degrees latitude up to 90 degree latitude is the Continent of Antarctica. There is no life of any type! You will find no occurrence of any animal, plants or insects. Not even a flake of a grass or algae grown. Anywhere your vision follows you will see snow and only snow! Do you have the idea of the temperature due to such situation there? It is freezing minus 57 degrees Celsius! What life will be created in such a temperature? What life shall exist at such a temperature?

How thick is the layer of snow in Antarctica, the south part of Earth?...

On Southern Pole after Chile and Argentina there is no human habitation at all! There is very less tract of land further, more of water and ice is found. How thick is the layer of snow in Kashmir or Himachal in India or Pakistan? It is at the most 15 to 20 ft. thick. But how thick is the layer of snow in Antarctica? It is almost as thick as **three kilometres!** This benefits the densely populated middle part of the Earth. It helps their existence by reducing the overall temperature there.

The situations on both the poles of Earth help control the temperature of the rest part of the Earth. So the life is dwelling happily on the Earth. Our existence is preserved due to these two poles of Earth. Such condition similar to Earth is not found on any other planet with surety. So we owe the life we are living today to the Mother Earth and her related twelve factors such as these.

See the prowess of global warming!...

Now a days there is much hue and cry about global warming. Sometimes the TV channels show the snowy cliffs of Southern and Northern Pole collapsing. After the collapse they showed it to be transformed into the water. The human on Earth is scared about the existence. What are the consequences of the increase in the Earth's temperature? Have a common man ever thought of it? There will be a chaos if the ozone layer on these poles reduces and the temperature of the Earth rises than what it is at present. The snowy cliffs on both the poles would start thawing and collapsing. As they melt eventually due to increased temperature, the level of water in Seas and Oceans will go up almost by 200 ft and it shall flood the land causing catastrophe and all life will be on the verge of destruction. With such enormous levels of water even the six foot tall person would vanish nowhere. Tall huge buildings on the Earth, the factories, roads, rails, airports, mines of coal and gold and silver_ everything will immerse under the water. Performing mass prayers, pujas or any rituals - nothing will work; no human will be left to perform these activities. No one will exist to compare who is wealthy and who is poor! Now you must have realized the importance of this sixth factor of Mother Earth i.e. both the poles are overall controlling the temperature of the Earth.

Would human keep in mind about the consequences if the snow of Antarctica melts?...

Yet without realizing this; the humankind is competing with each other about who is the richest of them all! For gaining that title of richness the governments are deceived and commoners are exploited. But these people must realize the cataclysmic effect of melting of the polar snow.

Your wealth, fame, position and grades are worthless!!!...

While describing each factor I have been trying to tell the egoistic people about their real identity. Who are you man? You may be a big industrialist, big leader, religious head or born rich; none of these things will come handy at the nick of time! Your breath is not going due to your position, wealth or fame. But you are breathing merely due to these twelve factors. Because you are the mixture of these twelve factors! Identify yourself! This is your golden chance! Make yourself and others happy and made the environment peaceful. Else you will just keep exploiting Mother Earth and leave one day without ever realizing the truth! This should not be the case and hence identify yourself through this book. Cleanse your past wrong doings and happily take leave of Mother Earth. Once gone, you will not return for sure!

****

4.7

The Seventh Factor of Your Creation means True Identity

Responsible For the Entire Life's Existence: Three Fourth Water on The Earth!

Part of Real LIVE GOD & signs of life and secret of birth and death is hidden in this!

The creation of all the animates and the beauty of nature means this seventh factor water! Your body is made up of ¾ water! Water is your real identity!!!...

Friends, we studied the six factors necessary for our birth so far. Now we shall know the importance of the ¾ water on the Earth. 'Water is life'. The sentence says it all. Your heart beats because just like the Earth, your 70% body is occupied with water. The human on Earth has not yet found any other planet in the universe with so much water. And even if there is one, cannot reach there to ensure it! So for the animates on the Earth, Mother Earth is everything! Each animate is the part and parcel of Mother Earth. No Earth, no animate!

What gives existence to water on Earth?...

The ¾ water on the Earth exists just due to the twelve factors of Earth! This water is held by Mother Earth by pulling towards herself through her gravitational power. Had Earth not got gravity, not a single drop of water would have remained on her surface! The environment clad by Mother Earth around self is important from the point of view of water's existence on her. This network of environment is a sieve filtering ultra violet rays of the Sun! It reduces the intensity of the Sun rays coming on the Earth. So the water is preserved on the Earth. Else from the creation of the Oceans till today the water would have got vaporized due to ultra violet rays of Sun and the vapors would have vanished in the space.

Not a drop of water would have existed on the Earth.

Out of almost 520 million km2 area of the Earth, 360 million km2 is just water and water only!!!...

Out of total area of Earth, which is 510 million 66 thousand km2 almost 71% means 361637000 km2 is occupied by water; while the tract of land is 148429000 km2 on which the life dwells barring cold desert. In this, the humankind census is almost 7000 million. Their existence is completely dependent on the water. Of course, all animates are born due to water.

Amount of fresh water is very less! Just 750ml fresh water for 100 litres of salty water!!!...

Though there is ¾ water on the Earth; barring aquatics this salty water is not useful for all beings. This salty water gets evaporated by the heat of Sun. Due to this process it is transformed into the vapors and clouds are formed from these vapors. We get fresh water after these clouds pelt down. But this fresh water that has rained down is negligible. On an average, for 100 litre of salty water we get just 750 ml of fresh water, means just 0.75%. This is the ratio of salty water to the fresh water. And on this fresh water the life on Earth's land is created and nurtured. Life includes all beings those get created and nurtured, including insects, plants, trees, animals and humans. So you must have understood the importance of the fresh water.

The ¾ water on the Earth is a very precious gift!!...

Though the ¾ amount of salty water is not useful for the human life, it has one important benefit. It has balanced the temperature on the Earth. Had this much water not been on the Earth, the temperature on the Earth would have risen too much. Perhaps the creation of the life would have been difficult. So this ¾ water is the big gift to the life on the Earth. Five Oceans and 113 Seas on the Earth are comprised of this amount of water. Most of the aquatics on the Earth have preserved their existence due to this water. Due to this water, our Earth looks like a beautiful blue sapphire from the space!

Including human, the body of each animate is made up from the water!!!...

The ¾ water on the Earth is responsible for our each breath. The eggs/sperms or the seeds of the living beings are nothing else but the mixture of the twelve essential factors including water. Also the immobile beings cannot reproduce without the use of water. I have informed about the two types of animates, mobile and immobile. 'Maize' is an example of an immobile animate. Unless their seeds are watered, they do not produce the saplings, the part of reproduction. Just sowing the seed in the ground won't produce anything. Without water it cannot germinate and reproduce. It needs to be watered regularly for its new creation and growth. Thus water is essential for the creation and happy dwelling of the life on the Earth. No animate on this Earth has the power enough to create a single drop of water without the essential twelve factors of Mother Earth!

The place on Earth! Not a single raindrop falls here despite the adjacent Sea!!!...

Friends, though water occupies ¾ of Earth's surface, there is a strange place where not a single drop of rain falls in hundreds of years! This strange place is the Atacama Desert in Southern American Continent. This is the famous desert in the country of Chile in South America. It's some part is spread over Peru, Bolivia and Argentina too. Atacama Desert means almost 966 KM long dry plateau spread between Pacific Ocean and Andes Mountains which is devoid of rains. It occupies the area of almost 181300 km2. Made up on salty sand and lava, this desert is 100 times dry than Americas' Death Valley. Friends, aren't you surprised to hear about its proximity with Pacific Ocean? It is a surprising fact that just adjacent to this desert lies the fathomless water of Pacific Ocean; yet not a drop of rain falls on this desert for centuries together! So no plantation is seen here. Just at the bank of Ocean, in the hilly area some algae or cactus like plants are seen due to the humidity in the air.

Just water is responsible for the cycle of 'Life lives on life'!!!...

The reason to describe the above example is that despite of huge water storage on the Earth, due to no drop of rain this area is not fertile for the creation of life. But wherever it rains, due to the favorable environment for creation, animals, plants and humans are being created there perpetually. Due to rains the immobile animates are created. As the rain causes the creation of greenery and plants, the mobile herbivores which survive of them are created and also the carnivores are created which survive on these herbivores. This keeps the balance on the Earth. Had these carnivores not been there, the herbivores would have overgrown in the number and their demand for food would have been large that would have caused harm to the availability of crop for the humankind. So, this is the greatness of the water on the Earth.

From getting up in the morning till getting into the sleep of night the human life depends on water. Without water human cannot survive a moment. The continuous thirst needs the intake of water. Human livelihood depends upon the fruits, grains, vegetables and all of them cannot be created without water. No life is created without water.

Here it is! The prowess of not getting water!!!...

The immobile or mobile, every animate on the Earth needs water for their existence. Once I was wandering at Maasai Mara in the country of Kenya in African Continent. I found the shrunk dead bodies of animals like lions, deer and elephants due to heat of Sun at different places. These were not killed by anyone. No one had hunted them. But they had died writhing in the absence of water during the summer!

The price of a drop of water is much more than your earnings of wealth, estate properties and fame!!!...

In truth even after getting the power of imagination and the thinking, the human being disobeys the creation structure's rules. The animate obeying these rules and living their life are far better than humans. Despite the gift of intelligence, the human does not realize that if he does not get the drop of water for his living; then the life time earnings of wealth, estate and fame is useless! If the drop of water is not available on the Earth, with his/ her wealth or fame they neither can get the drop of water nor can create it. Means without a drop of water, the value of these earnings including their own is a waste, a big zero!

Friends, the reason I am emphasizing this is, why is this real identity of a human not given to him/ her so far? I don't know, but through this book, I am trying to give this self-identity to all. This live body is made up of 12 factors. One important factor out of them is water. Without water you are nobody!

What is the biggest ignorance of the human being?...

The biggest ignorance of the human is they think of themselves as greater than other animates due to the gift of intelligence. But none of the animate can be created without the Earth related twelve factors. Human too is not an exception to it. If he identifies this, he too will not give undue importance to the god, silver, properties and fame. These things are not applicable or important to any animate on Earth except human! This is where the humankind looses the crux of the matter! Can you expect a buffalo to give half a litre more milk by keeping 10 KG gold in front of her? You must be laughing, because she has nothing to do with that gold! Its value is zero for her! She only has the connection with the twelve factors with which she is made. Give her the good fodder created by these twelve factors and she may give you more milk! But the manmade 13th factor is not acceptable to her! No man made factors are acceptable to the life around! Now are you getting your real identity?

****

4.8

Responsible for Life's Creation and The Life Giving Eighth Factor

THE OZONE GAS IN THE ENVIRONMENT: MAKING YOUR LIFE BEARABLE!

Part of Real LIVE GOD & signs of life and secret of birth and death is hidden in this!

THE LAYER OF OZONE IS RESPONSIBLE FOR YOUR AND EACH ANIMATES' BIRTH, EATING, DRINKING, ALSO FOR THE NATURAL BEAUTY ON THE EARTH AND THE EXISTENCE OF ALL!!!...

Environment and the thick membrane of Ozone in it is one of the root causes of the beginning of the life creation on the Earth. Today we see the life on Earth- different plants, tall trees, pitch green farms, variety of birds and animals, insects and human beings. The human inhabits on the different parts of the Earth. On this plane of Earth new life is created every day including human life.

WOULD YOU THINK BEFORE DEATH ABOUT WHAT GIVES YOU THE VISIBILITY OF ALL THAT YOUR EYES SEE?...

Friends, we-the intelligent beings with the power of thought, have ever thought of this? Do we ever get a question about what creates this living, non-living nature? What is the share of the ozone gas in it? Has anyone ever tried to know? That existence that you are enjoying, the food and beverages you are eating and drinking, the earnings you get of wealth and fame; also the other animates you see merrily roaming, getting their fodder, giving birth to new breeds - in short the entire life is thriving on the plane of Earth. What causes this? The Earth and her twelve factors are essential for the creation of life! One factor out of it is Ozone gas. How many of us are aware that, 'the breath of mine is going on due to the ozone gas!' Had ozone been not there, you wouldn't have been existing. It is no use to just have the layers of other gases, but you are there because layer of ozone gas is there. To know yourself, it is important to know the ozone gas.

Know the 'Ozone gas' that keeps you alive!!!...

The environmental quilt that Mother Earth has clad around herself has different 5 layers. Out of them, the ozone is present in the second layer, means from the distance of 7 to 17 KM from the Earth up to 50 KM. This ozone gas is responsible for our birth. Also the water you drink, the food you eat, the breath you take and the clothing you wear is due to this presence of ozone. Also the water in the Oceans and Seas is due to this ozone! Should I tell you more? The snowy continent of Antarctica and the northern pole are intact due to this ozone gas! The control of temperature of the Earth is maintained by ozone gas along with these poles! Means all the animation happening on the Earth has ozone at its root. Such is an importance of this ozone gas.

Talking about our solar system, no other planet has the ozone gas and so no other planet has created the life! So the beings on the Earth, specially the intelligent human should be thankful for the existence of ozone and consider it to be a god and pay the gratitude!

What will happen in the absence of the ozone? Or what if it fades away? See its prowess!!!...

Fading away of the layer of ozone gas is one of the main root causes for the hue and cry about the rising temperature on the Earth. Now just think, if the ozone gas vanishes from the Earth's environment, what would be the consequences? Due to the absence of ozone on the Moon, she has a temperature of frightening 105 degree Celsius! People, birds and animals die due to heat wave in countries like India when temperature crosses 45 degree Celsius! If the temperature rises further to what is on Moon, what will happen? But we are saved from such hot temperature because of the ozone. Our life is intact because of the layer of ozone in the environment! The absence of ozone has made other planets dry and barren and hence we don't see any life there!

See the ignorance of the human!!!...

I feel funny about human! He is not at all aware of the twelve factors to which he owes his birth, his nurturance, his existence! Forget about worshiping them, he is not even thankful to them. But he spends millions of money on the imaginary religion, spends entire life worshipping man made Gods, and has he improved himself with all this? But the live real God that you see with your eyes, experience her prowess, experience with each breath, eat and drink and merrily exist that true God, the Mother Earth and her twelve factors is never seen being worshiped or prayed for! Sigh! What humankind! So ignorant!!

Check the great task of ozone which is a gift to the humanity and the life on Earth!!!...

Friends, do you feel I am too much in love of some invisible gas? 'This happens' and 'that happens' due to this gas! It can't even be seen with the bare eyes! Well, just read on to know how it all happens due to ozone gas.

At first, it is necessary to know the intensity of the Sun light. Sun is the father of all planets in our solar system. We have seen his description earlier. This Sun is the huge ball of 4.4 million KM circumference, comprising hydrogen and helium gas. He is burning almost Four million ton hydrogen per second, the energy of which is reached through the Sun rays to all planets of the solar system. The distance between Sun and the Earth is approximately 150 million KM. Despite such huge distance, it takes 8 minutes 22 seconds for the energy of the combustion of hydrogen to reach the Earth in the form of Sun rays. Means it is marching towards Earth at almost the speed of 300000 KM per second. Due to the layer of ozone gas in the environment, these ultra violet rays get filtered before reaching the Earth. The sieve of ozone gas reduces the intensity of these rays before reaching Earth. So the Sun light is bearable, and nurturing to the Earth's life. The life dwells happily on Earth. Now do you get the importance of the ozone in the real sense? Till now we have seen how the life gets created due to ozone and how it is benefitted by ozone gas. Now we shall know the consequence of the absence of the ozone gas. It shall make the importance of ozone clear to us.

WHAT WOULD HAVE HAPPENED IN THE ABSENCE OF THE LAYER OF OZONE GAS IN THE EARTH'S ENVIRONMENT?...

Suppose, the ozone gets destroyed, then the ultra violet rays of the Sun will not be filtered and will directly hit the Earth's surface. There will be tremendous rise in the Earth's temperature. Moon does not have the ozone gas layer and she is roasting in the temperature of 105 degree Celsius! Such temperature will roast all the different species of animates on the Earth too. Is there ever a reproduction from the roasted seeds? There will be no creation at all. The nature's cycle of creation will totally stop. Immobile animates means grass, trees, plants will not be produced but even the existing ones will be burnt to the ashes. The snow on both the poles on the Earth will melt first and everything; all existence will be immersed in the water. It shall destroy the life on Earth. Later with the high temperature, the water on the Earth will be eventually evaporated and would be vaporized away in the space. Our Earth will become the barren planet like other planets.

And you know what? No man made God will come to stop this process of destruction. No one will be left to say the 'soul is immortal'. Now we got an idea about what will happen if out of these twelve factors, ozone gives such a jolt. Will your earnings, your name, fame, your property be of use at that time? No. So I say know yourself at least now! Who are you? Who created you? Who is moving the cycle of life? No one gave you your true identity so far. That opportunity has come through this book now, utilize it. If you don't identify yourself, no one will be as unfortunate as you!

****

The circular layer of ozone gas around Earth!!! Due to which our life breaths!!!

Our birth means the ozone gas...

Ozone gas constitutes the most important component of the environmental quilt which Earth has clad around herself. The creation of life dwells and is protected from the Sun's ultraviolet rays due to this layer of ozone around Earth. Just this layer of ozone gas helps preserve the snow on the south and north poles of the Earth. This in turn helps control the temperature on the Earth. If the layer of ozone gas perishes, the temperature on Earth shall raise enormously as ultraviolet rays shall directly hit the Earth's surface and the creation on Earth shall end. Such is an importance of the layer of ozone gas. You will get to read the detailed information in one of the factor 'Ozone Gas in the Environment' out of the twelve factors related to Earth.

4.9

The Ninth Factor of Your Creation means True Identity

The Environmental Quilt Clad Mother Earth!

Part of Real LIVE GOD & signs of life and secret of birth and death are hidden in this!

Friends, this is one of the main reasons for the creation of the life on the Earth. It is the fact that the huge ball of Earth is clad in the quilt of the Environment. With this quilt our Mother Earth revolves around the sun at the huge speed of 107000 KM per hour!!!...

After studying the Earth and the entire life system I realized that the 'atmosphere is the root cause of the creation!' Let us see the importance of the factor 'environment' or 'atmosphere' out of the twelve factors with which our body is created.

'Environment' is the main reason for the creation of animates!!!...

Without favorable environment no mobile or immobile animate gets created. No animate gets the body. Friends, this clearly means you and I are the part of this environment. As there is no atmosphere on the other planets no animate having eyes, ears, hands, legs, head including human is found or no plant, no pleasant breeze is found there.

Despite being gifted with the power of thinking & imagination; the human never tries to know about what the body is made up of or true identity of the self since birth to death. In the ignorance s/he goes after getting deeply engrossed in the mundane life. Now the importance of the environment that I am narrating is not just the introduction of environment but your introduction, introduction of your body and the identity or introduction of each animate on the Mother Earth in the true sense.

Noisy rivers, canals, pitch green mountains and large forests, huge oceans & seas, the flowers of different colors and aroma, snowy mountains, fruits having variety of tastes, crops, aquatics, animals, birds, multi-coloured insects, reptiles and humans like us-all that we see is just because of the environmental quilt clad by the Earth.

WHAT IF MOTHER EARTH LEAVES THIS QUILT OF ENVIRONMENT?...

Earth is the huge circular ball. She is clad in the multiple layers of gases spanning many kilometres from her surface. Due to her gravitational power she has pulled this covering of gases towards herself. Along with these layers of gases she rotates continuously around the Sun with huge speed of 107000 KM per hour. As other planets don't have the twelve factors like Earth, there is no question of environment's existence on them.

What makes our breath going in our life? Human doesn't think about this. If the covering that Mother Earth has held is left by her somewhere in the space during this huge speed of revolution, then what will be the consequences? Have you ever thought of it?

THE SKY THAT IS VISIBLE TO US IS NOT REALLY BLUE! THEN WHAT COLOR IT IS?...

We see the 'blue' sky, it is our illusion. The different gases in the atmosphere have given it the bluish color. If it is the illusion, then what is the actual space? The color of the true space is dark black! And to see it, you will have to cross the orbit or boundaries of the environment spread over hundreds of kilometres and go beyond. Then you will see it as pitch black.

HOW AND WHEN THE ENVIRONMENT WAS FORMED ON THE EARTH?...

Now we shall know more about the creation of the environment. Today our Earth is 4600 million years old. There was no atmosphere created till centuries after her creation. Hitting by other planets was common at that time. Due to these strokes of hitting, the gases and other factors in her belly kept coming out. So, she started getting cooler and the environment started forming.

Initially the environment of the Earth's land wasn't favorable for the creation of animates, but was somewhat favorable for the creation of aquatics. So at first there was a creation in the water of a single celled animate. Later as the favorable changes happened for the creation of animates on the land, the immobile animates were created i.e. the plants were created.

SEE HOW THE CREATION OF ENVIRONMENT FOSTERED THE CREATION OF THE ANIMATES!!!...

Before 450 million years from today (keep in mind the Earth's age of 4600 million years!) there were no animals or the plants of any type on the land of Earth. Only fishes were created in the water. And just 350 million years before the immobile animates means the plants were created. Later as the changes and development occurred in the environment the reptiles of 7-8 ft. length were created some 300 million years back. Flying insects like grasshopper having wings were created. After the further development of the environment, almost 230 million years back dinosaur like animals who were able to stand on two legs were created. Means from there onward the creation of mobile animals started.

WHAT CREATED THE HUMAN AND HOW S/HE WAS CREATED MUST BE YOUR QUESTION...

Thus with continuous development that kept occurring in the environment, the mammals like monkeys and elephants were created some 35 million years back. Now you must be wondering about when the environment became favorable to the creation of the human. You will be surprised to read; but after millions of year of Earth's creation means almost just 2.5 million years back **'Homo Habilis'** means the human with the hands was first created in the Africa on the Earth plane. Though he used to look like a monkey, he could hunt the animal for his living using the weapons made up of stone. In this manner as the environment became favorable for the creation of the advanced animates, the older animates perished to give a way to new animates.

The history of today's human!!!...

Has the human dwelling in today's world ever seen his/her history? Just 12000 years before, humans didn't know about cloth. Untouched by the knowledge of 'shame', both the genders used to be in the natural dress i.e. nude. That time they didn't know about farm and farming. Eventually they started forming relationships and living in a group. They started using leather to protect the body from the cold, winds and Sun's heat. Also they learnt making hut from the mulch and leather for a safe stay. When getting a prey for hunt became difficult, they turned towards farming.

The man-made adjectives of the modern times!!!...

Thus, with the change in environment the human too evolved to what we see in today's modern times. The adjectives of shame, honor, importance, rich, poor, smart and idiot are stuck to the today's human. They did not even exist in olden times. The simple answer to what created the human is **'environment'!**

The ignorant human poses the egoistic self-importance!!!...

The human dwelling in the modern era is stuck in the vortex of self-importance or ego. I want to ask them, 'Hey who are you? What is your root?' But after reading and realizing the importance of the twelve factors that I am describing, one would realize that one doesn't even belong to the self! And then your ego will be dropped. This body has resulted from the twelve factors and you claim it is yours! Human refuse to take notice of it.

The description that I have given has no meaning and utility to the other animates. But human is gifted with the power of intellect and thinking. So s/he should think that s/he is nobody! One is just a part of the environment. Due to environment you are born. When the link with the environment will be severed, your death is inevitable! This is your real identity.

So far we have seen and known how animates were created due to the environment and how their existence is preserved. Now we shall see what would have been effect of environment's absence.

What if environment would have been absent on the Earth?...

The human beings inhale the oxygen at each breath and so they are alive. They have got the existence. But with the absence of the environment no oxygen and not just the human but no animates would be alive! No one remain alive to show or boast and to also to see and listen the statements like 'I have 10 cars, I am a millionaire, I am country's prime minister, whole region is in my control or I am a great preacher of a great lineage…' etc. No persons who exploit others for their own benefits would have been born on this Earth!

In the absence of the atmosphere, there wouldn't have been any difference between the Earth and the other planets. Just like them, there wouldn't have been a single drop of water on the Earth. There wouldn't have been any existence of the rivers, canals, seas and oceans on the Earth. The biggest lake of fresh water 'Baikal' wouldn't have been created The greenery, forests, different types of grass and the insects and animals surviving on it and also the wild animals surviving on these herbivores -none would have been created. No variety of birds would have been created; their melodious coo wouldn't have been heard by any. Different crops, tasty fruits and food- nothing would have been created. No breeze would have been experienced on the Earth. The heat on the Earth would have risen to the point of melting the rocks. Earth too would have been a barren and dry land like Moon. And then on this Earth the thinker, the day dreamer human wouldn't have been born to think of the concepts of the solar system, galaxies and the universe and to research on this universe!

Well! Even these people wouldn't have been born in the dearth of the environment!!!...

The wickedly selfish persons who keep millions of people hungry by hoarding all the crop, wealth and resources created by Mother Earth; wouldn't have been created too!

The fanatic leaders wouldn't have been created, the heartless terrorists, blood sucking business bankers and preachers, destructive weapon maker industrialists and the misleading selfish politicians wouldn't have been created. Sometimes I feel taking birth along with these people is the severe punishment given by Mother Earth!

This is the true identity of the environment!!!...

So far we have seen and known how animates were created due to the environment and how their existence is preserved. We also have seen what would have been the nature of Earth without the environment's presence. Now we shall see what actually the environment is and how it is clad around the Earth. The information about the environment is given earlier in the astronomical description of the chapter 'Mother Earth'; still here is the generic information.

The hundreds of kilometres height from Earth the environment is spread over. It is divided in the five parts.

1. Troposphere - this layer is spread up to the height of 17 KM on the equator and 7 KM on both the poles from the surface of the Earth.
2. Stratosphere- further to 7-17 KM described above, this layer is spread up to almost 50 KM from the Earth's surface. It includes the ozone gas.
3. Mesosphere - from 50 KM up to 80 - 85 KM spread in the middle of all layers is this layer. Here the temperature decreases with the rise in the height.
4. Thermosphere- further to 80-85 KM almost up to 640 KM spread is this layer. But here with the rising height the temperature rises too.
5. Exosphere - spread further to 640KM this is the fifth outer layer of the environment. There is no definite boundary between environment and the space. Because these environmental layers fade away gradually into the space. But in the field of aeronautics 100 KM further to Earth's surface is assumed to be the orbit of environment which is called Carman Line.

Thus these are the different layers the Earth is clad in and due to which the life on Earth is birthing and getting nurtured in the continuous cycle of life.

We gathered the information on the 9th factor essential for the creation of life and its nurturance, existence on the Earth. Now we shall see the 10th essential factor the distance between Sun and Earth and know its importance.

****

Watch the environmental quilt the Earth has clad around herself in the pitch dark space!!!

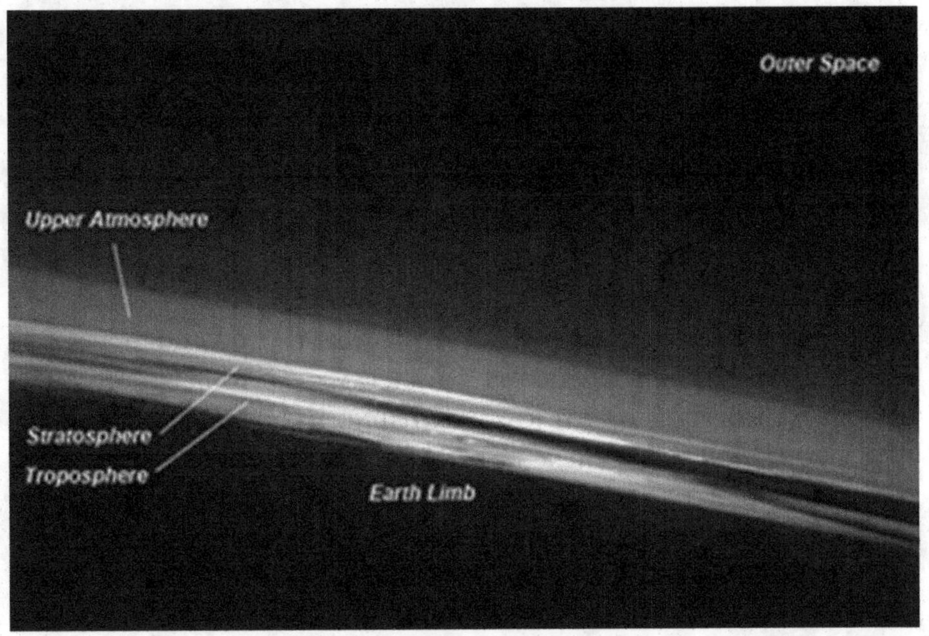

Our breathing means this environment ...

The important factor out of the twelve factors described in the book is 'environment'. The layers of environment spread over hundreds of kilometres are pulled towards herself by the Mother Earth with her gravitational force. She rotates around Sun with approximately 107000 KM per hour along with this environmental quilt. If she leaves wearing this quilt around herself we all will get destroyed. We can breathe only due to the environment. We are getting protected against the scorching heat of the Sun owing to this environment. You will get to read the detailed description about this in the factor 'Environmental Quilt Clad Mother Earth' out of the twelve factors related to Earth.

4.10

The Secret of Your Birth Revealed In This Tenth Factor

The Distance of 150 Million KM Between the Sun and the Earth

Part of Real LIVE GOD & signs of life and secret of birth and death are hidden in this!

The factor responsible for our birth is this 10th factor! Here is the canon! The birth of not just us, but of all animates, their existence and eating-drinking is related to this distance of 150 million KM from Earth to Sun!!!...

On our Earth, daily new animates take birth. These include mobile and immobile animates. No other planet has this process. The secret behind it is the 'Earth' 3rd planet from the Sun. The distance between Sun and Earth is approximately 150 million KM. Friends; you may wonder 'what is the relationship between our birth and this distance between Sun and Earth?' I have been stating continuously that for the creation of each animate twelve factors are essential. Let us see how!

Your wealth, your gold, jewels, your fame and your position has nothing to do with your being alive. See how?...

The person is so engrossed in doing something or the other that he or she has no time to contemplate upon the twelve factors. It is a human nature that the things easily available for being alive or existence are not given importance or any value. But they run after achieving the things like gold, jewels, fame, position which have absolutely no relation with being alive or existence. The entire life is wasted by humans after these things. The unimportant things get contemplated. They don't give time to the things on which his breath is dependent and find it boring!

No one knows and have no interest to know the secret of the twelve factors those I am discussing about which have given you the existence, due to which you have received the body. You won't find the religious scriptures or books talking about these twelve factors.

ALL HUMANKIND IS THE WORSHIPPER OF FALSEHOOD AND IGNORANT ABOUT THE TRUTH!!!...

In some Asian countries people shower their attention and affection on the preachers who colorfully describe the imaginary religious concepts and gods, give them the respect and fame. But never try to know the about what really keeps them alive. It is my experience that 'Earth' is the boring subject to people, but they are ready to bestow their life for some imaginary god, imaginary revengeful religious concepts on which the terrorism feeds! The human bombs are ready to die for some imaginary religious 'tasks' of destroying the humans of another religion! But they don't want to know about the reason of their being alive!

But no one occurs to at least pay gratitude or admire, worship the Mother who is responsible for our creation, our existence, on whom we feed, who just gives without any expectation and nurtures us! I have travelled the Earth. My observation is that the human throughout the Earth is the same! I used to that countries in Asian continent are poor and so that has a different psychological impact, especially my country India, but I found not much difference in the advanced nations. All humankind on the Earth is the same. In advanced countries too they are behind the imaginary religion. These religions have severely harmed the humankind and even today they are harming. Barring humankind, other animates do not have religions, casts, imaginary gods and legends and so they don't have destructive crusades amongst themselves. The African lions don't come to Indian lions to tell "Yours and ours religion/ race/ sect is different and we are better than you; so quietly accept our religion and give your land in our control else be ready for war!!" Barring humans no animals enter into the crusades killing millions of animals, destroying the precious wealth of Earth's resources. But exactly this is what the humankind has been doing since years in some or the other form! Terrorism also is a form of a crusade; they don't just kill humans for some imaginary concepts but also destroy Mother Earths' valuable resources. So certainly Mother Earth would be repenting to have gifted human beings with the power of imagination and thinking power. Perhaps she should have made the human to the same level as of other animals!

This book is your identity and Mother Earth Gift!!!...

In short, in the twelve factors I have found to create the human the distance of 150 million KM of Sun from the Earth is very important. Friends, please don't get lazy and read on about your creator. This book is written with a purpose to make you aware of your real identity and your creator's real identity. You will realize it after reading it from the beginning to the end!

The 150 million KM distance of Sun from the Earth is this nature of living and non-living beings!!!...

The animate on the Earth, including human is very fortunate to get life through Mother Earth! The factors responsible for your creation are related to the Mother Earth. Each animate is experiencing the life due to this and the 150 million KM distance of Sun from the Earth is responsible for this! Any difference in this distance would cause the destruction of the entire life on the Earth in no time. This distance of 150 million KM is responsible for the creation of an environment on the Earth. It created the air necessary for animates. This distance is responsible why the 113 Seas and five Oceans are full with water which has caused the birth of life i.e. plants, birds, animals including us and is a 'life' to all on Earth. The fresh water is created just from this salty water. Mobile animates live upon the creation of immobile animates i.e. plants. So the life cycle continues. This distance of 150 million KM is responsible for the modern life that the human is living today.

Check the consequences of the change in the 150 million KM distance of Earth from the Sun!!!...

Though the average distance is 150 million KM between the Sun and the Earth, on 22nd December the Earth is just at 147097000 KM distance from the Sun. At that time the northern hemisphere of the Earth has the winter and the southern hemisphere experiences the summer. And on 21st June, this distance is 152099000 KM. At that time the northern hemisphere of the Earth has the summer and the southern hemisphere experiences the winter. Now you may have realized what effect the difference is this distance would have on the Earth. Let us think, if these distances would have been constant, what would have been the effect? These changed distances would have caused perpetual summer on one hemisphere of the Earth and the perpetual winter on another hemisphere of the Earth. This wouldn't have been favorable to the creation of new life and the existing life would have started dying! Because the creation of the life on Earth needs favorable environment, natures cycle, rains etc. But having constant summer on one part of Earth would fetch no rains. In the absence of the water the new life wouldn't be created. Also constant winter on another part of Earth wouldn't vaporize the salt water. There would have been no creation of the clouds and no resulting rains. So fortunately the distance of 150 million KM of Earth from the Sun helps the life on Earth dwell happily keeping the cycles of season on. It helps creation of new life and nurturance of existing life by fostering the creation of farms for the human.

Check the effect of the combustion of hydrogen at the speed of 4 million ton per second on the Sun and his distance of 150 million KM from the Earth!!!...

Despite the 4.4 million KM circumference with the huge storages of hydrogen and helium and combusting 4 million ton hydrogen gas per second; the Sun's light reaches the Earth in 8 minutes 22 seconds travelling at the rate of

300000 KM per second speed from the distance of 150 million. So the Earth has life. Had it taken more time to reach the Earth, means had the Sun been on a distance greater than 150 million resulting in very less intensity of the energy, the life would have been absent on the Earth. Perhaps all the Earth would have been snowy. Contrary to this, if had taken lesser time to reach the Earth, say just 4 or 5 minutes, means had the Sun been at a lesser distance to the Earth, then with the blazing energy of the Sun rays, the life wouldn't have been created on the Earth. Earth would have been a hot ball due to high temperature.

Check the heat or coldness of the temperature due to more or lesser distances of the other planets from the Sun!!!...

How much would be the temperature on the planet Mercury which is having the distance of just 60 million KM? You won't even imagine, it is whooping 430 degree Celsius! Also the planet Venus has the huge temperature. The average distance between Venus and Sun is 100 million KM. The temperature on the planets nearer to the Sun is very high, whereas the planets far off from the Sun have very less temperature counting in minus!

The planet Mars 228 million KM far away from the Sun has the temperature from minus 5 degree Celsius to minus 87 degree Celsius. The Jupiter 778 million KM away from the Sun has the temperature of minus 150 degree Celsius. On Saturn it is minus 120 degree Celsius. Neptune, the planet far off from the Sun has the temperature of minus 220 degree Celsius. Now think, will you survive in the temperature of minus 220 degree Celsius? Will any animate be existed as a result of birth? Also you will not even exist where the temperature is 430 degrees. Life won't be born. Friends, we can conclude that the planets nearer to the Sun have very high temperature and the planets far away are very much cold! Springing of life in any form at these places is just impossible!

You have Now understood the importance of the 150 million KM distance?...

You must have by now understood the importance of the 150 million KM distance. So call the 10th factor to be responsible for the creation of the life forms and their on-going breath. You are born due to this factor. The day your link with this factor will be severed Sun's distance from the Earth will increase or decrease than 150 million KM-it is your death! No taking birth on this planet and no dying!

Do you want to know the real God?...

Your living real god is these 12 factors whom you feel with each breath of yours. You are fortunate enough to see and experience this god in your daily life. But the humankind is oblivious to this fortune! Making imaginary gods and worshipping them, humankind remains in the ignorance and leaves this world in the ignorance. The creator and savior is nothing else than these 12 factors and the Mother Earth! Your real GOD!

More than the manmade god, the 150 million KM distance between the Earth and the Sun out of twelve factors is the real god!!!...

Now we shall imagine if the Earth goes 30-40 million KM nearer to the Sun or goes away, what will be the consequence? If this happens, all the life on Earth will be destroyed. Also your concept of imaginary god will perish along with it! The rituals and prayers to the god in the legends will not solve the problem. The manmade god will not come to your rescue.

Reduction of just this one factor out of the twelve factors that I am telling about will completely destroy the life on Earth. The Mother Earth looking as beautiful as a blue sapphire will be dry like other planets.

Hey my brothers! The real secret of your birth, existence is embedded into this!!! To recognize this, include these facts in academic syllabus...

So human being! This has the real secret of your birth and existence embedded, hidden! Know that you are zero without these 12 factors! However tedious you may find this writing, but don't forget and deny that this is the root of your life! The information in this book should be included in the curriculum of the schools and colleges, because this has the secrets of life and death of humans and other animates. That is being revealed to you. One can keep aside the history of human, but the root of human and other animates must be taught to all.

****

The third planet from the Sun on the distance of 150 million KM means the Earth!!! The Moon at the distance of approximately 384600 KM from Earth!!!

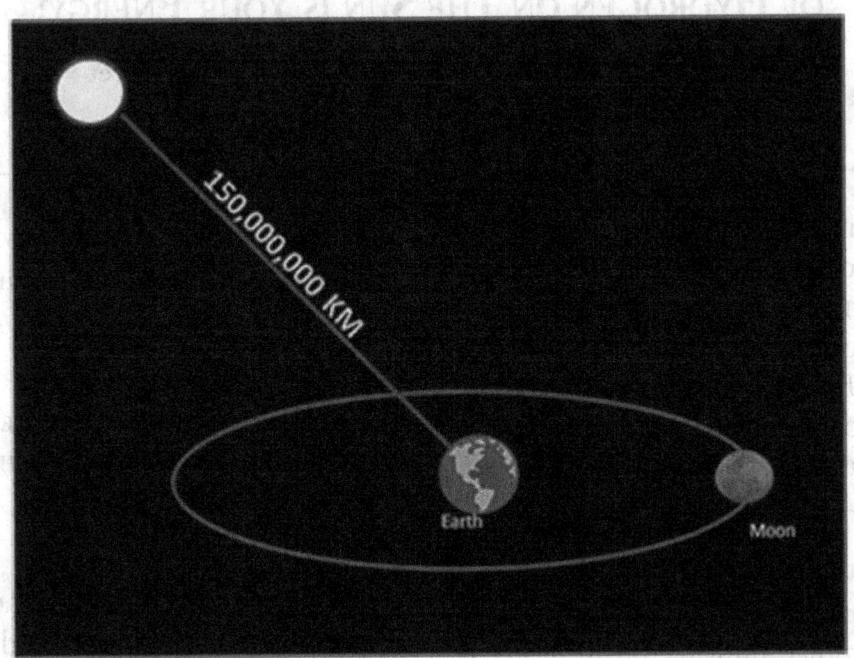

The speed of light and the distance of Sun from Earth is our life...

The above picture reveals to us that our Earth is 150 million KM far from the Sun. If we plan to watch the Earth from the actual Sun, she would appear to be of a size of sago! The rays of sunlight travel towards the Earth with the huge speed of 300000 KM per second! So just within 8 minute22 seconds the light reaches the Earth from Sun. The life creation we see on the Earth is due to the distance of Sun from the Earth of 150 million KM. You will get to read the detailed description about this in the chapter 'Distance between the Sun and Earth' of the Earth related twelve factors. The concept of the light year birthed from the speed of light. One light year is about 10 thousand billion KM. You will get to read the details in the chapter 'Astronomical Earth'.

4.11

The Eleventh Factor of Your Creation means True Identity

The Combustion of almost 4 million ton of Hydrogen on The Sun is Your Energy!

Part of Real LIVE GOD & signs of life and secret of birth and death are hidden in this!

The light, heat and energy received on the Earth is from the Sun. But do you know what process actually happens on the SUN? No? This is the eleventh factor responsible for your birth!!!...

What is the relationship between the combustion of hydrogen and your, mine as well as other animates birth? What to read about this combustion of the hydrogen? What a boring topic it is! My friends, this may be your question and natural reaction. But for your, mine birth and also the birth of all animates this eleventh factor is not only essential but is embedded into every ones' body! Like, due to this eleventh factor the mobile and immobile animates are created. Also when the connection with factor is cut, body of an animate gets cold, means one leaves the Earth permanently! (means death) Such is an importance of this eleventh factor.

The 70% of the water that we have in our body, due to which we are alive is just because of this eleventh factor!!

Despite having the gifts of imagination and thinking power the human being does not ever think about this important factor or no preacher describes its importance to the masses. The humankind is really ungrateful about this. Owing to this factor the Seas and Oceans are filled up to the brim! All mobile and immobile animates get the water due to this eleventh factor. The salty water of the Earth gets vaporized due to the Sun's heat. That create the clouds showering the fresh water on the Earth and this fresh water brings life on the Earth. You and I and the entire animates owe our birth to the water and this eleventh factor.

The creation of all plants and the food that we eat, the fire that is ignited in our kitchens and variety of sweet, sour, bitter tastes we get to taste are due to this eleventh factor means the combustion of hydrogen!!!...

All types of plants are created due to this eleventh factor and the mobile animates like human, animals, birds feeding upon these plants too are created due to this factor. The sunlight and energy essential for the creation and existence of the life on Earth is formed due to this eleventh factor. The fire that cooks your kitchen, the food that you eat and the crops that you grow all is possible due to the combustion of hydrogen on the Sun. Food grains, fruits and variety of eatables you enjoy due to the combustion of hydrogen. See the fun! Sugar is sweet; bitter gourd is bitter, lemon is sour, and chilly is hot and salt is salty! The creation of all these; needs the energy from the Sun. whatever your eyes see; all those things and animates are created due to the hydrogen burning on the Sun.

The life on Earth is dwelling happily due to the sunlight coming from the Sun. We have already got introduced to the creator of the energy, the Sun.

This is the area of the Sun just like the area of an Earth! We are breathing due to the hydrogen of 4 million ton amount burning on the Sun per second!!!...

Almost 100 times larger than the Earth means of the 1.4 million KM diameter and 4.4 million KM circumference; the huge ball having the storage of hydrogen and helium gas is the Sun. The area of the Sun is 6160 billion km2 which you might not have read anywhere. Due to this huge sized Sun our solar system including our Earth with our existence is rotating around the Sun. The sunshine that we get on the Earth or the energy that we get on Earth has its root in the combustion of the hydrogen on the Sun at the speed of 4 million ton per second. This energy provides the animation to the life on Earth.

What will happen with the combustion more than 4 million ton per second?...

Let us think. If more combustion than 4 million ton per second takes place, what will be the effect on the Earth and the life on Earth? All life will be burnt completely to the ashes! There won't be a drop of water on the Earth and all oceans and seas, rivers, canals, lakes will get dry. The environment on the Earth will vanish. This is the importance of the 4 million ton per second combustion or burning of the hydrogen happening at present on the Sun! Then it is necessary to give the information of this in the school curriculum. But it is never given. This fact is not even narrated in the religious scripts.

Less than 4 million ton per second combustion of hydrogen will freeze the Earth!!!...

Now let us think the other way round. Not increased, but decreased combustion means just 1.0 to1.5 million ton per second combustion of hydrogen gas takes place. Then what will happen? As due to the high heat the Earth and her life will be destroyed, very less temperature too shall destroy the Earth's life. Entire Earth shall be frozen due to freezing cold temperatures due to lack of energy in essential amount. The ice age will dawn but we shall not be there to see it! All the water on the Earth will be frozen to snow. The average temperature of the Earth shall be minus 150 to 200 degrees Celsius. Which animate shall be created in such cold temperature? All the planets in the solar system shall be very cold, without any life including Earth. No one will be created to discover the solar system or the concept of the Universe. No creation, no human created needs! Friends, sometimes it feels as if real happiness is in 'not being', non-existence. No needs, no sorrows. So the religious scriptures seem to lead to, desire for or beg for salvation! No cycle of birth and rebirth! In English it is said 'those who are unborn' are happy!

If the combustion that is happening on the SUN at present doesn't happen; with all the planets of the solar system the Earth too will get destroyed!!!...

The availability of the Earth related twelve factors those I describe the life on Earth is being formed and getting destroyed. Means the cycle of creation existence and destruction is continuously going on. Now we shall check if the combustion of hydrogen doesn't happen on the Sun, then what shall be the consequence? The entire life of living and non-living beings shall be destroyed and the existence of the Earth itself shall be in danger. Also if the excessive combustion happens than what is happening now and the storage of hydrogen on the Sun ends then along with Sun our Earth and the entire solar system shall be strayed away somewhere. Perhaps she will bump on the planets of the other solar system. As the gravitational power of Sun will end, none of the planet in the solar system shall be in place!

Dear Friends! Would you understand gravity of these facts? Will you know that your birth is not only for the wealth, belongings and fame?...

Think about it! Till the time the proper amount of hydrogen is getting combusted on the Sun your eating drinking and marrying is going on! Reproduction is going on. Your birth is going in acquiring the wealth, gold and silver. What gave you birth? What is the intent of the nature behind your creation? That is what you don't know! You are created here for a short period of time. After establishing one factory, you need another, if you get another then you need 10-15 more! If you become minister, you want to be the prime minister, if you are an executive, you want to be manger, if you become manger you want to be the general manger and if you get that too, you want to be vice president! Your greed is never ending! What an insane idea of the self-importance! Who counts you? You have come for a short while, how much do you want to jump? Made up of twelve factors, this is your recognition, your true identity! Not minister, prime minister, manager, general manager or vice president! You have so much greed; but one day you shall be existence less! Even if one factor out of twelve factors gets less, your existence is over! So these factors are important from your existence point of view. You don't have this real identity and hence this book is for ready reference!

CHECK THE EFFECT OF NON-COMBUSTION OF THE HYDROGEN!!!...

If there is no combustion of hydrogen on the Sun, then the light will not be created. Without the creation of light there will be no light on any planet. Means our Earth shall always be in the dark. There will be no morning, noon, afternoon or night! Years after years just night! Due to this no fresh water will be available on the Earth, because without the heat of the Sun there will be no vaporization of the salt water. So there will be no cloud formation and so no rain fall. Without rain fall there will be no drinking water for humans, crops no plants and trees grow. No animals will be created. Then Earth will be dry. For your life the combustion of hydrogen that is happening on Sun as of today is a must, else we shall face the above consequences.

TO DISCARD YOUR EGO, THIS KNOWLEDGE IS VERY IMPORTANT!!!...

So far you must have realized that the combustion of the hydrogen on Sun is very important in the magnitude it is happing for the creation and existence of the life on Earth. The twelve factors that I am informing about are interdependent. So the life is born on the Earth and everyone is breathing. Now wish to ask you a question, are you convinced of the importance of the twelve factors? If you are convinced, then shouldn't such valuable information be known by entire humankind? Don't you feel the necessity of this information? If you feel the necessity, shouldn't the children get this information from the childhood? Once this knowledge is realized the ego shall automatically be discarded. The intensity of the sorrows shall fade away. 'I' am not 'I' but these twelve factors are me! The need of the food is not for me but to these 12 factors embedded in the body. I am not shrinking or growing but the twelve factors are, this comprehension will increase.

ONCE THESE TWELVE FACTORS ARE PERCEIVED AS IMPORTANT AND UNDERSTOOD, THE MAN-MADE DIFFERENCES SHALL FADE AWAY. SUPERSTITIONS SHALL DISAPPEAR!!!...

I feel that if the importance of the twelve factors is understood by the masses, the enigma of birth and death shall be revealed and the difference between the humans will end. No one will believe in the superstitions, fate and miracles as these things will not get any base. If each human understands this reality, then the things like weapons and atom bombs shall not be needed. Root of any animate are these twelve factors. The difference of yours and mine in the humans is due to not having true self identity. It has spoilt the peace of mind and health of human today.

Well, this is not the imaginary or hearsay information. But the reality experienced by you all. Then shouldn't it be a part of the academic syllabus?

****

4.12

The Twelfth Factor of Your Creation means True Identity

THE GRAVITATIONAL POWER OF THE SUN!

Part of Real LIVE GOD & signs of life and secret of birth and death are hidden in this!

THE HUGE BALL OF 510 MILLION KM2 OF THE EARTH IS FLOATING IN THIS SPACE! BESIDES FLOATING, IS ROTATING AROUND THE SUN PERPETUALLY AT THE SPEED OF 107000 KM PER HOUR. WHAT IS THE REASON BEHIND THIS? KNOW THE TWELFTH FACTOR THAT ANSWERS THIS QUESTION. NOT JUST THE EARTH BUT THE PLANETS LARGER THAN EARTH LIKE JUPITER, SATURN TOO ARE FLOATING IN THE SPACE AND ARE ROTATING AROUND THE SUN, DUE TO THIS TWELFTH FACTOR!!!...

The humankind exists on the Earth but, no man made god gives them the birth. If that was the case, would the gods only see the Earth for this task and no other large planets? Why didn't they choose the other planets? If you claim that such god exists, then send 10-12 male-female pairs on the Moon and see if they create the animates! Forget about creating the animates; without taking oxygen or any of these twelve factors along they cannot survive for a moment on the Moon! To create the life, to give you the birth, only the Mother Earth and these twelve factors are essential. Without them no one can give you the birth and you wouldn't have been born without these twelve factors!

NO YOGI OR CHARLATAN CAN CREATE A SIMPLE DRY FLAKE OF A GRASS WITHOUT THESE TWELVE FACTORS ON THEIR OWN! THIS IS THE CANON!!!...

No power on this Earth, no so called God, preacher, religious head, or any quack can create a dry flake of grass without the interaction of these twelve factors! For its creation these twelve factors are essential. To ensure and convince yourself lock some quack in a closed room after strictly inspecting him and check if he manifest the things! I say, forget about the things; without these twelve factors such quack cannot even produce dry flake of a grass! Means so much deception goes on this Earth plane! With a jugglery someone can change the places of the things, but nothing is created by a miracle from nowhere-only the Mother Earth and her related interdependent twelve factors can do it! It is no task of any tom, dick and harry! If you properly study this book, you too will be convinced about it.

THIS HUGE BALL OF EARTH IS FLOATING IN THE SPACE ALONG WITH WATER WITHOUT ANY FULCRUM OR SUPPORT. CHECK WHAT CAUSES IT TO DO SO!!!...

The reason for this analysis above is that I am going to prove the relation of the twelfth factor that we are going to see; with the creation of life and preservation of its existence. So far we have seen the eleven factors responsible for the creation of entire life on the Earth including humans.

Now I am going to explain about the twelfth factor the gravitational power of the Sun which is responsible for your, mine and entire life's birth and their movement. How? I am explaining the doctrine.

Our Earth weighs approximately 5974 trillion metric ton! Means you will have to add eighteen zeros on the figure of 5974! And the area of our Earth is almost 510.066 million km2. The ball of this huge weight and area is gently floating in the space within specific limits, without any support! You must be curious about this fact. Also, she is not just floating but is rotating around her axis at a speed of 1610 KM per hour and revolving around Sun at the speed of 107000 KM per hour! What makes this possible? Just due to the gravitational power of the Sun! Having the gravitational power 28 folds more than the Earth's gravitational power; the Sun has pulled and held her towards him and kept her rotating at the speed of 107000 KM per hour around in the orbit at a distance of 150 million KM! Due to Suns' gravitational power the huge ball of an Earth is floating and rotating in a specific orbit in the space. Well, not just the Earth, but the other seven planets in our solar system too are floating at a specific distance in the space and are rotating around the Sun. Jupiter, the planet 13 times larger than the Earth too is rotating around the Sun from a specific calculated distance.

JUST DUE TO THE SUN'S GRAVITATIONAL POWER OF THE GREATER MAGNITUDE, THE EARTH AND THE LIFE ON HER IS DWELLING HAPPILY!!!...

Talking about Earth, we have already seen that her distance of 150 million KM from the Sun is essential for the creation of life on her. But she is floating just at this specific distance in the orbit and revolving around self as well as the Sun. Just this has caused the air, water and environment on the Earth. Also she gets the sunlight all around her. Different immobile and mobile animates are being born. Different colored flowers are blooming, fruits are coming to fruition. Forests are booming. You are getting water and foods of different tastes for your living. What makes this all? And what has created the happy user, the taster the joyous consumer of all these? Only one answer to these questions is that due to Sun's gravitational pull the Earth is floating in the space and rotating.

Due to Sun's greater gravitational power than other planets of the solar system, all planets are rotating around him at a calculated distance in a specific orbit. The gravitational power of the Sun is so awesome that anything weighing 100 KG on the Earth will weigh whooping 2822 KG on the Sun! So the existence of all planets is dependent on the Sun.

IF THE SUNS' GRAVITATIONAL POWER INCREASES THAN WHAT IT IS AT PRESENT, ALL THE LIFE ON THE EARTH INCLUDING HUMAN BEING SHALL PERISH AND THE EARTH WILL BE JUST BE A HOT BALL!!!...

Any increase or decrease in the present gravitational power of the Sun shall threaten the existence of the Earth's life. Suppose, if it increases and the Earth gets more pulled towards the Sun than where she is at present, then she will be a heated ball and the water as well as the entire life on the Earth shall perish. It will not be recreated. Contrary to this, suppose the gravitational power of the Sun decreases and the Earth gets pushed away at far distance from the Sun, then too the essential twelve factors to create the life shall perish. So the existence of the Earth's life shall end and the Earth shall be a cold ball devoid of energy. Friends, I hope you are not getting bored reading this, but this is the question of your life and death!

What will be the consequences of the end of the Suns gravitational power? Also the Sun is going to die one day like a human!!!...

Friends, Till now I have given you the idea about how the gravitational power of the Sun is responsible for the existence of Earth's happily dwelling life and also about the consequences of the increase and decrease in the Sun's gravitational power. Now a different thought has over taken my mind and it might have lingered in your mind too. What if the Sun's gravitational power is lost? I had described once earlier that the Sun too shall die one day like a human and you need not be surprised about it; because it is a rule of the universe, "Creation is the root cause of the destruction". Creation causes destruction too. Every creation of this universe has the seeds of its destruction. There is no exception. Our Sun too is no exception. Birth comes with the death. This is universal truth and each man made thing has an inevitable destruction. Let it be a huge dam or as beautiful and sturdy architecture as Taj Mahal. One day everything is going to perish. Earth itself has a death then what about the things on the Earth? Do we say that though we die our hands and legs shall be intact? Once the connection to the twelve factors embedded in the body broken, the life in all organs end.

If gravitational force of sun ceased in unforeseen circumstance, there will be panic in whole universe. All the planets in this solar system will be directionless and will collide with each other. Ultimately earth will ruin and destruction of human civilisation will occur. The survival of Earth nature is depending upon floating of sacred Earth.

Are you convinced about the importance of the twelve factors at least now? This is not the opinion of myself, but the reality friends!!!...

Are you convinced about the importance of the twelve factors at least now? Whatever is described above is not the opinion of myself or my feelings, but the reality that had not reached to you till now. So you weren't aware of this reality till now. I have given the description of the twelve factors in simple lucid language that can be understood by everyone. I have proven that you are nothing else but these twelve factors.

Your origin is the invisible sperm and egg, not of your parents but created by these twelve factors! This is your real identity!!!...

These twelve factors alone in reality are responsible at the root of your creation. It is not your parent's invisible sperm and egg that you get birth from, it is made up of these twelve factors. In the absence of the this knowledge we keep saying, "xyz is born and abc has died!" That egoistic 'self' that you assume is not yours, you are not yours; in this material world who are parents, daughters and sons, who are sisters and brothers, who are wife and husbands and who are relatives? Due to these twelve factors you are born and you will die. I am no one, but these twelve factors is my origin and if I don't belong to myself, how the lands, property, wealth that I have acquired are mine? The food that you eat is not eaten by your body but the twelve factors within you are eating. If the body was eating, the dead body too would have needed food!

Thus I have tried to give you the self-identity in these twelve factors. If you really have understood yourself, realized your identity then your life is worthwhile! Then you shall be free from the fear, worries and unessential needs and enjoy the life with true universal, natural laws in the real sense. You will not be afraid of the death.

****

5

Earth and Her Related Twelve Factors and the History of the Life Created From Them in Short!!

THE EXPLANATION ABOUT HOW THE ANIMATE IS CREATED BY AMALGAMATION OR COMING TOGETHER OF THE TWELVE FACTORS!!!...

Friends, I have introduced to you the origin of the twelve factors which I talk about i.e. Sun, Moon and the Earth and also the human on the Earth. You must have realized from it that our doer and the owner of the act everything is just the Mother Earth.

We have understood how and when our Mother Earth was born and about her body structure. Our root is our Mother Earth. Though she is 4600 million year old now, she gave the birth to her first animate in the water around 1100 million years after her birth, just to the favorable environmental conditions. Till date she has given birth to billions of animates.

THE EARTH HAS TWO TYPES OF ANIMATES, WHICH ARE THEY? CHECK HOW THE MOBILE ANIMATES ARE FED ON THE IMMOBILE ANIMATES!!!...

Two types of animates are observed on the Mother Earth. One type is the animate who are mobile or capable of movement, can migrate from one place to another. Means they are humans, animals, insects, birds, reptiles etc. Example is when it is freezing cold in the Europe, to save themselves from it some birds travel thousands of kilometres and migrate to the place of favorable environment. These are **mobile animates**. The second type of animates cannot move to other place once they are created in one place. These are **immobile animates**. These include entire plant kingdom. For example, we don't find the tree seen in front of our house in the morning, moved in front of someone one else's house at noon, isn't it? Immobile animates include all types of grass, plants, trees. Neither mobile nor immobile animates are created without the twelve factors as is observed by me and informed you. This is mere my observation and not the information gathered from any internet or research organization. So you will not read this information anywhere else other than this book.

Where and how the ancestor of today's human was born?...

The Mother of these two types of animates gave birth to the human very late means almost just 2.5 million years back from today. **Means after the age of 4597.5 million years she gave birth to the monkey alike human having hands. Just 12000 years back, the human was living as the barbarian or savagely.** Later he improved eventually. The leaving the nudity the human started using the leather as a cloth. To protect from the Sun, cold, rain and winds he started using mulch and leather to build the hut. When hunting became difficult, he started farming using the power of an elephant to prepare the land and continued his livelihood on crops received from farming. Means in his original savage state he was an carnivorous animal. Later he started sowing the plants, the immobile animates and using them as a diet to fill the belly. By then the twelve factors that we have been reading about were created. This is the history of the creation of animates.

Originally Earth is a hot ball! Then from where did the imaginary manmade gods came into being?...

When the environment became favorable for the creation of human, the human was created. Before that, there wasn't a trace of humans. So the question arises that there are concepts of God, super soul in the religious script. So when the first human was created on the Earth, where were these gods, super souls and soul of this human till then? And now almost 7000 million humans are on the Earth, where did their souls came from? **Multiplication is the rule of the nature.** Actually as the environment started getting favorable, the life started blooming on the Earth and also many life forms perished due to unfavorable environment for them. Means I feel there is no connection between the creation of life and the soul! Yet dwelling in 21st century human is stuck to the ideas of god, soul and super soul.

The creation of life forms on the Earth is not due to any imaginary god or super soul but just due to the Earth and the availability of twelve Earth related factors and the favorability of environment. When these things together became favorable, the animates were created on the Earth, this is the secret of the life's creation on the Earth.

THE REPRODUCTION OF MANY ANIMATES FROM A SINGLE ANIMATE OR MULTIPLICATION IS THE RULE OF THE LIFE STRUCTURE!!!...

I would like to share with you an incident. I had bought one melon. Due to some reason, for many days I couldn't use it to eat. Later after 8 to 10 days when I cut it, it had wiggly worms! How it entered in melon. Form where did the souls of these worms came from? Or they don't have soul? If it can enter into such closed melon, it can enter in the stones and the stones may start walking, isn't it? Do you have an answer to this? This means the twelve factors those I have described are animates. Grass shall foster grass. Lion shall birth the lion. Lion shall not deliver banyan tree! Human will reproduce human and not four legged animal! Would the Raspberry tree give Banana? In short the fraction or an atom of the reproduction of the animate will create the same animate. The seeds of groundnuts shall not grow walnut, but only groundnuts. One groundnut shall reproduce many groundnuts. Likewise, the animate reproduce many animates. This is the law of the life structure. There is no place for man-made gods or super soul. Till the time Earth related twelve factors exist, the life structure will go on the same way.

WATER IS NOT JUST H2O BUT ITS CREATION NEEDS THE ESSENTIAL TWELVE FACTORS!!!...

So I have been sharing with you that to know the secret of the life structure study the Mother Earth and just the Mother Earth! Understand Mother Earth. All these answers are hidden in the Mother Earth. Whichever things are visible to your eyes, they are nothing else but the part of the Mother Earth. It may be animate or non-animate object. For example water. In the science we are taught that the H2O means water. But in my opinion, water too is an animate. You will be surprised at this opinion, how is that? But in reality the water that you drink is not formed without the Earth related twelve factors. Just H2O doesn't create the water! Go on the Moon with just hydrogen and oxygen and show me the water produced there! I am not describing the twelve factors again, but these twelve factors are very essential.

Without the energy from Sun, the water will not be produced. Also if the Earth doesn't have gravitational power or the layer of ozone, the water will not be created. And so I say water is animate. Simply because the what is created by twelve factors is animate. So water is a part of Mother Earth. Which things are created due to Mother Earth is all just Mother Earth! Nothing is created without the Mother Earth! So if you study about whatever I have written from the beginning; you will realize that our root, our origin is Mother Earth!

THE FIRST HUMAN ON THE EARTH HAD NO ADJECTIVES OR LABELS MADE BY THE HUMANS TODAY. THE LIFE STRUCTURE HAS NOTHING TO DO WITH THE MAN MADE THINGS!!! UNDERSTAND THIS...

Did the first human created by the Earth have the soul or not? To which cast, creed, religion or race he belonged to? Which god created him? Whether he was rich or poor? Was he expert or ignorant? Will someone give me the answers to these? If this first human had the soul, where was it roaming before coming into this creation as first man on the Earth? If these questions remain unanswered then it is all man-made! The creative structure doesn't have anything to do with man-made things. Friends, I am not writing fairy story or tale or an imaginary story or a novel. I am not even writing this just because I felt like writing. But this is the reality we are into and the Mother Earth is motivating me to write such facts before you!

EVERY VISIBLE THING ON THE EARTH IS A PART OF MOTHER EARTH! EVERYTHING IS MOTHER EARTH AND JUST MOTHER EARTH!! SO 'I' AM NO ONE!!!...

To understand your own identity it is important to know when, how and why the first human was created. When these Earth related twelve factors were not created, there was no human alike animate created on the Earth. Due to the twelve factors the body form was created. So you must have realized that we too are not an exception to this. If thought about who am I? Who created me? Who provides me the things needed for my existence? Are the parents who gave me birth my real creators? From where did the sperm and egg that created me come into them? Actually it was created due to these twelve factors. So my body was created by the sperm which in turn was created by these twelve factors. So am 'I' really just myself? This body which I claim to be mine is created by the Mother Earth and her related twelve factors. There is no my own performance in that creation!

Means this body that I claim to be mine is just an atomic fraction of the Mother Earth. The day the cord from this body connected to the Mother Earth is broken, on that day this moving body is surrendered to the Mother Earth! She takes back the body she has given, because its association and relation with the twelve factors are broken!

ONCE YOU GOT THIS TRUE IDENTITY OF OWN; THE CONCEPTS OF BIRTH, DEATH, JOY AND SORROW ARE RELATIVE TO EACH ANIMATE! IN THE CREATION STRUCTURE THEY AREN'T EXISTENT!!!...

The one who realizes oneself this way will not get entangled in the emotions of joy, problem and sorrow during the limited life time that s/he has got. If I don't belong to myself, who is mother, father, wife, husband, daughter and son, sister and brother and all relatives! Everyone has got an independent body. According to the creation structure each animate comes independently, lives life independently and also one day leaves the body independently. Because everyone is made up due to these Earth related twelve factors. Joy, sorrow and problem all are personal ideas. The joy someone gets eating the sweet fruit, the other who is not eating will not get. Some scent may give you a wonderful aroma but it may be troublesome to the other. The fragrant insect repellers may be enjoyed by the humans, but makes the insects runaway or even die. So these are human ideas or concepts, not actually existent. Actually existent are the Earth and her twelve factors!

Now I am going to introduce the animates and the human on the Earth and also share the laws to be observed during the human life.

****

6

Made up of Twelve Factors

Modern Human on the Earth with the Thinking Power, Imagination and the Other Life on the Earth

So far the life has been created and is being created. The main reasons for this creation are Earth, Sun and the Moon. While living our common life, who is and what is responsible for the visible life around and the new born in our house? We don't think of this in detail. To create these, the Earth, Sun and the Moon along with the twelve factors created by them are responsible. The life is being formed just due to these twelve factors.

YOU MAY NOT HAVE READ ANYWHERE THE TWO TYPES OF ANIMATES!!!...

These animates are classified into two types. One those are moving who can move from one place to another, who have wings, legs means the **mobile animates.** Out of them, the one who has got the eyes, ears, two hands and two legs and who has got the more gift of thinking and imagination, intelligence than any other animate is the human being. And the other animates who cannot move or migrate from one place to another from their place of creation are the immobile animates. These include the entire plant kingdom on the Earth. There is no third type of animate on this plane of Earth.

YOUR BIRTH, YOUR LIFE IS CREATED DUE TO THE IMMOBILE ANIMATES!!!...

The livelihood of the mobile animates is dependent on the immobile animates. Also the creation of their bodies, nurturance and growth of their bodies and the existence is all possible due to the immobile animates. Out of all mobile animates only human has got the intelligence of cooking the food before eating. No other animate other than the human cook their food for eating. The knowledge of bitter, sweet, salty, sour and hot is only with the human and to satisfy his taste buds, the Mother Earth has created the immobile animates having these tastes. For example, chillies and spices for the hot taste, beet, sugar cane and different sweet fruits for the sweet taste, raw mango, ……so on. Thus different immobile animates are created on this Earth.

THE INTELLIGENCE, IMAGINATION AND THINKING POWER THE HUMAN HAS GOT ARE CURSES DUE TO THEIR MISUSE!!!...

No other animate has received the gifts of imagination, thought and intelligence like human. So compared to other animates, some beneficial and some unbeneficial traits are stuck to the human being. As the human gets benefitted by the intelligence, they have lost a lot due to misuse of these gifts and behave against the laws of the Mother Earth. To consider comparatively the other animates happily live their lives according to the natures law and take leave of this Mother Earth one day. But unlike this, the human keeps creating the series of troubles and sorrows and take leave of the Mother Earth with these troubles and sorrows. I sometimes feel that the gift of intelligence that is given to the human by the Mother Earth is not a boon but a bane. No other Animate is as wicked as human is!

SEE THE EFFECTS OF THE MISUSE OF THE GIFTS OF THOUGHT POWER, IMAGINATION POWER AND INTELLECT BY HUMAN!!!...

Only humankind is given these gifts by the creation structure. No other animate being is bestowed with it. But humankind has mostly been misusing the gifts. It also has caused the tremendous loss to the humankind itself. Even today, the humankind is on the edge of destruction due to the manufacture of destructive weapons. With this imagination power, thought power and intellect the humankind has created a chaos on the plane of Earth. The factory funnels are throwing up the smoke, the used chemical-mixed water is let in the rivers, Seas, and air is getting polluted due to excessive use of diesel and petrol. The trees are getting cut daily and causing the ecological disturbance. The fresh and clean springs and rivers of past times are now like gutters which flow the chemical-mixed contaminated water. Even the water of the river considered holy in Hinduism the Ganges is contaminated. Half burnt corpses, ashes and bones are immersed in her. The dreadful actions of humankind are marching to destroy all life dwelling on the Earth. Till now, due to the misuse of the thought power_ i.e. the gift given by the creation structure_ human was just killing other humans. But now breaking all the rules of the creation structure the human is shaking the roots of all the other innocent animate beings.

Actually if the human would have used the gift received wisely there wouldn't have been wars between the humans. No one would have been victimized and starved. Also other animates would have been dwelling happily on this plane of Earth. There wouldn't have been any danger to them from the human. Mother Earth must be repenting for bestowing the human with these gifts.

The happy, joyous and lively life of all animate beings including human depends upon the thoughts of the human. But looking at the tendencies of humankind, they have harmed themselves and created the danger of their own extinction. This is the effect of violating the rules of the creation structure.

Which is the most cruel and worst animal in the world?...

To share a funny experience, once we visited a city of Tokyo in Japan. We had gone to visit the great zoo in the city. Different animals from the different parts of the world are brought and nurtured here. Even the Lama, Alpacas appearing only in the ridge of Andes in South America were there. The animals like the Anaconda appearing in the valley of Amazon and Tiger, Lion, Elephants and Hyena occurring in different parts of the world are kept in this zoo. Watching the animals in each cage we came to the final cage. All different animals from different parts of the world were seen so far and so we were curious about which animal we get to see in the last cage. But there was no animal visible inside the cage. After going little ahead there was a huge mirror placed which was showing our own reflection. Just my eyes caught the statement written besides which was 'the worst animal in the world!!' Who was it? You have to identify, it is 'human'! After showing the all animal, the Tokyo city has given the true identification of the human! So I say that the 'intelligence' is not the gift the human has got but is the bane.

The 'human' on the Earth is the same everywhere!!!...

I have travelled a lot in the various parts of the Earth so far. During my travels, I used to curiously observe the humans nature at each place. What is the difference between the human at our place and their place? The human in the sub-continent of India has to do so many things to fill the tummy. I used to think that this may not be the case in other countries or parts of the Earth. But on the entire Earth, the human is the same! The needs and the emotions of thirst, hunger, happiness, joy and sorrow are attached to the human in all the nations of the Earth. An infant of the human, whether from the continents of Europe, America or any small country is the same everywhere. Same movements, same wailing and laughter, all is the same. All infants cry when hungry. The body structures of all male and female on the Earth are the same. There may be a change in the color or hair patterns, but no change in the body structure. So any man from any country if married to any woman in a different country, they will deliver a child for sure. This is the part of the life creation system. What I mean to say is that the six evils of anger, greed, desire, jealousy and selfishness are attached in some proportion to any human in any country from any continent. Also the mourning, joy, honor-insult emotions are the same everywhere. The tendency to run behind hospitality, dignity and fame is the same everywhere. The death of loved ones like parents; bring tears to the eyes of every human during the cremation whether in Uganda or America. I have seen it with my own eyes. In many countries I got to see the funeral procession. So the emotions of all humans worldwide are the same. These emotions are only in the human. You may not find them in the other animates. Other animates cannot express the joy and sorrow too, this is a good thing.

The human doesn't have the consciousness of the reality and hence has mountains of sorrow!!!...

Some calf of a deer just has started walking and is on mothers' milk. Some leopard sees him alone and attacks. The calf tries a lot to save himself but finally the leopard catches him by throat and starts tearing him apart. The mother deer of that calf is watching all this and is still. But then later when it is all over she starts grazing the grass. She doesn't mourn or doesn't have much sorrow of losing that calf. This is the big difference between the human and the other animates. The human sways in the emotions and invite the sorrow.

Thinking oneself very different than the other animates is the biggest ignorance of the human!!!...

One thing I noted in my observation is that humans think of themselves to be very different and special than the other animates. This is the great ignorance of the human, because as I have already explained, no animate can be created on this Earth without the twelve factors. According to the creation structure, the things necessary for the human's preservation of existence are also necessary for other animates too. Human doesn't need different things than other animates to preserve the existence. For example, all animates need air, food, water, light and coitus which are needed by human too. Though the human have the imagination and thinking power which other animates don't have, he cannot survive without the essentials like air, food, light etc. Is it that humans don't need water because they have intelligence? It is never so. Without water no life for all animates. Means according to the creation structure the human's intelligence alone is useless to preserve his existence. No human can survive without the basic needs. The laws of universe are same for all. So it is better for human to live the daily life keeping these things in the mind.

Have millions of animates died ever with the human like wars?...

Well, has the existence of other animates threatened ever without the humanlike intelligence and imagination power? Have they started dying fast? Have they started attacking on each other? Contrary to this, due to this curse received by humankind, there has been slaughter of trillions of human attacking each other in the war. It can go to the times as ancient as war of Kalinga during Ashok's time in India, wars initiated by Alexander the Great or as recent as our first and second world wars, the very recent war of Iraq to find some imaginary bio weapons! Have you ever seen such slaughters in the other animates? No, because they aren't cursed with the gifts of intelligence and imagination. There are many adverse effects of this curse on the human life.

The creation or cosmos doesn't work according to the man-made laws, but works according to the laws of cosmos!!!...

The cosmos has its own unchallengeable universal laws. The Mother Earth has created the twelve related factors that we have discussed earlier for the creation and nurturance of the life system. Also has resolved the issue of each animates livelihood. Creation has one law, the life lives on the life! To keep the cycle of creation perpetually on according to this law, one animate lives on the other animate for the existence. Had this system not been there in the nature of creation, the life on the Earth wouldn't exist. To feed the animates; there is another law of the creation structure that is one life creates many lives. So that each animate gets sufficient food on this Earth. But friends, you will be surprised; the human is an exception to this! Even after making provision of the food for all the human dies of hunger and malnutrition!! It is because few humans are challenging the rules of creation and makes their own rules by actions like hoarding more food grains than they need-- while others in Africa or Asia die with the lack of food! But they don't know that the cosmos, the creation works on its own rules and not their rules!

Understand this rule of creation, vegetarianism and non-vegetarianism!!!...

The one who reproduces is an animate. And one animate cannot survive without feeding on the other animate; this is the rule of creation! The rules of creation are so solid and beneficial which human never realizes.

Where the creation of immobile animates means fruits, crops or vegetables in is abundance the humankind can be fed on them for the livelihood. Means without eating one animate the other animate cannot survive. The rule of creation is applicable here because all plant kingdoms are animate. Some people give pretty name to this as 'vegetarianism'. But in short it is slaughtering the immobile animates and eating them. Also about the mobile animates, eating each other by the mobile animates is a 'non- vegetarianism'. These ideas of **'vegetarianism'** and **'non-vegetarianism'** are born in the fertile brain of a human! Now we shall see if the idea born in human mind is correct or the laws of the creation are correct.

Some people promote only 'vegetarianism' it is their ignorance!!!...

Some humans in specific religions justify **only vegetarianism** means just eating of immobile animates. These people consider eating of mobile animates as **'non-vegetarianism'**. But this difference is not agreeable to the creation structure. The cosmos has made the rules for the benefit of all animates. Not abiding by them would make the balance of creation structure collapse. If suppose all humankind decided to agree with the promoters of the 'vegetarianism' and start observing it totally, what will happen? Have they ever thought of the consequences? Getting fame from handful persons must be the motive behind it!

This is a complete ignorance! Here is the proof!!!...

We shall see the effect of eating just the immobile animates. Almost 3500 million years back first the aquatic was created in the water on this Earth. Since then billions of aquaculture is created in the water on Earth. One fish usually lays thousands of eggs. Had the entire humankind decided to not eat any aquatic listening to the promoters of vegetarianism, then what would have happened till now? According to the law of 'each animate born has the death' they would have died and as no one had taken them out of water to eat, there would have been the layers of millions of dead fishes floating on the surface of the sea or oceanic water. It would have covered the complete sea water. This would have arrested the process of vaporization of the salty water due to Sun's heat. Then the process of formation of natural water would have stopped! Since no fresh water would have been created, forget about the other animates, but even the promoters of vegetarianism wouldn't have stayed alive on the Earth in the absence of the water!

We shall see one more example. If embracing the vegetarianism animates surviving on the herbivores like deer and goats left eating them, then these herbivores would have outgrown in the numbers than humans. After the scarcity of the grass for such outgrown number they would have turned towards the grains in the farms and would finish them in a group! Then human would have no food left and hunger deaths would have been inevitable on the Earth. We can give such many examples. In short, if the human interferes the creation structures' rule of 'life is fed on life'; it will be self-harming to the humankind. So the promoters of vegetarianism should understand this law.

What not the human does to survive!!!...

Would share one more experience. I have visited the country of Norway near the Northern Pole. The majority of land of this country is covered with the snow for 8-10 months. There is scarce human habitation in such snowy region. You will never see the farms of cereals like wheat or maize. Whatever plants grow here is mostly consumed by the animal reindeer for his own livelihood. The same animal is used as a food by the humans dwelling in this country. As we dry the food in the summer to store it for use during the year, the scanty population of this region hunts reindeer and dries the meat with salt for the use during the year. Also his leather is used as a cloth. When moving out of house is difficult due to heavy snowfall and getting food outside is difficult, these people use the salted and dried meat of reindeer as food and preserve their existence. Thus the principles or rules made by handful of people are not applicable to the entire humankind. Also they don't apply to the other animates leaving humans.

I will share here more examples that might close the voice of promoters of vegetarianism! The rules of creation structure are so solid that the human intelligence or the man-made rules prove to be weak!

THIS IS THE PROOF! FOR SURVIVAL SOMETIMES HUMAN EATS HUMAN!!!...

The snow peaks of the huge Andes Mountain in South America which is larger than the Himalaya, are much higher than Himalaya. Over these mountains once the plane collapsed due to some technical problem. It was broken into pieces, and it was assumed that all the passengers travelling in it died. But out of the two close friends travelling in it, one was breathing. He was alive. No one was able to find where exactly the plane had collapsed because it had collapsed in the barren snowy peaks. So almost for the fifteen days after the collapse no one could reach there. The friend who was alive needed the food for survival, but there was no chance of getting any food. So he somehow spent some days by eating the meaty part of the close friends' dead body! When the search committee reached there, this fact was brought to the world. So the human should not give undue importance to the intelligence. In front of the creation structure the human intelligence is useless. To increase the self-importance and gain fame by exploiting the ignorance of the humankind some selfish people do such ado. They try challenging the laws of creation structure.

CHECK HOW HUMAN TAKES THE DISADVANTAGE OF ANOTHER HUMANS' IGNORANCE!!!...

In such way the exploitation happens in the society by creating the boogieman of fear in the minds of ignorant people by birth charts, predictions and religious rituals.

I have been describing the reality of how the animate was created on the Earth due to the twelve related factors since her birth? And how is the structure of creation? It has nothing to do with the bogus omens, predictions and man-made religion.

These things are the efforts by handful selfish people to gather unfathomable wealth by exploiting ignorant masses. If everyone studies the natures' creation in details they will not give any importance to such things. I have explained the creation structure in this book. I feel this information should be included in the school curriculum for the benefit of the ignorant masses that get exploited and also because the human is in the false ego of assuming himself different than other animates due to his intelligence, thought and imagination power.

Unfortunately human mostly uses his intelligence for the selfish motives, gaining fame and greatness. Other animates has absolutely no use. The selfish things are not reality. Whatever is agreeable to the creation and beneficial to all animates is the truth. For example, oxygen is needed by humans and also the by all animates. The entire life is dwelling on it. It is beneficial for all animates on the Earth.

What is the use of some big industrialist being filthy rich or prancing positions like royal, sir, duke and president to the humankind? Forget about the humankind, not even other animates have any use of it.

YOUR COUNTRY MAY NOT HAVE BEEN EVEN HEARD BY SOME OTHER NATIONS, AND THEN WHO ARE YOU? WHO KNOWS YOU?...

I have travelled entire Earth. I was amazed to know that the nationals of the country I visited didn't know the name of India. If the nation is not known, then who will know the minister, prime minister or a president, of that nation or the richest people? At least do you know the names of all the nations on this plane of Earth? And other animates have nothing to do with your ranks and positions! If I tell some buffalo 'hey, see this is our nations' prime minister!'; then what importance or recognition she has of it? Human has been using the gift of intelligence that's not with other animates for the selfish purposes. And it has created religions, fanatic religious heads, racism, superstitions of rituals and quakes. Other animates are oblivious of these things!

There is no difference between the life cycle of other animates and 'intelligent' human!!!...

The big ignorance of the humankind is that they think themselves to be different than other animates. Actually his life cycle too is similar to other animates. As any sapling of the plant takes birth, the human infant takes birth. Once roots of the saplings are firmly planted in the soil it stands on its own. Similarly the human infant grows and stands on its own feet. As the sapling grows, the human toddler too grows in the childhood and adolescence. As the tree gives fruits after its growth, human too marries and produces offspring in their youth. Now tree grows in a huge tree. Finishing the youth the human too enters into the late adulthood. As tree grows more and more old, human grows towards old age. Eventually the organs start losing their strength. As the old tree sheds its leaves and only a skeleton remains, means the life ends; the humans organ also give up one by one and one day he is declared as dead and is burnt or buried as the case may be! Same is with the tree. Someone cuts the branches of leafless tree and it gets flat on the ground.

Means mobile and immobile both types of animates were born, bloomed, grew into old age and ended their life. The life cycle for the both was the same. Friends, where is the connection of wealth and fame to this life cycle? Would these things change the human's life cycle? Tree and human have the same life cycle and there is no difference; because as I say both are created on this Earth plane due to Mother Earth and her related twelve factors. The creation structure doesn't discriminate between the human and other animates. But the human is ignorant and so lives in his own illusionary concepts in the life giving undue importance to fame, wealth, positions, anger, desire, jealousy, revenge and children without realizing the valuable human existence. And one day he leaves this world without realizing the reality!

DEAR 'RICH' HUMAN; IF YOU WANT TO BE FORTUNATE THEN UNDERSTANDS THIS BOOK!!!..

The purpose of this book of mine is to give the human his or her own realistic identity. The first thing in that is realizing the negligible existence of 'I' amongst uncountable animates born on the Mother Earth. Yours and any other animates' needs are the same. Balance unnecessary needs are created through your thinking, your imagination. They are really unnecessary for your happy dwelling. Other animates have no use of the needs you have created.

To the human who lives according to laws of universe, earning sufficient enough to comfortably meet the needs and living happy life enjoying the creation; has absolutely nothing to do with the unnecessary desires of 50 KG gold, silver, diamonds, ambition of getting high ranks and positions and felicitations from people, 5-10 bungalows or apartments, 20-25 factories, 10-15 cars!

Any lion or buffalo too doesn't have to do anything with these things. But the selfish and greedy human desiring these unnecessary things spends life and goes to any level by not understanding the real value of this invaluable human life. You keep hoarding till the last breath; deceiving poor masses, friends or your own nation and even own relatives and one day leave this world forever keeping all things here! Hey greedy human, isn't your life mulch if any of these twelve factors leave connection with you? Just think about it! Your real identity is just a negligible atom on this plane of Earth! Know this reality, know this real identity and walk your life in freedom by keeping aside unnecessary greed, jealousy, revenge and selfishness. Fill the cup of invaluable human life with joy up to the brim! Be happy and make other happy take leave of this world while giving others the joy. Just this will make your life worth for living!

****

7

The Laws Of Creation For Happy and Joyous Life

THERE SHOULDN'T BE A BIRTH. BUT IF YOU ARE BORN; TILL YOUR DEATH THE ENJOYMENT AND HAPPINESS OF YOUR LIFE WILL DEPEND UPON WHETHER YOU OBSERVE THE LAWS OF CREATION OR NOT!!!...

Friends, in the last chapter we have seen the illusion of the human birth and realized that getting birth is not necessarily a joyous and happy event. Of course it doesn't depend upon us. It depends totally on the minds of the reproductive animates. But once born, you must combine the laws of the humankind and the laws of creation architecture to lead the life of peace. The person who understands the creation architecture and study the twelve factors causing his birth of the Mother Earth will observe the laws to lead the happy and joyous life because of the realization of self-identity. She or he will be free from worries and will not be afraid of death

FOLLOWING ARE UNWRITTEN LAWS OF THE CREATION STRUCTURE. THERE IS AN ARRANGEMENT FOR SEVERE PUNISHMENTS FOR THE LAWBREAKERS! NOT JUST THAT, BUT DEATH TOO IS PART OF THE PUNISHMENT!!!...

Friends, while doing all this I have a suggestion that you understand the unwritten laws of the creation structure and act accordingly; because more than manmade laws, the laws of creation structure are more useful and 100 % beneficial to each animate. There is hundred and one percent punishment to those who break these laws of creation structure! You may get scot free from the superior court after breaking the manmade laws, committing the human crime. But there is sure shot punishment for the crimes committed by breaking the laws of the creation structure.

We shall see the laws and rules of the creation structure next.

If the human or any other animate has to sustain its existence, and wish to enjoy that existence, taste the life, want to reproduce; then creation structure has her own unwritten laws and rules. Anyone going against these laws will not be able to enjoy his or her existence. Also their existence will end. Means they shall die. If you want to survive, you must utilize the twelve factors which have given you your body. If you don't use any single factor or overstep it, that hundred percent leads to the end!

I have already analyzed many laws of the creation structure before this. Also know these rules.

1. To sustain your life on this Earth you must use the air means the oxygen. Not using it would cause danger to your existence or death.
2. The fresh water that is created from the ¾ water available on Earth must be in your body in right amount. Any reduction or increment in it shall lead to your death.
3. You must use the sunshine on the Earth. The death is certain to the non-user of this sunshine.
4. Earth revolves from west to east with a speed of 1610 KMPH. You must revolve along with her at the same speed. Rule-breaker will die.
5. Similarly the Earth rotates around Sun with the speed of 107000 KMPH. You must rotate along with her at the same speed else you shall die.
6. You must utilize the Moon for your sustenance. You cannot survive without Moon.
7. To sustain your existence your distance from the Sun must be 150 million KM. Any addition-reduction in this will cause your death.
8. The Earth on which you dwell has pulled you towards herself with the support. If you break this rule, your end is certain.
9. To exist on Earth the gravitational force of the Sun is necessary. Not using it will lead to death.
10. The snow of the north and south pole of the Earth should be intact. Its destruction is your death.

11. You stay on Earth. To keep you alive the existence of ozone gas in the atmosphere must be sustained. If it gets destroyed you shall roast to death.
12. This Earth is clad in the coat of gases. If this coat gets destroyed you will not be able to survive.

These are the rules for animates to sustain their existence. Now we shall see the rules after the creation happens.

1. Each animate is bestowed with the hunger. It is of a more or less magnitude according to each animate being. Human hunger is fixed. The other meaning of the hunger is need or necessity.
2. According to the creations' law according to the age & type of the animate being one must eat food necessary for the body. Eating in excess will meet serious consequences.

   Suppose if some sapling is cultivated with excess urea, the tree shall die. Also if any plant is watered in excess, the roots shall decay and it shall die.
3. Accordingly each human should have necessities of life, like food, money or home; just sufficient enough for the need. Anything more than necessity disturbs your health. It shall give sorrow in place of joy. It will create the enemies for you. Means the 'have-nots' will be your enemies.
4. Everything available on the Earth is the resource of livelihood for each and every animate being. It is created for all. If you keep collecting it alone, it is not agreeable to the creation structure. Collectors will have to suffer the punishment for it. It will be in such form that these hoarders will not even understand it. Those busy collecting wealth throughout the life must take lessons from this fact. They must check the position in the society of those who collect more than needed. No one should starve is the rule of the creation structure. She has made the arrangements for everyone by creating the availability of the resources for all. I have analyzed in detail the rules of the creation structure. Study them; follow them so that your life becomes happy.

Once born, there is nothing as valuable in this world as your happy and healthy existence! Just lead the life with this principle!!!...

Friends, once you are born, your cheerful and healthy existence is priceless in this world! It is the most invaluable thing in the world and in your life! This is the most important principle once you are born. If your life dwells around this principle, your life is worth! You must shun those vices that the humankind sticks to and dies in the chase of getting happy, joyous and healthy life. First thing to remember is this birth that you have received is just your illusion. Each thing that you see here is an illusion. Nothing is real. Once you lead the life realizing this, you will lead a successful life. Friends, why I call it an illusion? Because each thing here is perishable! This is the law of the universe! Change is the rule of the creation architecture. Nothing in this world is permanent.

Let us decide, from the invisible sperm to the flat body lying on the death bed which is real you?...

Friends, you are born from the invisible sperm; that is the origin of your birth. Then it took a form of a small fetus caused by the twelve factors which were supplied to you through your mother. After coming out of the mother's womb, the Mother Earth takes the responsibility of providing these twelve factors by herself. The umbilical cord with your human mother is severed and the one with Mother Earth gets connected! For the convenience of your animate type, i.e. humankind, you are baptized. Later growing through your toddlerhood and childhood you enter the phase of adolescence. Then you enter the youth to be a young adult. Then you reproduce and enter the late adulthood. You start entering the old age. Later your organs start giving up their functions one by one and you lie flat on the death bed. If you have captured this life cycle of yours in the camera, none of the photos taken in different phases would identify with each other! You look different at each phase. From a small baby, to the school going kid, to the rebellious adolescent, to the young adult, to the adult parent– there is no match! From the sperm to the dead body, through these stages of life which is real you? Baby? Or young adult? Or wise old man? Means all this is an illusion! Which is your real identity?

7.1

What Were You Before Your birth? And What Will You Be After The Death?

Each person on the earth curiously seeks the answer to the questions above; but I feel neither any saint, nor any religious preacher has answered these queries in a convincingly correct manner by establishing the doctrine in any religious scripture or holy books; nor seems to have anyone found the answer to it. I am giving these answers with doctrine through this writing of mine today.

Do you have the complete knowledge of the Earth on which you are born upon? ...

Some agree with the reincarnation and some do not. But no one has stated the reality or stated doctrine about the presence or absence of reincarnation. Just some imagination projected through one's own understanding. The fact remains that reality and imagination are worlds apart. First of all we all should know about the Mother Earth, upon which we ourselves and the other creation structure are born; no, rather know about 'just the Mother Earth' that birthed us along with the other creation-structure. In the true sense, even the bigwigs don't have knowledge about this. Does human race and the entire creation-structure or life exist only on our Earth? Why doesn't it exist on other planets like Mars, Mercury, Jupiter and Venus? Then what exists there? Once one knows the scientific answers to the questions above, the other questions discussed above could be easily resolved.

Why the life doesn't exist on the other planets like it does on Earth?...

Now let's think about why the other planets don't have the creation structure or life and see what is there. Other planets too are named by the Human being dwelling upon Earth. To name Mars, Mercury or Jupiter there is nothing on those planets. No one exists there to say " I am a being from Mercury or I stay on Mars!" No one other than human being knows whether someone exists there or not. Why? It is because there isn't anyone there. Means except Earth there is neither birth nor death on other planets. No one else other than human being on the Earth can imagine about these planets because there is nobody. Then what is there? The simple answer to this question is 'there is nothing!' No existence of life. 'Nothingness' is the principle of this universe! To imagine this universe or to call it 'universe'; except the mortal human being that is made up of Earth and her related 12 factors, there is no one in this universe. No other planet is in the position similar to Earth that has 12 factors, and so no other planet has the creation-structure similar to Earth.

Why life dwells only on the Earth? ...

If apart from Earth all other planets hold the principle of 'nothingness'; then why only Earth is an exception to it? I have researched it out. You must have studied this book of mine by heart so far. So far, I have given you the brief information about the Earth's creation till date along with the Sun, Moon and the 12 related factors created through her, in it. If you have deeply studied and thought over, you must have realized why there is no life on planets other than Earth? Why is it only on Earth? I have revealed this with a doctrine. **Just the twelve factors we studied so far are responsible for the existence of entire life, your birth on this planet Earth. These twelve factors are never mentioned so far by any saint or the holy books. Or none has preached the knowledge of this reality. So the humankind still lives in the ignorance.**

The twelve factors are responsible for giving you the so called existence!!!...

I have stated the doctrine about non-existence of the reincarnation. This is because, including human being, the birth of entire creation-structure on Earth doesn't happen due to reincarnation but just due to Earth and her related twelve factors and procreation of these animated beings. This means, if we minus these twelve factors, the

Earth too would carry the principle of 'nothingness', without any life on it like other planets. Just due to twelve factors, the life including human being births on this Earth for a short time. The mixture of the twelve factors is birth. After deducting the twelve factors what remains balance is 'nothingness' – the state of being nothing. Means the state of all animated beings along with the human being before birth is - 'nothingness' – non-existence. Means before birth you existed in no other form. Whenever you think about yourself, think about your existence, it means these twelve factors. To understand this thoroughly it is necessary to study Earth and her related twelve factors. Whatever life is taking birth on this Earth, it is nothing other than the play or dance of these twelve factors. With the fraction of reproduction that is held within human and other animate beings, along with the assistance of these twelve factors, creation (birth) takes place. Without the existence of these twelve factors no life will gain any form or existence. For example the root of every bird is the egg. But the creation of that existence, giving egg, happens through another bird. Means, before coming to the state of 'egg' that new bird is in the state of 'nothingness'. Egg brings it to some existence. Similarly all animals along with human are created through the drop of semen. Just one drop of semen is the root of humankind's existence on the Earth. And that too from other humans' semen you are re-produced or procreated. What were you before that? Did you have existence? Where were you? Were on you this Earth? Then how did you come to this Earth? You don't have answers to many such questions. So just from the drop of someone else's semen you are reproduced. That drop of semen too is formed by twelve factors. Wherever these twelve factors do not exist, neither drop of semen is created there nor is anyone born. **You are produced or birthed from other animate being. You weren't anything or anyone before that. This is the doctrine of your 'being nothing' before birth, your creation from 'nothingness'!** Your creation means you entered the illusion. This illusion continues till death. In short, before your creation you exist in 'nothingness'. If you understand this, you will be sure that you weren't anyone before birth. No drop of semen, no creation. It is the same thing with entire living beings. Fertilization of the drop of semen means birth. Was there any existence of you before this drop? It wasn't. Means it will be easier for you to understand that 'nothingness' was the status before birth. This drop of semen was created due to Earth and her related twelve factors. If these twelve factors weren't necessary, the creation structure, the life would have been visible on other planets too.

EARTH TOO HAS A PLACE WHERE DUE TO THE ABSENCE OF ALL TWELVE FACTORS THERE IS NO CREATION-STRUCTURE OR LIFE...

The principle of 'nothingness' doesn't merely apply on other planets. But Earth itself has a place of 14 million sq. km. where just one factor out of twelve factors is missing. That is, there is not enough supply of the sun light. This being the bottom part of the Earth, the sunrays fall askew on this part of Earth. **Due to the unavailability of the sunlight, which is the twelfth factor; this part Antarctica bears the temperature of minus 57 degree Celsius. Any of the life form including human being neither take birth nor die at this place. Not even the micro-organisms invisible to eyes like bacteria are created here. Just one thing exists there, 'nothingness'. If any God, Soul or Super Soul exists as is claimed, why nothing is born at this place due to their existence? If ten pairs of male-female are left at this place, will they be able to reproduce? No! Forget about reproduction, but their existence itself will end at this place. Birth or creation is just the magic of twelve factors! On other parts of the Earth the cycle of creation existence-extinction continues just due to the availability of twelve factors. So only state that remains without the connection of twelve factors is 'nothingness'. Also after severing the connection with twelve factors the status is 'extinction' means death, again 'nothingness'. This Earth holds the principle of reproduction and not reincarnation. Without twelve factors there is no**

reproduction or birth, this is the fact.

THE DOCTRINE ABOUT 'WHAT WERE WE BEFORE OUR BIRTH?'...

You must have realized with the analysis so far that our birth is nothing else but the mixture of the twelve factors. Even with the deduction of single factor creates the situation similar to Antarctica i.e. non creation. Nothing will be born. That means what remains after the deduction of twelve factors from us is 'nothingness'–non-existence. **Are you convinced now that we were 'nothing' before our birth? There is no reincarnation or rebirth, neither due to any Soul, Super Soul nor God. The birth takes place only due to Earth and her twelve factors. This is the answer to the question 'Who or what were you before birth?'**

THE DOCTRINE OF 'WHAT WILL YOU BE AFTER DEATH?'...

Now let us see about 'what happens to you after the death?' You got this birth due to Earth and her twelve factors, which doesn't happen on any other planet. **'Creation existence-extinction' is the law of creation-structure means twelve factors. The human being assumes the existence s/he has received between birth and death to be the reality, the truth and lives the life. And only the human race on the Earth assumes this temporary existence as the truth.** The other animate beings on the Earth do not run after wealth, fame assuming this existence to be the only ultimate truth. So the human being doesn't try to search the truth despite the intelligence it is gifted with. 'Creation-existence-extinction' is the form of twelve factors. The creation takes place due to twelve factors. After creation till death, the twelve factors grant the state of 'existence'. **The day this cord of the twelve factors is severed from you, all life or all animate beings; that day is your and all other animate beings' death or extinction. The end of twelve factors in you is your end. This means you are merged with the truth, the 'nothingness' means non-existence which is the truth.** The time period between birth and death is only an illusion of the humankind. Every human being lives in the illusion. Why do I call it illusion is because none of the events from birth to death are perpetual. What is perpetual or eternal is the truth. 'Existence' is just a delusion. Such delusion is mere illusion. Nonexistence or 'nothingness' is the truth.

Human being and other creation structure come to the illusion for a short time and again merge with the truth. These events happen on the Earth just due to the twelve factors and create illusion. You were nothing before birth. Birth means 12 factors and transformation of these twelve factors into extinction means death. **Means in fact you merge into the status of truth, 'nothingness' which was before the birth itself. There is no Soul, Super Soul, God or reincarnation involved in it. But it is only the creation, existence and extinction of twelve factors. This doctrine of mine is the reality, the truth because this is not my opinion or thought. The time period of non-existence is boundless, whereas the time period of so called 'existence' is short lived, momentary. That is what 'being or existence' is an illusion and 'non-existence or not being' is the truth about.** After you realize this, you will gain the knowledge of how to spend this short lived span of illusionary existence selflessly, without greed and jealousy. Human being will not run after power, wealth and fame. One must earn necessary enough to survive or exist. Anything else earned after that is a waste. Then why to keep collecting, hoarding and waste the life?

YOU MERGE INTO 'NOTHINGNESS' AFTER DEATH…

So the truth remains that you weren't anything before birth and you won't be anything after death. You need not die and experience to understand this. It is because you merge into 'nothingness'. If there is no rebirth or reincarnation then how will be the journey after death? Death ends the journey of so called existence. So there is no journey after death. Before birth, one is born from the 'nothingness'; due to twelve factors enters the so called state of 'existence' and after finishing this period one gets extinct as per the law of creation structure or nature, means 'nothingness is the final state again. Birth is only once and death too is only once. There is nothing before birth and after death. This is the reality. Being a doctrine this is difficult to falsify but in this society there are many conmen and many people who get conned. There is abundance of saints, holy-men amongst the humankind and religious scriptures, mythological holy books who take disadvantage of people. It is because they themselves live in ignorance and run their shops by fooling people.

HUMANKIND MAKES THE MISTAKE OF ASSUMING REPRODUCTION TO BE THE REINCARNATION OR REBIRTH...

Reproduction means producing many from one, which is the law of creation-structure. The perpetual cycle of birth and death continues due to principle of reproduction or procreation. When this process ends the Earth too shall merge into nothingness. But some people from humankind make mistake of assuming reproduction to be the reincarnation. Reproduction and after the end of reproduction, means before birth, and after death there is nothing and this 'nothingness' is the principle of universe. For any extinct or dead human there is neither universe, nor air, nor sun, nor moon, nor water, nor Earth and nothing about self. Just 'nothingness'

THE PERIOD FROM BIRTH TO DEATH IS A COMPLETE ILLUSION...

To lead a happy life human being struggles for entire life to earn property, wealth and fame. And this is his/her illusion, s/he lives in an illusion. Other animate beings or this creation structure has nothing to do with it. **In reality the rich, poor, saint, preacher, leader or prime minister are just the adjectives created by mortal human beings living a momentary life.** For example if some venomous snake is told that this man is a prime minister or leader or rich and don't sting him; that animal has nothing to do with these human created adjectives and he will go on doing his task. Such adjectives don't change the laws of creation-structure.

THE IMPORTANT MESSAGE FOR THE HUMAN BEING...

Oh human! You are gifted with this illusionary existence for a momentary period, how much will you dance within it? Just remember that you shall merge into 'nothingness' at last. One day you have to happily take leave of Mother Earth and her twelve factors, you have to merge into 'nothingness'; keeping this in mind without stocking anything you earn more than necessary while living life, live happily and let others live happily. 'Nothingness' is the principle of this universe... The human being who is gifted with momentary so called existence, that too illusionary, is nothing but a grain of poppy seed in this vast ocean of 'nothingness' in the endless expanse of universe. The idea of the universe's existence is mere manmade. Without human, there is no universe, Sun, Moon or Earth.

'NOTHINGNESS' IS THE ONLY PRINCIPLE OF THIS UNIVERSE...

The momentary existence of the human is not the principle of this universe, but 'nothingness' is the principle. So there is nothing before birth and nothing after death, this is the only truth. Rest things are just the illusionary ideas of human being, owing to his imaginary power.

COMPARE EACH EVENT WITH THE PRINCIPLE OF 'NOTHINGNESS' WHILE LIVING LIFE ...

We ourselves are responsible for the happiness or sorrow. Our actions create these both and everything is illusionary. Every moment of happiness, sorrow or difficulty is illusionary. Every such moment should be compared with the principle of 'nothingness'. Then you won't feel the intensity of any sorrow. This principle of 'nothingness' will be handy for you to live happy and peaceful life without hoarding. After all you shall be free to bid farewell to this Earth and her twelve factors happily. It is because you get merged with the original state, i.e. the state before your birth of 'nothingness', the state of truth.

****

7.2

What Is The Purpose of Creation Structure To Birth You?

Human Birth

Just One Illusion, Means Falsehood…

Creation Is The Root Cause Of Sorrow and Death!!

I have defined the rule of creation 'Creation is the root cause of destruction and sorrow'! What is birth? Birth is the selfishness of the creation structure. This causes the cycle of birth and death on the Earth. It is not pleasing but filled with the sorrow! So birth is not an event of celebration! By birthing someone you throw that person into the valley of trials till death and cause him or her unlimited sorrows! Have you ever thought of the price paid for your five minute inter-course fun by the new born? Now read O animate, your story of birth!!!…

The ceaseless cycle of life and death continues on our Earth since past 2.5 million years. At the birth time of the first human, all the Earth related twelve factors necessary for human birth were present. They also included the gravitational power of the Mother Earth. The first human that the creation structure birthed didn't have a developed brain and was in the wild state. According to the Darwinism theory of evolution, with the progress of the time the human brain developed further. We are seeing the evolved human of the 21st century today. Even today the body is not obtained without the Earth related twelve factors. All animates including human are nothing else but the mixture of these twelve factors.

Human is a mammal. When the man and a woman were created on the plane of Earth, the creation structure endowed the woman with the ability and responsibility of the new creation. During the intercourse between the man and woman the live sperms of a man help the egg in woman's womb fertilize which forms the fetus. By supplying the necessary Earthly twelve factors to this fetus through the umbilical cord, the woman nourishes the fetus. She delivers the full grown baby in due course of time. The umbilical cord connected with the human mother is severed after the birth as that with the Mother Earth is connected. Mother Earth nourishes the neo natal with the twelve factors. The creation structure has kept the responsibility of the nurturance and upbringing of the new born on its creator.

What is the root of each animate? The invisible sperm! The fraction of reproduction!!!...

The human infant is the new born animate. Despite being created through the fusion of sperm and egg of the male–female, no one on the Earth has got the power to create it from the air on their own! It is made up of the mixture of twelve factors which I described earlier in the last chapter. This egg or sperm is nothing else but the microscopic prototype of that particular animates' body. It has all the creative potential of that particular animate including the body parts. When this sperm develops into the miniature body, the Mother Earth takes the responsibility of it. You are only the medium! Take an example of the banyan tree. The microscopic prototype of the large banyan tree is embedded into its tiny poppy seed! Such seed gets the body with the help of twelve factors which grows further into a large banyan tree.

See how each animate reproduces! Two types of the mobile animates!!!...

According to the law of creation structure, the reproductive potential is embedded in each animate at its time of birth. This ensures the continuation of the cycle of reproduction on the plane of Earth. Once the animate grows to the adulthood from the microscopic existence, s/he reproduces again. This principle is applicable to every animate on the Earth. The immobile animates usually have their reproductive potential inbuilt with their seeds. Also the first existence of each animate is in the form of a tiny seed. The mobile animates have two broad types; mammals or vertebrates and egg laying invertebrates. It refers to two different methods of reproduction. Mammals reproduce through the female womb while egg laying animates reproduce by hatching the eggs laid by the female externally.

THE ONLY INTENTION OF CREATION STRUCTURE BEHIND BIRTH IS THE REPRODUCTION!!!...

Reproduction and continuation of the life cycle is the only aim of creation structure behind birthing of human or any other animates! Being rich, poor, achieving big business success, being prime minister or a quake or insane or philosopher none of this is intended by the creation structure! Just to continue the new life is the intention behind your birth. The life gained from birth to death is just for this cause. Once this is over your work is over as far as creation structure is concerned! Means 100% your death! If you read this book carefully and study the creation structure, you will realize that each birth of an animate is an illusion and illusion is always false. So being born is also false. This is the secret of the birth.

WITH THE BIRTH THERE IS DEATH AND IT IS A STATUTORY LAW OF THE CREATION STRUCTURE!!!...

According to the rule of the creation structure, 'creation is the root cause of the destruction.' **There is no animate on this Earth who is born and has planted itself here permanently! Death is inevitable to each animate. The birth may be an illusion, but the death is the truth!** Friends, what would have happened in the absence of the death? This cycle of creation structure will cease. This cycle is on because there is death along with birth. What causes birth? The Mother Earth with her twelve factors! There is no birth on Moon, Mars, Venus or any other planet. Twelve factors is birth. The absence or reduction increment of any single factor out of these twelve factors would halt the process of birth. This creation cycle will not be on.

Creation is the real cause of destruction and sorrow! Check my personal experience!!!...

Till now I haven't shared my personal thoughts in this book. But I would like to share here how I think that birth is a punishment. I am 69 years old as of today. If I look back at the challenges and trials I faced since my childhood till now, I feel the birth that I have received is a tremendous punishment! I recommend reading the chapter 'Me' in my 1st book 'Me, Earth and the Travel' for more explanation. After taking the birth whether one has come with a silver spoon in the mouth or is born clever, intelligent; s/he has to face the trial each day. Means facing trials, giving tests for lifetime is the punishment! After coming out of the mother's womb the survival needs start. To meet these needs one has to face various tests. For any animate birth is a punishment. The lioness gives birth to 4-5 cubs. An unbreakable relationship of affection is formed between the cubs and the mother. According to the creation structure, she has to nurture and grow these cubs by giving them necessary milk, food and care. Cubs too play with her affectionately, with abiding faith. They tease her; she teaches them and cares for them. Suddenly some other lion sees her, but she doesn't get ready for copulation as she has the responsibility of her small cubs. So the male, the lion removes the difficulty in the copulation, by killing these cubs one by one! Think of it. New born cubs loose their life as they or anyone couldn't protect them from the attack of the lion. If they weren't born, would they undergo this punishment? Such is not only the case of the lion. Even in humans, some mother carries the child in the womb for full nine months and leaves it in the dustbin. For that new born, this birth is such a tremendous punishment!

In my city Pune of India in Asia, when I halt at the traffic signal I often see the view of 4–5 nude kids begging on the road. I wonder if at a tender age such a tremendous punishment of asking alms, then what challenges their life would lead them further into! Well, this punishment is not just the case in a poor person's life. Even someone born rich may experience birth as a tremendous punishment.

I happened to visit one filthy rich family's house once. I was shocked to see one of their children. A body bent at various places was sitting on a chair. Perhaps she was around 20 years of age. Her hands, legs, eyes everything was bent! She couldn't do any movement without the help of other person. Seeing her thought crossed my mind – 'It is ok till her parents are alive; they will serve her but what after them? What a tremendous punishment the birth received by this girl is, isn't it?'

So I call birth a curse!!!...

Any animate whether born rich and healthy lives the life full of difficulties and necessities till the death! His needs are never fulfilled till the death. If someone has 10 factories he gets the need to start the 11th factory! But before fulfilling it, he dies! Someone dreams of being a prime minister but reaches to the minister ship somehow and dies without fulfilling the desire to be a prime minister! So the birth doesn't become a happy and fulfilled experience but a sad curse!

Well, this is not just the case with the humans, but even with the immobile animates! Some small sapling that has been planted looks so tender and green! But while growing it has to undergo so many trials. It has to endure the blazing Sun, beating rain storms, freezing and drying cold winter. Also with the blows of hurricane its branches can break or the tree itself collapses or one day some animal called human comes and cuts that tree into pieces! So, no animate that has taken birth is happy! Birth is a curse! That is why the saints of all religions have prayed to their Gods for the salvation! "O' God, Please liberate from the cycle of the births and deaths!"

Who is really happy, joyous and needless person?...

In English we say 'Who is happy? The one who is unborn!' Then someone may ask, "Then shouldn't anyone birth someone?" I will say, think ten times before birthing anyone! You have been given the desire of sex for the continuation of the cycle of the creation structure! We can say it is creation structure's selfishness! Well, in the evolved animates like animals and human; without the desire of sex would the cycle of birth continue? No!

WHY PEOPLE SAY DEATH IS BETTER THAN BIRTH?...

Every animate has the fear of some or the other thing till death, like diseases in case of humans. Accidents make someone lose their limbs or someone dies of pain. Some animates get cancer. The treatment method of cancer is so painful like chemotherapy or radiation that one would prefer the death to the pain of treatment! Patients die of the pain! In the human race, some find the traditions, rituals or even transactions so difficult to deal with their existence that they commit suicide! Like lovers who are not able to meet due to the barriers of traditions, race or nationality; or gays who are not able to cope up with the prevalent homophobic culture, or people who are unfit to cope up with the competitive society! They find the death better than continuing their life with the unbearable burdens.

FOR WHOM SHOULD WE TAKE BIRTH AND EMBRACE THE DEATH? IS IT FOR THE FILTHY RICH AND SELFISH PEOPLE?...

So many soldiers have died fighting the wars imposed on them by their selfish politicians, in the cute name of 'serving the nation'; and also while protecting these politicians! Who do they spend their valuable life for? For the selfish politicians and people who have no value of their martyrdom! And these politicians continue staying in posh ranches, bungalows and apartments, travel in luxurious cars, commit frauds and live on the blood of ignorant masses! Also the industrialists keep just the one intention–that of earning money from the masses by sublimely dumping unnecessary products and utilities on them! Why should the soldiers and security forces die for these selfish rich businessmen and leaders? What about the commoner? Their life anyway is a living death that they experience daily! So whether they die or not, doesn't make the difference! The protection is only applicable to the rich and famous and fraud politicians! But the commoners pay the taxes for this protection force!

SOLDERS DIE; THE LEADERS APPEAL THE MASSES FOR THE HELP IN DONATIONS BUT DON'T SPEND A SINGLE PENNY FROM THEIR TREASURE!!!...

During all riots the commoners suffer in any country! Have you heard of any rich, famous or politician getting injured or die during such cases? They are sitting in their protected air conditioned cars, offices or homes. The initiators of riots get the highest rank of protections. So for those commoners who die; the life becomes a curse! During the calamities the masses die in the number of thousands, the fraud politicians compete with each other under the vanity of their 'service' to the masses but appeal to the masses for financial help! They don't spend a single penny from their treasures to help the victims! I haven't heard so far about some politician or rich person's wealth being opened for victims of calamity, have you heard? On the contrary there are examples of the collected funds being fleeced by the politicians or the trustees! What kind of leaders are these! The commoners are getting poor and these leaders and the rich few feeding them are getting richer day by day. Is the life of a commoner destined to lift the burdens of these people? Are their lives to die in the wars of this group's egoism?

ARE THEY REALLY BLESSED?...

So many people, especially children die of malnutrition in various developing and underdeveloped countries. The leaders too call it a thing of shame. Then isn't the birth of these children a curse to them? Isn't here the 'creation' the root cause of destruction?

Out of 7000 million people on this Earth how many of them are truly enjoying the blessed life? So many of them don't have the shelters to live or proper food to eat or healthy fresh water to drink. Do they enjoy the life? If after birth they are living in such inhuman conditions, aren't their lives a curse?

So the one who has taken the birth should think ten times about his/her own conditions and if they themselves are not able to enjoy the life, why to birth someone and penalize their lives? So, in truth isn't the one who is not born actually happy? Hence the sages and saints have been asking for the liberation from the cycle of birth and death!

CHECK THESE FEW LARGE COUNTRIES! THEY ARE ENJOYING THE LIFE DUE TO LESS POPULATION!!!...

The copulation is the root of the birth of all animates. It is a curse for them! Is it correct to birth someone for your five minutes' pleasure? The societies with high population and their governments must consider this fact! It is better to have a lesser population from the point of view of everyone's benefit, their abundance. I have visited Australia-New Zealand twice. The country of Australia is almost two and a half times bigger in the size than my country India. But the population of this large country is just 20 million! India has a population of 1250 million! Australia's public enjoys the abundance of the resources due to less population ratio compared to the area and resources. The bus on route number 35 of city Melbourne is running free for the passengers (that is when I visited). The population of the country New Zealand is just 4.5 million. The people of this country are well to do. Each person carries a cattle wealth of 10 ships. There is an abundance of fruits and milk and milk products.

VERY FEW ADOPT POLITICS TO SERVE THE NATION OR MASSES IN THE TRUE SENSE!!!...

Contrary is the picture in the developing or underdeveloped countries. The population is inversely proposal to the area of the nation. The governments hesitate to control the population due to religious and traditional norms in such countries like Pakistan, India, China, countries of African continent. It is a fact that in some nations; politics is a profession or business rather than a means of public service! So the commoners birthed by the commoner cannot live their lives happily in such countries. One shouldn't be born. But if one is born in such conditions, considering the national conditions, what precautions should one take to lead a happy and enjoyable life? I am going to share my two cents about this further!

****

7.3

Just The Illusions From The Birth Till The Death!

Everything Has A Different Root!

All Vision Is An Illusion!!

'Everything that you see here is an illusion' understanding this is finding the way to the happy life!!!...

Everything that is visible to your eyes in this world is an illusion. The white colored sunlight as it appears too is an illusion, because sunlight is made up of seven colors. Combined together they give the white color. The green color of the leaves as it is visible too is an illusion. The leaf absorbs 6 colors barring seven colors of the sunshine, so they appear to be green as that unabsorbed color is reflected back to our eyes. If the leaves absorbed all the seven colors, they would appear white to our eyes! The root of every visible thing is different here. Sky appears to be blue but in reality it is black! Blue color which is not absorbed by the gases of the environment is reflected back to our eyes and hence sky appears to be blue. The fresh water that you drink has its root in the salty sea water. Water is the mixture of two gases but it doesn't stay after the decomposition. The food we eat, rice and bread has their roots in the rice and wheat. This too is the mixture of the twelve factors on the Earth. Without these twelve factors no rice, no wheat!

The rising of the Sun on the eastern sky and setting on the western sky too is an illusion. Sun is steady on its place. He doesn't budge an inch from his place. The phases of Moon is also an illusion which makes the Moon seems to be getting bigger for 15 days and getting smaller for another 15 days. In reality the Moon's size doesn't change. The lunar and solar eclipses you see in the sky too are the illusions. Actually real Sun and real Moon never gets eclipsed. The sizes you see of the Sun and Moon in the sky are also the illusions! Their actual sizes are different.

You feel your parents birthed you and gave you the body. But actually the sperm and egg that made you are made up of the mixture of the twelve factors which I described earlier. You have been birthed by the Mother Earth. So many such examples can be given. Whatever appears is not the reality and hence as you don't know your real identity, the life that you live too is an illusion. Anything that is visible on the Mother Earth is birthed by the Mother Earth and gets merged in her.

The things that you hold, the wealth that you gather, the fame and big positions which you achieve are all illusions. Who has taken along with them any of these things so far? Means the things s/he gathered never belonged to him/her but it was just the assumption of belonging! This is an illusion. 'I am not mine' this is the reality. You do not belong to yourself. Then who is wife, son or daughter? Who is rich and poor? Who is prime minister, major general or president? Everything is an illusion!

Check how the person lives in an illusion!!!...

Including human each animate is born in an illusion and dies in an illusion. So nothing here is permanent. The joy that you get or the sorrow that you experience, all is an illusion. My joy can be the sorrow of someone else. Some needy person receives a note of 100 dollars on the road. This can be a joyful thing for him, but the sorrow for the other who lost it on the road! You disdain garbage and the insects, pigs are fond of it. Someone's young son dies and he will be in the deep pain, but some one not associated with them would be oblivious to this pain, isn't it? This world would be a joyous and easy if each person realizes about how illusionary this world is! No one will do injustice with anyone else; no one will snatch from others. There won't be corrupt leaders and so no one will starve on the Earth! No one would siphon the funds raised for the good cause and there will be the proper utilization of such funds! No wars, no dumping tactics between nations!

What is the successful life?...

This world is much an illusion. While living in such world one must drop 'me' and 'mine' and enjoy the nature on the Earth. Earn with your own work sufficient enough for yourself. Once you have earned enough for your own needs, make an opportunity of earning available to others and one day happily take leave of the Mother Earth! This is truly successful life!

'Change' is the rule of the creation. We are living according to this rule!!!...

'Change' is the mother of the illusion! With death, the change is over and illusion too gets over. In this world, nothing is constant or steady. Feeling of steadiness is itself an illusion. You are staying on this Earth. You sit, stand, eat, roam and stay in houses. You feel the land you are staying on is steady. You traverse but you don't see the land beneath your feet traversing. This is such a big illusion! You feel you are steady. But you are not. This too is your illusion. The land beneath your feet is traversing at the speed of 30 KM per second around the Sun. So you too are traversing along with the Mother Earth at the speed of 30 KM per second around the Sun! Every second along with your other routine movements, you are also revolving with the Mother Earth. Means change is happening at every second!

What would have been the scene without 'change'? We wouldn't have been born!!!...

The steady thing is a dead thing! When someone dies, the twelve factors have left his body. So his movement stops and he is declared to be dead. You purchase someone's land. But before this transaction, the land belongs to someone else. S/he may have taken that land from someone else. There would be hundreds of owners of this place after you. Means change is permanent. So many people have born on this Earth and died so far. Further so many will be born and die. Till date, no one has stayed forever on this Earth. Then your imaginary God too is not an exception to this. Each day has a morning, noon, evening and night. This change is constantly happening. The crops grown are eaten and finished by animates. Again new crop is sown and grown. No crop has lasted forever so far. It is always replaced by the new crop. The same thing happens in case of each animate.

'Change' is life!!!...

Change is the nature of a human. We cannot sit constant at one place, we always need change. Then you will ask what about the immobile animates? Even if they appear to be steady, they aren't steady. Also if you observe carefully, you will see the minute changes daily in them. We don't like to eat same food each day, do we? We need the change, the variety in it. The fruits and vegetables too change with the season. You get mangoes, water melons in abundance during summer, while cherries, grapes are in abundance during winter. The Sun that you see too is not steady. He too is revolving around the galaxy along with his eight planets. Since all these planets are revolving with the same speed, the Sun appears to be steady to us.

Understand this significance of change!!!...

Change is the law of nature, of the creation structure! Now let us think, what will be the consequences in the absence of the change. There would be no reproduction from the sperm, because the sperm will remain as it is! It won't move or change to cause the formation of zygote and fetus. Means no one will be born. If there is no change, how will there be a new formation? And how will the existing people die? Because 'no change' won't cause any change in the age! If the existing people won't die, what will happen? Such a chaos it would be! Demons would still have still been existing and Nazi still would have been alive with his tyranny! The wars wouldn't have ended ever! Neither I would have existed to write this book nor would you have existed to read it!

Without change how the salty water would change to the fresh water? How new crop, new inventions would take place? Has anyone ever thought of this? No, never!

Due to change, the seasons change. It causes the creation of the new animates. Old leaves are dropped and are replaced by new foliage. There is a constant change in the life on Earth, the creation structure; the nature on Earth and due to this phenomenon of 'change' the life dwells on the Earth.

ILLUSION AND CHANGE ARE THE TWO SIDES OF THE LIFE'S COIN! NO ONE CAN GO AGAINST THIS LAW OF CREATION!!!...

Human is so engrossed with the mundane life that instead of checking on such questions related to their life they just spend their valuable time of life only in eating, drinking, possessing, earning fame and merry. No priest tells you, no preacher preaches you the laws of creation. Illusion and change are the two sides of the life's coin. No one can go against it. The human should realize using whatever intelligence s/he has got that all that is going on is an illusion! So as long as you are alive; nothing is as valuable as your joyous, happy and healthy existence. This must be imbibed in your mind and according should be your endeavors.

ON THIS PLANE OF EARTH NOTHING IS AS VALUABLE AS YOUR EXISTENCE!!!...

After taking the birth, this doctrine is very important according to the creation structure. This sentence has a great meaning embedded. But despite the power of thought, imagination and intelligence no human ever understands this value of happy and healthy existence. He just indulges into eating, drinking, collecting possessions for the entire life and departs from this plane.

Now I am going to explain here the importance of your happy and healthy existence. You may think that the existence of Sun, Moon, Earth and other stars is far greater than your own existence. But your healthy and happy existence is far greater than them! Your happy and healthy existence itself is this Sun, Moon, Earth, parents, kids, brothers and sisters, friends, wonderful snowy mountains, trees, soft bed, juicy fruits, tasty food. Everything is alive here on this Earth just due to your healthy and happy existence. If you have a good health, good cheerful clear mind, everything around you is good and cheerful, entire creation is soulful, spiritual! But if your health is not good and your mind is sorrowful, then the Sun, Moon and the Earth and nature are useless! If your stomach is upset and I serve you the great tasty food, would you enjoy it? If your existence ends, then no Earth, no Sun and no Moon, no tasty food and no possessions! No honor, no positions! So no parents, no relatives or anyone else is more valuable than your happy and healthy existence. I will explain this further in the next chapter.

7.4

My New Doctrine!

Nothing, No Relation Is More Valuable Than Your Happy and Healthy Existence!

This Is The Law Of Creation!

More valuable than prime minister, president or any millionaire industrialist is the happy and healthy existence!!!...

Friends, while living the life this principle must be remembered, rather around this principle should dwell your life that; when does the Earth, Sun, Moon and this world hold the value for you? Only when you have an existence! To the one whose existence ended or who is non-existent, none of these things matter! Earth, Sun, Moon or anything, everything will be a big zero to them. Let us think of a president. The title of presidency bears such an importance for the countrymen. But whosoever is carrying that position, is carrying it due to his or her existence. With that person's existence that position is important, not otherwise. More valuable than that position is the happy and healthy existence of that person. Would it be possible to label someone as 'rich', 'president', 'intelligent', 'number one' or 'minister' without the existence of that person? What is the validity of these labels? It is valid till the happy and healthy existence of that person!

One boy has healthy and happy parents and siblings. But he is bed ridden due to illness. So actually having healthy parents and siblings is of no use to this boy, isn't it? He cannot share their good health. Even parents cannot give their health to their child.

So priceless is your existence!!!...

It doesn't matter if you don't get fame or position; but your happy and healthy existence is important! Human race strives till the death for the name, fame, position and wealth but departs from this Earth and lies permanently flat one day. If we keep all his titles, positions, fame, property documents and wealth besides him and tell "this is what you have been struggling for lifelong, get up once just for two minutes and see it all at once"; he won't ever be able to do that. Means his existence was more important than all this, isn't it? Without his existence it is all useless to him. All his wealth and titles and clout with rich and famous cannot bring back his existence. So while living, even if anyone insults you, did injustice with you or caused you the loss or some close relative died– anything unpleasant or unwanted happens, you must live with the principle that nothing is as valuable as your joyous and healthy existence!

The person immersed in emotions cannot ever live a happy and joyous life!!!...

In front of above principle, all relationships are false, because each animate comes with an independent life existence! According to the law of creation structure, the mother has to birth and nurture the child. But their existences are pretty independent. They are not related to each other. Both have different hunger at different times. Feeding the child doesn't quench the mother's thirst and hunger. Both have to take their appropriate food separately. So if someone is swept in emotions; s/he seldom gets happiness and joyous life. The life must be lived and enjoyed with the awareness of a reality around. To live according to this principle, some rules must be observed in the life which I shall describe further.

This is my own principle; formed after the experience and observation of the life and I feel it is very useful to the human life.

Neither be too materialistic nor be too emotional. Here is the proof for this principle!!!...

Once I had gone to the market to buy water melon. I asked the hawker to check for melon to ensure that it would be red inside and will have a sweet taste. Accordingly he showed me one melon and said 'Sir, this is good' and told me the price. I bargained as I felt the price was high. But he wasn't ready for the bargain and told that it was a very good melon and so no bargain. So I accepted the price and asked him to cut the melon to check how it was. When he cut the melon, instead of having juicy red pulp which usually it has, it turned out to be clean white inside! So told him that I wanted the ripe, red melon but contrary to his claim this one wasn't the same and denied to purchase it. But then he was furious! He started arguing loudly and yelling at me. Since he had cut the melon, even if it wasn't good he insisted that I must pay him. I decided that the peace of my mind was more important than his fury and yelling and so I gave him the money and left the melon too with him! Rather than repenting on that money I was happy to get rid of that quarrelsome person! We do face such different situations in the life. The key is to value our peace, happiness and health and not money!

RESULT OF BEING TOO EMOTIONAL OR TOO MATERIALISTIC!!!...

Check what happens if we value the money over our existence. I knew a very healthy person. Once, one young man came to him for some recovery of money. He informed about the pending balance of two months. The healthy person denied it and told that he had already paid the money. But the young man was not ready to accept it.

The arguments came to blow and finally the person said "I won't give the money, no matter what you do!"

"You just step down below the building and see what can I do!" the young boy replied furiously and left the place!

This remark triggered the person's anger further and he picked up the receiver of the phone saying "you threatening moron! I will call the police!!" Before he could dial the number he got an intense heart attack and he sat back with the receiver in the hand permanently! He died on the spot! For a frivolous matter over money his existence ended forever!

IT IS VERY CRUCIAL TO KNOW THE IMPORTANCE OF FIRST AND THE LAST BIRTH THAT WE HAVE RECEIVED HERE!!!...

People go to the level of murders from frivolous arguments. If the people understand that nothing is more valuable than their happy and healthy existence, such incidents won't happen. Friends, I am writing this for you. Do use my principle that I stated earlier 'there is nothing as valuable as your happy and healthy existence!' For humans there is nothing really as valuable. You don't have past birth and you won't have further birth. All you know is this birth. You must decide how valuable it is, because you have received the thinking power, intelligence and imagination power.

I will be establishing the doctrine further of 'Only once you come to this life; there is no reincarnation'. So such an invaluable human birth cannot be compared to any manmade precious thing! Then perseverance and taking the joy of such life must be the motto of each person.

RATHER THAN TRYING TO TEACH THE WISDOM TO THE MEAN AND SELFISH RELATIVES, WIFE, HUSBAND, PARENTS OR SIBLINGS WE SHOULD GET WISE!!!...

We perform various roles in the life and deal with many relations like spouse, children, parents, close relatives and friends. Many times we don't get along with the closest of the relationship like spouse or siblings etc. Someone's wife may be very spiteful woman or husband may be male chauvinistic, irresponsible. Some relatives are very mean and selfish. Spouse is less educated, ignorant or stupid, immature. Everyone has more or less unpleasant nuances. Then how should one deal with such people? How to survive the married life with an incompatible in–law and spouse? You are married but the spouse is irrecoverable from his or her bad habits then what should one do? If making them understand is not going to work, if they are not going to improve; you should improve your way of dealing with them. Means the marriage should continue but if it is a quarrelsome marriage then you should seek the way out rather than wasting your life behind such person. Leave the expectations from the other person and find the harmless things that bring you the happiness in life. You need not break the marriage, but develop your own harmless lifestyle and keep the conversation limited to avoid the fights and arguments. You can develop good hobbies like music, going to concerts, painting, travelling and enjoying the nature. But you must deliver your family duties as husband or wife or son or whatever role(s) you are playing in the relationship. But don't waste your life for such relative(s). But this calls for a financial independence whether you are a husband or wife, man or a woman. Else you won't be able to live the life happily. How to be financially independent? I have explained this further.

So far I have travelled much all over the Earth. I have seen many married men or women travelling alone and enjoying the travel.

EACH ANIMATE IS BIRTHED SEPARATE AND INDEPENDENT OF EACH OTHER! NO UNDUE INTERDEPENDENCE! EVERYONE'S HAPPINESS AND SORROW IS DIFFERENT AND NO ONE CAN SHARE IT FULLY!!!...

Don't give undue importance to unnecessary things over your happy and healthy existence; because without such existence your life is a big zero! Suppose you birthed a moron son. With many efforts there is no sign or improvement in him. Then you must leave his life onto his destiny after doing the necessary duties possible towards him. It is useless to spoil your own invaluable life with undue worries and unnecessary wastage of the time on him; because you don't get this life again! Every animate is born independently and has independent life. Your own sorrows are to be endured personally by you; others cannot endure them for you.

Suppose someone pricks the pin to your child, he will have to endure those pains; you cannot actually sense and share them. Yes, you can apply balm, cuddle him affectionately and offer the words of courage. So everyone's joy, happiness and sorrow is personal, others cannot share it. These things are purely person dependent or relative. So in this world, your position, relation, and wealth nothing is more valuable than your happy and healthy existence. Lead your life by keeping this principle in the mind and lead the content, happy life so that you can also let other partake the joy and happiness.

****

7.5

One More Law Of Creation Structure

HUNGER MEANS THE LIVING & NON LIVING CREATION..!

OH HUMAN! THE ENTIRE LIVING AND NON-LIVING CREATION IS ENCOMPASSED IN THE SINGLE WORD 'HUNGER'. 'SATISFYING THE HUNGER IS LIFE AND UNMET HUNGER IS DEATH' THIS TELLS THE IMPORTANCE OF THIS WORD! FRIENDS, EVEN IF YOUR TUMMY IS FILLED AT PRESENT, LET US KNOW WHAT ACTUALLY IS THE 'HUNGER'?...

Actually human is very fortunate to possess the gift of thinking and imagination power which no other animates have. I am saying this because whatever I am going to explain should be known to everyone but barring human, it is of no use to any other animate. Other animates lack the intelligence, imagination power and thinking power. Of course, despite having these powers much of the humankind uses less or 'misuses' these powers. So it leaves less difference between humans and other animates! For example, I just said **'hunger means the 'living and non-living creation'**, did you understand how? If you understood it, very good, if not, please read on what I have explained further.

'HUNGER' IS THE LIFE, THE SPIRIT AND EXISTENCE. THE ONE WITHOUT 'HUNGER' IS A DEAD!!!...

This living and non-living creation happens due to 'hunger'. So I have made the sentence 'Hunger is the life and spirit, the one without hunger is as good as a dead.'

All mobile and immobile animates take birth with a hunger. Just within sometime after the delivery of the baby from the mothers' womb, it gets hungry. It cries to convey this need. It becomes quite only after getting mother's milk. Also amongst all animals what is the task of the calf or cub once it comes out of their mother's womb? It searches for the mother's breasts for milk! It is the hunger that gives it the natural instinct for this search! His or her existence depends upon feeding this hunger. So this living and non-living creation exists due to hunger. The types of hunger grow with the growth of the animate. Oh, yes! Forgot to mention here that 'hunger' is not just for food, but hunger is for many things. In short, 'hunger' means 'need'. Once the child is born, after meeting the hunger of milk it needs cloths to protect it from the cold, winds and Sun. As the body grows the types of hunger or demands grow. It needs toys and a food other than milk. Then it needs the knowledge of colloquial language, then notebooks and books. This is for humans. Other animates have different types of hungers for their existence. The wild cub needs the other food of meat after feeding on mothers' milk for some time. Also until the cubs are capable of satisfying their hunger independently, the mother has to feed their hunger. Then she teaches them to hunt and also fulfils the need of their protection in her own way. Else any other wild animal would eat these helpless cubs. More or less similar is the case of human kids.

Check how unmet hunger causes death!!!...

Of course there are many exceptions in case of a human. Sometimes the new born is thrown in the dustbin or sometimes the parents themselves end the existence of their kid. Sometimes the old parents are thrown out of their house by their own kids. We see such examples in the humankind. Hunger also exists for immobile animates. After the germination in the soil, the seed needs water and other twelve factors, support and food. Else that sapling will not grow. Without water it will get dry and its existence will end.

See how different types of hunger are created!!!...

According to one's age the type of hungers change in the human. During school days along with the hunger of food, clothing and shelter; there is a need for knowledge or education. After education the hunger of earning is created. During youth the hunger for companionship and sex arises.

Next arises the hunger for birthing offspring and then the hunger for their care, affection and love. Till death there are such many types of hungers.

Unmet hunger can cause the person to commit suicide! Here is the case!!!...

Much is encompassed in this single word 'hunger'. Not all people's hunger for whatever I have described above is always met. If the hunger is not fed, it affects the life adversely. Those who cannot feed their hunger and have no other way; turns to be beggars. Hunger is a thing that makes one do the strange things! You may be very intelligent, very knowledgeable; but in front of your hunger these things prove to be useless at times. I would share my own case here. Food was scarce during my childhood. No food was available enough to fill the tummy. In those days, I have literally eaten the banana peels thrown by the people on the road to fill my tummy! Later at a very young age I carried the responsibility to feed myself. The work I used to do those days wasn't able to feed my hunger two times. I used to attend the night school only on one meal after the work. One day after coming back from my porterage work I sat at the table in the regular inn at twelve in the noon as usual. Just then the new owner who had come there for some period in place of the old owner came to me and asked me to pay the balance amount for the month. I didn't have a single penny at that nick of time. I had no way to survive further. With the thought of 'getting food seems difficult henceforth' I tried to commit suicide that time. Just before the final action I thought of making a request to that owner once again and turned back. I convinced the owner about the money and he allowed me to have the only meal I used to have! The mention of this situation and the importance of hunger you will get to read in elaboration in my first book "Me, Earth and Travel" which is already published in Marathi language. Do read the book when it gets published in English.

'Hunger' is applicable to all animates. No king, rich or poor or intellectual person can escape from it!!!...

According to the rule of the creation structure all animates on the Earth are given the hunger. Hunger doesn't have discrimination. It doesn't happen that someone has great wisdom so he doesn't get hungry. Also it is unlikely that someone is a great king so he doesn't need to satisfy hunger. He too has the hunger. Accordingly even if someone is poor, insane from the human concept or disabled; each has the hunger to fill the tummy. Creations' rules are the same to all whether one is human or bird, animal or plant. All animates are same to her. We will not find any animate being on the Earth who does not have the hunger. Realizing this rule of creation, humankind must collect just sufficient to let others also get their share of food!!

There are yet more types of hunger!!!...

There are many types of hunger. Described above was the hunger of food. Similar to the hunger of food; all mobile animates have the hunger of the copulation or love making. The same hunger is expressed in a different way amongst the immobile animates. The reproduction takes place in immobile animates through pollination or air. As the animate being is given the hunger for food to sustain the bodily existence, the hunger for copulation is given for the continuation of the creation cycle. The mobile animates are divided between male and female for this purpose. Both are given the desire for copulation by creation structure. Through their copulation the new creation takes place and the cycle of creation continues perpetually. As it is important to satisfy the hunger of food, it is also necessary to satisfy the hunger of copulation. Dissatisfaction of this need can cause the wars amongst the mobile animate beings. Many wars among human race are caused for the 'female' so far or for the desired mate. The hunger for copulation is applicable to all living beings for reproduction and it is a rule of the creation structure.

These days this hunger for copulation has taken a different turn in humankind. Copulation with many females or many males can cause the disease of AIDS in males and females respectively. Earlier the kings used to maintain the harem but there weren't the viruses like HIV.

The root of human trafficking or prostitution is hunger!!!...

There is no country without prostitution, and human trafficking has different forms. These prostitutes, male or female as they are these days have no liking for this profession, but to feed the hunger of food for which they find no other way, or find this profession as an easier way; they agree to sell their bodies. Their existence is preserved by feeding the hunger of belly through this profession. It is not a surprise to note that many women in Asian countries like India satisfy the hunger of their old parents, younger siblings and run their livelihood by selling their bodies. Such is an importance of the hunger.

Hunger creates the relationships!!!...

This hunger has created the relationships like parents and children. Parents feed the hunger of their children and nurture them, raise them. Sometimes the situation is opposite. Sometimes for the food person steals. Actually any manipulation like stealing and lying is not inborn to the humans but the hunger and situations make them do such things.

The politicians and social elites are responsible for the hunger victims in Asia and Africa!!!...

Poor and developing nations in Asian and African continents always face hunger deaths. Some countries are so cultured, like India in Asia. But see the prevailing social systems and the politicians. So many children die of malnutrition in this country. But millions of tons of crop decays due to the lack of proper storage systems and policies. Politicians and elite socialites have nothing to do with this. In fact the elite businessmen await such opportunities to produce beer and wine from such cheap decayed crop. They are more interested in snatching the bite from the hungry people's mouth and produce wine and beer for their own inflated profits! Friends, do you know what type of 'hunger' they have? Hunger of hoarding lot of wealth by keeping others hungry! This is also a type of hunger, isn't it?!

PUTTING EFFORTS TO FEED THE HUNGER OR THE AVAILABILITY OF FOOD TO FEED THE HUNGER IS NECESSARY, ELSE DEATH IS INEVITABLE!!!...

Since the creation structure has given each animate the need of 'hunger' each one has to try to satisfy this need. If some lioness sits relaxed and bored under the shadow of tree saying 'let me leave that search for hunt and running behind it and who knows after so much running around whether you get it…better relax!' and sits without doing anything then due to not satisfying the hunger she and her cubs will die of hunger, isn't it? Not feeding the hunger means embracing the death. Some nations face a tremendous draught some year. During this draught, forget about the food but even a drop of water is hard to find! The wild lives in the forests i.e. lion, tiger, elephants die writhing in pain of hunger and thirst. Also due to hunger and thirst many tame animals like cattle of the farmers die. There are so many examples of human death due to non-availability of water & food.

BUT THE HUMAN HAS GOT A CURSE OF SO MANY TYPES OF 'HUNGERS'!!!...

Human race doesn't have only the hunger of food. Unlike other animates, the human is cursed with many types of 'hungers'. Someone has the appetite for power and are ready to do anything for that. Some have the hunger for wealth, more and more wealth! They work till death, ignoring their other duties towards family, friends or society. Some have the hunger of more and more profits. They create the vaccines, drugs which will entrap the common people in continuous health hazards; so these 'profit hungry' people can sell their medicines and mint money from the masses! Most of the drug making multinationals are into this. These profits are shared with the selfish politicians who just wish to control masses. Leaders are hungry of fame and credit! To get that fame they gather others and get themselves honored with phony awards and showy endeavors.

Some people have the giant hunger of snatching other's land and property with unfair means and they even commit murders for estate and property. With the appetite of power they murder the people who talk against them. They make someone else the scapegoat to save themselves of such heinous deeds. Some have the hunger of sucking the blood of poor people and they get work done giving meagre payments and make themselves rich.

There are yet many different types of manmade 'hunger'!...

Humankind has yet many types of 'hungers'. Out of that the hunger for love, education, travel, knowledge, music, singing, gambling and drinking are created through human mind. Such manmade hungers are not applicable to other animates. The animals in forests don't have degrees like Master of Arts or Commerce etc. Manmade laws and manmade hunger and adjectives like sane, insane, poor, rich, tall, short, black or white aren't acceptable for the creation structure. They aren't applicable to other animates except humans. But creation structures' rules and laws are applicable to all animate beings including human.

Only the natural – creation structure gifted hunger types are real! The man-made appetites are unreal and destructive!!!...

Thus sometimes hunger is destructive and also beneficial. Food, clothing, shelter are the basic needs, they are creation structure created. All other needs are man-made. Their absence doesn't harm the human existence. Friends, if you don't have 5-10 bungalows, 5-6 cars and positions and honors; will you die? No one dies in the absence of such needs! But without food, water, clothing or shelter one would die of hunger, thirst or cold. But whether poor or rich, no human understands this. Human has created unnecessary needs and has threatened own existence. The gifts or say curse of thinking and imagination power and intelligence of human are responsible for the exponential growth of these unnecessary appetites! Look at other animates! They don't have any unnatural appetites like humans. Once their basic needs are satisfied they are happy! They are manifold happier and content than humans, aren't they? The humans have grown their appetites and they are so costly that to buy a house you need millions of dollars. To meet this need the couple has to take the loan from some bank and keep repaying for the entire life! Whoa! What a human race and their appetites!

THE APPETITE OF BIRTHING MORE CHILDREN IN HUMANS HAVE PAVED A WAY TO MANY MORE APPETITES!!!...

The appetites of birthing more and more children for stupid reasons have grown so much! They want to grow their race, their religion or want a male child! So they keep producing more and more children despite their inability to tend them all. Such appetite is tremendous in Asian underdeveloped countries. To site an example of Indian appetite regarding this, the nation is small, but the population is huge i.e.1300 million! It is growing exponentially each day. They have highest per square inch ratio of population in the world! It is proving to be very harmful for the nation's wellbeing. Barring few fraud leaders, black mafias and industrialists almost 70 to 80% of population, means the couples as I mentioned earlier; need to mortgage their lives to the banks to lead the proper life! Yet their appetite to birth the children is tremendous! The socialites and politicians have nothing to do with it.

THE PRE INDEPENDENCE POPULATION OF 300 MILLION HAS GROWN EXPONENTIALLY TO ALMOST 1300 MILLION IN JUST 60 TO 70 YEARS!!!...

When the Britishers left the country, means in the year India got the freedom in 1947, the population was 300 million. After the independence it has grown to whooping 1300 million! What an appetite is this? And it is growing each day, every second! What endeavors of public awareness are undertaken by the elected leaders? Don't they understand the consequences? or there is no caretaker for such country? Or is it a gift of the independence? How much ever the crop is grown, the exponential increase in population eats that demanding more and shortening the benefits of all agricultural reforms! It must be controlled else it would lead to the destruction!

THERE IS A TREMENDOUS DIFFERENCE BETWEEN THE LIVING STANDARDS OF NATIONS LIKE NEW ZEALAND AND NATIONS LIKE INDIA, CHINA!!!...

I have traveled a lot throughout the Earth. I have observed that wherever the population is in limit or is less, those countries have a good living standards, good per capita income and people enjoy the life in a better way. They understand the importance of cleanliness, education, nutritious organic food. They understand the pollution free ecology. While travelling in New Zealand I found no pollution or no speck of dust. The cloths were so clean! The same white cloths were dirtied within seconds while travelling in India! This is the remarkable difference that the population makes.

THE 'GIANT HUNGER' OF THE RICH INDUSTRIALISTS AND POLITICIANS!!!...

We see so many examples of the giant 'hunger' of these few having the hidden agendas, if you understand what I am referring to. These elite few wish to possess as much as possible at the cost of squeezing the masses. Actual conspiracy is to keep the masses under control so they can be dominated and used for the benefit of these selected few. These things not discussed earlier and used to be hidden are open secret now! For example, everyone talks about the war of Iraq as an effort to destroy existing weapons to give a way for new weapon purchases and establishing the domination over oil resources. But who suffered in the war? Who lost their lives? Definitely not the leaders who called for the war! They are enjoying their lives while common masses of both the countries suffered. They bore the brunt of missile attacks, war deaths and inflation; they are paying the extra money needed in war time by paying taxes and are yet leading painful lives. The soldiers come from the masses. They lose their lives under the illusion of 'patriotism'! New weapons are being purchased; selected few will benefit from it and become rich! Masses will be fooled under the false notion of their nation being equipped with the latest weapons. When will masses realize the facts? Why do we need weapons? To destroy our own human race? Who benefits through this? Just think of it friends!

Same is the story of some industrialists. They make money cheating the masses and the governments of the nation. Friends, how many of us are aware of the fact that our bodies possess the self-healing capacity? In my city Pune of India, much hype was created about the 'swine flu'. The vaccine was made available but few responsible doctors came forward to explain that the flu virus was manmade and was created in the laboratories and released for test and the media created the hype despite the fact that so many die with other diseases too. But media would print even if single case of swine flu is present! It was a conspiracy of drug companies to mint money from the masses! They exposed the facts, tried to create awareness and masses were confused. But in truth while half of the patients adopted vaccination, rest half were cured automatically without vaccination with simple home remedies! So was that vaccine necessary? When humans will start believing in wise use of their own natural gifts such games will end.

The share market scams are well known. One reputed Indian company incepted new companies to collect capital from the masses. Without significant progress, they managed to hike the share prices manifold and sold them off to encash their profits. Later when the actual work started in those new companies, they were again merged with the original parent company and the masses were offered negligible price for the shares they had purchased! So many commoners lost their money in the process. The question is what is the real goal of such companies? Definitely not the benefit of masses or commoners but of selected few. The government regulations have many loop holes and the authorities ignore them to support the industrialists.

These are the examples of the 'giant hunger'. The hunger of fooling people to mint money! The hunger to be the number one rich person in the world by cheating government and masses! Friends, only us, the commoners, the masses can end this by realizing the facts and not being victims of the system.

WITHOUT THE 'HUNGER' THAT IS CREATED BY THE CREATION STRUCTURE, WE WOULDN'T HAVE WITNESSED EVEN A TINY EXISTENCE LIKE AN ANT!!!...

Friends, had the man-made 'giant hunger' been non-existent, the human life really would have been happier. But what would have been the consequence of the absence of the basic 'hunger' created by creation structure? Have you ever thought of it? As I described; the creation of Mother Earth and her related twelve factors have created the entire life on the Earth. But if animate was not given any basic 'hunger'; the hunger for food, water, cloth, shelter and companionship, then we wouldn't have seen even a tiny ant on this Earth! Without hunger there wouldn't have been the reproduction. There wouldn't have been the relationships, no question of work and farming would have arisen! Not a speck of any living thing would have been seen. Today we see the entire creation of living and non-living beings–huge mountains, plant kingdom having variety of trees, birds, animals, human colonies, large cities and green farms that we see are all created due to 'hunger'! This is the importance of the hunger!!

THE 'MAN-MADE HUNGER' MAKES OTHER ANIMATES STARVE!!!...

Barring humankind all other animates are dwelling happily by properly utilizing their basic hunger. The hunger or necessity of 'God' too is man-made. If it was the basic need given by creation structure, then all other animates too have had this hunger along with humankind. Human should control the hungers created by them. They must keep in mind that others too have the hunger. They shouldn't snatch the food of others to them by depriving others of it. Everyone's 'creation created' hunger must be satisfied. All animates should get the food needed by them. This is the law of creation. **Everyone is same for the Mother Earth.** Human must realize that they should acquire just good enough for their own needs or hunger. Mother Earth has cursed the one who eats more than necessary to feed his/her hunger. More than hunger means more than what is necessary, which goes waste. During the meal if you eat sufficient enough for your hunger it is ok, but if you eat more, it taxes your health and invites deadly diseases. Same is with earning more than necessary.

****

7.6

The Part Of Creation Structures' Law!

Ill Gotten Seldom Prospers!

Anything Gotten By Unfair Means Will Not Come To Fruition!

Anything ill-gotten will not be useful to you. This is an unwritten law of the creation. It mainly applies to the humankind, because barring human no other animate uses wrong ways to acquire things. Humankind lies, cheats, exploits the others and murders for getting things like property and wealth. No other animate does these things. So there is a principle of the creation structure which is 'ill-gotten seldom prospers'. Anything achieved using wrong ways is against the law of the creation and hence is punishable. Besides such thing never proves to be useful to anyone!

When lioness hunts the deer, everyone eats that in a group. Lioness doesn't say that it is only for her alone. But human is always claiming his possessions on anything. He never includes the third party and share whatever he has received. Even the herbivores in the forests don't accumulate and store the grass they are eating. The wild animals don't hunt 10–12 animals at once and store it! Whenever these animals get hungry, they eat at that time whatever is available to them. But the animal called human is different. He stores, accumulates everything. He keeps collecting for the lifetime. He collects manifold compared to his real hunger. He wants to accumulate for 400 to 500 generations of his family before death! Since he collects the things kept for others too, these others starve and die.

See these rich beggars! They keep begging to the society till death!!!...

Today we see the picture in the society that few people are so busy in collection of uncountable wealth that they are oblivious of any laws of creation structure or man-made morals. They just don't believe in adhering anything called 'principles'. These people sell the item of one dollar at the price of 80 dollar in the name of politics, business, black market by creating artificial scarcity and demand to exploit the masses. Without necessity, they are pulling the others' resources and earnings towards themselves. They cheat the masses and the society. The poor countries get under the pressure to import the things which are not needed, weapons are bought worth millions of dollars and the profits are shared between few elites while the taxes are recovered from the common people who have no use of anything of this! Then this unaccounted, unauthorized wealth is kept with the nations different than their own. They don't realize that they are snatching the bite from the needy ones and accumulating and building their own empires. Every person should think about whether the wealth accumulated really needed? Can they consume it themselves? Well, and finally without enjoying this wealth much, keeping it here they depart from this plane of Earth!

Each rich beggar is collecting enemies for the life time!!!...

The ill-gotten wealth doesn't get digested and needs to be left here itself. Also while collecting such wealth one is not living soulfully happy, fearless and worry free life. Since the wealth is collected by unfair means, the collector of such wealth also creates many enemies along with such wealth. So the fear is a constant companion to such person. So one cannot spend the precious life in happiness and contentment. If you peek into such people's personal lives, you won't find natural joy in their lives. They are unhappy in some or the other way, someone's young son dies in an accident, or is an addict or lunatic or someone in the home is bedridden, the daughter gets ill-natured husband or in–laws. They try to create an illusion of being a well to do, happy family in front of others but the entire home is in some or the other trouble. Such home has lost its character and divinity. Since they have snatched someone else's morsels, they repay the karmic consequences too. So anything more than necessity is a curse! Such fraudulent person cannot live a happy life as their family is always dwelling under the shadow of fear. The fearful existence is as good as a death.

Who is a real wealthy and phony wealthy and a beggar?...

I have seen so many examples in the society of the people who are destroyed, perished. Friends, do you think the possession of villas, cars and properties are the marks of life's success? No, not at all! Fraud or unfair means is not the way to make life successful. Someone who doesn't have these things but has sufficient enough for own needs, who eats the bread of fair earning, doesn't owe anything to anyone and has no enemies; s/he has no worries or fears. So he doesn't need some imaginary God to protection or lessening the guilt conscious. What is the need of blessings for someone who doesn't need a single unlawfully earned penny? Such people can dwell without fear in the society and enjoy their life with their head held high. It is not the case of the person who has earned the riches fraudulently. All vices get attached to such person. They don't understand the value of money and get into deeper vortex of misconducts. Public that praises in front of them always abuses such people at their back. I have seen such corrupt people having some handicapped or lunatic child or facing the bitter quarrels in the family; some or the other kind of serious punishment they endure!

The unfair wealth collection paves the way to demonic instincts!!!...

Once the unfair wealth collection becomes a habit, the development of demonic instincts is very easy. They want each thing free. The sense of good and bad is lost. The hesitation to exploit others ends. So the good friends of such people leave them. Good people in society stay away and also when such people are in trouble; their similar natured friends also avoid them! Thus finally without anyone's empathy, love or affection such person lives a lonely life and departs from this Earth one day. So one must observe the laws of the creation structure and dwell the life happily. Eat the bread of your own earning. You will live independently without fear. Always keep in mind that 'ill-gotten seldom prospers'. It is the rule of creation.

****

7.7

Creation Structure Doesn't Approve Manmade God! It's a Rule Of Creation Structure!

WANT TO SEE REAL GOD?

Here Is The Real Live God!!!

There is no other God on this Earth. Real God doesn't die. But when the Earth will be destroyed, the God proven by me too shall die. No animate being including human shall be alive that time to claim any God! Whether the manmade God is alive or not; it doesn't affect the humankind. But the destruction of any part of the God that I have discovered or any increase decrease in it; shall destroy the entire life on the Earth including human. This is the importance of the real God. This means the twelve factors which I have discovered! Since they belong to and exist on the Mother Earth only. Let us call Mother Earth the God

THE HUMANS CREATED THE CONCEPT OF GOD!!!...

The God is created by humans. No other animate has God! Daily millions of animals are slaughtered in this world, don't they have any God? This is not the monopoly of humankind. Just out of fear, worry, selfishness, greed and guilt consciousness of the human mind they have imagined a God. To satisfy different types of hunger the man needs God. Selfless, truthful person doesn't need lottery, birth charts, miracles, precious stones or God. He doesn't need the free golden locket or ring manifested by jugglery from any quack! It is because his needs are minimum and he can earn to satisfy them and is free from fear worries, tensions. Why he needs God? Actually so called God neither gives anything nor takes anything! God is created for begging to satisfy the man-made hungers! Barring human other animates don't have any such man-made or animal made hungers! Hence they don't need any God.

Except human no other animate needs God! All animates including human are created through Earth and her twelve factors. Then how is humankind different than the rest of them?...

Friends, have you seen any lioness praying to God 'Let me get the good, tender hunt today!' or any deer praying 'Let me not get hunted today!'? All other animates behave according to the rules of the creation structure, so they don't feel the need of God! So I say the human must study the creation structure to get the wisdom, watch other animates. Then humankind will understand themselves, and understand the laws of creation structure.

So far the man-made idea of 'God' has caused tremendous losses!!!...

Creation of this man made God separated and divided the humankind. But as other animates don't have God, they are still united between their respective types and live happily. Let us consider the example of the aquatics which dwell happily in water with the number of millions; despite the absence of the concept of God. Have we ever heard of any crusade happening between them? They don't have the concept of God, religion and race. All they know is to dwell happily in the water as long as they exist. Same is the case with all other animates except humankind! They don't have any weapons, any religious concepts, any fanatic religious leaders! But all these things the humans have due to the concept of God! Other animates seldom die of starvation due to the hoarding tendency of other animate except human! Other animates obey the limits of their own and other's territory. They neither encroach upon others' territories, nor do they want to impose their superiority or concepts on others! But friends, despite the intelligence, thought power and imagination; millions die of starvation within the human race including children! What creates this reality? Have we thought of this ever?

Check the gift of 'God concept' that humankind has received and its consequences!!!...

The volume or authority book writers didn't have much information about the Earth in olden days. In one of the holy book earlier then contained the information like "Earth is flat. If you go to the end of the Oceans or Seas of this Earth, your ship will fall down and will get lost somewhere! ...Sun too revolves around Earth!!" This was the ignorance till the seventeenth century; this proves the fact that they didn't have an iota of idea about the reality! In seventeenth century the scientist Galileo Galilee proved that the Earth is not flat but she is round in her shape and she is revolving around the Sun, not the otherwise! But since this was against the opinion of the priests at that time he was imprisoned. Those days everyone thought each thing written in the holy books' to be the absolute truth. The priests couldn't accept the opposition and with the notion that 'Galileo isn't larger than the holy book and he is against the God'; so they kept the Galileo and his daughter in the house arrest and tortured them to the death. This story must be mentioned that the scientist Galileo made a discovery for the benefit of humankind but due to the concept of God the humankind tortured him to the death! Shall we say this was the 'gift' received by Galileo from the humankind's concept of God?

Are we now wise enough to know and accept the reality; at least in the 21st Century?...

The human should understand the reality using the gift of intelligence and accept it by leaving the imaginary unreal ideas and concepts! For this you must study this book. Understand Mother Earth. Study the life dwelling on her and the creation structure. To birth you, to nurture you, to keep you alive, to keep your breath going and to provide you food no man made God but the Mother Earth and her related 12 factors are responsible. After understanding this, humankind too will never fight amongst themselves and dwell happily according to the laws of creation structure as all other animates do.

NOW LET US CHECK IF GALILEO IS CORRECT OR THE MAN-MADE GOD WAS TRUE AT THAT TIME!!!...

Friends, you too must be feeling sometimes that since dwelling in the imaginary world has caused such a loss to the humankind and it is of no use. To reveal this fact to you I have explained the Mother Earth and her twelve factors in this book, due to which the life on Earth has been dwelling happily so far. This is the truth and everything man made is false and imaginary!

Now I am going to describe how Galileo proved the statements in one of the holy book to be false and finally got his discovery accepted by the humankind. After 330 years of the death of Galileo means in the year 1982, the case that was filed against Galileo by the 17th century priests, for which he was prosecuted was reopened in front of Second John Pope Paul and again the discussions were started. Again the procedure of checking, cross questioning was conducted which went on for almost ten years. Finally on 31st October 1992 the christen priests agreed that Galileo's discovery was true. So though so late after the death of Galileo; he was finally given the justice. But if he was justified when he was alive, he would have made some more discoveries for the benefit of humankind. But the people swayed in the name of imaginary God, they killed the truthful person who was doing great work for the humanity and mankind.

Even today the humankind hasn't changed much! Under the name of 'hurting religious feelings' the persons talking the truth, writing the truth are tortured along with their family. They are asked to apologize. How fanatic and cruel humankind is! What stupid feelings are these! So I say that the power of thought, imagination and the intelligence that the human has received is more of a curse than the gift! On this plane of Earth the human is born after the birth of most of the other animates and yet humans kill each other. Isn't this a curse? There is no animate as ungrateful as human! How much ever you give to the human, whatever you do for them, s/he will enjoy that and will counter attack the benefactor. He will keep millions of poor and needy starving and blow millions of dollars on the imaginary concepts of God and religion to get the feel of salvation!

Friends, God has neither landed from the sky nor is created by the universe. It is birthed by the humans – not by other animates – to stifle the guilt of their own wrong doings, to feed the selfishness, to get imaginary escape from the fear and worries! So they taste the bitter fruits of their own creation – like starvations, mass slaughters in the wars, creation of atom bombs for complete destructions and so on!

DO YOU INSIST ON SEEING THE GOD? HERE IS THE TRUE LIVING GOD WHO HAS CREATED TRILLIONS OF ANIMATES SO FAR! HERE IS THE PROOF OF IT!!!...

So far we have been checking and observing how humans have been losing so much, killing each other's, starving each other due to the creation of imaginary God. You are neither going to die for not believing in the imaginary God, nor has he been created by the creation structure, nor is he the '13th factor' after the twelve factors, but is a man-made concept. But the same is not the case of the twelve factors described here in this book! Addition or reduction in any one of these twelve factors make imbalance and your death inevitable! Your knowledge is useless. Your fame, your wealth all becomes zero! It is because these twelve factors have not been created by any imagination. You are experiencing them at your each breath, with your open eyes. It doesn't need imagination. If you stop drinking water, you get dead. You stop taking oxygen, you get dead! If Sun stops giving you energy and light, you are dead! End of Sun's gravity, your life ends! If Moon of Earth vanishes, you vanish from the Earth! If Earth's gravity ends, your life ends! If the cycle of day–night stops seasons stop, your death is inevitable! This is the reality. This is the undeniable truth, not the imagination. The intact twelve factors that you experience at each breath keeps the life on Earth existent! Such is the significance of these twelve factors. If you just understand this, you had a glimpse of the real visible God! The one with whom these twelve factors are related, that is your real

God; the Mother Earth is your real God! To really know this real God let us look back little. Open the first chapter of this book which describes the real nature of the Mother Earth on which we are dwelling, due to which we are breathing. What was her real nature? The lump of the dust in the sky! That is her origin of which today we see the processed, evolved form. When she was born, means before 4600 million years; forget about the human, there wasn't any sign of animate on her. Where was human that time? Where was his man-made God and soul? 1100 million years after the Earth's birth and extensive & complex evolutions, the first creature originated in water due to the availability of favorable environment. No other mobile or immobile creatures were existent those days. After the origination of the first animate in water, for many millions of years animates were created just in the water. The surface of Earth wasn't conducive for the creation of animate on the land as the crust of Earth wasn't cooled.

NOW CHECK THE ROOT OF ALL ANIMATES INCLUDING THE HUMAN!!!...

Until 4250 million years back since the Earth's creation, there wasn't any type of vegetation or animal life on this Earth. Just 350 million years back the vegetation started on the surface of Earth; means the birth of immobile animates began. Almost 350 million years back the vegetation started on the surface of Earth; means the birth of immobile animates began. Almost 300 million years back the reptiles and gross hopper type flying insects were born. Millions of years passed before dinosaur like animals were created 140 million years back. Just 35 million years back the animals like monkey and elephant were created. This is the glory of favorable environment. This means as each factor was created out of these twelve factors, the plant and animal life on the Earth got created. Thus the environment kept changing and the creation of animates started taking place.

HERE IS THE HISTORY OF THE CREATION OF HUMAN RACE!!!...

Almost 4597.5 million years back, after the creation of the

Earth without the existence of soul the human like animal having two hands was created which is knows as Homo Habilis. It evolved further it started staying in a group around 0.5 million years back. Just 12000 years back from now, the nude, wild human, the ancestor of the human today was created who could hunt the animals for livelihood. Later evolved the changed human of today! The reason to take you back into this history is to stress that with the creation of the twelve factors necessary for life, the animates were created on this Earth including human. The root cause of the creation of animates are these twelve factors. So friends, which man- made God was available for the creation and changes since these 4600 million years? Shall we call this history completely false? Should we say the creation of living and non-living beings is on due to man-made God and there is no relation with twelve factors?

There is no other GOD; everything is Mother Earth and just Mother Earth! Here is the proof!

When the Earth was created, she was like a solid hot ball. Was the existence of human made God there at that time? Then why didn't he give birth to the human at the same time? If we consider the birth of man-made God, it is very recent in the lifetime of Earth. If 2.5 million years before there wasn't any existence of the human, when did the human created the God? He is referred as the creator of universe, the Almighty. It is said that God fills this universe and yet has remained balance. But the human hasn't yet found the life like Earth anywhere else and if it exists, going there to ensure the same is impossible. Then why didn't this man made God create the life on the other large planets like Jupiter, Saturn and Venus? The simple answer to that is the twelve factors of Earth are not found on any other planet yet! So, the truth is that no Almighty or man-made God can create the life on them. So in short the life on Earth is nothing else but the small prototype of the Earth, the image of Mother Earth! The real live God is the one who feeds you, supplies you with the resources that nurtures you and it is the one with twelve factors – the Mother Earth and just the Mother Earth! Friends, have you identified your live God at least now?

VEGETARIAN–NON VEGETARIAN, ATHEIST–THEIST, HOPE–DESPAIR SUCH THINGS ACTUALLY DO NOT EXIST!!!...

Some people ask me whether I am theist or atheist, hopeful or despaired, positive or negative, vegetarian or non– vegetarian. I say that people asking such questions are totally engrossed with material life. They don't know what lies next to their material or mundane life so they ask such questions, because these questions originally don't exist. Human has created these questions with his or her imagination. 'To get something' is the hope and 'will not get anything' is despair. I say about this that the Mother Earth has made the things available which are needed by you and they are available for all then what is to be hoped and what is not to be hoped for? Both are human ideas. They are not applicable to the other animates and the creation structure. They are created by the human mind. Except human does any other animate being or plant keep hope and despair? No, because these things do not exist in reality for them. The things which exist in reality are applicable to all that animates.

****

7.8

This Is The Law Of Creation Structure

Possessing Or Earning Anything More Than Necessary Is Not A 'Blessing' Given By Creation Structure But IS A 'Curse'

Excess Is A Curse, Not Boon!

The uncountable life forms dwell on this Mother Earth. But she has arranged for each ones food and drink and all resources that nurture and reproduce them. If all animates observe the rules of Earth's creation structure, not a single animate will starve. From tiny insect's link ants up to large animals like elephants and sky flying birds, aquatics all need food. Everyone's life and existence is dependent on food. The Mother Earth has been creating food for all these animates so far. So barring human no animate starves. Only human begs due to lack of food. Friends, have you seen other animates begging to each other? No, because they live according to the laws of creation structure. But the animate called human goes against and breaks the rules of creation structure. So the human has to beg to the human. Despite being created last of the lot, as an evolved being, the animal called human is full of greed and selfishness and hence many of them don't get food though Mother Earth has given in abundance.

The creation structure doesn't approve the human made needs!!!...

Human needs are vast compared to other animates. Actually they are created by humans themselves; which are not agreed by creation structure. Despite this human continues to collect more than necessary. So others fall short of food and die of starvation. What is the size of house needed for the family of an industrialist comprising husband, wife and two children? Considering their abundance and richness a house on a area of 4000 to 10000 sq. ft. land is more than enough, isn't it? How much space do four people occupy? But no, they possess houses constructed on larger plots valued at many thousands million dollars. And some other human in the same country may not have enough space to build a small hut. Getting plot is difficult. Such large is the gap between rich and poor that we can see in various nations and this is against the creation structure!

Contentment is the boon given by creation structure to the animates!!!...

It is amazing that we do find some family of four living in the small space of 500 sq. ft. area enjoying worry free, fearless and happy life! The creation structure has endowed such family with the gift of contentment, isn't it? They live capriciously. They do not bear any undue burden of avoiding taxes, hiding income, worry of raising capital for second factory or tightly busy business schedule and planning of exploiting others! They can spend time watching opera, theatre or roaming in the park and road without fear. There are no enemies; they freely enjoy the natures' beauty. No thoughts of deceiving others, the heart is very transparent. There is no artificial clouded element in living the life, no expectation of fame and no vanity. The family having the earnings just sufficient to meet the necessary needs can live such happy and simple life. I feel their life is the real successful life!

Everyone must surrender to the inevitability of death!!!...

So friends, hasn't creation structure given the blessings to such family described above? Contrary to this the rich man staying in the mansions of million dollars is riddled with many worries of the safety of wealth, need of investments; desire to lead the 'topmost rich men' list, busy schedules, night meetings and business travel worries. The lifestyle taxes them with different health problems much early in life and compel to live an artificial life dependent on chemical filled drugs. What worth all this trouble for?

The bogus definition of nations' progress made by economists! Then what is true 'growth' or 'progress'?...

Economists would say such rich people are needed for the growth or progress of the nation. Well, we still have nations with sky rocketing buildings, large airports, sky railways, big mansions of few, expensive areas, multiple flyovers and yet the people die of starvation! Can such country be called advanced country? What is real advanced country? progressed country? It is the country which doesn't have the people starving, where all public gets sufficient food and needs are met. It is the country where all basic needs of shelter, food and clothing are met for everyone. It is the country where there are no fraud selfish politicians, the country that has no loans of others. It doesn't matter if such country doesn't have the posh infrastructure described above. I call the country that enjoys the contentment and happiness of the masses as the advanced country, progressed country. Beside this, if there is such infrastructure, it is a real advanced country!

For whom such posh infrastructures are? They are meant for the 20 to 25% few! What about the rest?...

The countries like India and China too have such posh facilities and infrastructures, but just for selected few! If 700 to 800 million people are struggling with starvation and tax burdens in such countries; for whom are these facilities meant for? Is being the shelter place for beggars the real use of flyovers? What is the use of such flyovers to the illiterate labor, starving public? They won't even get to see the posh airports. They won't drive own cars on such flyovers to enjoy the ride! They don't need these facilities as it is of no use to them. Only handful rich would use them. Others don't have much use. The first necessity of each one is food, clothing and shelter. If these basic needs of each citizen are not able to meet then whatever improvements the government implements they will be only meant to fulfil the fancies of handful rich! They are useless and serve no purpose for those starving of food and struggling to meet basic needs!

If only ten people in the nation are eating full to the point of belching, the rest 100 who starved will not let them eat happily. This is the law of nature. The national resources belong to everyone, not to just handful! So anyone having in excess of anything that the creation structure has given, it is a curse. This is not only a good concept to be written in the books; just peek in the houses of these who have accumulated in the excess and you will know the reality. They live artificial lives; full of fear, worries, enemies and odd relationships.

If you want all the public to be happy, this is the 'remedy'...

If we plan to make the common man happy, some human made blocks need to be removed. The main block is bribery and wicked ways that is spread from top to bottom in all systems. But unless the humans realize the significance of creation structure and Mother Earth, it is difficult to change their nature. The capitalism has paved way to the hoarding, profit hungry economy and giant consumerism. The money is concentrated in the hands of few while majority struggles for daily bread and butter. Politicians, drug manufacturers, some religious fanatics have been successful with their conspiracy to keep the masses in ignorance and exploit them. How many of us know the fact that the cure for cancer has been available since years but in the indecisiveness of the conspiracy leaders about how the profits will be distributed; masses are deprived of it and many have died? The remedy to this is the education of masses. Increasing the awareness of masses. The more such things would come into light and when the real faces behind the mask will be exposed, this conspiracy will end. The key to this is not to believe things just as they appear! Know the illusion behind it. The present capitalistic economy has been systematically imposed on the masses and must be changed. The good news is that there are some changes underway in global economy.

If in your mundane life you have any philosopher, intelligent person, capitalist or president or prime minister would they ever think of these twelve factors? From their point of view, the presence or absence of the Moon doesn't make them any difference. But we have seen the chaos the absence of the Moon would cause on the Earth. But to understand this, studying the Earth and her natural system is necessary.

If the population keeps rising in the underdeveloped nations, such countries will never be able to progress! People will die lack of food!!!...

The biggest problem in front of nations like India, Bangladesh, China is exponentially growing population. There needs to be the education of masses about this fact and we need strict laws to implement the checks on population. Unless these countries check this uncontrollable growth, the majority of humans there will not be able to live happy life. We take the case of India and China. The area of the country India is almost 3.3 million km2 but the population is above 1250 million! The area of China is almost 9.6 million km2, means three times of India's area. But the population is 1300 million. Compared to other countries, these countries have whooping high population which nullifies the agricultural growth each year. Means no matter what the growth of agricultural produce is in these countries, since the population is growing exponentially compared to it, the production ratio to population remains negative. The huge population also impacts the other facilities. The growth for facilities planned for this population too never meet the needs. Same is with education. These and many such countries don't have proper facilities, no proper housing, proper food or clothing. Education remains remote thing to these citizens. With the natural gift of land these countries can supply food to all the world. But their own growing population eats out the excess produce and the shelter and other needs of this population fosters urbanization which in turn is reducing the available land for agricultural cultivation. The city I live in has been growing so much that each year lot of fertile agricultural land is turned into non-agricultural land to meet the growing housing needs!

The commoner like me understand these facts, shouldn't the socialites and politicians running the nations understand this? Everyone is just trapped into the vicious circle of excess to few people and nothing to masses! Like 80:20 rule! 20% have excess means 80% of the resources and 80% starve with just 20% resources! Friends, isn't this is the conspiracy against the Mother Earth and the life on her?

SO I STRESS ALWAYS THAT 'HAVING IN EXCESS' IS A CURSE IN SUCH SITUATION!!!...

Creation Structure has given specific 'hunger' to each animate for sustenance and also the resources in abundance. But barring human all other animals obey this rule. Only the human has acquisitive attitude, the attitude to store up and eat more than necessary on this plane of Earth. Human doesn't yet get the hidden danger in it; that eating more than necessary causes indigestion or gives unwanted consequences like obesity, diseases and also leads to death! It is better to let the others have it happily! Friends, do we see animals eating more than necessary? But yes, we do see so many people around us who hog the food, eat more than necessary isn't it? It is ignorance, false hunger, it is a disorder! Thus is wasted the food of the starved humans on Earth!

This attitude is seen in daily life of humans. Despite having taken birth for a short duration on this Earth, they keep struggling whole of the life to acquire more wealth, more land, more cars, more factories, more and more than necessity of anything that they can! The problem is they cannot use or enjoy many of these things either in their life time or after death! So these things anyway are a waste for that hoarder! But it is a curse to keep someone else in lack and acquire more than necessary for whole life. The hoarder cannot live life of peace, joy and contentment, but becomes a victim of greed, needs more and more always! Too much of anything is bad.

None should get more than necessary! No one should earn more than necessary! Else it shakes the balance of the creation structure!...

The person having things in excess seldom enjoys them all. Easy money spoils the thinking and mind of the spouse, children and people around, including the possessor of that excess. Too much vanity, wickedness and ego creeps in, they become enemies of the society. So no one should get in excess of their need or excess than the capacity to digest. Maintaining the balance is the rule of creation. Deteriorated balance ensures destruction. This principle doesn't apply to the wealth alone but to everything in life. If some person just keeps earning a degree after degree, when would he get the wisdom to get employed and earn?

See the result of getting in excess!!!...

Here I share a life experience. I knew a person aged 80 and his mother was 98 years old! Now one would say what a long life! But I feel it was a curse! One praises the long living individuals, but it is the life in excess. Well, this 80 year old person suddenly expired. When I went to their house, his 98 years old mother was weeping besides her old dead son. This mother saw the death not only of her husband but son, daughter in law, son in law, granddaughter! So what was the result of getting excess life? She got the sorrow of witnessing the deaths of her younger relatives too! So was this long life a curse or a gift to her? It is good to say good bye to this world in stipulated time. This asserts the saying 'anything in excess is bad'. So earn in your life for your necessity and spare the time to enjoy the life happily and leave in time!

Replacement of old by new is the rule of creation structure!!!...

Once you deliver the natural responsibilities given by the creation structure, you aren't needed here. Similar to other animates, once your reproduction i.e. your children become independent; your responsibility gets over. Means after finishing the task given by creation structure, your task on this plane of Earth ends. After a certain age, your routine remains eating, drinking and sleeping. What remains is a waiting for death! Regarding each animate this rule applies, that is your permanent departure and creation of new animate. This departure too should happen in time, else such living turns to be the punishment as I explained above. This punishment becomes must because there is no law or permission in the society for 'wilful death'! Getting more life than necessary is not a boon but a curse according to me. This reality applies to all humankind.

YOU HAVE BEEN GIVEN THE ORGANS ACCORDING TO THE NEED! CHECK WHAT THEIR EXCESS WOULD RESULT INTO!!!...

The body that Mother Earth has given you according to the rule of creation structure; its organs are good enough for living a happy life. Had they been in excess, check would have happened! If you had extra head or extra ears; would it have been good? When two eyes are good enough if you would have been given five eyes it would have been chaos. What if you had three mouths? And four five lips? Would you have been able to talk? You need just two legs to walk, to take you forward. But what if someone wanted extra leg and it was given? Could walking be easy and simple? Means all that you have been given by Mother Earth is for your own benefit! For your own easy utilization! We do see people around with such excess organs and then they undergo expensive operations, isn't it? It is classified under the category of 'abnormality or disability', isn't it? This law applies to all life and all transactions. Anything gathered in excess, received in excess makes life difficult. The life would be a waste!

ANYTHING EXTRA THAN NECESSITY IS DANGEROUS TO LIFE!!!...

The meaning of whatever I described above is that according to creation structure's law, to live normal happy life, easy life one needs just according to necessity. Not in excess. Birds have just one beak and two legs. He needs just two legs to walk and fly and one beak to eat. But if he gets extra leg and extra beak, it will be difficult to walk and easily fly and catch the prey! He won't live easy life, his existence will get in danger. Similarly, gathering of wealth, property, houses or any such thing in excess becomes dangerous for human's happy and joyous existence!

Simple example is if we don't turn the bread in the oven it will char and if we keep it for excess time; it will burn to a coal, isn't it? So many examples we can see in life. After observing this creation structure minutely I have come to my own principle i.e. 'anything gathered extra than necessity is dangerous to life! After getting life due to the twelve factors of the Mother Earth, I have been describing so far the laws of creation structure to get the simple and happy life till the death. We shall see some such laws ahead in the next chapter.

****

7.9

One More Law of The Creation Structure!

Thought Is the Mother Of Action!

Rich Or Poor, Both Are Beggar Without 'Wealth of Thought'

Though the human body is derived from the twelve factors just like other animates, the Mother Earth has not endowed other animates with humanlike thought power. It is bestowed only on the humankind. The humankind has certainly benefitted to some extent than other animals due to this.

You are enjoying the modern facilities only due to the wealth of thoughts of scientists!!!...

Many scientists emerged to serve the humankind by creating facilities for humankind's comforts. Louis Pasture, Darwin, Galileo, Isaac Newton, Thomas Edison are few to name out of these scientists. Utilizing their thought power they made many discoveries of benefit to the humankind. The humankind has been using the facilities and comforts created due to such discoveries. They have been enjoying life truly from their imaginations. As other animates don't have such thought power they are living in the same state as they have been since their creation.

But using the thought power the human is living a better modern life than other animates today. The humans invented airplane, rail and ships so that they can travel the destinations of long distances. He invented two wheelers, four wheelers. Using them he can travel to long distances easily. He built dams on large rivers and use that water all time wherever he wants. So he can create and use fruits, vegetables all times of the year. To get protected from winds, cold, rain and heat of Sun he built tall buildings for the shelter. This all was possible due to the wealth of thought power. It is not possible in case of other animates. They cannot live the comfortable life like humans. They have to depend upon the nature.

Only due to thought power human enjoys more comfortable life that other animates!!!...

It is the thought power due to which human could stay in a group creating colonies, villages, cities and nations. So he can live the life in a better style. Owing to thoughts; the arts giving pleasure to the mind like music, dance and painting could be created and learning them humans could entertain themselves. Discovering and developing different instruments they could amuse the mind. This all could happen due to the thought power given to them. Due to thought power human could create relationships like mother, father, sister, brother, wife and children and made the life easy. Twelve thousand years back human was living a savage life like other animates. He had not even discovered the fire then. So he ate raw meat. Took shelter at caves. But as brain developed he could strike new thoughts and implement them. That is why we are living such civilized and modern life today. Made up of the same twelve factors like other animates, but due to thought power the human is living a better life than and ruling the other animates, means the Earth. Till now we pondered upon the humankind and the thought power they have got. Now we shall know more about the personal life and thoughts.

The 'success and failure or God' of human is all dependent upon his thoughts!!!...

Once born, the success and failure of the life is all dependent upon the personal thoughts of the human. The human keeps asking and begging to the man-made God that could be from any religion; 'God, please give me this, God please let that happen and I shall do this for you, I will give that for you!' In reality on this plane of Earth there is no such God which gives you something or takes something from you. No animate has this 'dealing' of give and take with some 'God' barring humans!

Barring humans, no animate has this 'dealing' of give and take! Just due to the thoughts of selfishness of humans these 'deals, fate and God' are created!!!...

If two three lionesses hunt some big prey, four five other lions too share it to satisfy the hunger. Do they make a deal like 'today you eat my prey, tomorrow we expect you to repay this'? Not just in the lions, no other animates have this kind of 'deals' of give and take except humans. These deals have crept in the human life due to selfishness. The vice of selfishness is stuck just to humans and it has created the concept of 'God'. God is needed because 'something is needed'. Same is the thing with the fate. Fate doesn't say 'without doing any work I will give you the windfall!' This too is the human concept, created through selfishness. The one who remains under the notion that 'If it is in my fate, I shall get it and then I will eat' will starve for the life. The tendency of eating free, expecting something without efforts has created the concept of 'fate'. It is only man made. Such things are not acceptable to the creation structure! Leave the selfishness, leave the tendency to eat without own efforts or expect unless you deserve. Then you don't need the company of fate or God! All you need are the constructive thoughts. **Thoughts are the mother of your success and failures! First thought, then their implementation and then a certain fruit!**

The creator of your success and failure are only your thoughts!!!...

Think of the thoughts which are constructive and useful to you and act accordingly so you certainly will get the fruit of the same. There is no need of any God or fate. What is the desired fruit? It is getting enough to meet your necessities. Your need may be fulfilled with one thousand dollars but you expect to get ten thousand! Why do you want those nine thousand dollars which you don't need? Just whatever is you need just that much is your own, and actually of use. To act according to your thoughts you also should know your worthiness. If you dream to be an industrialist or president without the worthiness, it is a stupidity! Every success comes in phases. If you leave the stairs in between and try to directly jump to last step at height you will fall! So using your constructive thought power and act according to your capability and worthiness will surely lead you to the success!

'Thoughts' and 'action' are the two sides of the single coin!!!...

'Thoughts' and 'action' are the two sides of the single coin. Your success and failure depends upon it. Without thoughts no action would happen. Then live the life like a stone! Such is the significance of the implementing thoughts into an action. Happy successful life and sad sorrowful life is all dependent on your thoughts. With the good thoughts and good actions you shall lead to the good, happy life. But wrong thoughts and stupid actions will lead to the misery and troubles.

Wealth of thought is more valuable than material wealth and money! We recognize the person due to his or her thoughts and actions!!!...

Friends, we give Mahatma Gandhi the credit to get Indians the freedom from the British rule and cultivate the virtues for the world. But it happened because he implemented his thoughts, he put them into action. This is the result of thoughts. The thoughts are more important than the wealth and money in each one's life. We identify the person with his or her thoughts. For example Hitler's thoughts were harmful to the humankind. He is recognized as selfish, fanatic and cruel and is known as a 'bad guy'. Whereas Mahatma Gandhi, Nelson Mandela are recognized for their pure, clean and helpful thoughts and are known as 'virtuous guys'. So good or bad is decided upon one's thoughts. Each moment human needs to think in the life. It is your test of success and failure. Generally after the childhood is over the human needs to think for living his life and the further life depend upon that thinking.

Some student doesn't study despite the reminders of the teachers and parents. His thoughts revolve around playing and hooliganism. So instead of study he gives priority to vagrancy and to gambol. The thought of responsibility doesn't touch him at all. So he lags behind in studies and in further life. Whereas some other student obeys the parents and teachers. He thinks that not listening to them and not studying will result in his failure. Then he thinks if he fails his relatives won't respect him and more important is that in his further life he will not be successful. With such thoughts he studies with responsibility and achieves success in the education, in the life. But the wandering student gets failure in life and makes his parents and himself unhappy. This means the future of human's life is dependent upon thoughts and action. Just keeping faith on God and dependency on fate doesn't bear the desired fruit. Getting good results depends upon your thoughts and their implementation. Parents, well-wishers and teachers are just guides and can wish you well but the success needs your own complete involvement.

Your thoughts are your saviors or destructors at each moment!!!...

The human life on the Earth depends upon the thoughts. On each phase of life the thoughts are needed. Whether in your studentship, your youth, whether in earning money or any deal or in old age; without right thoughts you cannot live good life. Each time the thoughts save you or destroy you. Someone with very poor economic conditions may surprise you by rising to heights with their good thoughts and actions. If you read the chapter 'me' in my another book "Me, Earth and Travel" you will know that whatever I am today, the credit goes to my wealth of thoughts.

At the age of sixteen, I came to city from a small village after passing the seventh standard. The economic condition was very poor at home but I had tremendous ambition of getting education. But those days I wasn't able to get even two times meal. Without proper shelter and food getting educated seemed impossible. But I had a great wealth in that age, my thoughts! I could think that if I gave priority to food; I won't educate myself! Without education I would not be able to change my status and waste my life working as some worker in a mess. At one inn when the owner rejected my preposition to attend the night school though I was ready to slog for any work given. I tried to work as a water carrier in some bungalow or sometimes worked as a part time compounder. But since it didn't give me enough earning, I worked as a porter at one press and got admission in the night school! But the wages were insufficient to meet the expense of education and two times meal so I continued education on one time meal. Porterage in a day time and education at night time was my routine. Later with a better wage as an office boy the two times meal was possible. I accepted sleeping under the benches of a mess after dinner. Thus each time I made decisions according to my thoughts and behaved accordingly.

Later I realized that I needed to do something else. Then I thought of adding the skills, acting upon it I learnt typing. This way climbing ladder one step at a time I progressed enough to open my own office of typewriter repairs and sales in the city and next I owned almost 200 typewriters. Later upon my own thought power I started business in estate dealing. First foot path, then the benches of a mess, then a hut and then one room and next I could build my own bungalow in 20 years. All this was possible due to my wealth of thoughts. Due to correct thinking I didn't get into any addiction or bad company. After getting economic stability, I longed to see the real 'God' i.e. the Mother Earth. Implementing the thought I visited all places on the Earth and wrote my first book about it. Now to make the human realize his own real identity and to share my comprehension about creation structure with others this second book is written. The root for all this is my wealth of thoughts.

I have written these two books for the happy and joyous life of the human race. Please share them with your children too. I am 100% confident that after reading this book you will understand about how to live happy and joyous life and you will know the importance of the thought power.

EVEN IF YOU DON'T HAVE GOLD, SILVER, MONEY OR PROPERTIES; THE CONSTRUCTIVE THINKING AND ACTIONS RESOLVE ALL THE PROBLEMS!!!...

If you don't have gold, silver, money or properties it is fine, but If you have the wealth of thoughts you won't be devoid of anything. You shall resolve many problems with thoughts. You will get things with your thoughts. But just thinking is of no use; it needs action too. Getting the things that you think of needs persistence, sincerity and purity for self and others. Deception seldom works. If you have these things then getting your desired results is not difficult. Please do read my other book to ensure yourself about this fact.

Now I will change the subject a little. Check how this is related with the thoughts.

A THOUGHT – 'I DON'T BELONG TO MYSELF'! THIS TOO IS A LAW OF CREATION. THE CAUSE OF ALL PAINS AND TRIALS IS 'GETTING THE BIRTH'!!!...

As I have said earlier creation is the root of all misery and destruction. The root of all miseries in the 'birth'. So all saints pray and demand to their 'God' for liberation from the cycle of births and deaths. Birth means trouble and misery. Then it doesn't matter whether it is a son of reputed leader, or a son of priest, saint. He cannot avoid the miseries and sorrows of his share. This is true from the human perspective. But this rule is applicable for all creation structure. But since human is more intelligent and emotional and has the ego to think of himself as someone special; perceives these sorrows and misery more than other animates. In reality, sadness, trials, joy and happiness are created from the human imagination and feelings. These are neither part of and nor agreeable to creation structure.

SEE HOW THE ROOT OF SORROW AND TRIALS IS JUST 'BIRTH'!!!...

I read a news in the paper on 22nd May 2012. One woman was admitted to the hospital and she had 1.5 years daughter along with her. During the treatment the woman died. No one came forward to claim her dead body. Now the question was what to do about the small kid along with her? Humans have been given the thoughts so, a sympathetic feeling about that small girl without parents was natural. She was an innocent, naïve and helpless kid and was orphaned after her mother's death. All those who read the news must have felt sad about her. The photograph of that innocent girl was printed in the newspaper. Everyone must be thinking, 'now who shall support and take care of her?' All such emotional thinking only the human would entertain. The creation structure doesn't have anything to do with it. So many animates take birth and die like this. Some get enough food to eat and some starve. Such so many beings are suffering on this Earth. But barring human other creations doesn't have anything to do, no emotions, no thoughts! All these ideas are limited to human beings. **They do not exist in reality!** Well, so from the point of view of that small kid, taking birth means trials and sorrow! Do you get it, how taking birth is an invitation to miseries? So all religious books have been demanding 'no cycle of birth and death'! All saints have been trying to convince the humankind of this.

HOW YOU DON'T BELONG TO YOURSELF?...

Friends, you must be wondering that when the title of the chapter is 'thought is the mother of action' why we strayed away from the subject? The reason is, one shouldn't get birth and if you are born, I have been telling how to deal with it till the death what restrictions and rules you should observe. This is a part of it. After the birth when you are entering into the mundane life if you keep the thought 'I do not belong to myself' and be sure about it and live your life; your life will be much easier, peaceful, happy and healthy which shall help you to be successful. This thought may sound strange to you initially. It is because you have been engrossed by the material things. But I shall explain you how you do not belong to yourself!

Have you read everything that I have described in the book from the beginning? How the Earth was created? What are the Earth related twelve factors on this Earth? How the human was created due to these twelve factors? Friends if you have read this by heart, you would understand the thought that in reality you don't belong to yourself. Do you know the root of all the people you see around? This is a crazy question. The root is nothing else than the invisible sperm. Everyone is made up of the sperm. What is the root of the sperm? You will say your parents, but no. There is no animate on this Earth who can create anything on his own. So this sperm or egg doesn't actually belong to your parents but is made up of the mixture of Earth related twelve factors. The process of the creation of sperm or egg doesn't take place of any other planet than Mother Earth! The zygote created by sperm with the help of mother's egg develops in her womb for nine months. After nine months the fully developed human fetus comes out of mothers' womb. After finishing the childhood this body enters into youth, then mature adulthood. Next is the old, wrinkled body which ends in death. Thus the body created lies flat permanently one day. Now can you tell from this journey of a sperm to the flat dead body lying in the bed, which is real you? None of you in each of this stage is finally real you! So I say 'I don't belong to myself', you don't belong to yourself. Not even the sperm because it is made up of the Earth related twelve factors. Any increase or decrease in these twelve factors won't create the sperm. If this is the reality, you are no one, I am no one! I am explaining this again and again because human being doesn't leave the 'self' the 'ego', the false identity as 'me' and 'mine'; till the death!

IF YOU ARE NOT YOUR OWN, THEN WHO IS YOUR WIFE, YOUR DAUGHTER, YOUR SON, YOUR PARENTS? IF NONE OF THEM ARE YOURS THEN WHOSE BUNGALOW, CAR AND FAME AND PRIDE!!!...

If you think and realize your true self identity, then you will think about the fact that if you don't belong to yourself, the who is your mother, father, wife, daughter or son! Forget about other relatives! Once this is understood, the human will not get involved into any relationship deeply to create sorrow. This is about the relationships. Same is the case with so called 'your' possessions. If you are not your own then what is 'your' car, fame, bungalow, wealth and property? So without wasting your life in collecting these things more than necessary you will not give importance to sorrow, trouble, fear and enemies. Means you shall earn just enough for your existence and while enjoying this life fully by letting others too enjoy, you shall take leave of this world happily. This will happen only when you shall comprehend the thought 'I do not belong to myself'. It shall ensure you that if I am not mine own, I don't belong to myself, then running behind this 'me' is useless! Then your life won't have place for things like greed, selfishness, hoarding, ego and allurement. So I keep telling that the wealth of thoughts has such a great importance in the human life. From thoughts itself you understand yourself, realize yourself and recognize your true identity. Now tell me which sorrow, which joy and what death and what trouble and worry? To whom it is for? If I am not mine then whose birth and whose death? In front of this thought who is president and who is industrialist, capitalist, rich man? Due to not having this knowledge and identity of self the human remains ignorant!

YOUR THOUGHT IS DEVIL AND DIVINE!!!...

Getting the gift of thought and imagination power and intelligence hasn't been of any use! You will object this statement of mine. But this objection is only due to your engrossment with the materialism. You may think that you have received the thought power and imagination and intelligence for earning facilities, comforts, wealth and good food is the benefit of for which you have received the thought power! But despite the capability of understanding the thoughts described above the human gets trapped into the vices of greed, hoarding, fame, jealousy and selfishness. Due to misuse of this thought power the human has been killing the human. So good thoughts have a great importance in the life. Your thought makes you a thief, selfish, cunning person. It creates in you the devilish tendencies. Your greedy thought keeps the poor ones away from the food and makes you rich and fraud. Your thought itself makes you create atom bomb. Your thoughts make you ready for the war and get responsible to victimize the millions of innocents. Your thought makes you break the laws of creation structure, becomes the cause to kill each other, exploit nation and masses. The thoughts make you take the false support of the quackery, astrology and also the gambling, human trafficking, stealing and lying. Behind any tyranny and misdeeds are your thoughts. The root of all evil is your wrong thinking. So what you should be in life, whether a thief or a gentleman; depends upon your thoughts. Your thought decides your place in the society. Once, instead of the evil thoughts the good thoughts are implemented, brought in action; you have become a saint, the God!

Don't eat single morsel of earning from misdeed. Earn enough for your needs with good means and let others too earn. If you behave in compliance to the laws of creation structure these thoughts make you a saint, a God! If anything in your life is important, they are your thoughts. So I say, thought is the mother of action and your thoughts make you devil or God!

What is the need of God, quakes, fate and astrology?...

Your thoughts create atrocious questions in your life. Living peaceful, joyous and happy life also depends upon your thoughts. If all good and bad things are dependent upon thoughts, then what is the need of God, quakes, fate and astrology? When your thoughts make you, why one needs the other external supports? Due to thoughts itself the beggar becomes a king and also a king becomes a beggar in no time. Your thoughts give you the title of a 'murderer' in one moment! To live happy, tension free and content life your good thoughts have important role. Match all these things with your thoughts and you will get your own identity! This is the identity from the material thoughts. But your true identity is Earth and her twelve factors!

This book is for giving you your true identity. You will not read anything that gives you such real identity of yours. This book is not based on reading 14/15 other books. But the two books I wrote are written after spending many years' experience of life in observing and studying the Mother Earth, Creation Structure on Mother Earth and human and animates on the Mother Earth. Out of them, I hope this book will prove to be useful to help the humankind live peaceful, healthy, content, tension free and joyous life! This is not an imaginary novel. It is based on truth, the facts. So I wish this book to reach to entire humankind. Of course, some selfish people may not like these things, because their fame and means of earning are dependent upon keeping masses in ignorance. I know this!

Rich and poor, both are beggars!!!...

Someone is very rich and famous. There is no shortage of anything. Lot of wealth is available. But he doesn't have the wealth of thought. Also someone is very poor, a beggar. If he too doesn't have the wealth of thoughts, then these two – rich and poor, both are beggars!

****

7.10

Contentment Contains All Riches!

Friends, since birth as one grows into adulthood all relatives, parents and society teach the person about NOT to 'give' to others and how to strive to collect more and more wealth. With such mind condltioning since the childhood, the person runs after wealth so much that he forgets everything, including himself. If one shop starts doing good business, he feels proud in starting second, third and fourth shop. But while doing all this he ignores everything, doesn't take care and give needed love & affection to parents, wife and children and doesn't care for his own wealth of health. His all time is spent in thinking about how the one million that he earned can be turned into two million, two million to three million and so on. His this multiplication never ends in his life. Whatever he earns he cannot use in his life and also doesn't let his parents and family enjoy it. By not paying attention to whatever he 'has'; he strives till the end of his life behind what he doesn't 'have'. The multiplication, with which his wealth grows, brings his death near with the same multiplication of years! He never understands this and one day he lies flat forever according to the law of creation structure; not using whatever he kept earning! Is this called successful life?

I know an acquaintance who is suffering from diabetes. He owns a factory and despite of the great earnings his wife is very ambitious. They have a daughter and a son. Once he had visited my home and said "I really admire you. Though you were a simple house servant, you earned good successes in life and had luck of visiting various nations in different continents of the Earth. Not just alone, but you travelled with all the family. How could you do this? I can't resolve this riddle. Despite much desire I can't do it!" I told him, "After getting a particular amount I immediately closed my business that was giving me lot of profit. I sold the assets I had and converted them in money and decided not to do any business which deals with people. So just dealing with government and banks, without touching the main amount we spend the returns we get from it. So we don't have any worry of earning or worry of recovery from anyone. We don't have any business where we need to deal with the people. So we all in the family live happily. Whatever earnings we get, our entire family is completely content. There is no desire to add to the wealth that we have. We just think about spending the rest of the life happily. According to the creation structure we live in the present. We don't think of the future much. So you feel like admiring me."

So he said, "due to factory I live a very troublesome life. I have to face various issues daily. I just cannot live life like yours!" So I asked a casual question, "What is the market price of the factory that you are running at present?" He told that if he sold his factory it shall be priced at 60 million. I said, "If you can get so much then what is the need of living the troublesome life? If you invest that much money in government bonds and banks, you shall get around 0.6 million monthly which is not less to live a good comfortable life! Then no life full of trouble and issues! But unlike me, you may not have courage to close the running business like this!"

Living troubled life despite having everything in life has the root in the lack of wealth of thoughts. While living routine life, instead of looking at life from emotional angle it must be lived from the view point of reality. Also avoiding the competition, the priority must be given to the peace, happiness and contentment of the self. Whatever wealth the other has, what we got to do with that? Living in peace, happiness and contentment is the biggest wealth of all. If you have the greed of getting more wealth than whatever is sufficient to you, you will never be happy and peaceful in the life. Over ambitious nature is a block in the contentment, happiness and peace. Means you should be content after getting whatever is necessary to live the happy life. All wealth is contained in such contentment. Whether the person lives in one room or earning minimum, if he has the gift of the contentment, there is no other content and happy person than him! If some rich person doesn't have the contentment, there is no 'rich beggar' than him. It is the 'curse' that he has got. Whatever alms he gets, he cannot fill his tummy with it! Then he is rich beggar. So at least after some age one should learn to enjoy the life. There is nothing valuable than your happy and healthy existence. After your existence, all your wealth is useless, because it is never yours. So earn as much is necessary and enjoy the life fully. So I say contentment contains all riches.

****

7.11

Kindness

A key to life that is fearless, happy joyous and free from worry...

"If I were in your place, what would have been done?" Thinking this ends the problems of the life.

'Kindness', in this one word that encompasses the happiness, joy, contentment, freedom from fear, jealousy, anger, and worries; all kind of freedoms from unwanted, bad traits. **Kindness** is necessary for this freedom. Actually other than human no other animate need these adjectives or traits, because other than human no other animates transact in 'give and take' deals. Only humans are the one who cannot avoid the give and take since birth, even if they wish to! So humankind must have and develop the trait of the kindness in them. It makes you live your life in happiness.

In all relations of the human life like servant–owner, doctor–patient, lawyer–client, leader–public, judge–client, shopkeeper–customers, owner– tenant, student–teacher, friend and all relatives each moment each one is interacting with one another in various ways. From these interactions quarrels, deception, anger, jealousy, murder and beating all such mis-happenings are taking place in human life. But this itself is the invitation to the sorrow and trouble. But I shall tell you one thing that if these things are not to happen then each one should consider imagining oneself in the place of other person during such transactions. If everyone deals with each other with kindness then the anger, jealousy, competition and greed would not be created and everyone will be able relish the life happily.

We can give many examples. But let us look at some examples. Suppose, if it is a real estate transaction, the seller and buyer both can consider themselves in each other's place. The seller should imagine himself in the place of buyer and think and act. Means while purchasing the property I need a clear title, reasonable price so I get the complete return of the money spent which I would expect. Also the buyer should consider himself in the place of the seller and think and act. Means if I was a seller, I would expect that I should get money in time, there shouldn't be any deception. He should think about if "I was the owner of the place, what would have been my expectations from the buyer?" thinking and acting accordingly is the 'kindness'. Means now I too should think like the place owner and act accordingly!

Millions of deals take place like this. But if each one thinks about each other no problems arise while dealing. But selfish thinking does create the problems. It leads to the issues and you lose your peace.

We shall take a simple example in daily life. Most of us have house maid. But she too is a human like you are. The only difference is in the economic condition of yours, you are moneyed and she is poor. But just like you; her life is also full of challenges. Suppose if her son is not well and she doesn't come for the work, the lady of the house shouldn't taunt and scold her. Instead check on her and considering her difficulties; if situation desires extend the helping hand. In such situations instead of cutting her salary the kind consideration is needed. The lady of the house must think about if she were in a place of the house maid what behavior she would have expected from the owner; and act accordingly. One shouldn't treat the servants' mere as 'servants' but treat them as a human first. Owner and the servant both are the same, just they differ in the nature of their work. Also the servant should consider the kind treatment given by the owner from time to time and shouldn't create difficulty for owner by fooling them for selfish reasons. This would create the harmony in the relationship.

Everyone in the family should cultivate the habit of thinking about each other by considering themselves in the other person's shoes. This will eradicate the situations of quarrel and resulting unpleasantness. The kindness will bring so much smoothness to your life!

If everyone cultivates the kindness, no one will starve on this Earth. No one would trouble the others, attitude of capitalism would end. The basic reason of difficulties is lack of kind heart, absence of kindness.

The trait of kindness will attract peace, happiness and contentment in your life!!!...

Since you wake up in morning till you go to the bed at night; you encounter many different situations in your life. If you decide to behave kindly in these situations you will live a tension free, quarrel free and joyful life and get peaceful sleep. Always considering one another in each other's shoes will solve so many problems. See how the regular use of this 'key' of kindness will attract happiness, peace and contentment in your life! Such great is the importance of the 'kindness'.

Without giving joy to others no one can enjoy peaceful, happy and joyous life for oneself!!!...

By throwing others in the problematic situations or doing the deals difficult for others one cannot be happy. This is the law of creation structure. Without giving others the happy, joyous and peaceful life one cannot enjoy the joy, peace and happiness in the life. But the happiness that is visible to your physical eyes is not real. Show of joy is not always real joy. Always put yourself in the other's shoes which will give you better insights, help shine the light on the situation and act accordingly which will bring real happiness and joy in your life. How I would have behaved if I were in your place? What I would have expected? Considering this if you keep your behavior, no argument, quarrel, and unpleasantness will arise. For this you should remove the anger, greed, selfishness and jealousy from your nature, from your intentions. So there won't be quarrel, pain and troubles and no contact with police, lawyer or court staff! Friends, isn't this the key to happiness in life?

****

7.12

Human Mind

What Is Mind?

Friends, what is mind? No one can answer this question properly. In the mundane life we use the word mind in various references like, "In my mind I thought so…, this depends upon your mind…, mind is not ready to accept this…!" But what exactly is the mind? I have formed my own opinion about the mind while observing the twelve factors of Mother Earth and the animates created with them. First it is the brain, the intelligence created from it and the thought or image created through that intelligence. The mixture of all these things is the 'mind'. We name each and every visible item in the life. But 'Mind' is not a visible or tangible thing, like bread. We call one thing served in our lunch or dinner as 'bread'. But it is not made up of one thing. First it is the wheat or any such grain made up of twelve factors. Later with the manual work it is converted into the flour in the flourmill. Then it is converted into the dough that is formed after mixing some other ingredients in it along with the water. Later it is the round, square or oval shape that is given to it by patting. With the energy given to it through fire for roasting it is deliverable and consumable as a part of our meal. The making of a simple daily bread needs so many factors! Thus making of the 'mind' too demands combination of many factors. Then 'mind' is formed. The same 'mind' cannot be created in the dead body of any animate. It gets dead forever with the body!

Barring human some other animates do have 'mind' but in a very limited nature. Suppose if a lion is chasing a group of deer and they decide of a collective counter attack, the lion will run away! If each animal uses their 'mind' or say their 'intelligence' in this way, the lions will starve and won't get their prey! To avoid this; the creation structure has given the 'mind' of a limited nature to these animals! Else such use of a mind will break the chain of survival. The hunted animals wouldn't have been available as prey to the hunting animals. This is the difference between the 'human mind' and the 'other animal's mind'. So far I have been saying that the thought, wisdom and imagination powers are the gift given to the humankind, though human has been misusing it. Every creation through human hand is the 'mind's creation'.

****

7.13

The Manmade Predictions, Miracles, fate, Soul, Super Soul and Reincarnation Are not Agreeable To The Creation Structure, Mother Earth...

Friends, till now we read about the description about the creation of the Earth, about the twelve factors related to her and the living and non-living life that is created owing to them.

This is the importance of the twelve factors! It means yours and mine birth–death!!!...

Only due to the Earth and her related twelve factors we have the life that we have received and the breath that is going on. Any imbalance or any addition–reduction in these twelve factors will halt our breath, will end our existence. Also the life on Earth shall end. Each animate on the Earth is made up of these twelve factors.

As I am writing this, it is the month of April here in India and there is such a blazing Sun outside that one doesn't even wish to go outside! Everyone is just waiting eagerly for the rainy season to start. Just think of it, what will happen if the heat that one feels today continues forever? The animate won't get the water and food to sustain their existence. In the absence of water the existence of plant kingdom will be in the danger. Trees will get burnt. Without water and the unbearable heat, the lives of birds and animals would come to an end. Only skeletons of the wild animals would remain behind. How will the living and non-living creation would survive in the absence of fresh water? At such time, neither any God would be useful to give life to this creation nor would any charlatans' trick work. The charlatan himself won't survive!

There is a hue and cry about the global warming. Even if the layer of ozone gas within the environmental quilt that is clad by Earth starts getting dispersed; it won't be long before end of the life of the Earth. Formation of any new animate will stop. The water from all Seas and Oceans will vaporize away in the space. This will stop the formation of clouds and the water in the Oceans, Seas, rivers and lakes will deplete and dry up. It will change the form of today's Earth. She will get dry and barren like other planets. Moon doesn't have the environment and ozone and so gets directly hit by the blazing Sun rays which makes the temperature there as high as 105 degree Celsius. Same will be the position of the Earth in the absence of sufficient ozone. No one will survive to read whatever I am writing right now. Human never thinks of these things while living routine life. Today gold and silver is valued in the market and so he wastes all his life collecting it. But when the balance of the twelve factors would shake, your heart beats will stop forever and then no one will be alive to value the gold, silver and precious stones. No existence, no gold, silver and flat or bungalow! Nothing will have value! Will human ever understand the importance of the twelve factors?

I have described these twelve factors in detail. If you study that properly you will know that these twelve factors are your breath, your existence, the food you eat, the water you drink, the oxygen necessary for your life, the energy and the light you get. It means that when the things necessary for the creation of the life on the Earth and its sustenance and nurturance would end; the existence of the life on the Earth too will end.

If this is the truth, you must know the importance of your existence. Once you realize this, rather than giving the place to useless things like selfishness, possessive attitude, greed, fate and miracles for living happy, joyous and content life; you must observe the things agreeable to the creation structure so that your life will be easier in a real sense.

WHAT IS THE NEED OF FATE, PREDICTIONS OR GOLD--SILVER FOR THE PERSON WHO DOESN'T WANT A SINGLE ILL-GOTTEN PENNY OR EASY MONEY?...

Friends, you have thought and pondered over the things discussed in this book so far. If you have realized the reasons behind the ongoing cycle of the creation structure and your existence; then you will note one thing that there is no relation of these reasons with the prediction, miracles or manmade God or fate in this whole system. These things are created by some people in the humankind for their own vested interests. What I have to say is though some quack takes out a golden ring for you with his jugglery and if you are not selfish and not interested in the ill-gotten, easy money; then not just the ring, but will you have any business with such quack even if he takes out the golden bricks for you? Why do fall at the feet of such quack? Does he give you that golden ring? Even if he gives, why he would choose YOU? So many needy people are there in the world, why doesn't he create useful things for them?

IF MIRACLES CREATED GOLD, SILVER AND PRECIOUS LOCKETS AND RINGS IN REALITY; THEN GOVERNMENT SHOULD HIRE A SQUAD OF SUCH 50-60 CHARLATANS, QUACKS SO THE FEDERAL TREASURE WOULD ALWAYS BE FULL EVEN WITHOUT RECOVERING THE TAXES FROM PUBLIC!!!...

Government carries and uses the wealth received from you– the commoners–given in the form of taxes and duties recovered from you. Instead of recovering such taxes and duties and levies from the public and printing notes or minting coins; the government should permanently hire a squad of such 50–60 charlatans or quacks or any such 'miraculous' persons and fill the treasure using their miracles, isn't it? Why the factories and workers are needed? The treasure can easily be filled saving all those expenses! No searching for the gold mines and no spending of enormous money on that would be needed, isn't it? Why do we need all those things if we get such charlatans and miraculous quacks? With their existence how the masses would die of starvation? Isn't it?

No one can create a speck of dust on this Earth!!!...

I tell you with guarantee that there is no power in any animate on this plane of Earth that can create even a speck of dust with a miracle, forget about gold!

If you consider the whole creation structure, you will realize the truth behind my claim. None of the things on this plane of Earth can be produced without the Earth and her twelve factors! This canon applies to the creation of anything, even your own creation!

No animate has got the power to create even a flake of a dried grass. That too doesn't get created without the Mother Earth and her twelve factors. The misfortune of the humankind is that there are few people who fool others and also there is no dearth of people who get influenced by such conmen and get fooled happily worshipping them! This is such a simple thing, if there was any such power of creation then even the lions in jungles would get their hunt without any efforts with the help of miracles.

So who is real saint, real holy man?...

The person who is disinterested in the ill-gotten wealth or easy money, the person who is free from the vices like greed, selfishness, possessive attitude; such person doesn't need the fortune tellers, man-made Gods, fate, architects and such other things. Then I will say such person doesn't need any saint or holy man for his guidance and protection. Because such person himself is the saint, the holy man!

If you study this creation structure, this Mother Earth deeply; then you will realize that all such concepts are just the fads with which the society is infested!

Vastushastra (an Indian concept) theory is just created as a business to make money out of quackery! Check yourself...

Can you note one thing that if you give house to the family whose children have been sleeping in the open sky facing cold winds, hot Sun and rains; they wouldn't be concerned with which direction you are providing them the doors, windows or kitchen platforms.

They need the shelter! They actually will be very happy to get the shelter irrespective of its 'auspicious' directions. They won't see any harm from such house. Contrary to harm they will get protected from natural troubles of scorching Sun, chilling cold and wetting rains. The need of a house according to the Vastushastra (an Indian concept) is the fad of someone who has got more than enough money in his pockets! The needy person doesn't think of such things, but the one who has more money than necessary can think of it. Twelve thousand years before the human was staying in caves, he wasn't checking which side was the entrance of the cave! He only needed the protection from the wild animals, Sun, rain and cold and it was the only thing important to him. I have already given my own example regarding this in the previous chapters of this book.

The way of the creation structure!!!...

In last chapter I have convinced about the thought 'I am not mine'. If I do not belong to myself then whose fate am I taking about? Whose fortune is to be told and why is the need of quackery? What is the necessity of miracles and Vastushastra? These things are needed by the greedy and selfish people. The human lives within the limits of two types of laws. One is the law of the creation structure according to which your life is on a sort of autopilot! Breaking these rules of the creation structure is your end! This is the way of creation structure! It says, if you want to live, you must breathe! You must drink water! You must eat food! Avoiding these things will hundred percent lead you to the death!! Second types of laws are manmade laws which are made by handful of humans for other handful of humans. Other animate and the creation structure have nothing to do with it! For example, the law of monogamy is applicable in most religions, but the Muslim religion has got nothing to do with it. It is also not applicable to the other animates in the nature. No human will die disobeying this manmade law because some group of people has made it for their own social reasons.

During my visit to Singapore I observed that spitting on the streets had a fine of 5000 Singapore dollars. This is not applicable in all nations, especially in some Asian countries including my country India you would find the staircase corners of some buildings are colored due to habit of spitting. Thus the man-made laws are not applicable to entire creation nature, forget about just entire humankind. Animates don't die due to the no observance of such laws.

THE CONCEPTS OF BIRTH CHART, PROPHECIES, MIRACLES, VASTU SCIENCE AND QUACKERY WHICH IS CONCEIVED BY THE FERTILE HUMAN MIND ARE NOT APPLICABLE TO OTHER ANIMATES AND ACTUALLY HUMANS TOO!!!...

It is a law of the creation structure that one must eat just enough to meet ones' bodily need. But the human keeps stuffing more than necessary even when not hungry and also dies sometimes due to this overeating. The reason behind giving such examples is that as I have been mentioning, the concepts of birth chart, prophecies, miracles, vastu science and quackery are not applicable to the entire humankind! But some people in the humankind are totally taken away by these ideas. These things are not at all applicable to the other animates. Has rooster or hen ever tried to know their future through a fortune teller, that when will she be cut to get roasted? Has lioness ever checked her fate or sat idle thinking that if she has the hunt in her fate she anyway will get it? Has sparrow and other birds ever thought about the 'auspicious directions' before building their nests? Or have you seen animates wondering whether to take shelter of this tree or that tree or which direction the tree faces? Or has any fox gathered other foxes to fool them by showing the jugglery of creating the mouse from the air for meals? These things are not agreeable to the creation structure. Few people in the humankind seem to have taken the contract of such things for their own benefit! Due to selfishness, certain things are not digestible by few in the humankind. As if the Mother Earth has given the feelings only to them, so they retaliate as their 'feelings get hurt' when the truth comes to the surface! Such 'hurt' people behave against the laws of the creation and victimize the truth seekers. Didn't they kill truth bringers like Galileo?

So friends, if everyone studies the Mother Earth and her twelve factors you will be cocksure of the how harmful are these false concepts created by handful people. Then no one will be taken over by such people and they will not be supported. Even if such selfish people get hurt, don't leave the search for and the path of the truth! Use your own brain, not the brain of the selfish con-men! Follow your own heart, you will be not wrong.

THE MOTHER EARTH AND THE CREATION STRUCTURE ON HER DISAGREE WITH THE 'TENSE' - PAST TENSE, FUTURE TENSE - ONLY 'PRESENT TENSE' IS VALID! WHATEVER HAPPENS, IT HAPPENS ONLY IN THE PRESENT TENSE!!!...

Remember one thing, the Mother Earth is neither concerned with the things that have happened in the past i.e. the past tense, nor is She concerned with the things expected to happen in the future i.e. the future tense. Both of these are not agreeable by Her. Also as it is illustrated by famous Eckhart Toll in his book 'Power of Now'; barring humankind no other animates on Earth has anything to do with these 'tenses' or 'time'. No animal in the forests stores the food thinking of the future need! Neither have you heard a lionesses hunting 10 or 15 deer at once and storing them, nor have you ever heard them suddenly dying due to no storage of food! Also no lioness remembers the past tense that she had hunted a bull and had lot of trouble hunting it! The animals don't have past tense or future tense but handful humans are stuck with fate, future and miracles. Just because of the greed & selfishness they need the concepts of fortune and fate. These are mere human ideas.

The creation structure, the Earth and the other animates on her barring human - agree only with the present tense! 'Present' exists. The only truth is what exists 'today'. 'Yesterday' and 'tomorrow' are false as you have only 'today'.

So without dwelling in the future or past the human should live in the 'present'; just like other animates. Staying in present or

'now' will lessen your burdens, difficulties and sorrows. You will get peace of mind and health. Living in 'present' you shall enjoy the life. Else you will keep brooding about 'this fellow had abused me last year' or 'this fellow had duped me two years back" and waste your joyous present. Who are you to think about what will happen tomorrow? Are you larger than Mother Earth? She is the 'accomplished' one. She has our threads and we must dance to her music! She has created all animates. If she doesn't have the 'past' and 'future' tense who are you to have it? There is no as miraculous power as She is. It is so difficult to rain in the desert but there is snow fall sometimes, though rare. Only Mother Earth can do this miracle. So my human friends, earn just enough for the needs, be content with it. Dwell each present moment of your life happily. Don't waste your time peeking in the future. Also don't waste the time in sorrow by remembering the past. Don't cry over the spilt milk. Don't whine over past tense blaming whatever happened in the past. I shall explain how this is not agreeable to the creation structure.

CREATION STRUCTURE DOESN'T AGREE WITH THE PAST OR FUTURE TENSE. IT IS AGAINST THE RULE OF THE CREATION STRUCTURE. THIS IS THE DOCTRINE!...

Friends, we know that the Earth revolves west to eastwards around herself. She never revolves otherwise. She doesn't look at the past. If she ever would do it, all the life on her will be perished. Earth never gets into the past tense, it is not agreeable to her. Also she never looks into the future. She needs twenty four hours to complete the revolution around self; she never hurriedly completes it within eighteen hours to peek into the future, isn't it? She always revolves in the 'present'. You can get such many examples of the creation structure. Creation structure doesn't agree with the past tense, future tense or the miracles created by human; because she knows for sure that human cannot perform the miracles! These hints are just one thing that one must keep away from quackery. Instead learn to curb such selfish attitude in the society. Such attitude destroys the health of the society.

Oh human, would the apple tree ever bear the fruits of orange? Even the creation structure cannot perform this miracle!!!...

Such a powerful and huge Mother Earth, but she too cannot usually change the creation structure. She cannot perform miracles against the creation structure. Have you ever seen the apple tree laden with the oranges? Has Mother Earth ever performed such miracle? Has human womb ever delivered an elephant? Has the roots like potato grown on the tree like tomato? If it is not possible for the Mother Earth to perform such miracles then is it possible for the human whom she has given the birth and exists due to her? Why should the human believe such miracles? Human has received the power of intelligence and thinking so if he studies and understands the Earth and the creation structure and live life according to her rules; after dwelling happily he would be able to take the leave of Mother Earth one day happily.

Friends, with this description you would have understood that things like fortune telling, vastu, fate man-made God or miracles on this plane of Earth aren't agreed by Mother Earth and creation structure. These things are created by the selfishness, greed, fear and worries created by the humankind, they don't exists in reality.

****

7.14

This Too Is The Law of A Creation Structure

NO ANIMATE HAS THE REINCARNATION!!!

The Plan of Creation Structure Is That Of Reproduction! Not of Reincarnation!

NOT REINCARNATION BUT REPRODUCTION!!!...

Is there reincarnation for animates including human being? There had been fruitless discussions in the legends, religious scripts and various other books of authority. But I assert that the reincarnation is not agreeable to the creation structure! This is just the ignorance of the humankind. Here it is explained!!!

To understand this thing, the ignorance of the human of considering himself different and greater than the other animates created by the Mother Earth, is the hindrance. Due to this ignorance the ancestors of some humans have believed in reincarnation. If you read this book by heart from the beginning to the end and study it properly, you will get the answer to the question whether there is reincarnation or not.

WHAT NEXT AFTER DEATH? UNDERSTAND THIS PROCESS OF REPRODUCTION!!!...

Not understanding the architecture of the creation structure and the Earth, most of the humankind have dilemma about 'what next after death?' No proper illustration or scientific explanation has come in front of the humankind. To reveal about the reincarnation one must understand 'why' and 'when' the first animate was created on the Earth. After that, means after the 3497.5 million years of the creation of the first animate, the first human being was created. **It wasn't the reincarnation or rebirth of the first human because there wasn't any human animate born on this Earth before that.**

What is reincarnation? It means after the end of first birth getting the second birth. This understanding gave the term 'reincarnation' or 'rebirth'. But when the first human was born, it wasn't preceded by his birth. Then from where did the concept of 'rebirth' came into the picture? And if there is no rebirth then from where did the soul and super soul came into the picture? The creation structure came into existence on the Earth. The root of that Earth is the hot ball. On such hot ball where the soul or super soul exists? If it exists on such hot ball then it must also exist on the dry planets like Venus, Mars, Saturn and Moon. So according to the doctrine of immortality of the soul, if we send 10–12 pairs of male–female there should be rebirth and reproduction. But in reality would reproduction happen there? I say never! It is, because after the hot ball of the Earth was cooled, the twelve Earth related factors were born first.

The Ignorance of some humans is that they think of the 'reproduction' as 'rebirth or reincarnation'! But it is not acceptable to the creation structure!!!...

Due to these twelve factors the first animate was born on the Mother Earth. Later after 3497.5 million years the first human was born on the Earth. Later male–female two separate identity were created. Due to the emotion of sexual attraction between them the reproduction journey began. Some humans seemed to be in great ignorance that they started calling this reproduction as 'reincarnation'. The creation structure doesn't accept this concept of 'reincarnation' that has birthed in the human mind. When the old authority books were written the human intelligence wasn't developed as much as it is today. He wasn't aware of the reasons behind the creation of the animate including human. The main point here is what is next after death? It is nothingness. End of everything for good. No coming back, no going back, complete salvation! Human was ignorant about the Earth those days. The good example about this is one holy book. Even today the human doesn't have deep knowledge of the Earth, this is the big ignorance. After reading this book from the beginning will ascertain this true fact.

In the holy book of some it was written that the 'Earth is flat. On such flat Earth there are Seas. If any boat sails to the other bank she will fall down'. Also, 'the Sun, Moon and the stars are rotating around the Earth'. Such things of ignorance were mentioned in the holy books of olden times. This knowledge was proven wrong by the scientist Galileo with his doctrines proving that the Earth is not flat but round and rotates around the Sun and not that the Sun rotates around her; in front of the priests of the church for which he got life imprisonment. I have mentioned this earlier. This means no matter which time period the human belongs to; he is allergic to the truth. Even if someone proves them the falsehood of the traditional knowledge and wrong beliefs, they are very fond of and engrossed with them that they will kill the truth-teller no matter how much ever s/he tries to prove, but will not leave their wrong beliefs.

THE ORIGINAL HUMAN HAD ONLY ONE SOUL, THEN FROM WHERE DID THESE PRESENT 7000 MILLION SOULS CAME FROM? THIS IS THE PROOF OF THE ABSENCE OF THE SOUL!!!...

The first human animate was born just 2.5 million years before. To the people who firmly believe in the existence of the soul I wish to ask a question that even if we assume that this first human had one soul then from where did the 7000 million souls of present population came from? Because the original soul was just one! Before that there wasn't any soul on this plane of Earth, because the Earth was a hot ball. So there wasn't any human. So the concept of reincarnation has come from the traditional thoughts. The people ignorant about the creation structure should keep one thing in mind. That is, the creation structure doesn't create new souls each day to feed all from one type of soul. So I am explaining ahead about the process of new creation through the creation structure.

Soul is not the reason behind the reproduction! So no one is born again!!!...

There is no reason for the creation of soul. So called soul doesn't give birth to anyone or animate the body. If that was the case then there are so many rocks and stones lying on the Earth in which they could have entered and they would have got the consciousness. Why does this so called soul need the body of only a human? Other than human, there are so many millions of animates on this Earth, don't they have souls? Doesn't hen have soul? Doesn't the groundnut or the tree of mango have soul? Doesn't wheat or oats have soul? Such a vast life dwells on Earth doesn't it have soul? Worms are found in the rotten fruits. Within such packed flesh of fruits from where does the soul come in that wiggly worm? If it can go in such closed fruit then why can't it go in the rocks and stones? If it enters them they too would animate because according to your traditional belief the reincarnation depends upon the soul, isn't it?

Nothing like soul exists! Here is the doctrine!!!...

The animation or the movement that we see in each animate is not due to the soul but the Earth and twelve factors related to her. Each consciousness or the animation of each animate depends upon these twelve factors. We shall take an example of the water out of these twelve factors. What happens if some animate doesn't get the water? We all know that devoid of water the animate dies. If there is soul in the body then what is the reason for death? You claim that the soul animates the body! But at least do you accept that if the Earth doesn't rotate around the Sun then all animates will die? Then what is the role of the soul? What about the soul in the body that is animating at that time? The animate should be alive due to the soul even if the Earth doesn't rotate! But it doesn't happen. If the Earth doesn't rotate all the animate beings will die. Also there will be no reincarnations. So what is the role of the so called soul? Just like this the animate is created, birthed, breathes not due to one or two factors but the Earth related twelve factors; not due to the soul!

So soul is mere a human abstract idea not a reality! So there is no question of reincarnation.

Sun too doesn't have anything called soul! Once the storage of the hydrogen gets over, he too will die forever!!!...

Human is so engrossed in the mundane life that s/he doesn't have time to observe and study the Mother Earth and the creation structure on her. There is one more important principle of this universe which I have mentioned time and again; that is creation is the root cause of destruction for good to which even our Sun is not an exception. Then where comes in the picture the soul and the super soul? If everything that gets created is perishable then it doesn't matter whether it is manmade, universe made or Earth made. When this is the reality from where the soul and super soul comes in the picture? The first animate created on this Earth, then whether it may be a human, a tree or aquatic; while getting created it comes with the potential of the reproduction. The potential of reproduction is inbuilt in each animate. So for the continuation of the creation structure there is a cycle of reproduction, not reincarnation. 'Creation of many from one' is the principle. The creation structure acts according to this principle. Check how.

Creation of many animates from the single type of animate is the rule of the creation! So the soul is mere an imagination!! Check this doctrine!!!...

One animate reproduces many animates. This is the rule of the creation structure. No animate is an exception to this rule. From one grain of the maize hundreds of maize grains are created. Do hundreds of souls get created accordingly? 'Creation of the soul' is not the law of the creation structure! And so there is no reincarnation.

First one human was created on the Earth. Now almost 7000 million humans dwell on this Earth. These are not created by reincarnation but by the principle of 'many from one', just like from one pea many peas are created. Otherwise according to this so called soul, there should be just one animate on this Earth!

According to your imagination about the soul the same soul should rebirth. Means always just one human should be created. There wouldn't have been the creation of many from one. So reincarnation and soul are the human concepts. Creation structure has nothing to do with it. Even today for the creation of any animate the environment is mainly responsible. If there is no environment on this Earth then which soul and who would reincarnate here?

OUT OF TWELVE FACTORS, 'ENVIRONMENT' IS THE MAIN RESPONSIBLE FACTOR GIVE BIRTH TO THE ANIMATE! NOT SOUL!!!...

So I have created my own doctrine that atmosphere is the root cause of the creation. If the temperature on the Earth rises to 70 degree Celsius, all animate beings would die. Then where will the soul go? Who will be reincarnated? The ignorance about the reincarnation and soul is just because of not having the deep knowledge about the Earth and her creation structure. These are many of the long running misunderstandings within humankind. But humankind has given the important place to such wrong beliefs and embraced them. Such wrong beliefs are not beneficial to the humankind but are harmful. But knowing this if someone tries to prove such traditional beliefs to be wrong; he attracts the animosity of the humankind. Such has been the ungrateful attitude of the humankind so far! But after the death of that truth teller they shall worship him by decorating his photographs with garlands! The best example of this is Galileo. Today they name the satellites or ships 'Galileo'. After his death he was worshipped. But during his life time he was tortured to death.

HOW THE LIFE ON EARTH IS CREATED WITHOUT THE SOUL? HERE IS THE DOCTRINE FOR THE SAME!!!...

Now I come to the point and explain about the process of creation of the life on the Earth.

I have already told you that there are two types of animates, immobile and mobile. Out of these the animates who birth through the mother's womb are the mammals or vertebrates and those who take birth through eggs are the invertebrates or oviparous. The ones only taking birth in the water are aquatics. Also some animates are born due to temporary environment creation like the insects growing in the rainy season, centipedes and millipedes, flying insects around the light bulb. Some animates are created on the dirt or rotten environments like wiggly worms in rotten fruits. Whereas immobile animates means the entire plant kingdom ranging from algae to huge trees.

Any living being is always born on Earth with its element or fraction of reproduction!!! Here is the doctrine!!!...

Every animate being on Earth is born with its element of reproduction. No living being is an exception to this. This is an important facet of creation structure works.

Here let's see an example of an immobile animate being. We shall see how a mango tree is born.

The basic form of a mango tree is its seed from which saplings of mango tree are prepared for cultivation. This seed has a hard outer covering. After germinating the seed in the soil and providing it with necessary 12 factors, water, fertilizers etc. its reproductive fraction sprouts and its tender leaves are visible. As its stalk grows, these leaves too grow. It eventually develops into a sapling. The roots of this sapling start spreading through the ground. They grow deep in the ground as the sapling grows and strengthens the support. The outer cover of the mango seed is supporting sapling in this process. It expands as the roots spread in the ground. As the roots grow and sapling firmly stands in the soil, the task of seed regarding reproduction gets over and it merges in the soil. The original mango seed germinated in the soil is never seen again. It is disintegrated in the soil.

What created the sapling of mango tree? It's because of the reproductive element or fraction present in the germinated seed of the mango tree. The new sapling is born as a result of fruition of the reproductive fraction within. Not just due to mango seed. What is the role of the germinated seed in this process? It is just to support the sapling till it stands firm on its own. The body of seed plays this role.

I will explain you in a different way to make you realize what birthed the mango sapling.

If we remove the reproductive fraction or element from any animate being, then that being will not be reproduced!!! Then what is 'soul'?...

Now, let us think that we cut the reproductive element or fraction present in the seed and germinated the seed in the soil, provided it with ample water and fertilizers. But even if we wait for many days, that seed will not sprout and new sapling will not be born. That mango seed shall decay and disintegrate within the soil. Means there will be no reproduction through that mango seed. When does reproduction take place? Only when it has the reproductive element or fraction present in it! Once you took away the reproductive element in it, it did not reproduce or create. New sapling wasn't born. The reproduction stopped after discarding the reproductive fraction. Now tell me, here what is the role of so called 'soul'? Where did it come from? This process of reproduction applies to all living beings, including humans too!!!

The live sperms in the semen are the root of reproduction! There is no birth and no soul from the dead sperm!!!...

The new life is formed only due to the presence of the potential of production within the living animate. If this potential, this fraction of reproduction gets destroyed, none of the animate will be formed on this Earth. Then where is the question of the so called soul and the reincarnation? The same process applies to the human being. Laws of the creation structure are the same to all animate beings. In human race all male and females come with the fraction of reproduction. Their offspring are born only due to the potential of reproduction contained within them, due to the sperms and egg in male and female respectively. Only the live sperms can fertilize the egg and cause reproduction. The important part is liveliness of the sperm and egg, if they are not live, they cannot produce. So only the live animates can reproduce, dead animates cannot reproduce. Regarding this I have cited an example of a woman in the one of last chapters. For reproduction only living animate beings are needed. Reproduction happens only through animated.

Fresh and new fraction of the reproduction gives new birth. Stale semen isn't capable of birthing!!!...

I gave an example of the mango seed above. But if I just keep this seed as it is for 10 years and plan to use it for sowing after 10 years; it won't reproduce. Any seed, any grain needs to be fresh and new for the reproduction to take place. Reproduction doesn't take place when it is stale and out-dated. Young parents would give birth to healthy offspring.

It doesn't happen in the old age. To reproduce many animate beings from one animate, the existence of the reproductive potential is essential. This is a part of the creation structure that births the life.

Another proof of non-existence of reincarnation and soul!!!...

After sowing the seed it germinates and sprouts and perhaps the so called soul enters into its new form. But if we cut the apex of the seed, the seed doesn't sprout. Then where does that soul go? This means there is nothing called 'soul' and if you insist on its existence you may call it so to the original seed which was sprouted, otherwise you are just burdened with this concept. You may call the fraction of reproduction the 'soul' but if it too gets out-dated there will not be any reproduction, then where is the existence of 'soul'?

As I gave an example of the mango seed, we shall take an example of the groundnut. What creates handful of groundnuts with single groundnut? If we observe minutely we shall find that the radical–the embryonic root of the groundnut has the potential of the reproduction hidden. This part of the single groundnut is responsible for producing the handful of groundnuts. If you check it separately you shall find the leaves of the groundnut in it in the micro form. In short, the fraction of reproduction of the groundnut is this part – the radical of it. If we cut it off and sow the groundnut in the soil and nurtured a lot with fertilizers and water; it will be useless. The new sapling will not be formed from it. This means that the whole groundnut does not reproduce. But the radical, the tiny fraction of reproduction within the groundnut reproduces. Then whether it is a human being or any other animate, they birth the new animate due to the fraction of reproduction within them. You may call this reproduction as reincarnation as you like. But the body that reproduces neither has the reincarnation nor the soul. If some man or woman undergoes vasectomy they will never reproduce. It means the fraction of reproduction within the male and female births the new offspring. If you want you may assume this as the reincarnation of male or female. But not so called 'soul' within the body of an animate causes the reincarnation. Within these illustrations you must have understood that we don't reincarnate. We don't reincarnate means there isn't any 'soul' or 'super soul'!

EACH ANIMATE IS BORN ONCE AND DIES ONCE! NO BIRTH AND NO DEATH AGAIN!!!...

Once the original mango seed or the groundnut is sown in the ground, they will not come back again. In short their existence ends. This law of the creation structure is applicable to all the life on the Earth. Take an example of the birds. Through the copulation of the male–female, the female bird lays the eggs. The prototype of the bird is formed after they are hatched. The parent male–female birds nurture the hatchlings by feeding them the worms, grains and insects until their growth. Once the fledglings get enough strength in their wings they fly away. Considering all this creation structure, after the reproduction, the responsibility of feeding and nurturing the new animates until they form their own independent existence is mainly given to all animate beings. After fulfilling this responsibility the task on the Earth of these animate beings ends. Once the task ends, the animate perishes to which we call death.

Such perished animate doesn't have a rebirth or soul or super soul. Such cycle of the creation shall continue until the Earth and her related twelve factors are favorable. When any one factor out of these twelve reduces or increases creating an imbalance, the existence of the Earth shall end and the life on her and this creation cycle on her too shall automatically end. Where shall be the soul at that time?

To understand this and ward off the superstitions this knowledge must be imparted in the childhood from the schools and colleges!!!...

While this is the reality, few in the human race take pleasure in adding to the ignorance by spicing up and narrating the legends of the reincarnation. So I have mentioned at many places in my book that without understanding their basic similarity with other animate beings, the humankind considers themselves different from them. Due to this ignorance, the human cannot enjoy their life fully. **Not understanding the difference between two animate beings the human is engrossed by the vices of greed, selfishness, jealousy and sad emotions and wastes the valuable life. So I desire that to give the knowledge of this reality to the students from the primary schools and college levels; this book may be included in the academic curriculum.**

Due to the stupid superstitious ideas like this the humankind is at a tremendous loss!!!...

Due to traditional false ideas, the humankind has been at a tremendous loss, day by day the superstitions are getting stronger. Though the human is marching towards the 21st century s/he is not ready to leave the old traditional superstitious beliefs, there has been the addition in it, quackery is increasing. Forget about the commoners, the politicians and learned masters too are enamored by such quacks. At least now you should reconsider your thinking about these superstitions and reincarnations. Just say good bye to the superstitions!

If the Sun too doesn't have the reincarnation or soul then how human possesses the same?...

Whatever is created gets permanently perished one day on

this plane of Earth. Just as the Sun is created; but he too shall die someday permanently. After his death the 8 planets rotating around him and their satellites too are going to die. They will never get created in their original form. Our Earth too is included into this. This means even these huge celestial beings don't have the reincarnation. No soul and no super soul. And then are these applicable only to the humans on the Earth? We have read in the earlier chapter on Sun about how Sun is going die one day and how his existence will end one day. Once he dies there is no reincarnation to him. If he doesn't has the 'reincarnation', then how the human who is born upon the energy of Sun can have the reincarnation? If all this is understood, automatically the idea of reincarnation in your mind shall perish.

'Just as we drop the old shirt and change to the new shirt, the soul of the animate being drop the body after it gets old and wears the new body' –this is the doctrine mentioned about the soul in the old scripture. If there is a real existence of the soul then why does this so called soul changes the body impulsively without waiting for it to get old? For example why does the soul leave the body out of the fetus when it is still in the mother's womb? Or what is its reason for leaving the tender body of 4 month old neo natal or a new born? Don't we see a 4 month old baby dying? Or even a youngster in early twenties dying? Why does the soul leave the young body? So many animate beings die on this plane of Earth just after taking birth or when they are young. Then if we consider the doctrine in the scripture, why does the soul leave the body when it is young? Means there is no meaning to this doctrine in the authority book! In reality the soul doesn't exist, it is the human imagination! This is the second proof I add to the earlier proofs I have already given.

As we change the shirt, the 'soul' changes the body is a myth! Check how?...

The scriptures mention that like we change the shirt worn on the body after it gets old, the soul changes the body when it gets old. I say, this is where the human errors. The error is differentiating between the body and the shirt. I say that the twelve factors that made the body and the shirt are the same for the both. Shirt hasn't fallen from the sky. Its birth took place out of twelve factors of the Mother Earth. Similarly the formation of the human body too takes these twelve factors. Reduction of even a single factor would neither have created the shirt nor the body. So I have mentioned earlier too that 'differentiating between the self and others' is the big ignorance of the humankind. In reality there is no difference. Now I shall explain how the shirt and the body are the same. We shall first know how the shirt is created. The seed of cotton is sown in the soil. It grew into a sapling. Sapling grew into a tree. At appropriate stage of its growth it gets laden with the bolls. The cotton is created from these bolls. Then processing that cotton the final product is shirt. For this entire process the twelve factors were needed. Means the cotton too is one type of animate like human. From one immobile animate the shirt is made. Similarly the human body is created through the sperm made up of the same twelve factors. Just like the human body is made up with the factors like - Sun light, rotating of the Earth, air and water; the body of shirt too is made up from the cotton that needed these twelve factors. So there is no difference between the human body and the shirt. As the shirt shall perish one day, the human body too shall perish means die one day. The only difference is that one is the mobile animate and the other is immobile animate being. So both the beings have the inevitability of death. Both of them have nothing called 'soul'. So it is better to keep the stories of the scripture to the scripture itself.

Shouldn't we teach this true knowledge to all young and elder ones? Friends, just think about this please!

THE CREATION STRUCTURE HAS BIRTHED YOU ONLY FOR THE REPRODUCTION. NOT FOR GETTING VARIOUS ADJECTIVES LIKE RICH, POOR, ROYAL, MASTER, ENLIGHTENED, WISE, INSANE, PRIME MINISTER OR PRESIDENT OR FOR STAYING HERE PERMANENTLY BUT TO LEAVE AFTER YOUR TASK OF REPRODUCTION GETS OVER; THIS IS THE REASON BEHIND EVERY ANIMATE BEINGS' BIRTH! UNDERSTAND THE DEFINITION OF THE BIRTH!!!...

The creation structure has given you the birth only for the reproduction! After reproduction, nurturing the offspring to make it independent and getting old after finishing this and taking leave of the Mother Earth is the only rule of the creation. The birth of an animate is not for eating, drinking and getting rich but to continue the cycle of creation. Without this intention the creation structure would have ended. There wouldn't have been any animate being visible on the Earth. Earth would have been barren. So she has made the provision for your eating and drinking and given you the desire of copulation. What would have happened without it? So the only intention of the creation behind birthing you is birthing many from one. Understand this creation structure.

****

7.15

The Enigma Of Death!

What Is Death? What Is After Death?

Life means death! This too is the law of the creation structure. 'Creation is the root cause of destruction'. From the point of view of the animate being the death is one moment of joy, the moment of salvation!!!...

What is death? Have you thought about it? Does the one fearing death know about the death? Death is the end of some creation that took place in this universe. Death is inevitable. Means creation is the root cause of the death. Creation or life is death; this is the simple definition of the death. Something that is never created doesn't have the question of death. According to this principle, whatever is created on this Earth, including Earth; it all certainly has a death!

All the life created on the Earth since her creation, including manmade God, all have died! Anything that is manmade or the nature created, are perishable one day. So instead of looking at death from an emotional, painful and sad angle it should be looked upon and accepted as an inevitable reality of the life. Owing to their ignorance, many from the intelligent human race question 'what next after death?' According to their fancy there is something next to the death! But there is nothing next after the death.

The body made up of twelve factors! As there is a death to the body according to the law of creation, each organ of the body too has the death! After taking the birth and delivering the task of reproduction and nurturance that is given by the creation structure; each organ of the body slows down which gives the old age to each animate being. Then whether they are the tree or an animal, bird or a human or the lion in the forest; the parts of each animates' body slow down after a period. The body animates through the organs due to the twelve factors. When the bodily organs stop receiving the twelve factors, the animate is said to be dead. Because twelve factors means the life! Ending of twelve factors is death! This process is applicable to all the creation in the universe. The existence of Sun depends upon the gases of helium and hydrogen upon him. Just like any animate, the combustion process of hydrogen is going on Sun too. Due to some reason if it increases and the storage of hydrogen ends on the Sun, it means the death of the Sun. As there is a death to the Sun, there is a death to the human being.

Someone's death may cause sorrow for some and the joy for others! Means this is all person dependent!!!...

Humans cannot tolerate the idea of the death of the near and dear ones and dreads it. The main reason behind it is the companionship, emotions, attachment and selfishness. On this Earth many lonely people die each second but no one cries for them. The reasons behind crying or wailing over someone's death is that the dead one could be young, could be the only bread winner for the family, having many dependents on him and so a thought that after his/ her death who will look after these dependents or who will feed after him or her; the presence of such some or the other selfish intents are always there. Passing away of that person harms this selfish intent somewhere. So the sorrow, sadness is expressed about such person. The death of a smiling, good natured, honest and harmless person creates genuine sorrow. But sometimes though people may express sorrow over the death of troublesome, manipulative, exploiting natured goon outwardly; inside they know that troublemaker is gone and are happy to get rid of such a person! Someone's death may cause such reactions in the society. There is a close relation between the death and emotions in the human race. Someone's death creates an emotional outbreak. Someone's death may deeply affect the immature people to the extent that they themselves embrace the death! When I was around 18 -19 years old, the sudden outbreak of the news of India's Prime Minister Jawaharlal Nehru's death was difficult to tolerate for some people. It was so intolerable to some overemotional people that they committed suicide! This kind of act happens only from the over-emotional, ignorant and immature persons.

EACH PERSON OR ANIMATE BEING IS BORN INDEPENDENT OF ANYONE FROM THE CREATION STRUCTURE'S POINT OF VIEW AND DIES INDEPENDENT OF ANYONE ELSE. THERE IS NO CO-RELATION BETWEEN ONE ANIMATE TO OTHER IN THIS RESPECT!!!...

In reality each animate is born independent and lives life independently. There is no co-relation between two animates about this. Human race has created relationships from own imagination. These relationships establish emotional bonds of each human with the other humans. But creation structure does not accept these relationships or emotions. Suppose, one baby and her birth giving parents is the relationship established from the human concepts; but their hungers are different. Baby's hunger doesn't get satisfied if mother eats or father eats; or due to baby's satisfied hunger parents hunger doesn't get satisfied. Suppose if the baby falls down and gets injured while playing, the pains of the bleeding wound are to be endured by her alone. Birth giver parents cannot share baby's pain. They at the most can medicate her, cuddle and hug her and try to divert her attention from the pain. But the baby's pain cannot be divided and shared. **So every ones' creation, existence, joy, happiness and sorrow is independent.** Each animate being in real sense is not related with each other with this respect.

JOY, SORROW, HEALTH, PEACE ARE PERSON DEPENDENT THINGS. THEY DON'T EXIST IN THE CREATION STRUCTURE!! 'DEATH' IS NOT AN EASILY AVAILABLE THING!!!...

Suppose I eat a sweet apple sitting in front of some one. The joy I am getting of that sweetness of apple cannot be enjoyed by the person sitting next to me. So joy, happiness, health and peace too are not related to the relationship. These things are independent for each person. The sharpness of sorrow gets blunt after living the life with this understanding. Accordingly each person's death too is independent. Death of one person is not related to the other person according to the rule of the creation structure. Once this rule is understood one need not get swayed away in excessive emotions. One's lifestyle is not dependent on someone else's lifestyle. In fact getting death is not that easy. There are so many diseased, bed ridden people waiting for the death on this plane of Earth; but death is not ready to accept them. In this world so many disabled, mentally affected people are living life for they don't get death. Here the emotions of the human being come in between. Whether the emotions given to the human are boon or bane could be a subject of a big debate. But since other animate beings don't have the emotions there is no sorrow or grief felt by them.

EMOTIONS ARE ONLY ATTACHED TO THE HUMAN BEINGS. IN THIS CREATION STRUCTURE, IN ANY OTHER ANIMATE BEINGS NO ONE GETS EMOTIONAL!!!...

Once while wandering in the Crawford market of the city Mumbai in India I saw some 20–25 live hens kept in the basket with their legs tied together and the person sitting beside was swiftly cutting each hens' head with his sharp knife and keeping the cut head on one side and the writhing body in one vessel. I casually thought that had this been happening in case of humans, there would have been such a commotion! There would have been the huge outbreak of the human emotions. But since the hens don't have emotions they didn't have feelings; the hens in the basket had no grief towards the hen whose neck was under the sharp knife. No emotions so no joy and no sorrow.

ONCE THE REPRODUCED ONE GETS STABLE, YOUR TASK ON THE EARTH GETS OVER! THEN YOU SHOULD GET LOST FROM HERE, MEANS ACCEPT THE DEATH THIS IS THE LAW OF THE CREATION STRUCTURE!!!.

Besides human being, so many animate beings die. But no one grieves for one another. Their life routines go on according to the nature's law. The humans also have the attachment to the life as some of them have the attachment towards collecting gold, money and properties. They never want to die. They feel dread with the mention of death. Actually this is their ignorance, because death is inevitable. After the reproduction task is over and the offspring gets stability, the first creation's work gets over. After your task gets over according to the creation structure's law you should empty that space for the new creation. Should you live just to eat the bread and butter of the Earth? This is not acceptable to the creation structure. So there is a provision of the death. Despite someone's being rich, wise, brave, clever, king, quack or even so called God; one has to face an inevitable death. Why should there be such a long stay here? Leave after the task gets over, there is no point in staying longer as a guest. Each animate has come here as a guest. So without keeping any attachment you should move your seat from here permanently!

IN THIS LIFE THERE HASN'T BEEN ANY ANIMATE WHO LIVED THE HAPPY LIFE WITHOUT NEEDING ANYTHING! EVEN THE GREAT SAINTS, GREAT WISE MEN AREN'T AN EXCEPTION TO THIS!! NO BIRTH OF ANY ANIMATE BEING IS HAPPY; THIS IS THE LAW OF THE CREATION STRUCTURE!!!.

End of anything that is created is the law of creation. No one's principle, no one's thoughts or no animate being is greater in front of this creation. Once this principle is understood, all questions will be solved. Creation is the root cause of the sorrow and demise. According to this principle every animate is born along with death. Also the sorrows and problems come along with the birth till the death. Neither any animate being is created without problems or sorrow having a life full of happiness, devoid of neediness, who never cried till the death since birth; nor would such animate will be born after this.

In the recent century there was a widely accepted person birthed in India. He was very devoted, elegant, pious and so truthful preacher that he practiced the preaching himself first. Not just this, but also it is said that he used to actually talk to the 'Goddess'. Despite all this he was infested by cancer in his last days. So enduring the unbearable pains this person died. All I want to say that however great someone may be from the point of view of the human thought or idea; the birth taken by that great person is never joyous or full of happiness. Many examples like this can be cited. Means the birth is one type of penalty for each animate.

I have already discussed this in the chapter called 'Birth'. Till the death, each animate is stuck with the needs and sorrow. No animate has the control on when, where and in what condition the death should be faced. We see in the society that even after all the tasks in the life are over, one gets bed ridden waiting for the death. Nothing brings the death closer and till then the tremendous penalty has to be endured.

HERE IS ANOTHER PROOF. BIRTH IS JUST THE ILLUSION OF THE 'JOY'. IT IS A GREAT FORTUNE TO GET THE DEATH IN A GOOD CONDITION!!!...

I had a friend aged 75 years and I had occasions of foreign travel with him 2–3 times. The introduction during the travel led to the friendship. He was regular at exercises besides being a nutritious diet observer since his childhood. So he enjoyed the robust health devoid of any common health problems like hypertension or diabetes even at the age of 75. He used to say 'I still feel like 10 year old and would like to play marbles.' He was such a person with great health. Once he visited the place called Mathura in India for Krishna festival along with wife and some friends. The festivities went on very well and they boarded in the train for return journey. In the morning the train reached at Zanshi station and his friends found that one side of the body of my healthy friend wasn't functioning from head to toe! He had got an attack of paralysis during his sleep. They somehow reached to Pune and he was admitted to the hospital. After knowing this I went to see him at the hospital. I was shocked to see the person once in the robust health in a paralyzed situation that he couldn't move at all. Neither could he get up and sit nor could he toss from one side to another. All nature calls were catered on the bed itself. In that situation he gave me a look and the tears started flowing from his eyes. Perhaps he had recognized me in that state. As there wasn't any effect of the treatment even after 2 months, he was brought home. He had wife, son and daughter–in–law who used to be at his continuous service. But my friend wasn't recovering from the disability. Even after the year passed there wasn't any improvement in his health. Since I was close to the family, his family members used to frankly tell me that they were bored of serving him on the bed without any signs of recovery, their lives were bounded to that task of tending him and there seemed no way out. Almost for one and a half year my friend was bed ridden in that miserable state. He was waiting for the death and even his family members too were waiting for his death. But the death was cheating him.

The 75 years of the life were spent nicely; but he might have felt the last one and a half year as hundred and fifty years long! This is the scene of the animate beings' life! I have already said that the birth is a bane rather than a boon! Like we see in this example, his family members were waiting for his death eagerly. But he wasn't getting death. Means from their point of view, his death was a joyous moment rather than being a sad event. They were relieved the day he died. Now tell me who says death is a sad and bad event? Today there are several of lives in this world who are waiting for their death. But they aren't getting it easily! So knowing this pre–death situation isn't it fortunate to get the death when your eye sight is good, legs and hands are giving you proper work? This thing I am saying for all animate beings on the Earth and not just only for humans. This writing is done while keeping all animate beings on the Earth in the mind. All are same for the Mother Earth.

While roaming in the forests of Africa I saw the lion on the verge of death. Once upon a time the roar of this king of jungle might have shattered the whole forest! But death wasn't ready to accept him easily. Now you must have understood that getting the birth is not much a happy thing! Facing many hurdles after the birth one has to wait for the death too. There are many people who are in coma for years together, but the death doesn't even touch them!

But some people are immensely scared of death...

Some people are shit scared of death! So the thoughts about death are dancing in their minds, 'what will happen if I die? Will they take me to the graveyard? Who all will keep crying near my dead body?' such many thoughts engross their mind during the day and at night these thoughts often mugged up reflect in the dreams in the form of pictures of graveyards, gathered people igniting the pyre of fire etcetera. Such strange and fearful dreams the person manifests. The saying 'the dreams are but the reflections of mind' isn't prevalent for nothing. Accordingly ghosts too are the creation of human imaginations. Actually there is no ghost. To the fearless one, who never behaves wrong in his life, doesn't indulge into ill – gotten things; has no fear at all. Actually death is permanent salvation. It is freedom from all things like needs, fear, troubles and worries. Death means getting rid of a curse.

In the beginning of this chapter many eyebrows would have been raised reading the title 'death means a moment of joy'; many must be thinking 'why the author is talking insane?' But there are so many beings waiting for the death on this Earth and if you see them closely, you will know and will surely understand the meaning of my statement. The one fearing the death is engrossed in the mundane life.

At least now will you be convinced about the necessity of euthanasia?...

Actually one shouldn't get birth and if at all born then it should end in joy at the right age. Taking birth is in no one's hand. But the human in this animate creation must get the right to end the life received happily. Then there will be the right use of the gifts of thought and imagination powers, wisdom and the intelligence that human has received. So I am going to convince about the importance of the euthanasia. Someone who is engrossed in receiving the hospitality here may find my thinking as negative. After the hospitality gets over they will find my thoughts positive. Today I too have completed the 70 years of my life. My task on this Earth has ended. So I too am waiting for that happy moment means the death eagerly. In fact had the law of euthanasia been existing in my country, I would have embraced the death at the age of 58 itself! But the law structure and the society in my country does not permit the joy of this moment. So I have described the importance of the euthanasia next and demanded it. I hope you shall agree with the same and shall demand for the same.

Death is inevitable for each animate being that is born. The period since birth till death is mere an illusion and illusion is false. But when any animate being dies, that death is true. It is not an illusion. 'Not being' is the truth, but 'being' is an illusion. Death means end of an illusion and getting the true state. Always keep this principle in mind so that the intensity of labor of existence lessons and the mind gets prepared to welcome death. Nothingness is the universal truth. Till now so many animates birthed here on this Earth and they perished permanently. Means 'being' was an illusion of the animate beings born here till now. After the end of illusion, they submerged into the truth means 'nothingness'. This is the enigma of death.

BIRTH MEANS ENTERING THE ILLUSION FROM THE TRUTH AND AGAIN GOING BACK TO THE TRUTH; MEANS GOING BACK TO 'NONEXISTENCE' WHICH WE CALL DEATH...

So far we got to know about the Earth, creation-structure and Earth's related twelve factors. The creation of animate beings started on the Earth after the creation of environment favourable for creation and the twelve factors. Before that there was no animate being on this Earth. That too the human being was first created recently; means approximately 2.5 million years back on this plane of Earth. So considering the Earth's age of 4600 million years, if we subtract 2.5 million years from it; there was no trace of human being before approximately 4597.5 million years. The animate being gets created on this plane of Earth in accordance to the laws of the creation-structure due to the twelve factors. And since the duration of his 'non-existence' is greater than the duration of 'existence'; the life from birth to death is just an illusion. It is because there is no provision for rebirth of any animate in the creation structure. Rebirth is not the rule of the creation-structure. I have already given the doctrine that the new creation happens due to the twelve factors. If you understand that doctrine; it will be easier for you to understand the fact that birth is an 'illusion' and the death is the 'truth'. Death is the permanent end. You don't get birth again on this plane of Earth. Means the duration after death is the duration of absolute 'non-existence'. Means 'non-existence' is the truth before birth. And from birth to death all is just an illusion and mere illusion. It means merging into the truth again after the death. The huge period of 'non-existence' passed billions of years before the birth. Including human every animate being's birth is an illusion and death is the truth since it is merging into the 'non-existence'.

'Existence and visibility' is not true; it is an illusion. But 'non-existence' is the perpetual truth. Like on the planets like Moon or Mars or on any other planet of the solar system, there is nothing called 'existence', there is no one; so no question of 'existence'. There is perpetual 'non-existence'; that is the truth. The temporary illusion created by twelve factors on the plane of the Earth means the birth of the animate. He again merges into the reality of 'non-existence'. So each 'visible and existing' thing is an illusion. So the death of each animate is the truth.

In front of the vast period of 'nonexistence' the illusionary period of 'existence' is negligible means actually nothing; so the birth is an illusion. The thing that temporarily appears is an 'illusion'. The truth of 'non-existence' starts after the end of this illusion. Birth is like a dream, a mirage and like a drama. It is because the dream is never a truth but an illusion. Once you understand that the birth itself is an 'illusion' then you will realize what misery is, what honour and grandeur is, who is stupid, who is wise, rich or poor and who is leader and a priest!!! Everything is man-made and momentary! These are just the ideas of the human being born for a short period and living an illusionary life.

SEE THE ENIGMA OF THE DEATH!!!...

Once the body organs end their capacity to utilize the twelve factors; the illusion ends and each animate being goes into the state of truth, it is the real state. Each animate lives the life embracing the illusionary things till death. But if the principle of the creation structure is understood, it makes life happy and joyous. Experience it!!

****

7.16

Ghost is not in Existance But Manmade Illusion!

Friends, you have been reading this book so far in which we have seen how the human being is created by the creation-structure. Any animate being whether immobile or mobile needs the Earth and twelve factors related to her for its creation. Without these factors nothing can be created on this plane of Earth. Also anything once created any animate being; will perish one day. It means 'the creation is the root cause of destruction' - is the law of creation. Show me a single example that any big saint, leader or big politician – anyone having big labels – has returned back to the Earth after the death. This has never happened because the things like soul, reincarnation do not exist. I have given this doctrine in this book. The body of any animate is made up of these twelve factors which I have mentioned and after the death, that animate being's body is again merged back into these twelve factors. Without these twelve factors no animate, animal or ghost can be created. In the creation-structure, on this plane of Earth, only the being called human is coward. So he conceived the idea of ghost which is created from his perversion. Ghost is not the reality. Actually the Earth and the twelve factors related to her do not give birth this animal called ghost. **How then one that is not born can exist?** The concept of ghost is acceptable to few people in the humankind.

If according to these people the ghost exists and if it is nature's creation; is it exclusively for the human? Why it doesn't exist for other animate beings? It is because it is not real. If this so called ghost would have existed, it would have existed for all the animate beings. According to the law of the creation-structure, unless one animate being consumes another, it cannot keep its existence. Accordingly the human has been keeping his existence by killing billions of animals daily. On the plane of Earth every day the necks of millions of lambs, pigs, cows, fishes and hens are being cut with sharp edged knives. Then how many ghosts of these animals should be formed daily? Has humankind ever got the proof of any such ghost so far? If you cut and eat chicken does its ghost ever wanders around your home? So many animals get killed daily, do you find their ghosts? I have given the definition of immobile animate being in this book earlier. The mobile animates keep their existence by consuming immobile animate beings. Daily immobile animates like wheat, barley, oats, maize, vegetables and grass are killed each day. You cut the fodder to feed your cattle each day. The ghosts of these immobile animates don't frighten other animates with the indignation, "You finished our existence by cutting, grinding and killing us". Why aren't the ghosts being created when one animate being is openly killing other animate being? But ignorant human sticks to the idea of ghost and gets afraid of the non-existent thing.

Another example of non-existence of the ghost is that in the jungle the wild animals like tiger and lion maintain their existence by eating animals like deer, bull and bison etc. They have no choice other than killing and eating other animals. When any tiger or lion catches and eats any animal, that hunted animal endures unbearable pains till death. Then the ghost of that animal should haunt the tiger or lion. So it means that lion or tiger should get troubled to see the ghost of that hunted animal in front of their eyes continuously. Had the thing like ghost been in existence; all the animals killed by any lion should have made the life of that lion miserable by haunting as ghosts. But it doesn't happen that way. Have you ever heard that some lion is troubled by ghost or some lion is haunted by the ghost of a bison he killed? Even after killing so many animals, no ghost troubles him, or they don't get illusion of any ghost. The main reason of this is that the creation structure hasn't created anything like ghost. But it is the concept created by fertile mind of human being out of fear.

Had there been anything existing like ghost, it would need the twelve factors like any other animate being. Without these twelve factors nothing is created on this plane of Earth. The people who have experienced the ghost should answer my questions. If the ghost is created by the creation, it should need food and water like other animate beings. Also it should breathe like other animates. Then have anyone seen him breathing or eating or drinking water? Each animate created on this Earth has received the density or inertia. Accordingly, can you tell the weight of the ghost you saw? No animate being on the plane of Earth can vanish suddenly. The animate beings have age. With all these facts, how come the ghost manifested from human imagination vanishes suddenly? According to the law of the creation structure, no animate being can suddenly manifest and vanish suddenly. With all this analysis you must have realized that in the creation structure; the thing called ghost doesn't exist. But it is an idea created through human perversion to create fear.

With above analysis it is proved that on this plane of Earth the creation structure hasn't created any thing called 'ghost'. If the idea of ghost is real then it should have birth and also death; because according to the law of the creation-structure for destruction there should be birth and for this process the twelve factors are necessary. Have you ever seen the birth and death of any ghost? In reality there is no existence of ghost on this plane of Earth. This thing is just the ignorance of the humankind. Taking advantage of this basic ignorance, there are some selfish people who add fuel to this ignorance. Not just the manmade ghost but instead of prohibiting society from the superstitions, child marriages, religious wars, racism and such other adverse manners; the so called educated, reputed businessmen, authors, newsletters, entertainment industry and media encourage it for their own benefit and fame. But in front of their selfishness they forget the fact that they are adding to the ignorance of the innocent masses. Actually such mediums should educate the society against wrong things and help create fearless society by removing the ignorance. The promotional media should help ward off the fear in the humankind by keeping the truth in front of masses. The novels, movies, stories created so far have shown that the only the human has committed wrong things under the name of ghost. No one has proven so far the existence of ghost and no one will be able to prove; because ghost is not created by creation structure. Those who wish to ensure the non-existence of ghost should deeply study the creation-structure.

Without the twelve factors which I have discovered not even a flake of grass can be created or it doesn't get any existence. Then how come the huge ghost will automatically be created? No animate being is created without the spirit or life in it. Then without the spirit how the ghost will be created? If the ghost believers study the twelve factors they will be convinced about the nonexistence of the ghost and will be sure that it doesn't get created. Everything that gets created has an existence. Without the existence anything is imaginary. The existent thing has birth and the death too. But since the ghost is without an existence it neither gets born nor dies. Non-existent thing neither has birth nor death.

Watch the living ghosts haunting in the society!! They have taken every one by the scruff of neck!!!...

Though I have put up the doctrine on non-existence of the ghosts, there are many living ghosts who have taken the Indian public by the scruff of neck. They have spread free after the independence. Our innocent public is troubled the most due to them. The most horrible ghost that has been haunting is 'exponential growth of population'. No one is there to control this ghost. Every political leader & party is busy in serving themselves. Who knows when this horrible ghost of population will be destroyed? Another big ghost is the hypocrite leaders – from small lanes to the capital of nation - wearing the mask of social service. It is rare to find any public representative or leader who will not misuse a penny of the nationals!

Third ghost is the hoarder - leaders who hoard the hard earned money of nationals under the name of national service and another one is the civil servants who help such leaders for self-interest. Without bribe no work gets done in government offices. There are plenty of such ghosts haunting the nationals and are at various places. The effects of these ghosts are hunger death, malnutrition and child-deaths, illiteracy amongst masses as the public money is in the hands of few people. The ghost of corruption should be destroyed. If the uncountable hoarded money is freed back to the nation; Indians may experience the condition contrast to present i.e. sixty dollars will be equivalent to a single rupee. And the ghost of terrorists has haunted the nation just due to the short sightedness of the corrupt leaders!! Such many live ghosts are present in the countries like India who have been troubling the masses. Only Mother Earth knows when these will get destroyed and the when country gets back the prosperous state!!

All the political parties are the ghosts that have taken the public by the scruff of neck. All parties are dodgers! They just think of their own interest and parties benefit before the benefit of the nation and nationals. That is what has made India the poor country in the world. More or less this happens in many countries. The unworthy people sitting on the higher positions are the deadly ghosts who have taken the nation by the scruff of neck. In the world no nation should allow the government of single party continuously. In democracy the masses should give opportunity to other parties too. So they won't have to tolerate the frantic administration of the single party. They should not allow such franticly administrating party to haunt them. To prove the truth behind this there is a rule of creation-structure which is - 'Change is the rule of nature'. This is applicable to democracy too. So instead of selecting the hodgepodge parties; the public should decide two parties who can be given the chance to serve the nation alternatively. The public must be haunted by this wisdom! These other ghosts are more horrible than the man-made ghosts and are galloping entire nation and humankind. One must throw these ghosts off the neck and trample them under legs to destroy them.

Now you must have realized which are the real and false ghosts and would have known that these live real ghosts are more horrible. But it is the public who births these ghosts! For this reason at first the ghost of ignorance must be destroyed that has caught the public by the scruff of neck.

****

8

The Key To How The Poor and Middle Class Can Get Rich In A Constructive Way!!!

HERE IS THE WAY OF FINANCIAL PLANNING ALONG WITH LIFE PLANNING FOR THE HUMAN RACE; TO LIVE HAPPY, CONTENT, PEACEFUL, CAREFREE, DISHONESTY FREE LIFE THAT IS FREE FROM THE HUNGER!!!...

The mobile and immobile animate beings take birth and die on this Earth. Similarly humankind too takes birth and dies. This period between the birth and the death is very important in the human life. This is what we call life. The human needs start with the birth. During the childhood the intensity of the needs is not felt because parents take care and provide for them. But after the end of the childhood there are piles of the needs in front of each human. Those endowed with the financially sound parents do not find any difficulties. But those with average or poor financial conditions need to prioritize their needs. Means when and what importance should be given to any particular need? This understanding is necessary for ones' own good. So using the gifts of thought and imagination power, intelligence which you have received since that age are very important. The good and bad of your life depend upon it. Then realizing your present family and financial conditions; planning the time you have in the hand becomes necessary.

ARE YOU A POOR STUDENT WHO WISHES TO LEARN FURTHER? CHANGE THE POOR CONDITIONS? THEN YOU MUST READ THIS!!!...

Hard work has no shortcut if one wishes to raise oneself from the poverty to better financial status. Combine it with your gifts of intelligence and imagination to walk further. In such time, to fulfil the need of your education invest in whatever hard efforts possible for you. During education the good use of the time is necessary in such situation. It means while adjusting the school time one should find the ways of earning by doing possible small tasks. Because the biggest hurdle in the life is money! The biggest hurdle in maintaining the existence is that of food; means the first need is to get enough food to fill your tummy. It needs money. Without getting food you cannot do anything. After fulfilling the need of food, the next necessity of such age is education! Rest of the needs like notebooks, books, cloths and other things; these expenses can be met easily if there is a thoughtful planning. If you are not able to buy new cloths, you can request the neighbors and other acquaintances living in a good condition to provide you the used old cloths. Perform small and sundry tasks to meet the school expenses. This expense should be done bare minimum to the necessity. Those who cannot buy the new books can buy the second hand used books and complete their aim of education. It is necessary to study whenever time is available keeping the aim of education in the mind. As you march forward, with the help of your intelligence and thought power you should face and solve the problems in the life.

WHETHER YOU ARE POOR OR RICH, WITHOUT THE WEALTH OF THOUGHTS YOU ARE JUST A POOR!!!...

In my opinion, while resolving these hurdles, the wealth of thoughts that you have is more important than the wealth of money. This wealth of thoughts will take you far ahead in life! It doesn't take time to destroy your property, estate and wealth due to stupidity or thoughtlessness! So to the aspiring youth I have to tell that their difficulties in the life will be better solved by the wealth of thoughts than the material wealth. At each step of the life if you use the wealth of thoughts and act accordingly, no one can bring the barriers to your progress. So there is English saying 'thought is the mother of action'. If you read my first book 'Me, Earth and the Travel' then you will be convinced that the thing that makes you great is not the money but the thoughts and your action. Then you can realize any dream of yours.

The human is neither rich due to possession of money, nor is poor due to lack of money!! But only due to the wealth of thoughts he is rich! He is clever! Accomplished and gentleman This is the proof of it!!!...

To cite my example, I was born in a village to a poverty struck family. Devoid of food to meet the hunger, cloths to cover and protect body, oil to hair and shoe to bare foot–in such situation I worked as a child labor in the farm and completed my education till seventh standard in the village itself. Then I arrived at a city. There were no arrangements for living and food in the city. Not a single penny in the pockets. In that young age I accepted the work of collecting and washing used dishes in the inn. But when it too became hurdle in the education, I worked as a porter in the day, had just one meal and attended night school. In such situation if some fortune teller would have predicted that this boy would build his own bungalow in future life and would own vehicles, would roam internationally on the Earth, visiting cities like London, Paris, Buenos Ire's, Melbourne and Johannesburg; everyone would have laughed at him or her. But thoughts and action have played important role in manifesting this to a reality. This was all possible not because of money but because I used the gifts of thought & imagination power & intelligence received from the Mother Earth. I could reach these heights due to these things. Only my wealth of thoughts is responsible for this. Nobody ever helped me in cash or kinds.

To be successful in the life, the planning of your life too is very essential along with the financial planning...

Particular things must happen at particular age in life. It calls for the proper planning of life. Considering my example you can imagine how hard it must have been to get educated as I had to shoulder the responsibility of my own nurturance at a very tender age due to poverty struck family. But in that age, if I would have ignored the education blaming the economic conditions, my whole life would have been a waste. Uneducated person doesn't have any other option than the labor work and needs to struggle hard to fill the tummy. The village dweller would work at farms and get the earnings. The city dweller would work as a porter and earn. This means the uneducated human has to simply waste his or her life by working hard to fill the tummy. So education has to be of the utmost importance during the childhood. After being birthed as a human, the education has the prime importance to be able to live like a human. In such situations, you must have a firm intention to give education the priority over filling your tummy.

Just due to my wealth of thoughts I could plan my life and reach the desired heights in the material success!!!...

'Change' is the motivator of law of the nature. According to this law, after some time you can change that economic situation in which you starve due to poverty. In such times if you give priority to filling the tummy you shall lose the education. To avoid it even if you have to starve for one meal, you can find your own way and never leave the education. During my poor economic conditions attending the day school wasn't possible for me so I chose the option of working as a porter in the day to earn and attended the night school. During that earning of the day even two times meals wasn't affordable. As I had no shelter, the inn owner used to take 10 rupees for sleeping and 17 rupees for one time meal out of the 30 rupees I earned during the day. Means only one time meal was possible. I spent three months attending night school and having just one time meal. But later as I started earning 50 rupees, according to the saying 'change is the rule of the nature'; despite giving priority to education over filling the tummy, my economic condition improved due to my wealth of thoughts and I could get two times meal and also my education continued. The reason behind mentioning this here is that we do face such difficult times in the life. But going by the saying 'where there is a will, there is a way'; you shall find the way and overcome the difficulties. Had I taken a fulltime job in the inn, I could have fed myself two times. But then I wouldn't have been able to write this book in the absence of education. So according to the stages of your age; taking correct decisions for the success in life and proper planning is necessary. This is the part of determination and diligence.

YOU SHOULD LEARN SOME ART OR SKILL WHICH SHALL ENABLE YOU TO EARN WHILE GETTING EDUCATED!!!...

If you don't have any financial backing from the family, you will not have shelter, land, home or any such property and so you must learn some art, some skill which will enable you to get good earnings while you are continuing the education. Just bookish knowledge is of no use in the practical world. Along with this academic knowledge you must learn how to earn and learn some skill by recognizing the need of the society that you can fulfil through that art or skill. Possessing such skill combined with the academic knowledge makes earning for needs easier.

As typing had demand in those days, in addition to daily porterage and night school I had learnt the skill of English typing. It landed me to the job of typist in a reputed business house like Sakal Papers-a popular news daily in the Pune city, else I would have continued being the 'delivery boy' or 'office boy' which I was before that job! I have narrated this experience of mine with the intention that it may motivate and be useful to you.

ONE MUST MAKE A THOUGHTFUL DECISION ABOUT AT WHAT TIME WHICH NEED SHOULD BE GIVEN THE PRIORITY IN THE LIFE...

Later I passed the pre–degree exams externally. I was staying in a slum at that time. In between I got a good government job due to my good typing skills. It helped me live in a rented room in the suburb area leaving the slum. I used to leave the house at 6.00 AM in the morning to attend the class within the city. After class I used to attend the office. It was a very laborious routine for me. There were more educated people than me who had bachelors and masters' degrees, who were double post graduates at the place of my work. Their level of work was same as mine. I used to get the salary equal to them. I used to think those days about this that those people were so educated but they were getting the same salary as mine. My laborious routine for attending the morning class cycling long distances was to earn the bachelor's degree. But then after putting so much effort what was the worth of that degree education? I saw no benefit! So with these thoughts I said good bye to the further education and concentrated on earning more money utilizing that time. But say fortunately or unfortunately I was separated from the job due to health reasons. Then I thought that I should start a business that may give me more earning than the job and I started earning accordingly. Then with one business I started another business.

Success can be fetched like this!!!...

According to the times and situations I thought about the needs of society and the law, I achieved success in the other business chosen. The previous situation was completely changed. There was no shelter to stay when I had come to the city of Pune, no food to eat. But later I built my own bungalow, owned two four wheelers. Once I collected the sufficient money to meet the needs of the family, one night I suddenly stopped the money giving business. So I could enjoy from the bottom of my heart travelling throughout the Earth. Today my age is 71. But during this time period in life I achieved the success and enjoyed the happy, joyous life. Whatever decisions I had to take from time to time for all this, they were possible only due to my wealth of thoughts. While attaining the heights of success I observed many regimens. Just getting the art of earning money doesn't mean getting the successful life. Your life becomes successful only if you have the art of avoiding the ill–gotten money and earning money honestly.

The life is not a mere patterned block but it should be multifaceted, multi-dimensional. Such life is called the real life!!!...

Instead of being a simple square block if the life is multi-dimensional, multi-angled, it is called the real life! I will neither call the person an 'accomplished' who has only learnt to earn the money with whatever labor just to fill the tummy; nor will call such life a successful life. But to live a beautiful, multi-dimensional and completely content life one should observe some rules, follow some laws. Having the tendency to develop good traits, avoiding wrong things by picking only the virtues, not following phony life styles of others, holding your own special principles and following them, living the life in the bracket by observing the manmade and creation structures' laws, understanding the real meaning of life; these are all things necessary to live the happy and successful life. I am going to explain them to you. So you too can make your life successful and enjoy it fully.

AUTHORS' ADVISE ABOUT HOW THE COMMONERS SHOULD IMPROVE THEIR ECONOMIC CONDITION AND WHAT RULES SHOULD BE OBSERVED FOR THE SAME!!!...

The commoners are most affected with the difficulties of economic conditions. The inflation rate crosses new high each day and the necessities too are increasing with changing socioeconomic life style. Meeting these needs is getting harder.

In most parts of the world, the children finish their education by early twenties and earning becomes the main aim for the young generation. One must start by choosing the job or business suitable to their educational qualification. If the parents have not arranged for the accommodation, staying in the city becomes a difficult task for the young people. Collecting and keeping aside some cash by serving in some job or through self-employment becomes the need at such time. To meet the demand of shelter one needs to spend in some millions these days. It is difficult to get the place in cities like Mumbai, New York, or Shanghai even in some millions. Such a complex problem needs to be faced. My advise to the young people in such situation is that instead of blocking large amounts in buying an apartment in the beginning, they can resolve the problem of accommodation by investing small amounts in rented apartments. Instead of buying, have a rented apartment. Instead of investing large sum in apartment, make a fixed deposit with some bank. It will give you a certain monthly income. You can use it to pay off the monthly rents.

The concept of 'ownership' is unmaterialistic at least in the case of home. Actually there should be synchronization between the earning you get in the human life and your needs. If you spend most of your earnings just to meet one need, then what about your rest of the valuable life? When will you enjoy it? So in my view if you wish to be fearless, healthy and live a joyous life that is free from worry and tensions irrespective of your present economic conditions; I give you the important key word. It is just spend some years in the same condition that you are presently in. Don't spend a single penny of your present earning on luxuries, non-productive things. Continue your life for some time as it was before when you weren't earning. Just spend on the necessary things like food and clothing. To maintain the existence these are important things.

THE MOST IMPORTANT THINGS NEEDED TILL DEATH IS 'FOOD'; SEE HOW YOU CAN ARRANGE FOR THE SAME...

You must first permanently arrange for the basic necessity i.e. for food and clothing. Suppose if you are a family of three including husband-wife and a child; then you need a particular fixed amount say of 5000 dollars monthly for the food and clothing. In order to get this amount monthly, you need a certain large amount say of one million dollars to be invested in a bank or some such reliable scheme which will bring you the monthly amount of 5000 dollars that meets the food and clothing needs of your family. In such hypothetic case, till you collect the large sum of one million dollars you need not invest the money in other unwanted things like TV, furniture etc. It doesn't matter if you don't have these things for some period; but once you raise the amount of one million, you will have resolved the question of food and clothing for the family for the life time. Once the question for food and clothing is resolved for the life time you can relax. This amount must be kept completely aside. Remember not to touch this amount and the returns of this amount. If you don't use this amount, considering 10% interest on an average, you will grow this amount roughly to 1.8 million after 7 years span. Then it won't matter if you use your complete monthly earning for the other needs of family, because with this amount you will get the additional earning that is almost equal to the monthly salary. Moreover, this amount keeps growing in next coming years. By bearing a small discomfort for a short period, you will be arranging for the big thing in life. You may not have an idea of the position of people whose kitchen can't lit the fire to cook food. When such situation arises, your relatives or friends or even society might solve this question of yours just for few days, no one will take your permanent responsibility, isn't it? To avoid such big trouble, such provision is very important in the life.

JUST OBSERVE THE ROUTINES SUGGESTED BY THE AUTHOR FOR THE CAREFREE AND HEALTHY LIFE AND SEE THE EFFECT!!!...

1. Never compare with your acquaintances, neighbors or relatives. Don't try to equate or compare if the neighbors got air conditioners or new car or use expensive clothes or his wife wears lot of golden ornaments so your wife too desires to have it etc. You decide the direction of your life yourself.

2. As far as possible, don't buy anything with loan. Don't spend a single penny from your earnings on the interest. Until you get the financial strength, avoid the desire to live in luxury or use expensive luxury items. Contrary, increase your sources of income to strengthen your financial base. Start side business or a part-time job. After increasing the income when you collect a sizable amount, plan for the returns on that amount without touching the basic amount. This is the planning of the young age.

3. When you turn old and cannot work; instead of depending

on someone for the financial help you should plan for the necessary old age funds when you are young and have the capacity to earn.

In India the government has offered the facility for the provision of old age through public provident fund (PPF) account. Every nation may have such facility which needs to be found out. Open such account as early as possible in your life. According to their 2012 rule at Indian PPF facility you can deposit the amount of 100,000 each year in the name of each adult. This amount is completely tax free under income tax code 80C rule. Means you can save that much amount from incurring the tax. Second benefit is that each of you will receive the interest on this amount, which is added to the original amount and compound interest is calculated on the total amount. This interest too is tax free. After six years from the opening of an account you can withdraw some amount from it. But I suggest that you forget the amount deposited in this account. Remember never to touch that amount. For fifteen years just keep depositing the money. After that you can close that account and withdraw entire money. Here too I will suggest you that you need not close the account if not in immediate need and you may continue the account by paying as little as 500 each year.

Suppose someone opens the account at the age of 25 and deposits 50000 each year in a row for 30 years, by the age of 55 according to current interest rate the amount in this account will keep growing double after every eight year three months. If you keep depositing money like this for thirty years, the collected sum of 10 million can be handy if you plan foreign travel or any other such expense in the old age. You can withdraw the 12% of the balance each year out of the balance amount collected in the account after 15 years. Means you get the facility like a pension at the age of 58 years. Each year you withdraw the amount the interest 8,80,000 @ 8.80 percent, yet your original amount remains intact. Means the monthly pension of almost 75000 you will keep getting and important thing is you will not spend a single penny as an income tax. Your heir will get this amount after your death. Thus you also provide for the next generation making them millionaire. They don't have to spend a single penny income tax while getting this amount back.

The person for whom it is not possible to invest as described above should open the PPF account and deposit the amount of hundred thousand at the beginning of each financial year for consistent 8 years. As per today's interest rate at 8.80%, the deposit amount will grow to 1191000 after the eighth year. Next 8.5 years will make it 2.4 million and next 8.5 years will grow it to 4.8 million. After first 8 years of depositing the amount of hundred thousand each year consistently, even if you later just deposit 500 each year without withdrawing anything, you will have a deposit of 5.0 million at the end of your age 51. This investment of 5.0 million will certainly fetch you the amount of 40000 each month. This is like your pension of 40000. If you keep depositing sizable amount even after 8th year then your this deposit sum will grow. But after completing 15 years you must keep renewing the account at every five years. Also remember never to withdraw the amount from this account. This certainly shall end the financial stress of yours.

Due to this PPF scheme, I am enjoying completely tension free life with my family in terms of our financial needs. Savings in such account creates a big financial support and makes life tension free from the financial point of view. Such schemes are gifts for commoners but many don't know about it and so can't use it. You can find out information about such schemes from your nationalized banks or post office and such government facilities.

I have described the two schemes in Indian provident fund. I trust that following them finishes the financial instability for commoners in India. They can live the happy and joyous life. One thing must be kept in mind that there is no need to make high risk investments for financial stability.

After making such arrangement why do you need more wealth?...

Why do you need more wealth after making such arrangement? What to do with the gold-silver? Having home for comfortable life and the financial arrangement as described above makes the person wealthy enough to live happy and joyous life, isn't it? After getting such financial stability that meets your mundane needs, what more you need than getting to enjoy the tension free, happy and joyous life fulfilling your desires that the creation structure has bestowed upon you? Rather than investing into some high return high risk investment options, if you invest as is described you will never fall short of anything in life. You are your own boss! If you are happy and content, how does it matter how rich someone else is? There is no reason to compare with someone else! If you have understood the meaning of life, it is sufficient! According to the law of the creation structure, the one with the greed for more cannot be happy and content in the life and also cannot enjoy the life fully. It is because having in excess is the curse; you must have understood this after reading my book by now.

Some more tricks to earn money!!!...

There are some more tricks to earn money. Keep in mind the principle of the economics. The money begets money. You need not cross the steps of your court yard to get money. It means if some person collects a sizable amount and invests it in a planned proper way; besides fulfilling all the needs of the family he can also tend to his hobby. Means if someone loves travelling, he can easily cater the expenses for the same. For this if the person invests in the share market and the real estate, he can surely and easily earn money. If some plot is bought outskirts of the city or in some nearby village after enquiring and ensuring the title and the proper deal; one can earn good money after selling it. Of course, purchase and sale of the open plot is a risky business due to the cheating which goes on in this profession. But you can get ahead if there is certainty about it. Or you can also invest in the booking of ownership flats in the suburb area as the initial booking rate during the construction time is low. Later you can sell off the booking after you get possession of the flat. You will earn more than interest.

The third way of earning the money!!!...

Third option is share market. I dealt in share market many times. I also lost many times. But I shall share with you what I learnt through it, so you can avoid such losses. What I observed and studied of the share market, I have found that after 3-4 years the market sky rockets. The share prices go up. There is sudden boom and also a slump after that. Many people buy shares during the boom and sell off due to fear during slump. When the market is up and the people are purchasing, we should sell off the shares we have and deposit the money in the bank. Don't get into the temptation of buying immediately. Usually after each 3-4 years the market collapses. When the market collapses and the Sensex is very much down; without fear buy the shares at such time. After selling the shares during boom, don't purchase shares even if market doesn't come down for 3-4 years. When the market is down you must study properly and invest in the shares of reputed companies which have good track record for years together, after discussing with the share market experts. The shares of such companies definitely give returns after 3-4 years.

After doing these arrangements you need not wait for marriage because you have now understood the principle that money begets money!!!...

Follow the money begets money principle and invest. Such advise is given to make you financially stable while you are young.

Now you are ready for the marriage. After marriage it is natural to have the offspring. If you wish to enjoy the life fully and wish to give such joy to your offspring too, then I will give you a valuable but free advise that whether a boy or a girl, stop after giving birth to one offspring. Giving birth to more offspring you shall put them in misery. And will spend your life too to tend them. The life will be troublesome for both of you. So develop just one offspring properly, spend on his/her good education. Let him or her enjoy the life along with you. From financial point of view if you concentrate only on single child, it shall definitely live happy life and you too shall be happy for it. I have observed in the society that the siblings are good towards each other until they are under the wings of their parents. But once financially independent, they don't stay with each other. Not just that, they also stay separate from parents. They don't even enquire about the old parents. So many people face this problem today. So while birthing the offspring think ten times. You will not be 100% satisfied with more than one child. You will have to spend the valuable life of yours to tend their needs and develop them. You will miss your own health and joy in the process. Sorrow will be unavoidable. To understand this read this book by in depth. Then you will know who you are and understand why I am suggesting this.

IF YOU OBSERVE REGIMEN AND RULES BELOW REGARDING OFFSPRING AND FINANCE; POSSIBLY YOU MAY NOT FACE ANY DIFFICULTIES!!!...

If regarding your children and the finance you observe some rules and regimen; probably you may not face any difficulty in the life. You shall spend your life happily and take leave of the world with contentment.

What principles and rules are necessary for the life? They are such as,

1. Ill-gotten seldom prospers
2. Change is the rule of nature
3. Anything in excess is the curse
4. Thought is the mother of action
5. Creation is the root cause of destruction and sorrow

And most important is–

6. There is nothing more valuable in this world than your cheerful and healthy existence.

and so on.......

I have analyzed above principles already in this book. Adopting these principles in your life will definitely help you live in a better way.

If you wish to plan your finances and life, possibly select some relevant small business. You can earn more in the business than job and also can enjoy your hobby whenever and however you wish in your life. You can spend the life time nicely. After gaining desired wealth you can retire from your business-job and enjoy the national international trips to your heart's content and in full measure. With proper planning you don't face the barrier of your finance or job-business. In the rest part of the life due to the availability of the money and time visiting different countries on the Earth makes the life enriched.

All the wealth on Earth belongs to the Earth; not to a specific person! So all should be benefitted from it!!...

Suppose ten people are overeating. The food for hundred people is stored with them. But other ninety people are starving. Then according to the rule of the creation structure, these ninety people will not let those other overeating ten people happily eat. Those ten will not have any power over these ninety people. When needed; the food will be snatched from those ten people. Even after that if those ten people do not consider about the other ninety people, then there will be a revolution and whosoever out of these ten will not open the food-stores in their possession will be killed. This is the rule of the creation structure. Hunger is not one person's privilege. All corrupt politicians, capitalists, exploiting money lenders and black mafias should not behave against the rules of the creation structure. All the wealth on the Earth belongs to the Earth. It doesn't belong to one person. The wealth received by misuse of the intellect and thought power is the injustice to the starved ones, hungry ones.

If you peek into such peoples' houses; their house is always under some or the other shadow of the sorrow or fear. Mother Earth doesn't let these people enjoy the health.

THE HUMAN HAS JUST INVITED THE SORROW BY CREATING THE ADJECTIVES THROUGH HIS OWN THOUGHTS!!!...

Since only humankind has received the gift of thought power, imagination power and the intellect, wisdom it itself has created the adjectives. The human is recognized by applying the adjectives like clever stupid, accomplished-ordinary. Of course this is limited to the humankind. Other animates don't have anything to do with these adjectives. Out of these adjectives, there is an adjective 'accomplished'. Who is applied this adjective? The person who has earned and collected lot of money in a short time, have purchased many houses, display or show 10-12 cars in front of his house, has started 10-12 factories, has procured many lands, someone who is a big builder, owns helicopter and lot of wealth! Such person is considered as an accomplished human and the society too admires him by honoring him with garlands in public functions. No one labels a simple man 'accomplished' - who honestly earns just sufficient to meet his needs and is happy, isn't it?

THE ONE WHO EARNS MONEY WITH HONEST EFFORTS PUTTING HIS LABOR AND SWEAT IN THE TASK IS THE REAL 'ACCOMPLISHED' HUMAN! BUT THE SOCIETY LABELS THE PEOPLE WHO GET FILTHY RICH MISUSING THEIR THOUGHT AND IMAGINATION POWER AS 'ACCOMPLISHED' OR 'CAPABLE'!!!...

First, the fact is no man gets filthy rich by labor work, sweating out in efforts. Had it been otherwise, the farm-labor works hard under scorching heat of Sun, in water of the rain, in cold winters; but he neither gets filthy rich as described above nor can send his children for education abroad. He can never buy his own house or farm in the life. He cannot even give good education to the children. Would anyone label this farm-worker as 'accomplished'? But our society labels to the builders and industrialists who get rich by misusing their thought power and intellect, emptying others pockets by selling goods at very high price, exploiting government and masses; as 'accomplished'. Government too plans the policies which will benefit this 'accomplished' lot, by supporting them and widening the gap between the poor and rich; making rich richer and the poor poorer! Had this not been the fact, there wouldn't have been the hunger or malnutrition deaths in Asian and African countries. 500-600 million people wouldn't have been homeless and starving. The person labeled 'rich' only exploits the work from the commoners and society till his death. Society too honors such people as 'accomplished'. In reality, these people along with the governments are responsible to keep masses starving, illiterate and homeless. For whom is the freedom & progress of the nations? For these handful billionaires! What is the use of freedom to the poor class? There are no representatives in the cabinets, parliaments or state councils from the poor masses who are homeless, starving, illiterate and sweating till the end of life under the pressure of unending hard work. All political parties are behind filthy rich, all local representatives are behind exploitation of the mass-funds. On one side, around 20000 people die starving each day in India and on the other side there are politicians, legislators devouring the delicious food in government canteens at subsidized prices. These leaders are not ashamed of this inequality! What protagonists of the masses! What right they have to use government vehicles, government properties and resources? But they have robbed the masses under the pretext of leaderships and politics. They get ample honorariums and perks. Do poor masses get these perks? Despite being large in numbers, there is no savior for the poor masses.

The human in India has created such nuisance that old citizens say "Golden were the days before the independence!!!"...

Those who experienced the pre-independence period always claim after looking at the present status of my country India that pre-independence days were better. What was achieved after getting freedom? Freedom for speech or abusing is not the freedom. It doesn't fill the tummy of starved ones. Real freedom is enjoyed by politicians, industrialists, their staff, all government and semi-government servants. But what can be said about the common masses? Have they received any benefit of freedom? One class affords planes, cars, helicopters and the other class cannot even afford a simple cycle!

Is it a freedom that common citizen enjoy?

What an 'accomplished' filthy rich people!!!...

Cheating the government and the masses, cleverly siphoning billions of dollars by avoiding taxes; the corrupt Indian politicians and industrialists have kept sizable black money in foreign banks and even government has accepted this fact. It has kept the masses of this nation on half stomach. Children are dying of starvation and malnutrition. They neither have home to stay nor clean fresh water to drink nor proper education and lack of health care centre people are victim of unknown diseases. Are these the fruits of independence for countries like India? Isn't this the picture observed by and large in each country with more or less difference? Such is the society today that holds the black money mafias in honored position labeling them 'accomplished' for the money they hoard! Are these really 'accomplished people'? No, but they are the prime enemies of the nations and the common innocent masses world over! They are also the enemies of the Mother Earth who created them! In reality when the creation structure has arranged for the food and water for everyone; these enemies have robbed & hoarded the food, shelter and clothing of trillions of people!

I am writing with such fervor because I too had gone for suicide once in dearth of food!!!...

Have these people experienced poverty ever? I speak with such fervor because I too am born in such poor family. In dearth of food I too had the suicidal thoughts. Who was responsible for it? These handful 'accomplished' people! Friends, just think about it, you call this freedom! From the head of a small village to the president of this nation, all are the servants of that nation. This is what the Indian constitution says. But the situations in this nation are totally reversed today. All politicians are the owners of the masses. The masses are caught in the hands of such butchers like poor cattle. Who should be called real 'accomplished'? S/he is the one who earns and keeps just enough to meet his or her necessities and returns the excess to the masses, to the nation. The one who keeps collecting from the masses and nation till death is the biggest traitor! He is not accomplished or capable.

To avoid the above defects the economic growth must be all encompassing!!!...

According to the law of creation structure, it doesn't approve of the boundaries or borders. All Earth belongs to all animate beings dwelling on her. But the human has created the borders. Whichever country one is born into enjoys the equal rights over all the natural resources and wealth of that country. Nation cannot belong to the handful people. Or just handful people are not given the contract by Mother Earth or creation structure to enjoy the rights on the resources and wealth. The Mother Earth doesn't tell that just handful people's children should learn in the good schools, hoard uncountable wealth and enjoy it alone or snatch the things of other's right by misusing your intellect! The present technique is to capture the power by hook or crook, then to ruin the poor masses and trouble the middle class, make them mortgage their life in the bank for their living space and throw them into the ditch of poverty. While I am writing this, the prices of all goods like cooking gas, petrol and other vital essential commodities, goods have sky rocketed. Medical services are becoming unaffordable, public transport is untrustworthy; and with such situation the middle class is perplexed; whereas the poor farmer is committing suicide. Kids are dying of hunger and malnutrition. This is the condition of independent country like India. Then who is real happy in such country? Only the rich businessmen, industrialists, who have made lot of money, are the happy lot. There is no question of money for politicians. They don't have place to keep the money in India so they are keeping it in the foreign banks! Industrialists are only bothered about how to make 10 factories out of one factory. Also they are behind how to start ten businesses in place of one-two businesses and make uncountable money. Government officials get increase in the dearness allowance from time to time. They don't feel the heat of inflation. But the unorganized labor class, farmworkers, disabled, private job holders who don't have any scope for corruption or those who do not have the means to earn extra money; all these classes are perplexed with the inflation. Who enjoys the resources and wealth of the nation? They are the handful rich people! Not all can get into politics and also not everyone can indulge into corruption like politicians do. For the real progress of any nation, rather than just handful people, each citizen should be progressed. It doesn't matter if your nation doesn't have the huge posh flyovers, eight fold highways or sky-scraper buildings!

IF THE PEOPLE ARE STARVING WITHOUT FOOD, WHAT KIND OF MISLEADING BOGUS PROGRESS THE NATIONS CLAIM ABOUT?...

The bogus facilities are useless if the people are starving of food in your country. It is not the sign of a progressive country. Actually according to the rule of the creation structure, each citizen of any nation must get the home to live, fresh clean water to drink, good food to eat, cloths to cover and protect body, good education for children and proper health care means of livelihood for all; such all-encompassing progress is the real progress of that particular nation.

UNTIL THE SELFLESS, PATRIOTIC NATIONAL SERVANTS DON'T PRESENT GOOD EXAMPLES TO THE MASSES; THE NATIONS WOULD TRAIL IN UNWANTED DIRECTIONS!!!...

The resources of the nation should be equally shared by all citizens of nation. The real national servants would be the ones who would care for the future of masses in the nation, their safety and security and be considerate about how the masses can be happy and about their welfare. No country having the self-fulfilling selfish politicians, who take politics as a business would progress ever in reality. The masses of such nation would never be able to live happy, carefree, tension free life. Peace would never dwell in such country.

Politics is not a business where one invests 20 million to receive 5000 million!

UNLESS TODAYS' FORM OF POLITICS AS A MEANS OF 'GETTING RICH FASTER' IS DESTROYED; THE COUNTRIES DO NOT PROGRESS!!!...

At least the country India has such situations today, but I know that this is the situation by & large with most of the countries of this world. There is no ideal savior to these nations. The politicians have given the form of 'means of getting rich faster' to the politics today. When the 'business' form of the politics will end, when the corruption under the name of 'development' shall end; there will not be any homeless, starved, poor citizen in that country. It will be an all-encompassing development of the country and it really can be called 'developing' or 'developed' country in the real sense. After the freedom India was declared to be a secular country, but owing to politics even today the power is captured with the politics of religion, cast, race and the masses are held for ransom!

THIS BOOK IS THE MASTER KEY TO THE HAPPINESS!!!...

After reading this book from the beginning and reflecting and contemplating upon it and acting upon it you shall find the master key to happy and joyous life. This master key means you shall be introduced truly to the self or 'I' that you assume. After this true knowledge of the self you shall not get stuck with the manmade ideas and materialistic and illusionary things. Spending the life bestowed by Mother Earth and the creation structure happily in true sense you shall be ready to take leave of this world one day. I have suggested you the ways from the practical point of view from birth to death.

I give the credit for being able to write two books to my wealth of thoughts. So I shall tell the young generation with an authority that even if you don't have money but the wealth of thoughts and the ability to act upon it, you shall overcome the lack of money. And then the success shall follow you; I assure you of that!

****

9

Population – From 300 Million to 1300 Million!!

This Is The Gift of Independence For India...

ONE VERY IMPORTANT LACUNA THAT I NOTICE ABOUT MY COUNTRY INDIA; THAT IS NEITHER ANY SOCIAL ORGANIZATION NOR ANY POLITICAL PARTY PAYS ATTENTION TO THE BURNING PROBLEM OF TREMENDOUS POPULATION GROWTH. IT MULTIPLIES THE OTHER PROBLEMS IN THE COUNTRY. WITH REGARD TO AREA, INDIA STANDS 7TH IN THE GLOBAL RANKING BUT WITH REGARD TO THE POPULATION IT STANDS FIRST IN THE RANKING!!! DESPITE THIS, NONE OF THE POLITICAL PARTY UTTERS A WORD AGAINST IT! WHY? THE VOTE BANK IS MORE IMPORTANT FOR THEM!!!...

From the perspective of land area, India has a seventh ranking in the world. Means, there are six countries which are area wise larger than India. But despite this, as far as population growth is concerned, India almost stands first amongst the 200-250 countries in the world. Out of 7000 million people of the world, 1250 million belong to India. With this, will India ever be a developed nation? But it is marching rapidly with regard to population growth. Along with the obstacles for progress I mentioned earlier, population growth is proving to be the biggest obstacle. When would our politicians realize this? If the population growth is to be arrested in India, the strict measures like those in China must be implemented. Though China's population is little higher than India, it must be noted that her area is three times larger than India's area.

The obstacle of the population growth must be first eradicated for India's highest progress, all round development so that her public enjoy the fruits of her progress. This will automatically lessen the corruption and corrupt people will not enter the politics. The society too will not let them enter. All will get to taste the fruits of the progress. All will get the opportunities for good education, employment and business. As all will get the means of earnings, no one will remain poor and homeless. All people will get enough food. Farmers will not commit suicide. The sufficient crops for all could be grown in the fields. Excess imports of petrol and diesel will stop. The country will have an economic independence; the nationals will get rid of the burdens of loans. Law and order shall be maintained. Security forces will never be stressed out. With the spread of happiness, contentment and joy amongst masses; genuine, patriotic and selfless representatives will be honest elected from the masses. The chaos that we witness in the assembly houses of government, disgusting and hateful allegations and counter allegations etc. will never be seen again. The nation and the nationals will get health & peace. This necessitates laws for population control and corruption eradication; ideal responsible leaders, genuine and selfless representatives, and industrialists. Only this would help the nation's all-encompassing progress in real sense!!

The obsolete laws and judiciary framework of old British times must be changed. Everyone is first an Indian. Then comes the cast, religion and cult of the house! Same laws should be applicable to each Indian and they should not differ with cast and religion or groupism!! But when will it happen?...

Every citizen living in India should be under equal law. Things like cast, religion and cult should not stand against the national benefit. The laws should be designed keeping the national and mass benefit in mind. All British time laws should be abandoned or modified appropriately. Here I explain an example of an obsolete British time law. According to Hindu religion, after marriage the bride inhabits in the house of in-laws. Later if her husband keeps illicit relationship with another woman and that woman bears kids; the married lady cannot take any legal action against them despite the other woman's kid bear the name of her husband on their birth certificate due to the existing obsolete British time law. Such law was made by British rulers in those days for their own benefit! But it is still active as it is in the Indian judiciary system. Means the law of monogamy or law of prohibition for polygamy is existent only on the papers for the Indian woman. So in the above case, the lawfully married woman cannot take any lawful steps against her husband except the right for demanding divorce! This is paradox of democracy!

In short if the obstacles coming in between the national benefit are removed, the nation shall make all-encompassing progress and each citizen shall taste the fruits of nation's independence and benefits of progress.

HUMANKIND ITSELF HAS CREATED THE ADJECTIVES LIKE RICH-POOR, SORROW-JOY. THE CREATION STRUCTURE AND OTHER ANIMATE BEINGS DON'T HAVE ANYTHING TO DO WITH THESE ADJECTIVES...

This Earth and her related twelve factors have created the each animate being. After this creation, the survival necessities like food and facilities to meet the other natural hunger are also created for each animate being. Even today, except human, no animate remains hungry. Whether it is elephant or lion in the jungle or small ant at home; we never hear them die of hunger. Though these animals die natural death, they die only due to imbalance between the twelve factors. For example, animals die of thirst without water during the summer time due to excess heat. Even human too is not an exception to it. But no animate being dies without food except human.

THE HUMAN BEING ON THIS PLANE OF EARTH IS CRUEL! DESPITE ABUNDANT SUPPLIES OF FOOD, EACH DAY SOME PEOPLE DIE OF HUNGER!!!...

Misusing the powers of intellect, wisdom, imagination and thoughts, some people without the need hoard the food of millions of other people to themselves. If any hungry man approaches to such hoarder for food, he is beaten and is given to police as a 'thief'. Such is the law of humankind! So despite the abundance of the food, some humans die of hunger. The magnitude of this is greater in India. Actually though Mother Earth has made abundant food available for her children; the most cruel, greedy, selfish human being does not allow his own brothers & sisters their share of food, does not allow them to partake from the excess storage they hold.

Have we ever heard of some animals like tiger, elephant or deer being very rich and some being very poor amongst the other animate beings?...

In human beings the machinery called 'government' doesn't work for the hungry people. On the contrary, it protects those who have abundant food supply and lets the hungry people die and use the power of law against the hungry people. Such machinery called 'government' doesn't exist in other animates; so they don't die of hunger. Such a huge elephant, what a huge body he has! But he never dies due to lack of food. When the food is not available easily on the land, he just plucks the big trees from ground and consumes the green leaves. But in the humankind, the rich human doesn't let his own brother - the other poor human fill his midget tummy. He leaves the poor man to death. This feeling of rich-poor does not exist in any other animate beings except humans. Have you ever heard that some tiger or deer is very rich? These man-made adjectives are not at all applicable to other animates. So the distance of rich-poor doesn't occur amongst them anywhere on the Earth. Since other animate beings do not have any man-made adjectives, they live the life according to the law of creation-structure. The adjectives like poor-rich, sorrow-happiness etc. are all created by humankind and hence some people in the humankind bear the bitter fruits of it due to some ungrateful and piggish people.

The person who gathers more than his or her requirement is the real beggar!!!...

The day human being shall give up the misuse of his/her imagination, intelligence and thought power and embrace the laws of the creation-structure; that day all humankind shall live life full of happiness and satisfaction. The idea of grief and happiness shall be wiped off. The one who has enough food, shelter, clean water, air and clothing for the existence is the real rich, happy and content human. The one who has all these available and yet devoid others of their bare necessities by hoarding these things without necessity is a real beggar, poor and cruel. These adjectives that human has created are responsible for the human sufferings. Owing to such laws of humankind some infants, like I was, who was born to the so called poor person, starves without being a criminal. Without reason he has to struggle for the existence. So the root of sorrow is with the humankind and not with the Mother Earth or creation-structure. The idea of 'rich' is only with the humankind. Why only the human is the creator of the cruelty, injustice, selfishness, thoughtlessness and greed? It is because he is endowed with the power of imagination, intelligence and thought. Human should contemplate on this. By dwelling according to the laws of creation structure he should destroy the valley between rich and poor. Human should not let the population grow like herds. The facilities created by Mother Earth should reach to each human. Such governance should be created amongst humans. Then the imagination, intelligence and thought power given to the humankind by Mother Earth shall be worth. Humankind should imagine what Mother Earth would feel seeing her children die without food. So all the adjectives which exist – like wise-stupid, illiterate-literate, clever-mulish, rich-poor, good-bad – all are just manmade adjectives. They aren't acceptable to the Mother Earth. Besides, except human, no other animate has anything to do with these adjectives. There has been deep injustice with many of humankind due to these adjectives!!! So while living the mundane life, one shouldn't use these adjectives much. The wellbeing of the humankind lies in delivering the responsibilities planned by creation-structure and delivering the natural duties accordingly!!

I have already analysed & discussed all the laws of creation structure before this.

10

Personality Cult Is Detrimental To The Country & Society!!!

According to creation-structure each animate is made up from the twelve factors. So each animate is similar. Barring human no other animate entertains personality cult or hero-worship. It is prevalent only in the humankind. Who wins and who loses fighting with each other? This thing is not acceptable to the creation structure. In the countries monarchy or royal rule, we don't see any hero-worship other than honouring the kings. But surprisingly in a democratic country, the personality cult is seen in each corner, lane and town. Whosoever shall study this book seriously, will notice that all animate beings are created through the twelve factors and human too is not an exception to it. Then who is big who is small? Who is wise and who is stupid? Honour and grandeur are all stupid ideas sprung from the human mind. So despite having democratic rule, countries like India entertain the wide spread personality cult. Such heroes don't have the shortage of 'yes-men' or hirelings around them. So such leaders may have taken the responsibility of the social or national service, but it remains aside. Instead these people, their egos need to be taken care of. Instead of being of the service to others, he becomes the owner or boss of all those linger around. He pretends to be a service-man only during assembly elections to win the votes from masses. After he gets elected; instead of getting public work done from him, our public starts worshipping him with garlands. So instead of giving service, he takes service from the public! Actually he gets the conveyance, honorarium and other perks from the wealth of masses. Besides this, with corruption he makes the arrangement for many of his future generations. In addition, he siphons money to foreign banks and keeps the extra money. Public too serves him like devotees and elects him year after year throughout their life time! As if this is not enough, his photographs decorate the showcases of every home as an ideal person! What a public and their leaders! What a democracy in the countries like India!!

Indian constitution has given the definition of the public representatives as the 'servants elected by masses for the service of masses and nation'– which are so called leaders of today. Including the heads of small village to ministers or prime ministers and president, including their staff like secretaries and cleaners – all are supposed to be servants of nation, servants of public! But contrary to this definition it is seen that these so called servants of nation, servants of masses take the service from nation, from nationals instead of serving them. Perhaps there may be some who really serve public and nation according to the constitution. But very rare! Only those should be elected who really wish to serve the masses and nation. They shouldn't take any benefit of government facilities after the completion of their tenure. Only with this condition they should take the challenge of the national service, else there is no dearth of real public servants in such nations. India is a poor country. So the public servants for such countries should represent the poor class.

Once I had asked the main newspapers to publish the following type of narrative before parliamentary elections – "I am the servant of nation, fighting this election as a public and national servant. The citizens of this nation are my owners. I wish to publish here about how I will serve you, so you should vote and elect me as your servant" Such narrative that declares each candidate as public servant as per the Indian constitution should be published by each candidate to inform their manifesto to the public. But none of the newsletter took cognizance of it. Does it mean that the Indian public should worship these leaders spread over lanes and towns like so called 330 million Gods with garlands and acclamations? This is nothing but mockery of democracy!! How many of Indian nationals have clearly understood the real meaning of democracy? The real meaning of democracy is that we have given the role of servant to the elected person. If he doesn't deliver his or her duty properly the citizens have the right to throw them out. But on the contrary should we worship the persons who make public their servant and are corrupt? And decorate our houses with their photographs? What a leadership of India?

This is about leaders! But in the society there are many charlatans, con men who deceive masses with jugglery. There are many who make quick bucks in the name of God. Not just the common men but high positioned officers and successful leaders too prostrate in front of them. What ideal such leaders keep in front of public? Instead of teaching reality to the masses they teach to get addicted to such conmen. Explain these twelve factors to the masses. Who is human? What is human made up of? Identify yourself and also make other human beings identify themselves! Leave so called 'leadership' and just serve the public. Is it that without such corrupt leaders the nations like India won't be happy and prosperous? Absolutely not! If the nation has to be happy, hunger free and prosperous; the masses should stop the personality cult and start getting the duties properly done from their leaders, public representatives. Anyone interested in the personality cult shouldn't stand for the elections. In this country there is no dearth of selfless serving people. With the eradication of personality cult many such deserving candidates will get the chance to serve the nation.

At least today the personality cult believers have stopped the deserving servants of nation and social workers. With a minor difference we see the same representatives and party leaders at municipality, state council and parliament. Despite their aging they aren't ready to leave their seats for the new people, young generation. As in USA the President gets to fight the election only twice and serve the nation; countries like India too should have such provisions made through their constitutions. The Indian public doesn't get as much returns as it spends on its leaders. The nation is laden with burden of loans due to this. Farmers are committing suicide and millions of children dying without food. With these facts, why does nation need such leaders? India's population is increasing day by day in the world. So we all must decide that the personality cult in the India must be stopped. The country doesn't need charlatans, con men and deceptive leaders at all. So the masses should stop worshiping such people and abandon them. Else this thing badly and adversely affected our country. Whichever country has such personality cult, that country has suffered severe losses; for example what happened to Iraq, Libya, Egypt?

The political entrants should have a limit of ten years. The law should retire them from the public life after winning maximum 2 elections. We shouldn't see the same faces year-after-year! All desirous of serving the nation should get the chance. This is healthy democracy. Else we see the corrupt politics with the same corrupt politicians who ruin the nation. The limitation of ten year tenure shall prohibit the corruption to a great extent. Before corruption they should be thrown out of the politics. This book of mine must be studied properly to know the real identity of human. Then you will realize the importance of my thoughts.

No one is greater or smaller in this world. Everyone must dutifully deliver the work of their own share. Else the society should throw off that person; this will leave no scope for the personality cult. The cleaner's work is as important as is any prime minister's or president's work. No work is of lower or higher standard. I have seen this spirit in many foreign countries. During my New Zealand visit the driver of my bus was an expert engineer. There seems no differentiation between the grades of engineer and driver. India has a situation opposite to this. In the society who is rich and who is poor? The law should be the same for both. But it doesn't seem so. Despite the serious offenses in politics there is no punishment for the corrupt representatives. On the contrary the masses elect those politicians again and again; this is the misfortune of the country and its countrymen. At the same time some poor person languishes in the prison for a minor offence. This is the result of personality cult!

In the society there are many con men like politicians. If their worth is noted in reality, they aren't worthy of any position yet the public honours and worships them. Do the illusions they spread amongst the public real? No one studies to find the reality? The position of Indian public and society is like the flocks of sheep that blindly follow each other. Does anyone check the depth of wisdom of such con men? No! Let it be charlatan, or leader or preacher! No one checks the depth of their wisdom, knowledge. But worship them like God. So the country should be made free of personality cult attitude.

****

11

Everything Is Earth!!!

Every Animate Means Earth...

Wow! How marvellous is the mother Earth!!!...

The description you read so far was all about the Earth. Everything visible to your eyes; means the green hills, snow-clad hill ranges, the desert spread over miles, fathomless water of the oceans, large rivers, tall trees, greenery of the farms, millions of animates in the sea and oceans, big cities, sheer blue sky, variety of colourful birds, uncountable animals and the human on this plane of Earth; all are the parts of this Mother Earth. Without Earth nothing exists. All the description in this book from the start to end is related to Earth. If you study it by heart you will be convinced about why I say 'Earth is everything!'

The root of humans and animates is just the Earth and her related twelve factors- means this living & non-living creation!!!...

The root of all animate beings is the twelve factors and the root of these twelve factors is the Earth. Anything that your eyes see is Earth. You will say what about the stars, planets, Sun & Moon? But it is Earth that enables you to see them. Does anyone exist on the other planets to see the Sun & Moon? The root of human is the sperm. That sperm means the Earth. The blue sky visible to your eyes means the layers of many gases. What is the reason of the existence of this sky? Just the Earth! Due to her gravity the sky is visible around her. Due to absence of the layers of gases, you will not see the blue sky on other planets. But you will see the pitch dark space there. As the sperm is made up from the twelve factors, the foetus in the mother's womb is too Earth. The new born that comes out of mother's womb remains alive due to the twelve factors related to Earth. Since it has growth, whether it is 2 year old toddler, 14 year old teenager, 40-50 year old adult or an old man; all are just Earth. The last stage, the dead body laid flat forever too is Earth. There is nothing else without the Earth in this living & non-living creation. Earth, Earth and just Earth!! The things so valuable for the human like gold, silver, diamonds, emerald or any precious thing all is just Earth. No Earth, no precious things. So called God, soul, super soul all are Earth. Without Earth, neither you nor other things exist. All things are Earth-made. Other than Earth no other planet has anyone stating such definition. No one exists on these planets to claim 'I am Sun', 'I am Moon', 'I am Mars', 'I am Jupiter'.

After realizing the principle that 'everything is Earth'; who is 'mad'? Who is 'wise'? Who is rich and who is poor? What is prime minister, leader, minister and who is charlatan or preacher or scholar? All are creations of twelve factors!! But some act so pricey!!!...

If humankind understands this principle, there is no reason for someone to starve. No one is rich-poor, wise-mad, beggar, literate-illiterate. Actually the creation structure of Earth doesn't approve of these ideas. Life means Earth, death too means Earth. The food that you eat, water that you drink, your each movement everything is Earth. Why is it so? If you read my book by heart then you will understand my thought. There is nothing else on this plane of Earth other than Earth herself. Everything is Earth, Earth and just Earth. Understanding this truth will make you realize that there is no difference between Human and other animate beings on this Earth. It shall melt the human's ego and which will make him/her tension free, happy, fearless and joyous. Not understanding the principle that 'everything is Earth' has caused the wars. If you want to understand this, you need not study anything else. Just study the Mother Earth in depths. This book is for the same purpose! To the animate beings here, 'everything is Earth'. Despite this truth humankind has been wasting its life by running behind mirage. It is spending millions of dollars in the name of God. Instead of taking care of the homeless, beggars, starving and illiterate children of the Mother Earth; the trillions are spent on the imaginary Gods. Humankind finds its worth in this activity! When will it realize this stupidity and when the change will happen? If you need to spend the money, spend it on these needy brother-sisters of yours. Mother Earth will regard you as her real child!

What this Mother Earth hasn't given to the humankind? But despite giving everything the human remains unfortunate!!!...

All the things that will make each moment of the life happy and joyous are given by Mother Earth to the human. The sunny day is created to enable the routine work from morning to evening. You can remain active in that sunlight to meet your needs of shelter, food, clothing and other things. The living and non-living creation gets full of life throughout the day. The movement of all the animate beings start. With the dawn all animals, birds and plants brighten up and blossom with the joy. With the inkling of dawn the cock of the bird species awakens the human and other birds welcome the dawn with their sweet chirping. The exhilarating chill air of morning freshens up the animate beings. All animates start searching their daily food. To rest the body that is tired from the whole day's work; the provision of night is made from Sunset till Sunrise. While half of the living and non-living creation is resting in sleep; the Mother Earth is still revolving around self without any rest for all the animate beings. This enables life and its existence for all the living beings along with human.

Not just this, but the Mother Earth has also arranged the food and water for all animates created by her. She has ensured that no one would starve. All the immobile animates have been facilitated with the water, light and food juice through soil. The herbivores are created for the carnivorous mobile animals. For herbivores; the water, Sunlight and immobile animates like plants are created. Over and above she has pampered the humans most of all. Fruits and plants with different tastes are created to savour his tongue. To fulfil the sour taste lemon, gooseberry, tamarind are created and Kokum(Garcinia Indica) are created and for salty taste the waters of all seas and oceans of the Earth are made salty which give humans their salt. It is an important ingredient in the human diet. So many fruits are created to fulfil the sweet taste like sugarcane, Mango, Banana and for bitter taste vegetables like bitter gourd are created. Besides taste, so many other things are created to fill the tummy; i.e. grains like barley, oats, wheat, rice, maize and animals like hen, pigs, ducks, fishes. The beauty is filled to the brim in the nature for human entertainment. Pitch green forests, white snow clad hills, fathomless seas, flowing springs; all such valuable treasure is created for human and other animate beings.

Such a great arrangement the Mother Earth has made for her children; that has no limits! This all is created in ample amounts to facilitate all the animate beings.

THE HUMAN BEING HAS BEEN SPENDING TRILLIONS ON THE SO CALLED GOD BY KEEPING MILLIONS STARVED! BUT THE HUNGER OF THIS 'GOD' IS NEVER SATISFIED. HIS DEMAND IS INCREASING EACH DAY!!! WHEREAS AFTER GIVING SO MUCH; THE MOTHER EARTH NEVER DEMANDS ANYTHING!!! SHE HAS BEEN JUST GIVING, AND GIVING!!!...

Very important thing to note is that the humankind keeps spending trillions of dollars on so called 'Gods'. Still the hungers of these man-made 'Gods' never gets satiated! Their 'intake' goes on. But Mother Earth keeps giving to her children by working hard. She never demands anything to you or never takes anything from you. No one remembers or worships such selfless Mother Earth owing to whom we breathe and we live! The humankind never thinks about why we live and owing to whom we live, who feeds, who makes us wealthy; on the contrary they assault her! Such ungrateful is the humankind!!

I SAY EVERYTHING IS EARTH, EARTH AND JUST EARTH!!!..

Now tell me, is there any exaggeration in the slogan I have made or whatever I have described above? What is wrong? So human, your real God, your real aegis is only Mother Earth. So for you and me and all of us everything is Earth, Earth and just Earth!!!

THE DESTRUCTION THAT IS GOING ON ALL OVER THE EARTH IS JUST DUE TO THE MISUSE OF IMAGINATION, INTELLIGENCE AND THOUGHT POWER GIVEN TO THE HUMAN!!!...

After reading the description above, some scholars may ask me a question that according to the slogan that 'everything is Earth, Earth and just Earth'; aren't the murderer, corrupt public servants and politicians, ministers, leaders and selfish rich people who make other starve – all are Earth too? My answer to that is, on none other animate being, but only on the human being; Mother Earth has bestowed the intelligence, imagination and thought power. According to the saying 'thought is the mother of action'; how to use this gift bestowed by Mother Earth to the human is a decision of the human. He thinks of murdering someone and acts accordingly to become a murderer. With corruption he amasses a lot of wealth and becomes corrupt. Implementing the individual thoughts, each one creates own image in the society. The Mother Earth and the creation-structure don't have anything to do with it. The solution Mother Earth has for this, is according to the law of creation-structure, she doesn't allow such people live their human lives happily and peacefully. Such people are always ridden with worries, fear, disturbed and full of enemies. They die one day in the same miserable condition!!

HAVE YOU EVER HEARD THAT THE TIGER, LION OR OTHER ANIMALS OF FORESTS OR FISH AND OTHER AQUATICS HAVE COMMITTED A MESS?...

No one is affected with such things except human being because they aren't gifted with the imagination, intelligence and the thought power like human. So there is no question of misusing it. Due to this have you ever heard that some corruption occurred in the dense forest of amazon or among the trees of African jungle? Or that the tigers of African jungle have messed up something? Since so many years the fishes are dwelling in the water; have you ever heard that they murdered each other? So whatever happens between human beings, only human is responsible for that. Earth is not responsible for it and so 'everything is just Earth'.

DESPITE SO MUCH ABUNDANCE ON THE EARTH WHY IS 'HUMAN' STARVED?...

Despite abundant fruits, vegetables, crops on the plane of Earth how does human starve? Humankind itself is responsible for this. Some human hoards everything to self and keeps other human starved. Human has been killing another human. Not the Earth but the human is responsible for this. Earth does punish such people in her own way but just that they don't realize it! Means such misdeeds get punished. Such is the importance of the Mother Earth!

****

12

Euthanasia For The Painless, Joyous Death!!!

The Dire Need of Painless and Joyous Euthanasia To Make The Life Of Human Endowed With Thought Power, Imagination Power and Intelligence Successful!!!

HAVE YOU EVER THOUGHT IN DEPTH? WHAT IS THE ORIGINAL MOTIF OF THE CREATION-STRUCTURE BEHIND BIRTHING YOU AND OTHER ANIMATE BEINGS? YOU ARE NOT BIRTHED FOR ACQUIRING POSITIONS, RANKS OR TITLES LIKE RICH, POOR, PRIME MINISTER, PRESIDENT, NUMBER ONE LEADER, BIG INDUSTRIALIST, GREAT KING OR QUEEN OR VERY BRAVE ETC. HAD THAT BEEN THE REASON, YOU WOULD HAVE STAYED HERE FOREVER. THERE WOULDN'T HAVE BEEN ANYTHING CALLED DEATH. SO JUST REPRODUCTION IS THE SINGLE MOTIF!!! THE ANIMATE BEINGS SHOULD LEAVE THE EARTH PLANE FOREVER AFTER FINISHING THAT WORK -- IS THE ONLY RULE OF CREATION!!!...

Do you know why Mother Earth has created each animate being? The motif of creation-structure behind birthing each animate being is just the reproduction. The main intention of each animate being's life is not eating drinking, sleeping and being merry; but the creation-structure has put up each animate with the responsibility of reproduction. For this reason each animate is birthed here as a guest. To facilitate the reproduction, the Mother Earth and the creation-structure have given hunger and thirst to each one and also have arranged for its fulfilment. After getting physically capable of reproduction, each animate being is given the emotion of sex. Whether mobile or immobile, each animate must deliver the task of reproduction. Once they reproduce, each animate is also given the responsibility of upbringing, care taking and providing for the newly delivered existence till it gets physically capable.

Next, with the birth of grandchildren the task of

grandparents get over; the return journey starts and one has to leave the Earth permanently. No one is allowed to wait here!! This is the law of creation!!!

After the grown up new creation itself reproduces, the task of old creation naturally ends. Means after the reproduction of grandchildren; the creation-structures' purpose of birthing the grandparents gets over and their return journey starts after the task is completed. To allow the new creation the needed space and facilities; the old creation has to empty the place and take leave of this world. This is the structure of the creation. Creation structure births you, feeds you to get this work done from you. This doctrine is applicable to every animate being whether it is a male or a female. After taking the work from you, the creation structure ends your existence here. Each animate being's body structure is designed accordingly.

After delivering the responsibility of your offspring's upbringing, you automatically start getting old. Each organ of your body slowly starts giving up. Eyes can't see, legs start giving up walking, digestion system starts collapsing and so on. The body undergoes the suffering. Due to diminished immunity in the old age, the diseases attack one by one. Some humans get diabetes, cancer, ulcer, arthritis and high blood pressure. The diseased person gets perplexed with pains. Whether rich or poor he awaits the death eagerly. But the death too dodges these people. There are few lucky ones who die of heart attack or cardiac arrest. But the diseased person neither can die immediately nor can live properly. Some people get financially and emotionally orphaned as children ignore them and it is hard to see their dire conditions. While some diseased persons become the obstacle in letting their children live good life.

Now you decide whether the law of euthanasia is necessary or not? Check this example!!!...

I share here an example I have seen. I know a gentleman who is married and doesn't have any sibling and also any brother or sister. His mother is dead. He has purchased the home on loan. Both the husband and wife have to go out for work to ensure the timely repayment of home-loan instalments. You may not have felt any seriousness in the story so far! Where does the question of euthanasia come here? But the real twist in the story is that this person has an old age father who is bed ridden due to paralysis. He is not recovered with the medication. Forget about sitting on his own, the old man has to answer all calls of nature in the bed itself! Since this gentleman and his wife need to go on their respective jobs, they keep the water and all necessary things near the bed of the old father and lock the home from outside. After returning from office they clean and change the dirty bed and cloths of father. They spend their valuable time in tending to their bed ridden old father. This is the routine. How long it shall continue? It is unknown. Even after delivering the task of reproduction and upbringing of the reproduction; the death is dodging the old father of the gentleman.

In the society there are so many such bed ridden people with the diseases! Some have ulcer, some have paralysis and some have cancer and so on. The near and dear ones of these people too suffer in the today's world of inflation. The people can neither enjoy joyful living nor are the old bedridden persons rescued by death. Every one faces the health challenges in the family that is barely able to meet their needs. And don't ask about the old ones, who don't have anyone to look after them! They really live a very miserable life! Some people are in coma for years together. They don't have consciousness to know whether they are in this world or not. As if to add to the miseries; we are now challenged by the disease like AIDS. AIDS affected people too keep waiting for the death to rescue them from painful, miserable life. To get rid of these pains, the government of Holland have passed the law to allow the painless death. The population of Holland is very less compared to Indian population. So comparatively situation in India is much pathetic. Almost 500-600 million people are living below poverty line.

What right does that government & society have to deprive the opprèssed people from euthanasia; which cannot protect or take responsibility of them?...

Considering human rights, the fact remains that society or government cannot make arrangements for the oppressed poor, cannot take care of their medical expenses, resolve their problems of food or tend them anyway. Then what is the problem in giving such people the rights of euthanasia? Government doesn't even try to check the population growth. It cannot afford to provide for the daily necessities of these people. Then how can it deprive them their right to willingly embrace the joyous and peaceful death? Why you file a criminal suite against them? What kind of justice is this that neither allows to live nor to die!!

I feel the Indian government is afraid of the misuse of such law by the people who would kill the wealthy people to embezzle their wealth.

One nurse has been in coma for last 30-35 years. The court was approached to allow her death, but the court denied it. The societal questions cannot be resolved by getting emotional. Whosoever completes their task according to the creation structure's design, has the right to joyful death; s/he should be given the right to euthanasia.

Let them happily live who have the longing to live within pain. No one is forcing them. But in order to save them, why to stop those who wish to embrace 'happy and peaceful death' willingly?...

Similar to the longing for wealth and property, some people also long to live. Some fear death. No one is forcing these people for death. Let them miserably wait for the death if they desire so! But the ones who willingly want the happy and joyous death; they should have the right for the same and society and the government should allow them. For this the aware public should raise the movement and fight for the 'right of euthanasia'. Those who don't understand what birth and what death are; they should get the knowledge from this book and clear the path for euthanasia. The government and society shouldn't look at this question from the emotional angle but think practically. Cancer is usually incurable. Its treatment is very painful. Even after the painful treatment, one has to accept the painful death. Then if any such patient willingly desires to accept the joyful death, fulfilling his/her wish is the duty of the society, government and the relatives alike. So as soon as possible the law of euthanasia should be passed and implemented.

The principle of creation-structure should be taken into consideration. Creation-structure has given birth only for the task of reproduction. So those willing to embrace peaceful death should not be prohibited. Many countries in the world are implementing such law. Enforcing someone to die a miserable, painful death is not called the 'human rights'. The true 'human right' is that which allows the right to a suffering human to willingly and peacefully embrace the death without troubling anyone else.

****

AUTHOR'S INTRODUCTION

I am Eknath Kisan Wani, the author of this book, born on 1st June 1945 in a very poor family in an undeveloped small village in India. Despite the intense scarcity of food, I completed the education till 7th standard in the same village. Then I migrated to Pune with the help of the elder brother. I came to the big city of Pune but there was no one to help and no backing of money. Forget about the staying arrangements, it was hard to get the food for two times. But despite such situations I continued education in the night school. I passed the 11th standard by working in various roles like as a porter, plate-cleaner in hotel, domestic help, and office boy etc. during the day. Later I continued the education at Night College for one-two more years after getting a reasonably paying job. But later giving more Importance to sort out the financial problems I gave up the education. More details about me has been mentioned in my first book 'Me, Earth & Travel'. After getting financially settled I started getting the view of the real God of this creation structure, our Mother Earth. I completed the desire of getting the view of Earth during almost 25 years by travelling in main countries of all six continents. Then I published a 680 pages book 'Me, Earth and the Travel'. This became very popular amongst Marathi speaking readers. It got such admiration from all spheres that its two editions of 2200 copies finished within a short time by only mouth publicity.

The chapters 'Astronomical Earth, Geographical Earth and the Human and Animate Beings on the Earth' were not much understood by the readers. But according to the saying of famous scientist Albert Einstein - 'Imagination is more important than knowledge' I discovered the real live God owing to my observations during travel and the thought (imagination) power and realized how prevailing notions are wrong. So with the intention to clear up the ignorance and for the wellbeing of all humankind which is laden by the traditional misunderstandings I have written this book in a simple and understandable language. I have brought forth the things that are not resolved by the humankind so far. I am sure that if the principles and information contained in this book are actually implemented the human will have no fear or problem left in his/ her life. I am also sure that if the copies of this book reach to the corners of Earth, It will clear up the ignorance, illusion and fear of the humankind and make their lives immaculate.

I wish that at least 10 million copies of this book be sold all over the world and 50% of the royalty (excluding expenses) per copy that I would get be spent on charity.

Author : Eknath Kisan Wani
Email : wanibook@rediffmail.com

Bibliography

1. www.wikipedia.org
2. http://www.nasa.gov
3. http://www.morguefile.in
4. https://pixabay.com
5. http://allthingsplants.com
6. http://science.nasa.gov
7. http://eoimages.gsfc.nasa.gov
8. http://www.hq.nasa.gov